Auditing Cases

An Interactive Learning Approach

FIFTH EDITION

MARK S. BEASLEY
FRANK A. BUCKLESS
STEVEN M. GLOVER
DOUGLAS F. PRAWITT

PEARSON

Boston · Columbus · Indianapolis · New York · San Francisco · Upper Saddle River
Amsterdam · Cape Town · Dubai · London · Madrid · Milan · Munich · Paris · Montreal · Toronto
Delhi · Mexico City · Sao Paulo · Sydney · Hong Kong · Seoul · Singapore · Taipei · Tokyo

Editor in Chief: Donna Battista
Acquisitions Editor: Stephanie Wall
Editorial Project Manager: Christina Rumbaugh
Senior Managing Editor: Cynthia Zonneveld
Production Project Manager: Carol O'Rourke
Senior Operations Supervisor: Diane Peirano
Printer/Binder: BindRite Graphics, Robbinsville

10 9 8 7 6 5 4 3 2 1

PEARSON

ISBN 10:   0-13-256723-7
ISBN 13: 978-0-13-256723-7

TABLE OF CONTENTS

SECTION 1   Client Acceptance

CASES INCLUDED IN THIS SECTION

SECTION 2   Understanding the Client's Business and Assessing Risk

CASES INCLUDED IN THIS SECTION

SECTION 3   Professional and Ethical Issues

CASES INCLUDED IN THIS SECTION

TABLE OF CONTENTS

SECTION 4   Accounting Fraud and Auditor Legal Liability

CASES INCLUDED IN THIS SECTION

SECTION 5   Internal Control over Financial Reporting

CASES INCLUDED IN THIS SECTION

SECTION **6** The Impact of Information Technology

CASES INCLUDED IN THIS SECTION

SECTION **7** Planning Materiality

CASES INCLUDED IN THIS SECTION

TABLE OF CONTENTS

SECTION 8 Analytical Procedures

CASES INCLUDED IN THIS SECTION

SECTION 9 Auditing Cash, Fair Value, and Revenues

CASES INCLUDED IN THIS SECTION

SECTION **10** Planning and Performing Audit Procedures
in the Revenue and Expenditure Cycles
An Audit Simulation

CASES INCLUDED IN THIS SECTION

SECTION **11** Developing and Evaluating
Audit Documentation

CASES INCLUDED IN THIS SECTION

OTHER CASES THAT DISCUSS TOPICS RELATED TO THIS SECTION

TABLE OF CONTENTS

SECTION **12** Completing the Audit, Reporting to Management, and External Reporting

CASES INCLUDED IN THIS SECTION

ALPHABETIC CASE INDEX

ACKNOWLEDGEMENTS

We would like to thank our families for their understanding and support while writing this casebook. We would also like to thank Jonathan Liljegren for his excellent work in the design and layout of this casebook as well as Christina Rumbaugh and Stephanie Wall for their editorial support.

We are grateful to the research assistants both past and present who have helped write, revise, and review the cases in this edition. We especially thank Jace Garrett and Aaron Jacob for their assistance with this latest edition.

PREFACE

Auditing educators continue to look for opportunities to increase their emphasis on the development of students' critical thinking, communication, and interpersonal relationship skills. Development of these types of skills requires a shift from passive instruction to active involvement of students in the learning process. Unfortunately, current course materials provided by many publishers are not readily adaptable to this kind of active learning environment, or do not provide materials that address each major part of the audit process. The purpose of this casebook is to give students hands-on exposure to realistic auditing situations focusing specifically on each aspect of the audit process.

This casebook contains a collection of 48 auditing cases that allow the instructor to focus and deepen students' understanding in each of the major activities performed during the conduct of an audit, from client acceptance to issuance of an audit report. The cases are designed to engage the student's interest through the use of lively narrative and the introduction of engaging issues. In some cases, supporting material in the instructor notes allows the instructor to create a "surprise" or "aha!" experience for the student, creating vivid and memorable learning experiences. Many of the cases are based on actual companies, some involving financial reporting fraud. Several cases give students hands-on experience with realistic audit evidence and documentation.

Each case contains a series of questions requiring student analysis, with numerous questions related to the guidance contained in several new authoritative auditing standards, including the PCAOB's recently issued Risk Assessment Auditing Standards (up through AS No. 15, Audit Evidence) and recent standards issued by the Auditing Standards Board (up through SAS No. 121, Revised Applicability of SAS No. 100, Interim Financial Information). The instructor's resource manual also provides references in the solutions to many of the recently revised SASs that are part of the ASB's Clarity Project. Several cases require students to gain a clearer understanding of the specific requirements contained in the Sarbanes-Oxley Act of 2002. Other cases provide additional exposure to the role of information technology in today's environment, including a focus on Trust Services. One case incorporates actual excerpts from transcripts of testimony provided in court related to a financial statement fraud to illustrate the importance of following audit principles and procedures. Finally, cases new to this edition highlight the challenges of auditing fair value estimates, audit decisions related to the use of sampling when performing tests of controls and substantive testing, audit deficiencies in the highly publicized Satyam fraud, and opportunities for providing assurance on sustainability reports.

The cases included in this book are suitable for both undergraduate and graduate students. At the undergraduate level, the cases provide students with active learning experiences that reinforce key audit concepts addressed by the instructor and textbook. At the graduate level, the cases provide students with active learning experiences that expand the depth of their audit knowledge. Use of the casebook will provide students with opportunities to develop a much richer understanding of the essential underlying issues involved in auditing, while at the same time developing critical thinking, communication, and interpersonal relationship skills.

The casebook provides a wide variety of cases to facilitate different learning and teaching styles. For example, several of the cases can be used either as in-class exercises or out-of-class assignments. The instructor resource manual accompanying the casebook clearly illustrates the different instructional approaches available for each case (e.g., examples of cooperative/active learning activities and/or out-of-class individual or group assignments) and efficiently prepares the instructor for leading interactive discussions. To access this manual, log on to www.pearsonhighered.com/beasley5e.

FIFTH EDITION

UPDATES TO PRIOR CASES

Cases from the prior edition have been updated to reflect changes in professional standards. Cases based on events at real companies have been updated to reflect recent developments. Dates in the hypothetical cases have been set in calendar year 2012 with audit procedures performed on the 2011 fiscal year information and/or interim procedures performed on the 2012 fiscal year information. When appropriate, we have changed underlying data in the hypothetical cases so that the cases differ from prior editions.

NEW TO THE FIFTH EDITION

The following cases have been added to the fifth edition to expand coverage of audit topics and provide timely coverage of recent high profile accounting-related events.

This case highlights the accounting fraud at the Satyam Computer Services Company based in Hyderabad, India whereby senior management manipulated the company's IT-based accounting system to orchestrate a $1.1 billion fraud. Students learn about techniques used by senior executives to manipulate revenues and profitability and the importance of maintaining control of the entire confirmation process.

In this case students research standards on auditing fair value and then have the opportunity to consider the appropriateness of Morris Mining's fair value estimate for a patent obtained in an acquisition. Students get hands-on practice at considering sensitivity of the fair value estimate to changes in the model inputs. Morris Mining Corporation is a hypothetical company.

This case provides students the opportunity to apply audit sampling concepts in determining the nature and extent of testing. Students evaluate and perform tests of controls and tests of details on selected samples in an accounts receivable setting. Students also consider the benefits of risk- and coverage-based substantive testing prior to applying audit sampling. Hooplah, Inc. is a hypothetical company.

This case presents students with the opportunity to explore the emerging area of sustainability reporting. Students gain knowledge of the Global Reporting Initiative Framework for sustainability reporting and use it to evaluate the sustainability report of an actual company. Students also gain knowledge of the AICPA Attestation Standards and International Standard on Assurance Engagements that would be used to provide assurances on sustainability reports.

Client Acceptance

Ocean Manufacturing, Inc.
The New Client Acceptance Decision

MARK S. BEASLEY · FRANK A. BUCKLESS · STEVEN M. GLOVER · DOUGLAS F. PRAWITT

LEARNING OBJECTIVES

After completing and discussing this case you should be able to

[1] Understand the types of information relevant to evaluating a prospective audit client

[2] List some of the steps an auditor should take in deciding whether to accept a prospective client

[3] Identify and evaluate factors important to the client acceptance decision

[4] Understand the process of making and justifying a recommendation regarding client acceptance

INTRODUCTION

The accounting firm of Barnes and Fischer, LLP, is a medium-sized, national CPA firm. The partnership, formed in 1954, now has over 6,000 professionals on the payroll. The firm mainly provides auditing and tax services, but it has recently had success building the information systems consulting side of the business for non-audit clients and for audit clients that are not publicly traded.

It is mid-January 2012, and you are a newly promoted audit manager in an office of Barnes and Fischer, located in the Pacific Northwest. You have been a senior auditor for the past three of your five years with Barnes and Fischer. Your first assignment as audit manager is to assist an audit partner on a client acceptance decision. The partner explains to you that the prospective client, Ocean Manufacturing, is a medium-sized manufacturer of small home appliances. The partner recently met the company's president at a local chamber of commerce meeting. The president indicated that, after some difficult negotiations, the company has decided to terminate its relationship with its current auditor. The president explained that the main reason for the switch is to build a relationship with a more nationally established CPA firm because the company plans to make an initial public offering (IPO) of its common stock within the next few years. Ocean's annual financial statements have been audited each of the past 12 years in order to comply with debt covenants and to receive favorable interest rates on the company's existing line of credit. Because the company's December 31 fiscal year-end has already passed, time is of the essence for the company to contract with a new auditor to get the audit under way.

The partner, Jane Hunter, is intrigued with the idea of having a client in the home appliance industry, especially one with the favorable market position and growth potential of Ocean Manufacturing. Although there are several manufacturers of small home appliances in the area, your office has never had a client in the industry. Most of your office's current audit clients are in the healthcare services industry. Thus, the partner feels the engagement presents an excellent opportunity for Barnes and Fischer to enter a new market. On the other hand, knowing the risks involved, the partner wants to make sure the client acceptance decision is carefully considered.

The case was prepared by Mark S. Beasley, Ph.D. and Frank A. Buckless, Ph.D. of North Carolina State University and Steven M. Glover, Ph.D. and Douglas F. Prawitt, Ph.D. of Brigham Young University, as a basis for class discussion. Ocean Manufacturing is a fictitious company. All characters and names represented are fictitious; any similarity to existing companies or persons is purely coincidental.

BACKGROUND

Ocean Manufacturing, Inc. manufactures small- to medium-sized home appliances. The company's products include items like toasters, blenders, and trash compactors. Although Ocean's common stock and other securities are not publicly traded, the company is planning an IPO in the next few years in hopes that it will be able to trade Ocean's common stock on the NASDAQ. You have been assigned to gather information in order to make a recommendation on whether your firm should accept Ocean Manufacturing as a client.

Ocean wants to hire your firm to issue an opinion on its December 31, 2011 financial statements and has expressed interest in obtaining help to get its recently installed information technology (IT) system in better shape. Ocean also wants your firm's advice and guidance on getting everything in order for the upcoming IPO. During the initial meeting with Ocean's management, the following information was obtained about the industry and the company.

The Home Appliances Industry

Over the past several years, the domestic home appliances industry has been growing at a steady pace. The industry consists of a wide variety of manufacturers (domestic and foreign) who sell to a large number of wholesale and retail outlets. Though responsive to technological improvements, product marketability is linked to growth in the housing market. Retail outlets are served by both wholesale and manufacturer representatives.

Ocean Manufacturing, Inc

Ocean's unaudited December 31, 2011 financial statements report total assets of $76 million, sales revenues of $145 million, and net profit of $3.4 million. In the past, the company has not attempted to expand aggressively or develop new product lines. Rather, it has concentrated on maintaining a steady growth rate by providing reliable products within a moderate to low price range. However, Ocean hopes to use the capital from the upcoming IPO to aggressively expand from a regional to a national market. Ocean primarily sells its products in small quantities to individually owned appliance stores. Over the last few years the company has begun to supply larger quantities to three national retail chains. Two of these larger retailers started buying Ocean's products about two years ago. In order to handle the increased sales, Ocean significantly expanded its manufacturing capacity.

Though shaken by recent management turnover and ongoing difficulties with the company's new accounting system, management feels that Ocean is in a position to grow considerably. Management notes that earnings have increased substantially each year over the past three years and that Ocean's products have received increasing acceptance in the small appliance marketplace. Three years ago, the company received a qualified audit opinion relating to revenues and receivables. Ocean has changed auditors three times over the past 12 years.

Management

In October 2011, the company experienced significant management turnover when both the vice-president of operations and the controller resigned to take jobs in other cities. The reason for their leaving was disclosed by management as being related to "personal issues." A new vice-president, Jessica Wood, was hired in November, and the new controller joined early last month. Jessica is an MBA with almost 12 years of experience in the industry. Theodore Jones, the new controller, has little relevant experience and seems frustrated with the company's new IT system. The company's president, Andrew Cole, has a BBA and, as the founder, has worked at all levels of the business. Mr. Zachery, who is principally in charge of the company's procurement and manufacturing functions, meets weekly with Mr. Cole, as does Frank Stevens, who has served as vice president over finance for the past eight years.

Accounting & Control Systems

The company switched to a new, integrated central accounting system in early 2011. This new system maintains integrated inventory, accounts receivable, accounts payable, payroll, and general ledger software modules. The transition to the new system throughout last year was handled mainly by the former controller. Unfortunately, the transition to this new system was not well managed. The company is still working to modify it to better meet company needs, to retrain the accounting staff, and to adapt the company's accounting controls to better complement the system.

Problems still exist in inventory tracking and cost accumulation, receivables billing and aging, payroll tax deductions, payables, and balance sheet account classifications. The company stopped parallel processing the old accounting system in April 2011. During several brief periods throughout 2011, conventional audit trails were not kept intact due to system failures and errors made by untrained personnel.

The company's accounting staff and management are both frustrated with the situation because, among other problems, internal management budget reports, inventory status reports, and receivables billings are often late and inaccurate, and several shipping deadlines have been missed.

Your office has never audited a company with the specific IT system in place at Ocean. However, your local office's IT team is fairly confident they will be able to diagnose Ocean's control weaknesses and help Ocean overcome current difficulties.

Accounts Receivable, Cash, and Inventories
The sales/receivables system handles a volume ranging from 2,900 to 3,400 transactions per month, including sales and payments on account for about 1,200 active credit customers. The six largest customers currently account for about 15% of accounts receivable, whereas the remainder of the accounts range from $1,500 to $32,000, with an average balance around $8,000.

Finished goods inventories are organized and well protected, but in-process inventories appear somewhat less organized. The company uses a complicated hybrid form of process-costing to accumulate inventory costs and to account for interdepartmental in-process inventory transfers for its four major product lines.

Predecessor Auditor
When you approached Frank Stevens, Ocean's vice-president of finance, to request permission to speak with the previous auditor, he seemed hesitant to discuss much about the prior audit firm. He explained that, in his opinion, the previous auditor did not understand Ocean's business environment very well and was not technically competent to help the company with its new IT system. He further indicated that the predecessor auditor and Ocean's management had disagreed on minor accounting issues during the prior year's audit. In Mr. Stevens' opinion, the disagreement was primarily due to the auditor's lack of understanding of Ocean's business and industry environment. According to Mr. Stevens, the audit partner indicated that because of the accounting issues, he would be unable to issue a clean opinion on the financial statements. In order to receive an unqualified opinion, Ocean had to record certain adjustments to revenues and receivables. Mr. Stevens believed the adjustments were unnecessary but felt forced to make them to receive a clean audit opinion.

Mr. Stevens noted that Ocean's management feels confident that your firm's personnel possess better business judgment skills and have the knowledge and ability to understand and help improve Ocean's IT system. Mr. Stevens also indicated that Ocean wants to switch auditors at this time to prepare for the upcoming IPO, noting that companies often switch to larger accounting firms with national reputations in preparation for going public. Your firm has been highly recommended to him by a friend who is an administrator of a hospital audited by Barnes and Fischer. After some discussion between Mr. Stevens and Mr. Cole, Ocean's president, they granted you permission to contact the previous auditor.

During your visit with the previous auditor, he indicated that the problems his firm had with Ocean primarily related to (1) the complexities and problems with Ocean's new IT system and (2) management's tendency to aggressively reflect year-end accruals in order to meet creditors' requirements. The auditor also disclosed that the dissolution of the relationship with Ocean was a mutual agreement between the two parties, and that his firm's relationship with management had been somewhat difficult almost from the beginning. Apparently, the final straw that broke the relationship involved a disagreement over the fee for the upcoming audit.

Client Background Check

A check on the background of Ocean's management revealed that five years ago Ocean's vice president of finance was charged with a misdemeanor involving illegal gambling on local college football games. According to the news reports, charges were later dropped in return for Mr. Stevens' agreeing to pay a fine of $500 and perform 100 hours of community service. The background check revealed no other legal or ethical problems with any other Ocean executives.

Independence Review

As part of Barnes and Fischer's quality control program, every three months each employee of Barnes and Fischer is required to file with the firm an updated disclosure of their personal stock investments. You ask a staff auditor to review the disclosures as part of the process of considering Ocean as a potential client. She reports to you that there appears to be no stock ownership issue except that a partner in Barnes and Fischer's Salt Lake City office owns shares in a venture capital fund which in turn holds a private equity investment in Ocean common stock. The venture capital fund holds 50,000 shares of Ocean stock, currently valued at approximately $18 a share. The stock is not publicly traded, so this value is estimated. This investment represents just over a half of one percent of the value of the fund's total holdings. The partner's total investment in the mutual fund is currently valued at about $56,000. No other independence issues were noted.

Financial Statements

You acquired the past three years' financial statements from Ocean, including the unaudited statements for the most recent year ended December 31, 2011. This financial information is provided on the pages that follow. The partner who will be in charge of the Ocean engagement, Jane Hunter, wants you to look them over to see what information you can draw from them, paying particular attention to items that might be helpful in determining whether or not to accept Ocean as a new audit client.

REQUIRED

[1] The client acceptance process can be quite complex. Identify five procedures an auditor should perform in determining whether to accept a client. Which of these five are required by auditing standards?

[2] Using Ocean's financial information, calculate relevant preliminary analytical procedures to obtain a better understanding of the prospective client and to determine how Ocean is doing financially. Compare Ocean's ratios to the industry ratios provided. Identify any major differences and briefly list any concerns that arise from this analysis.

[3] What nonfinancial matters should be considered before accepting Ocean as a client? How important are these issues to the client acceptance decision? Why?

[4] [a] Ocean wants Barnes and Fischer to aid in developing and improving its IT system. What are the advantages and disadvantages of having the same CPA firm provide both auditing and consulting services? Given current auditor independence rules, will Barnes and Fischer be able to help Ocean with its IT system and still provide a financial statement audit? Support your conclusion with appropriate citations to authoritative standards if your instructor indicates that you should do so. *Extend of time, Independent issue. might not have the knowledge, even do, get more job.*

[b] As indicated in the case, one of the partners in another office has invested in a venture capital fund that owns shares of Ocean common stock. Would this situation constitute a violation of independence according to the AICPA *Code of Professional Conduct*? Why or why not? *No. not in the same area.*

[5] [a] Prepare a memo to the partner making a recommendation as to whether Barnes and Fischer should or should not accept Ocean Manufacturing, Inc. as an audit client. Carefully justify your position in light of the information in the case. Include consideration of reasons both for and against acceptance and be sure to address both financial and nonfinancial issues to justify your recommendation.

[b] Prepare a separate memo to the partner briefly listing and discussing the five or six most important factors or risk areas that will likely affect how the audit is conducted if the Ocean engagement is accepted. Be sure to indicate specific ways in which the audit firm should tailor its approach based on the factors you identify.

Ocean Manufacturing, Inc.
Balance Sheets as of December 31, 2009-2011
(In Thousands)

	(Unaudited)		
	2011	2010	2009
ASSETS			
CURRENT ASSETS			
Cash	$ 3,008	$ 2,171	$ 1,692
Accounts receivable (net of allowance)	12,434	7,936	6,621
Raw & in-process inventories	11,907	10,487	10,684
Finished goods inventories	3,853	4,843	7,687
Other current assets	1,286	1,627	1,235
Total Current Assets	32,488	27,064	27,919
PROPERTY, PLANT, & EQUIPMENT	53,173	46,664	39,170
Less accumulated depreciation	11,199	9,009	7,050
Net PP&E	41,974	37,655	32,120
OTHER ASSETS			
Deferred income taxes	714	547	339
Other noncurrent assets	1,216	1,555	735
Total Other Assets	1,930	2,102	1,074
TOTAL ASSETS	$76,392	$66,821	$61,113

LIABILITIES AND SHAREHOLDERS' EQUITY

	2011	2010	2009
CURRENT LIABILITIES			
Accounts payable and accrued expenses	$12,285	$ 9,652	$12,309
Current portion of long-term debt	3,535	3,054	2,899
Income tax payable	865	565	295
Other current liabilities	872	847	988
Total Current Liabilities	17,557	14,118	16,491
LONG-TERM DEBT	20,000	17,234	11,674
TOTAL LIABILITIES	37,557	31,352	28,165
SHAREHOLDERS' EQUITY			
Common stock (10,000,000 shares auth.)	10,675	10,675	10,675
Additional paid-in capital	5,388	5,388	5,388
Retained earnings	22,772	19,406	16,885
Total Shareholders' Equity	38,835	35,469	32,948
TOTAL LIABILITIES AND EQUITY	$76,392	$66,821	$61,113

Ocean Manufacturing, Inc.
Statement of Earnings for Years Ended December 31, 2009-2011
(In Thousands)

| | (Unaudited) | | |
	2011	2010	2009
Sales	$145,313	$104,026	$92,835
Cost of sales	95,906	69,177	63,870
Gross profit	49,407	34,849	28,965
Operating expenses	41,414	28,607	24,601
Operating income	7,993	6,242	4,364
Interest expense	1,700	1,473	699
Provision for income taxes	2,821	2,246	1,592
Net Earnings	$3,472	$2,521	$2,073

Ocean Manufacturing, Inc.
Statement of Retained Earnings as of December 31, 2009-2011
(In Thousands)

| | (Unaudited) | | |
	2011	2010	2009
Balance, beginning of year	$19,406	$16,885	$14,812
Cash dividends paid	(106)	0	0
Net earnings for year	3,472	2,521	2,073
Balance, end of year	$22,772	$19,406	$16,885

Average Industry Ratios for Comparison

	2011	2010
Return on Equity (ROE)	20.33%	26.22%
Return on Assets (ROA)	6.62%	8.10%
Assets to Equity	3.30	2.82
Accounts Receivable Turnover	7.49	6.96
Average Collection Period	41.25	44.35
Inventory Turnover	8.09	6.90
Days in Inventory	38.16	43.86
Debt to Equity	2.38	1.90
Times Interest Earned	1.62	2.37
Current Ratio	1.29	1.44
Profit Margin	10.58%	10.82%

Understanding the Client's Business and Assessing Risk

Your1040Return.com

Evaluating eBusiness Revenue Recognition, Information Privacy, and Electronic Evidence Issues

MARK S. BEASLEY · FRANK A. BUCKLESS · STEVEN M. GLOVER · DOUGLAS F. PRAWITT

LEARNING OBJECTIVES

After completing and discussing this case you should be able to

[1] Identify business risks for Internet-only business models

[2] Recommend internal control improvements for an eBusiness-based company

[3] Understand selected eBusiness related revenue recognition issues

[4] Identify accounting issues that arise when Internet-only companies exchange banner ad services

[5] Recognize issues surrounding the privacy of customer information

[6] Describe audit implications when transaction evidence is solely electronic

[7] Recognize threats to eBusiness strategies, which rely solely on the delivery of services via the Internet

INTRODUCTION

After being in business for only two years, Your1040Return.com has quickly become a leading provider of online income tax preparation and filing services for individual taxpayers. Steven Chicago founded the company after a business idea came to him while shopping for individual tax preparation software. As he stared at all the software packages on the shelves at a local computer supply store, the following thought kept racing through his mind:

> *"With all of the tax law changes from year to year, why should I shell out $50 for a CD that will be obsolete next year, not to mention the $20 I have to pay to file my taxes electronically over the Internet? I'd rather pay a company a small membership fee to use continually updated tax preparation software."*

Not long after his shopping experience, Chicago, an entrepreneur at heart, decided to create such a company. Less than one year later, Your1040Return.com began operations in time for the next tax season.

OVERVIEW OF YOUR1040RETURN.COM OPERATIONS

Your1040Return.com is an entirely Internet-based tax preparation website for preparing and filing federal and state individual income tax returns. Most of its revenues come from individuals seeking to avoid preparation of a paper-based tax return and who are willing to "rent" access to a popular tax preparation software package through Your1040Return.com. Other revenues come from individuals wanting to electronically file an already prepared paper-based return.

The case was prepared by Mark S. Beasley, Ph.D. and Frank A. Buckless, Ph.D. of North Carolina State University and Steven M. Glover, Ph.D. and Douglas F. Prawitt, Ph.D. of Brigham Young University, as a basis for class discussion. Your1040Return.com is a fictitious company. All characters and names represented are fictitious; any similarity to existing companies or persons is purely coincidental.

For a minimal fee, Your1040Return.com provides an interface for individuals to electronically file their returns with the appropriate federal and state regulatory bodies. Typical users come from middle class households wanting to simplify yearly tax return preparation tasks. These users are generally searching for an accurate, easy, and economical alternative to other professional tax services.

Individuals can access these services through Your1040Return.com's website. To log on, customers must first register for a user name and password. Once the customer indicates that he or she wants to register, the website asks the customer to provide information including full name, mailing address, Social Security number, birth date, phone number, email address, and a major credit card number. This registers the individual on Your1040Return.com's website and initiates the credit card approval process. Once the credit card number is validated, customers select from one of three service packages: Silver, Gold, or Platinum.

The Silver package provides basic tax services, including electronic access to tax forms, schedules, and publications. Customers can enter tax return information directly onto the forms and schedules, and Your1040Return.com will file the completed materials electronically, eliminating the need for mailing paper copies to tax agencies. The Silver package also provides a service that allows customers to apply electronically for a return extension. The Silver package, however, does not give subscribers access to the tax preparation software package.

In addition to the benefits of the Silver package, the Gold package grants customers online access to a commercially developed and continually maintained tax preparation software package. The package helps customers easily prepare tax returns ranging from the simple 1040-EZ to a complex return, such as one filed by a self-employed businessperson with nationwide real estate investments and actively traded securities. Both the Gold and the Silver packages provide access to services for one tax season only.

Premium services are offered through the Platinum package, which allows customers to sign up for Your1040Return.com membership ranging between two to five years. Through this multiple-year package service, customers receive year-round access to the tax preparation software provided to Gold customers, which allows them to continually track changes to their tax basis in securities and periodically evaluate tax implications of possible transactions. Furthermore, Platinum customers receive personalized attention and real-time tax support from qualified income tax specialists, who work on a contract basis, via an online instant messenger program.

Your1040Return.com experiences high seasonal demand for its services from early February to the filing deadline of April 15. Because Your1040Return.com allows customers to apply for filing extensions online, the company also experiences strong demand for its services just before extension deadlines.

If the IRS finds a problem with a return submitted through the company's Web service, Your1040Return.com does not correct the problem, but informs the customer of the problem so that the individual can correct the error and refile the return free of charge. The estimated frequency and cost of expected refilings are factored into the price of the service packages.

Your1040Return.com does not handle tax refund or tax liability payments. If a customer is eligible for a refund, the IRS remits the payment directly to the taxpayer. If a customer is required to pay income taxes, the IRS simply charges the appropriate amount to the customer's credit card number that is electronically submitted with the income tax return or the customer can provide bank draft information to electronically transfer funds from the customer's bank account to the IRS. Your1040Return.com assumes no liability for inappropriately filed returns or the tax positions of its customers. All liability resides with the customer who prepared the return.

Your1040Return.com recognizes revenue differently for each product. The revenue for the first year of Platinum service is recognized immediately after the customer selects this option. The company assumes customers will use the package for an entire year without cancellation even though Your1040Return.com has a fairly simple cancellation policy. All revenues from subsequent years of Platinum service are recognized in like manner. For the Gold package, a portion of the revenue is recognized when the customer accesses the tax preparation software package via the Internet for the first time. The company recognizes the remaining revenue when the customer submits the return to the IRS. The company does not recognize revenue for the Silver package until the customer submits a return to the IRS.

In addition to fees generated for its individual tax preparation services, Your1040Return.com engages in ad swapping with a number of major Internet companies. For example, Amazon.com swapped a significant amount of advertising with Your1040Return.com from January to April of this year. Amazon.com placed a banner ad on its website reminding visitors to visit Your1040Return.com for all of their tax needs. In exchange for this ad, Your1040Return.com placed a similar ad directing its visitors to shop online at Amazon.com.

SECURING CUSTOMER INFORMATION

Protecting unauthorized access to customer information is a high priority at Your1040Return.com. The company houses its web server and microcomputers, which run critical applications, in a key-coded room accessible only to the programmer and Chicago, the CEO. The web server is also protected by a proxy server firewall to prevent outside hackers from attacking the database. In addition to these security measures, all customers are required to create alphanumeric passwords that are at least six characters in length, to prevent unauthorized access to customer accounts.

Your1040Return.com does not maintain a "bricks and mortar" storefront or interact face-to-face with customers. The company engages in all transactions electronically and stores all purchase orders, sales invoices, and advertising contracts in electronic form. The company backs up data daily, but the backup data are not readily available at all times. After six months of soft storage on the company's server network, backup files are removed from the network to free up the limited storage capacity. The files are downloaded to DVDs for storage and future retrieval. A significant upgrade of Your1040Return.com's limited information system is in the planning stages.

The company has hired several tax experts who monitor tax code changes and help ensure the underlying tax preparation software is accurate. In addition, Your1040Return.com engages a national CPA firm to review the accuracy of the tax preparation software. The company contracts with a software design firm that develops the actual tax preparation online tools. Two of Chicago's nephews – Nathan Randall and Matthew Gilbert – oversee the operations of the information technology platforms that host the tax preparation software and Your1040Return.com's internal applications, including the company's financial accounting system software. Both of them have some prior experience in IT operations; however, each has less than 5 years of relevant work experience following their completion of undergraduate degrees in computer science. Emily Parkin serves as the company's CFO, responsible for Your1040Return.com's accounting and financial reporting activities. She joined Your1040Return.com after three years of audit experience with one of the Big Four international accounting firms.

Given the growth in the number of individuals using Your1040Return.com's services, several marketing executives have recently begun to offer Chicago large sums of money to purchase Your1040Return.com's customer lists. Although Chicago has yet to formally draft an official privacy statement for his company, he feels responsible for the privacy of his customers' information and is unsure if he should sell the lists. The cash offers have been tempting, however, given that the money would allow him to move ahead with planned information system upgrades. In the meantime, Chicago arranged a line of credit with a local bank to fund the upgrades. As part of that financing transaction, the bank has required an audit of Your1040Return.com's annual financial statements.

REQUIRED

[1] You are an audit senior with Gooch & Brown CPA, LLP, a local accounting firm specializing in audits of information systems and financial statements. Your1040Return.com engaged your firm to perform its financial statement audit. You have been asked by the partner to perform the following tasks:

[a] Describe to Steven Chicago why it is important for your firm to have an understanding of Your1040Return.com's business model.

[b] Identify Your1040Return.com's major business risks and describe how those risks may increase the likelihood of material misstatements in Your1040Return.com's financial statements.

[c] Indicate what Your1040Return.com should do to improve its internal control.

[d] Explain what audit implications arise if you decide that the controls over electronic records at Your1040Return.com are inadequate to ensure that records have not been altered.

[e] Authoritative literature provides guidelines for proper revenue recognition policies for transactions such as those discussed in the case. Analyze Your1040Return.com's revenue recognition policies for the three package services. Provide appropriate citations to authoritative literature.

[f] Explain how you can obtain evidence that ad swapping actually occurred between the Your1040Return.com and Amazon.com. Describe accounting issues that arise when Internet-based companies swap ad services and identify relevant authoritative literature.

[g] Address a memo to Steven Chicago detailing the appropriate contents for a customer privacy policy. (You may want to visit other company websites, such as www.cpamoneywatch.com, to see an example of a privacy policy). Why is it important for Your1040Return.com to have an explicit privacy policy? How might the lack of a policy affect Your1040Return.com's financial statements in the future?

[2] Auditing standards provide guidance for auditors when evaluating electronic evidence. What are the implications for an auditor when a client's accounting system produces and stores transaction evidence only electronically?

[3] Your1040Return.com's main business strategy involves the delivery of services via the Internet. What are some threats to the viability of Your1040Return.com's business strategy?

[4] When customers register for the Platinum package, they have online access to tax professionals who are paid on a contract basis. If you were in Steven Chicago's shoes, how would you compensate those professionals for their services? What controls could Your1040Return.com implement to ensure that the company does not overpay for those professional services?

Dell Inc.
Evaluation of Client Business Risk

MARK S. BEASLEY · FRANK A. BUCKLESS · STEVEN M. GLOVER · DOUGLAS F. PRAWITT

LEARNING OBJECTIVES

After completing and discussing this case you should be able to

[1] Describe the implications of an audit client's business risk on the audit engagement

[2] Describe the types of information relevant to evaluate an audit client's business risk

[3] Identify and evaluate the factors important in assessing an audit client's business risk and risk of material financial misstatement

INTRODUCTION

Dell Inc. (Dell) is a worldwide provider of innovative technology products and services that enable customers to do more. Dell offers a broad range of product categories, including servers and networking products, storage, mobility products, desktop PCs, software peripherals, and service.[1] The company conducts operations worldwide. Dell has manufacturing facilities in Austin, Texas; Penang, Malaysia; Xiamen, China; Hortolândia, Brazil; Chennai, India; and Lodz, Poland. Net revenue for fiscal 2011 was $61.5 billion and net income was $2.6 billion.

Dell common stock is traded on the NASDAQ national market, and Dell is required to have an integrated audit of its consolidated financial statements and its internal control over financial reporting in accordance with the standards of the Public Company Accounting Oversight Board (United States). As of the close of business on March 4, 2011, Dell had 1,906,749,664 shares of common stock outstanding with a trading price of $15.60.

INFORMATION ABOUT THE AUDIT

Your firm, Smith and Jones, PA., is in the initial planning phase for the fiscal 2012 audit of Dell for the year ended February 3, 2012. As the audit senior, you have been assigned responsibility for gathering and summarizing information necessary to evaluate Dell's business risk. Your firm's memorandum related to the client business risk evaluation has been provided to assist you with this assignment. Assume no material misstatements were discovered during the fiscal 2011 audit.

---

1 The background information about Dell Inc. was taken from Dell Inc.'s Form 10-K for the fiscal year ended January 28, 2011 filed with the Securities and Exchange Commission.

The case was prepared by Mark S. Beasley, Ph.D. and Frank A. Buckless, Ph.D. of North Carolina State University and Steven M. Glover, Ph.D. and Douglas F. Prawitt, Ph.D. of Brigham Young University, as a basis for class discussion. It is not intended to illustrate either effective or ineffective handling of an administrative situation.

REQUIRED

[1] Go to Dell's website (http://www.dell.com) and click on the "About Dell" link. Review background and investor information provided about Dell. Click on the "Investor" link in the About Dell section and read the most recent SEC Form 10-K provided for Dell.

[2] Based on the information obtained from the website and your knowledge of the industry, prepare a memo discussing the following items:

   [a] Dell's:
   - Sales
   - Net income
   - Cash flow from operating activities
   - Total assets
   - Number of employees

   [b] What are Dell's products?

   [c] Who are Dell's competitors?

   [d] Who are Dell's customers?

   [e] Who are Dell's suppliers?

   [f] How does Dell market and distribute its products?

   [g] What is Dell's basic business strategy (cost leadership or differentiation)?

   [h] What are critical business processes for Dell given its basic business strategy (for example, supply chain management)?

   [i] What accounting information is associated with the critical business processes and how does Dell measure up on that information?

   [j] What accounting methods does Dell use to report the accounting information associated with critical business processes and what is the risk of material misstatement?

This memo is to be used as a foundation document for the preliminary business risk assessment. In evaluating Dell's performance and assessing the risk of misstatement, please be sure to describe your reasoning. Your memo should be double-spaced and addressed to the partner for the engagement (your instructor). Your firm demands polished, concise, professional analyses and writing. Be thorough, but get to the issues without unnecessary verbiage. In describing your analyses and conclusions, please consider relatively short "punchy" or to-the-point sentences. When appropriate, consider using bullet point listings.

[3] Professional auditing standards provide guidance on the auditor's consideration of an entity's business risks. What is the auditor's objective for understanding an entity's business risks? Why does an auditor not have responsibility to identify or assess all business risks? Provide some examples of business risks associated with an entity that an auditor should consider when performing an audit.

Smith and Jones, PA.
Memorandum: Business Risk Evaluation

This memorandum provides a general framework for firm personnel when evaluating client business risk for purposes of determining the nature, timing, and extent of audit procedures. Knowledge about the nature of the client's business activities and related business risks provides a basis for the auditor's assessment of the risk of material misstatement. The auditor's assessment of the risk of material misstatement is used to determine the nature, timing, and extent of audit procedures. The intent of this memorandum is not to suggest that this framework must be followed on all audit engagements. The appropriateness of this framework must be determined on an engagement by engagement basis, using professional judgement.

Client business risk is the risk that a client's business objectives will not be achieved. Business risk results from the interaction of internal and external business forces. Clients achieve business objectives by setting strategies and then designing and implementing processes to execute those strategies. Strategies represent the overall approaches used by management to achieve its business objectives. Business risk is reduced when the client effectively aligns its business strategy and processes with the external business environment. Business risk is increased when the client does not effectively align its business strategy and processes with the external business environment or when new external business conditions emerge to weaken the alignment.

The dynamic nature of today's business environment requires that clients do more than develop processes to execute their current business strategy. Clients must also develop processes to monitor the changing business environment and reorient their strategies and processes as environmental business conditions change. Clients must continually scan their business environments for changes that may threaten achievement of their business objectives.

To assess the risk of material misstatement auditors must understand the client's current business strategy and environment along with emerging business forces that may require reorientation of its current strategies and processes. A proper analysis of a client's business risk requires an understanding of the client's business strategy, the client's internal business processes, and emerging business forces. Important aspects of understanding each of these dimensions are discussed below.

Understand Emerging Business Forces
The starting point for performing a business risk analysis is to understand the external business environment in which the client operates. This analysis is an essential first step because it allows the auditor to properly frame the subsequent analysis of the client's strategy and internal business processes. Understanding the client's business environment enables the auditor to assess the sustainability of the client's business strategy and to identify critical business processes.

External business forces influencing business risk are:
- **Customers** – aspects to consider include size and number of customers in industry, availability of competitor products or services, similarity of competitor products or services, ability of customers to switch to competitor products or services, complementary/substitute products or services, and desired qualities/features of products or services.
- **Competitors** – aspects to consider include number and size of firms in industry, maturity of products or services in industry, production capacity of firms in industry, required capital investment to enter industry, availability/access to distribution channels, and legal or regulatory barriers to industry.
- **Suppliers** – aspects to consider include number and size of suppliers in industry, number and size of customers for supplier products or services, relative importance of supplier products or services to client's products or services, similarity of supplier products or services, complementary/substitute products or services, and cost of switching suppliers.
- **Labor** – aspects to consider include required competencies of employees, availability of employees, and other employment opportunities for employees.

- **Capital market** – aspects to consider include availability of investors and creditors and alternative investment opportunities available to investors and creditors.
- **Regulations** – aspects to consider include nature of and changes to regulatory oversight and global differences in regulatory oversight.

Understand Business Strategy

The next step in evaluating the client's business risk is to understand the client's strategy to gain a competitive advantage. The sustainability of a client's competitive advantage is dependent on the external business environment. Changes in the external business environment may render the client's current business strategy ineffective. An understanding of the client's business strategy is also necessary to identify critical business processes for the client.

Business strategies influencing business risk can be broadly categorized as:
- **Cost leadership** – objective is to supply products or services at the lowest cost. Clients using this strategy have organizational structures and processes that promote cost control. These clients are primarily concerned with efficient production processes, lower input costs, lower overhead costs, and simple product design.
- **Differentiation** – objective is to supply product or service that is unique on some dimension valued by customers. Dimensions clients may use to differentiate include product/service quality, product/service features, product/ service variety, product/service image, product/service support, or product/service delivery. Clients using this strategy have organizational structures and processes that promote creativity and innovation. These clients are primarily concerned with research and development, engineering, and/or marketing capabilities.

Regardless of the business strategy selected by a client, the other differentiation dimensions cannot be completely ignored. Clients focusing on cost leadership still must have products that customers desire and thus cannot completely ignore the product/service dimensions valued by customers. Similarly, clients focusing on differentiation still need to deliver their products or services at a reasonable price.

Evaluation of Internal Business Processes

The final step in evaluating the client's business risk is to understand and evaluate critical business processes. Success of a business strategy is not automatic. Business strategies fail because of changes in the external business environment and/or flawed client business processes. Clients must implement business processes that develop and maintain the core competencies necessary to execute the business strategy and sustain competitive advantage.

Internal business processes influencing business risk are broadly categorized as:
- **Control environment** – organizational processes concerned with integrity and ethical values, commitment to competence, board of directors and audit committee oversight, management's philosophy and operating style, organizational structure, and assignment of authority and responsibility.
- **Risk assessment** – organizational processes concerned with identification and analysis of risks associated with achieving business objectives.
- **Control activities** – organizational processes concerned with the execution of business strategies and achievement of business objectives. This includes core business processes related to product/service development, production, marketing, distribution, employee relations, supplier relations, and customer relations.
- **Information and communication system** – financial and non-financial information concerned with the measurement of the progress toward achievement of business objectives.
- **Monitoring system** – organizational process for evaluating the design, operation, and effectiveness of business processes.

Approved: June 10, 2009

Flash Technologies, Inc.
Risk Analysis

Mark S. Beasley · Frank A. Buckless · Steven M. Glover · Douglas F. Prawitt

LEARNING OBJECTIVES

After completing and discussing this case you should be able to

[1] Identify and understand the implications of key inherent and business risks associated with a new client

[2] Understand and link audit-client's risk to accounts, assertions, and the audit plan

[3] Appreciate the degree of professional judgment involved in analyzing risk related to the audit of a rapidly growing company in a high technology industry

INTRODUCTION

Flash Technologies, Inc. has recently engaged your firm to perform the annual audit for the year ending December 31, 2011. Flash has determined that its current auditors, Adams & Adams LLP, cannot provide the international support that Flash now requires with its increased investment in Korea and Canada. Partners from your firm have discussed the prior audits with the engagement partner at Adams & Adams, and everything seems to be in order. Your firm also met with executives at Flash in December 2011 and January 2012 and a verbal (but informal) agreement was reached regarding fees, timing, scope, etc. Your firm has decided that additional analyses are needed before finalizing the details of the engagement (assume that it is now late January 2012). On the following pages you will find (1) a memo from the audit manager of your firm to the planning files regarding background information, (2) an industry article, (3) industry ratios, and (4) the draft annual report for fiscal year 2011 that Flash has prepared.

REQUIRED

[1] Perform a risk analysis of Flash Technologies and document your findings in a written report. Use the two-part solution template provided on the next two pages (an electronic version of the template is available on www.pearsonhighered.com/beasley5e). The template is organized by General Business and Industry Risks (e.g., foreign ventures, high tech, etc.) and Financial Accounting/Reporting Risks (e.g., unusual ratios or significant increases in balances). Using only the information provided in the case (e.g., memo, annual report, and article), identify key business objectives and strategies and then map those on the template from business risks to the potential effect on the audit plan.

Auditors are required to specifically assess the risk of material misstatement whether caused by error or fraud. The AICPA's and PCAOB's "Risk Assessment Standards" may be useful source materials for your risk analysis. In addition, to help you identify risk factors, you should also perform analytical procedures based on the company's financial data and compare those results to your expectations and general industry ratios and trends. You may attach your analytical procedures to the solution template. Please provide polished, concise, professional analysis and writing. Get to the issues without unnecessary verbiage.

You will find an electronic version of the following template at www.pearsonhighered.com/beasley5e

SUGGESTED FORMAT FOR FLASH TECHNOLOGIES MEMO

GENERAL BUSINESS AND INDUSTRY RISKS

As illustrated in the table below, provide an analysis of business objectives and strategies and how they map to business risk, audit risk, related accounts, and their potential effect on the audit plan. For the two business objectives illustrated below, identify one or two additional risks associated with each objective and complete the remaining columns for all risks (note that the template has been partially completed).

Business Objective and Strategy	Business Risks	Audit Risk (auditor's concern)	Related Accounts and Assertions	Potential Effect on the Audit Plan
1. Continue Expansion Internationally (acquisitions in other countries)	Foreign Currency Risks.	Gains/losses not properly calculated or accrued on hedging activity.	Gains/Losses from currency hedging: Valuation Accuracy Classification	Gains/losses: Increase the number of hedging contracts tested with particular emphasis on contracts in currencies with less developed countries. Examine unrealized and realized gains/losses to ensure that they are properly classified.
	Lack of understanding of culture and business practices.			
	Identify one or two additional risks…			
2. Be a leader by having the latest technological advances and releases in the flash memory market	Insufficient number of existing and new customers accept the new technology	Overstatement of accounts receivables through fictitious sales.		
	High amounts of R&D expenses cause margins to diminish and cause concern among investors.			
	Identify one or two additional risks…			

ADDITIONAL GENERAL AND INDUSTRY RISKS

Provide a list of additional general and industry risks you identified. Only list the risk, no need to fill out a table as shown above. You should identify at least three additional risks beyond those listed in the table above and provided in the example immediately below:

- DCI experiencing losses
- There is pressure to increase sales to be a leader in the flash memory market
- *Identify at least three additional general/industry risks…*

FINANCIAL ACCOUNTING/REPORTING RISKS

Fill in the table below by completing the final box for the first risk and by identifying two additional financial accounting/reporting risks through examination of Flash's financial statements and related disclosures (e.g., significant or unusual increases in ending balances, unexpected patterns such as slower growth in accounts receivable than sales, unexpected differences between Flash's ratios and the industry averages). The two additional risks included in the table below should be the financial accounting/reporting risks you consider most significant.

Financial Accounting/Reporting Risk	Audit Risk (auditor's concern)	Related Accounts and Assertions	Potential Effect on the Audit Plan
Inventory turnover is much lower than the industry	Overstatement of inventory due to obsolescence. Is inventory properly valued at the lower of cost or market?	Inventory: Valuation Existence	

ADDITIONAL FINANCIAL ACCOUNTING/REPORTING RISKS

Provide a list of additional financial accounting/reporting risks you identified. You need only list the risk, no need to fill out a table as shown above. You should identify at least three additional risks beyond those listed above.

- *Identify at least three additional financial accounting/reporting risks…*

Reference:	A 8
Prepared by:	ASG
Date:	1/7/2012
Reviewed by:	

Flash Technologies, Inc.
Memo to the Planning File by Audit Manager—General Information
12/31/2011

General Background Information

Emanuel "Manny" Schwimez, is the CEO and chairman of the board of Flash. Mr. Schwimez is originally from Tel Aviv. He has an impressive resume, including a master's degree from the London School of Economics and many years of executive-level experience. He has led several high technology companies in the U.S. and abroad since the early 1980's. In 1993 he became president of Seatac Inc., a start-up company in Seattle, Washington, which manufactured and sold font cartridges for printers. In 1996 Seatac agreed to merge with Boston Printing of Massachusetts. In 1997 the combined company was incorporated in Massachusetts as Flash Technologies, Inc., and began developing and commercializing font cartridges for laser printers. Headquarters for the company are in Binex, MA. Beginning in 2002 the company began to shift its emphasis from font cartridges to the growing market for flash memory cards, USB flash drives, and solid state hard drives with flash memory. Flash memory is a rugged, lightweight, device inserted into a dedicated slot in a broad range of electronic equipment that contain microprocessors, such as personal digital assistants, laptop and tablet computers, digital audio players, digital cameras, mobile phones, and vehicle diagnostic systems. Although Flash Technologies, Inc., is still a relatively small player in the industry, it has enjoyed impressive success. The company's stock price has grown 300% over the last 5 years. In 2008 Flash's stock graduated to the New York Stock Exchange. The stock recommendation from analysts following Flash's stock is currently "strong buy." However, I did some market research and noticed short positions in Flash stock have increased during November and December 2011.

While I was researching the stock, I visited the Google™ Groups Page and located information on Flash Technologies. The Groups Page is a place where interested parties can discuss the future prospects of the company and share information about it with others. The Groups Page is not connected in any way with the company, and any messages are solely the opinion and responsibility of the poster. Most of the posts on the Groups Page are positive and suggest investors are bullish on Flash stock. However, there were a few posts from someone who goes by the penname, "Mr. Truth," that were very negative with respect to Mr. Schwimez. Mr. Truth calls Schwimez a "pathological liar" and referred to alleged wrong doings by Mr. Schwimez in the late 1970's when he was a journalist for an Israeli newspaper and in the 1980's when Schwimez was an executive with a Swiss company in Geneva. To this point, our local background checks for Mr. Schwimez (e.g., local bankers, attorneys, business associates, vendors, etc.) have been positive. I mentioned the negative allegations to the chief financial officer (CFO), Jane Murphy, and she indicated that she had also heard similar allegations. She indicated that Mr. Schwimez is an aggressive, successful businessman and that because of his particular style of business not everyone likes him. Ms. Murphy believes the allegations are baseless and are simply the result of envy and jealousy. Although the CFO is probably correct, we may want to conduct a more thorough background check on Mr. Schwimez.

New Product

In the 4th quarter of 2011 Flash began shipping a new product "Flashwall 2011." It is a computer encryption device for notebook computers. Sales for fiscal year 2011 amounted to about $2 million. The company is attempting to keep the details of this card relatively quiet for a few more months for competitive reasons. Due to design advances developed by Flash's research and development team, these new cards have an extremely low cost (less than $20). However, they are currently selling for about $300. To date, all sales of Flashwall 2011 have been made to one customer, CCB Computers, which is located in New Hampshire. Mr. Schwimez indicated that CCB and Flash have an excellent working relationship. The president of CCB, Andrew Jolsen, is a long-time associate of Mr. Schwimez. Mr. Jolsen will be joining Flash's Board of Directors within the next few months.

Reference:	A 9
Prepared by:	ASG
Date:	1/7/2012
Reviewed by:	

Flash Technologies, Inc.
Memo to the Planning File by Audit Manager—General Information (continued)
12/31/2011

Plant Tour

After a December 23rd meeting with Flash, I visited the Massachusetts manufacturing facility just outside Binex. This is one of the original manufacturing facilities and thus is not as "leading edge" as Flash's other manufacturing facilities around the world. I was somewhat surprised at how much of the product is still assembled manually. I saw a lot of people assembling cases for solid state hard drives with rubber mallets. Nonetheless, I was generally impressed with the organization and efficiency of the facility. It appeared employees were well trained. In one assembly line, I was particularly interested in the inspection team over product quality. They were examining the welds on the flash hard drive casings. I watched the process for several minutes (and several hundred drives) noting no faulty product during that time. I examined a casing that was in the "reject" bin due to a failed weld. When a weld did fail, the inspection team member indicated most of the time the casing could be rewelded without any spoilage. I noticed all the reject casings were empty (no electronics inside). An inspection team member told me that after the casings are inspected and rejected, the "insides" are removed for cleaning and are then carefully reprocessed in a static-free environment.

In the employee dining area, I overheard some disgruntled employees talking about the pressure they were under to ship customer items. When I inquired further I was informed that Mr. Schwimez had just decided to send out large holiday baskets of fruit and candy to show the company's appreciation to valued customers. Because of the rush to get the baskets in the overnight mail, Mr. Schwimez asked the shipping department to take care of the packing and shipping. Employees indicated that what Mr. Schwimez wants, he gets.

Major Contract

Mr. Schwimez informed me that Flash is close to sealing a deal with AT&T for a satellite tracking system for truck fleets that could be worth up to $300 million. He is very excited about the deal and believes it will really put Flash Technologies "on the map." He indicated that when the formal announcement is made it should boost the stock price even higher. Because the deal is so close to completion, he has been disclosing the information to investors and some in the financial press. Industry publications have mentioned the possibility of a big AT&T contract for such a tracking system, but AT&T has thus far declined comment and no agreement has been announced.

SEC Investigation

The CFO, Ms. Murphy, informed me that Flash has received informal notification from the SEC that it is performing a review of Flash's financial statement filings. The client has indicated this is a routine process that is common for rapidly growing companies, particularly high technology companies. The CFO indicates that many high technology companies have recently received comment letters regarding their accounting for in-process R&D.

"FLASH MEMORY MARKET EXPLODING"

By Jessica Mara Jayne
October 23, 2011, *Financial Times and Seasons*

In 2002, when flash memory was an emerging market, I suggested that it wouldn't surprise me if flash memory had a larger market share than either HDD (hard disk drives) or RAM in ten years. I was almost right. Today, HDD and RAM are both about $30 billion each, while flash memory is a $20 billion market. But HDD and RAM are not growing, while flash memory is continuing to grow rapidly. The real takeoff is just beginning.

Why is the growth of flash exploding? Because flash memory is everywhere, in cameras, camcorders, MP3, GPS, gaming, USB flash drives, e-books, mobile phones, notebooks, netbooks, tablets, and servers. And the stage is set for some of these categories to really expand, like smartphones. People want to store a lot of data on their mobile phones, and that's only going to increase as mobile internet grows with technologies like 4G. With the growth of cloud computing, people are also storing a lot of their data on remote servers. And they will want backups of a lot of this data on personal flash memory products, either for safety reasons, or for using them when there is no connectivity to the internet.

Also watch for solid state drives (SSDs) to replace HDDs that have rotating mechanical discs and suffer wear and tear. The price of solid state is now at a reasonable level to be more broadly adapted. With operating shock loads of 20Gs, solid-state memory devices have clearly superior durability to rotating memory devices. In applications where durability is of extreme importance (including some military applications), flash memory is the preferred technology at any capacity. SSD's are fast, rugged, and use less power than traditional rotating hard drives, and flash memory never crashes. PC makers are able to make smaller notebooks and netbooks.

Worldwide market consumption of flash memory cards is growing at incredible rates, well over 50% in last three years. Because of the enormous potential for this market, there may be opportunities for smaller niche players to be successful.

Industry Ratios

	2011	2010
Current Ratio	1.50	1.30
Quick Ratio	1.10	1.06
Debt to Equity Ratio	29.00%	28.00%
Inventory Turnover	8.10	8.60
Profit Margin	14.60%	11.18%
Return on Total Assets	5.03%	4.97%

Flash Technologies, Inc.
Annual Report, Management Discussion of Financial Condition, Report of Independent Auditors, and Notes to Consolidated Financial Statements
For the Year Ending December 31, 2011

Annual Report

OVERVIEW

Flash Technologies, Inc. (the "Company") designs, manufactures and markets an extensive line flash memory cards, USB flash drives, and solid state hard drives for computers and other electronic devices. Flash memory is a rugged, lightweight device inserted into a dedicated slot in a broad range of electronic equipment that contain microprocessors, such as portable computers, telecommunications equipment, manufacturing equipment and vehicle diagnostic systems. The Company sells its flash memory primarily to original equipment manufacturers ("OEMs") for industrial and commercial applications. The Company's flash memory provides increased storage capacity and programmed software for specialized applications.

The OEM market served by the Company has rigorous demands for quality products, technical service and support, and rapid order turnaround. The Company provides its OEM customers with comprehensive flash memory solutions, including in-house design, programming, engineering, manufacturing, and private labeling. The Company believes its ability to provide a full range of services, rapid order turnaround, and manufacturing flexibility to accommodate both large and small production runs provides a competitive advantage in servicing the OEM market. The Company sells into a broad range of markets, including: Communications (routers, wireless telephones, and local area networks); Transportation (navigation, vehicle diagnostics); Mobile Computing (hand-held data collection terminals, notebook computers, personal digital assistants); and Media (digital cameras and digital audio players). The Company has sold its products and services to over 250 OEMs, including 3Com Corporation ("3Com"), Bay Networks, Inc. ("Bay Networks"), Lucent Technologies, Inc. ("Lucent Technologies"), Philips Electronics N.V. ("Philips"), Trimble Navigation Limited ("Trimble Navigation"), Digital Equipment Corporation ("Digital"), Sharp Electronics Corporation ("Sharp") and Xerox Corporation ("Xerox").

The Company was incorporated and began operation in 1997 to develop and commercialize font cartridges for laser printers. Beginning in 2002, the Company began designing, manufacturing and marketing flash memory and gradually de-emphasized the marketing and sales of font cartridges in order to focus on the rapidly growing flash memory market.

RECENT DEVELOPMENTS

In September 2011, the Company entered into an agreement to form Flash Technologies (Korea) Limited ("Flash Korea"), which will provide contract manufacturing services for third parties, as well as serve as an offshore manufacturer of flash memory. Under the agreement, the Company will acquire a 51% interest in Flash Korea in exchange for $1.25 million in cash. The remaining 49% will be held by an unaffiliated company. The Company expects Flash Korea to begin operations by May 2012. No assurance can be given that Flash Korea will commence operations on schedule, or that it will not experience significant and unforeseen expenses, costs, and delays.

In January 2012, the Company purchased a majority interest in Design Circuits, Inc. ("DCI"), a contract manufacturer for OEMs. DCI has a June 30 fiscal year-end. For the six months ended December 31, 2011 and the fiscal years ended June 30, 2011 and 2010, sales at DCI totaled approximately $7,000,000, $9,070,000 and $8,482,000, respectively, and net income (losses) totaled approximately ($509,000), ($1,418,000) and $171,000, respectively. The Company acquired approximately a 75% interest in DCI in exchange for approximately $3.2 million in cash and 125,000 shares of the Company's common stock (the "Common Stock"). The remaining 25% of DCI was acquired by outside investors for approximately $2.4 million.

The Company believes that DCI and Flash Korea may benefit from the Company's existing supply relationships and customer contacts. In addition, the Company believes that it may benefit from exposure to the products and customers of DCI and Flash Korea.

TECHNOLOGY AND INDUSTRY BACKGROUND

In recent years, digital computing and processing have expanded beyond the boundaries of desktop computer systems to include a broader array of electronic systems, such as mobile communication systems, communications switches, network switches, medical devices, navigation systems, cellular telephones, portable computers, digital cameras, and portable data collection terminals. Flash memory characteristics, such as shock and vibration tolerance, low power consumption, small size, and higher access speed, better meet the requirements of these emerging applications than do traditional hard drive storage solutions. In addition, flash memory can provide features, such as additional or specialized memory technologies, that previously resided on computer add-in boards or required external hardware devices. The Company believes that demand for flash memory will increase from increased adoption of next generation electronic devices.

The Company primarily targets OEM customers in the following four industries: Communication (smartphones, routers); Transportation (fleet data recording, navigation, auto diagnostics); Media (cameras, media players); and Mobile Computing (notebooks, tablets, netbooks).

CUSTOMER SALES AND MARKETING

The Company targets industrial and commercial applications for flash memory in the communications, transportation, media, and mobile computing industries. The company has a direct sales force of 12 people with offices in Massachusetts, California, Canada, England, and Germany.

The Company's sales staff and engineers often work with OEM engineers to design and engineer flash memory to OEM requirements, which often leads the Company to provide custom-designed flash memory for specific applications. The Company also markets its products to corporate end-users directly and through value-added resellers. Corporate end-users purchase flash memory to provide additional memory to store customized software for encryption and other specialty applications.

MANUFACTURING

The Company's flash memory manufacturing process includes programming, production, assembly, ultrasonic welding, cleaning, final assembly, labeling, and packaging. Nearly all of these operations are conducted at the Company's manufacturing facility in Binex, Massachusetts. The Company's manufacturing facility has generally operated on a two-shift, five-day-per-week basis.

Manufacturing Flexibility. The Company has designed its manufacturing facility to accommodate its customers' requirement for rapid order turnaround. The Company's manufacturing process may be converted to accommodate the production of different products with minimum down time.

In fiscal 2011, the Company subcontracted a small portion of its manufacturing to a Canadian electronic-assembly contract manufacturer with specialized manufacturing capabilities, which include wire bonding and ceramic printing. The Company believes its ability to subcontract a portion of its manufacturing will give it greater flexibility with respect to manufacturing capacity.

Product Quality and Testing Procedures. The Company continually seeks to improve product quality. The Company's zero-defect policy, implemented in April 2010, is designed to ensure that there are no defects in flash memory products shipped from the Company's facility. In connection with this effort, the Company hired additional production and testing engineers and established additional quality control checks throughout its manufacturing process. In October 2010, the Company became a certified ISO 9001 manufacturer with respect to its Binex, Massachusetts facility. Certification requires that the Company undergo an annual audit of certain policies and procedures.

Manufacturing Efficiency. The Company places a high priority on maintaining efficient operations. The Company is upgrading manual production lines to automated production lines in order to reduce cost and increase throughput. For example, the Company uses ultrasonic welders that encase the Company's flash memory more efficiently than manual labor and produce a more rugged product with better protection against electrostatic discharge.

Flash Technologies, Inc.   **DRAFT**   **For Internal Use Only**

SOURCES OF SUPPLY

The Company has, from time to time, experienced shortages in components used to manufacture flash memory, specifically crystal oscillators. The Company expects such supply shortages to continue. The Company purchases certain key components from sole or single-source vendors for which alternative sources are not currently available. The Company does not maintain long-term supply agreements with any of its vendors. The inability to develop alternative sources for these single or sole-source components or to obtain sufficient quantities of components could result in delays or reductions in product shipments. The Company relies on certain sole-source suppliers to provide components used in certain of the Company's products. The Company seeks to maintain close working relationships with its suppliers to ensure timely and reliable delivery.

COMPETITION

The Company competes with manufacturers of flash memory and related products, including SanDisk Corporation and Smart Modular Technologies, Inc., as well as with electronic component manufacturers that also manufacture flash memory, including Mitsubishi Electronic Corporation, Intel Corporation, Epson of America, Inc. and Fujitsu Microelectronics, Inc. Several of these competitors also supply the Company with raw materials, including electronic components that are from time to time subject to industry-wide allocation. Such competitors may have the ability to manufacture flash memory at lower costs than the Company as a result of their higher levels of integration.

The Company expects competition to increase in the future from existing competitors and from other companies that may enter the Company's existing or future markets with similar or alternative solutions that may be less costly or provide additional features. The Company believes that its ability to compete successfully depends on a number of factors, which include product quality and performance, order turnaround, the provision of competitive design capabilities, success in developing new applications for flash memory, adequate manufacturing capacity, efficiency of production, timing of new product introductions by the Company, its customers and its competitors, the number and nature of the Company's competitors in a given market, price, and general market and economic conditions. In addition, increased competitive pressure may lead to intensified price competition, resulting in lower prices and gross margins.

| Flash Technologies, Inc. | DRAFT | For Internal Use Only |

Management Discussion of Financial Condition

The Company was incorporated and began operation in 1997 to develop and commercialize font cartridges for laser printers. Beginning in fiscal 2002, when the Company began designing, manufacturing, and marketing flash memory, the Company gradually de-emphasized the marketing and sales of font cartridges in order to focus on the rapidly growing flash memory market. The Company's sales increased from $6.3 million in fiscal 2008 to $37.8 million in fiscal 2011. Net income has correspondingly increased from $442,000 in fiscal 2008 to $4.9 million in fiscal 2011.

Sales increased to approximately $37.8 million in fiscal 2011 from approximately 12.4 million in 2010, primarily as a result of increased sales volume of flash memory. Sales of flash memory as a percentage of total sales increased to approximately 98% in fiscal 2011 from approximately 86% in fiscal 2010. The growth in the Company's flash memory sales resulted primarily from expansion of the flash memory market, increased sales and marketing efforts by the Company, and the broadening of the Company's flash memory product line. The increase in the Company's flash memory sales was partially offset by a decrease in sales of font cartridges.

Gross margin increased to approximately $14.2 million in fiscal 2011 from approximately $5.6 million in 2010. As a percentage of sales, gross margin decreased to 37.5% in fiscal 2011 from 45% in fiscal 2010, primarily due to an increase in the cost of electronic components used in the Company's products and to the continuing shift in product mix from font cartridges to lower-margin flash memory. The cost of these components generally stabilized during the latter half of fiscal 2011. Flash memory sales may comprise a lower percentage of the Company's total sales in future periods due to the recent acquisition of DCI, a contract manufacturer, and the commencement of contract manufacturing operations at Flash Korea, expected in May 2012. The Company expects to realize lower gross margins associated with its future contract manufacturing services than those realized from the sale of its flash memory.

SIGNATURES

In accordance with Section 13 or 15(d) of the Securities Exchange Act of 1934, as amended, the registrant caused this report to be signed on its behalf by the undersigned, thereunto duly authorized.

Date: December 31, 2011

Manny Schwimez, Chairperson of the Board, Chief Executive Officer, and Secretary

Ronald J. McDonald, President and Director

Jane M. Murphy, Chief Financial Officer (Principal financial and accounting officer), and Director

Flash Technologies, Inc.   **DRAFT**   **For Internal Use Only**

Report of Independent Accountants (*copy of prior year's report*)

To the Board of Directors and Stockholders of FLASH TECHNOLOGIES, INC.:

We have audited the accompanying consolidated balance sheets of FLASH TECHNOLOGIES, INC. and subsidiaries as of December 31, 2009 and December 30, 2010, and the related consolidated statements of operations, stockholders' equity and comprehensive loss, and cash flows for each of the fiscal years in the three-year period ended December 31, 2010. These consolidated financial statements are the responsibility of the Company's management. Our responsibility is to express an opinion on these consolidated financial statements based on our audits.

We conducted our audits in accordance with the standards of the Public Company Accounting Oversight Board (United States). Those standards require that we plan and perform the audit to obtain reasonable assurance about whether the financial statements are free of material misstatement. An audit includes examining, on a test basis, evidence supporting the amounts and disclosures in the financial statements. An audit also includes assessing the accounting principles used and significant estimates made by management, as well as evaluating the overall financial statement presentation. We believe that our audits provide a reasonable basis for our opinion.

In our opinion, the consolidated financial statements referred to above present fairly, in all material respects, the financial position of FLASH TECHNOLOGIES, INC. and subsidiaries as of December 31, 2009 and December 30, 2010, and the results of their operations and their cash flows for each of the fiscal years in the three-year period ended December 31, 2010, in conformity with U.S. generally accepted accounting principles.

We also have audited, in accordance with the standards of the Public Company Accounting Oversight Board (United States), the effectiveness of FLASH TECHNOLOGIES, INC. internal control over financial reporting as of December 31, 2010, based on criteria established in Internal Control—Integrated Framework issued by the Committee of Sponsoring Organizations of the Treadway Commission (COSO), and our report dated March 14, 2011 expressed an unqualified opinion on management's assessment of, and the effective operation of, internal control over financial reporting.

Adams & Adams, AUDITOR. Boston, Massachusetts.

March 14, 2011

Flash Technologies, Inc.   **DRAFT**   **For Internal Use Only**

FLASH TECHNOLOGIES, INC.
Consolidated Balance Sheet

	Unaudited Dec. 31, 2011	Dec. 31, 2010
ASSETS		
Current assets:		
Cash and cash equivalents	$ 6,181,520	$ 970,446
Available-for-sale securities	4,932,763	—
Accounts receivable, net of allowance for doubtful accounts of $230,000 and $122,200 at Dec. 31, 2011 and 2010, respectively	12,592,231	3,932,170
Inventories	18,229,317	8,609,492
Current portion of notes receivable	3,680,750	767,758
Deferred income taxes	211,100	209,300
Other current assets	2,362,887	670,812
Total current assets	48,190,568	15,159,978
Equipment and leasehold improvements, net of accumulated depreciation and amortization of $822,011 and $299,355 at Dec. 31, 2011 and 2010, respectively	4,698,616	1,322,637
Notes receivable, less current portion	—	1,072,939
Investments	2,472,381	—
Other assets	170,392	266,658
Deferred income taxes	121,300	126,000
Intangible assets, net of impairment costs	128,918	250,944
Total Assets	$ 55,782,175	$ 18,199,156

	Unaudited Dec. 31, 2011	Dec. 31, 2010
LIABILITIES AND STOCKHOLDERS' EQUITY		
Current liabilities:		
Note payable	$ 4,683,876	$ 1,153,167
Current portion of long-term obligations under capital leases	336,058	102,645
Accounts payable and accrued expenses	3,494,693	3,570,519
Income taxes payable	614,036	591,265
Deferred revenue	—	175,000
Total current liabilities	9,128,663	5,592,596
Long-term obligations under capital leases	366,944	161,134
Deferred income taxes	241,600	—
Stockholders' equity:		
Common stock, $.01 par value; 15,000,000 shares authorized 8,315,935 shares issued and outstanding at Dec. 31, 2011 and 5,591,288 shares issued and outstanding at Dec. 31, 2010	83,159	55,913
Additional paid-in capital	38,883,677	10,213,517
Retained earnings	7,078,132	2,175,996
Total stockholders' equity	46,044,968	12,445,426
Total liabilities and stockholders' equity	$ 55,782,175	$ 18,199,156

Flash Technologies, Inc.   **DRAFT**   **For Internal Use Only**

FLASH TECHNOLOGIES, INC.
Consolidated Income Statements

| | Years Ended Dec. 31, | | |
| | Unaudited | | |
	2011	2010	2009
Sales	$ 37,847,681	$ 12,445,015	$ 8,213,236
Cost of goods sold	23,636,299	6,832,927	4,523,186
Gross margin	14,211,382	5,612,088	3,690,050
General and administrative expenses	4,468,387	3,275,315	1,837,514
Impairment Costs	122,026	90,437	51,088
Research and development costs	1,433,765	752,654	567,248
Income from operations	8,187,204	1,493,682	1,234,200
Other income (expense):			
Interest income	352,606	9,944	8,159
Interest expense	(369,584)	(73,952)	(169,755)
Loss on sale of receivables to factor	—	—	(76,892)
Amortization of discount on bridge financing	—	—	(247,500)
Total other income (expense)	(16,978)	(64,008)	(485,988)
Income before income taxes	8,170,226	1,429,674	748,212
Provision for income taxes	3,268,090	555,958	284,320
Net income	$ 4,902,136	$ 873,716	$ 463,892
Earnings per share: Primary	$ 0.67	$ 0.16	$ 0.14
Weighted average shares outstanding: Primary	7,338,906	5,511,606	3,325,000

Flash Technologies, Inc.　　　　DRAFT　　　　For Internal Use Only

FLASH TECHNOLOGIES, INC.
Consolidated Statement of Cash Flows
Years ended Dec. 31,

	Unaudited 2011	2010	2009
Cash flows from operating activities:			
Net income	$ 4,902,136	$ 873,716	$ 463,892
Adjustments to reconcile net income			
Depreciation and amortization	522,656	246,714	141,585
Impairment on intangibles	122,026	90,437	51,088
Provision for loss on accounts receivable	280,000	162,200	49,000
Discount on bridge financing	—	—	247,500
Compensation from option grants	19,875	52,650	—
Tax benefit related to stock option exercise	614,322	—	—
Deferred income taxes	244,500	(219,593)	(76,506)
Changes in operating assets and liabilities:			
Accounts receivable	(8,940,061)	(2,432,829)	(981,064)
Inventories	(9,619,825)	(5,238,039)	(1,115,211)
Notes receivable	759,947	(1,840,697)	—
Other assets	(1,595,809)	(564,033)	(58,726)
Accounts payable and accrued expenses	(75,826)	2,954,790	(974,411)
Income taxes payable	22,771	74,854	75,070
Deferred revenue	(175,000)	175,000	—
Net cash used for operating activities	(12,918,288)	(5,664,830)	(2,177,783)
Cash flows from investing activities:			
Capital expenditures	(3,898,635)	(862,396)	(525,438)
Purchase of available-for-sale securities	(8,913,741)	—	—
Proceeds from sale of available-for-sale securities	3,980,978	—	—
Notes receivable	(2,800,000)	—	—
Purchases of investments	(2,272,381)	—	—
Net cash used for investing activities	(13,903,779)	(862,396)	(525,438)
Cash flows from financing activities:			
Cash overdraft	—	—	(54,398)
Net borrowings under line of credit	3,530,709	1,153,167	—
Borrowings from sales leaseback of equipment	691,034	319,735	—
Payments on equipment financing	(251,811)	(55,956)	—
Net proceeds from exercise of stock options	698,671	149,550	—
Net proceeds from exercise of warrants and representatives' warrants	5,193,785	3,809,630	
Net proceeds from public offerings	20,928,753	—	4,637,589
Net proceeds pursuant to the underwriters' over-allotments	1,242,000	—	26,100
Net proceeds from private placement	—	1,140,476	—
Proceeds from bridge financing	—	—	550,000
Repayment of bridge financing	—	—	(550,000)
Payments on notes payable	—	—	(925,000)
Net cash provided by financing activities	32,033,141	6,516,602	3,684,291
Net increase (decrease) in cash	5,211,074	(10,624)	981,070
Cash/cash equivalents at beginning of the year	970,446	981,070	—
Cash/cash equivalents at end of the year	$ 6,181,520	$ 970,446	$ 981,070

Flash Technologies, Inc.   **DRAFT**   **For Internal Use Only**

NOTES TO CONSOLIDATED FINANCIAL STATEMENTS

SUMMARY OF SIGNIFICANT ACCOUNTING POLICIES

Basis of Presentation. The consolidated financial statements of Flash Technologies, Inc. (the "Company") include the accounts of the Company, all wholly-owned subsidiaries and majority-owned subsidiaries. Investments in companies in which ownership interests range from 20 to 50 percent, and the Company exercises significant influence over operating and financial policies, are accounted for using the equity method. Other investments are accounted for using the cost method. All significant intercompany balances and transactions have been eliminated.

Industry Segment. The Company operates in a single industry segment: the design, manufacture, and marketing of flash memory used primarily by original equipment manufacturers for industrial and commercial applications. In September 2011, the Company entered into an agreement to acquire a 51% interest in a joint venture. The joint venture intends to manufacture flash memory and provide contract-manufacturing services.

Revenue Recognition. Revenue from product sales is recognized at time of shipment.

Warranty Costs. Costs relating to product warranty are expensed as incurred. In addition, on sales to certain wholesalers, the Company offers a stock rotation policy. The Company has not experienced material costs associated with its warranty and restocking policy.

Research and Development Costs. Expenditures relating to the development of new products and processes, including significant improvements and refinements to existing products, are expensed as incurred.

Cash and Cash Equivalents. The Company considers all highly liquid investments purchased with an original maturity of three months or less to be cash equivalents. The Company has no requirements for compensating balances.

Concentration of Credit Risk. Financial instruments which potentially subject the Company to concentration of credit risk consist principally of trade receivables. If any of the Company's major customers fail to pay the Company on a timely basis, it could have a material effect on the Company's financial position and results of operations.

For fiscal 2011, two customers, whose individual sales exceeded 10% of total sales, accounted for an aggregate of approximately 25% of the Company's sales. At December 31, 2011, these two customers accounted for approximately $4.7 million, or 38% of the Company's accounts receivable balance.

No one customer or group of related customers accounts for more than 10% of the Company's sales in fiscal 2010 and 2009. At December 31, 2010, two customers of the Company accounted for approximately $1.4 million, or 35% of the Company's accounts receivable balance.

Approximately 12%, 23% and 22% of the Company's sales in fiscal 2011, 2010 and 2009, respectively, were outside the United States, primarily in several Western European countries, Israel and Canada. No one area comprised more than 10% of the Company's sales.

Inventories. Inventories are stated on a first-in, first-out (FIFO) basis at the lower of cost or market.

Equipment and Leasehold Improvements. Equipment is stated at cost. Major renewals and improvements are capitalized, whereas repair and maintenance charges are expensed when incurred. Depreciation is provided over the estimated useful life of the respective assets, ranging from three to 10 years, on a straight-line basis. Leasehold improvements are amortized over the lesser of the term of the lease or the estimated useful life of the related assets. When assets are sold or retired, their cost and related accumulated depreciation are removed from the accounts. Any gain or loss is included in the determination of net income.

Intangible Assets. Our intangible assets consist of trademarks, copyrights and a covenant not to compete. The FASB's Accounting Standard Codification (ASC) Topic 350 requires that intangible assets be evaluated for impairment at least annually or more frequently if events or circumstances indicate that the asset might be impaired. Impairment is measured by comparing the intangible asset's carrying amounts to the fair values using methods outlined in ASC Topic 350 and ASC Topic 820.

INVENTORIES

Inventories consisted of:

	December 31, 2011	December 31, 2010
Raw material, primarily electronic components	$ 8,994,805	$ 4,511,892
Work in process	1,637,519	1,814,599
Finished goods	7,596,993	2,283,001
	$ 18,229,317	$ 8,609,492

The Company maintains levels of inventories that it believes are necessary based upon assumptions concerning its growth, mix of sales and availability of raw materials.

NOTES RECEIVABLE

Operating Activity. In fiscal 2010, the Company sold approximately $1,040,000 of accounts receivable and $1,000,000 of inventory to an unrelated party for $200,000 in cash and two promissory notes. The notes with an original aggregate principal amount of approximately $1,840,000, are collateralized by the assets of the unrelated party, bear interest at 9% per annum and are payable in equal quarterly installments in 2010 and 2011. At December 31, 2011 and 2010, the balance of these notes receivable was approximately $1,081,000 and $1,840,000, respectively.

In fiscal 2010, the Company recognized gross margin of $75,000 from this transaction and deferred $175,000 of gross margin. During fiscal 2011, the Company recognized this $175,000 deferred gross margin as income, as scheduled payments continued to be made and an agreement was reached in the fourth quarter of fiscal 2011 that certain payments were to be accelerated. These notes receivable are classified as an operating activity in the accompanying Consolidated Statement of Cash Flows.

Investing Activity. During fiscal 2011, the Company advanced funds to affiliated and unaffiliated companies that generally develop technologies complementary to those of the Company. At December 31, 2011, the notes receivable balance due from these companies was approximately $2,600,000. The Company made eight such loans, all of which are evidenced by notes (promissory or convertible). The terms of these notes are one year or less and bear interest at rates ranging between prime and prime plus 4%. These notes receivable are classified as an investing activity in the accompanying Consolidated Statement of Cash Flows.

To date there have been no defaults associated with the terms of the outstanding notes receivable.

EQUIPMENT AND LEASEHOLD IMPROVEMENTS

Equipment and leasehold improvements consisted of the following:

	December 31, 2011	December 31, 2010
Equipment	$ 4,302,016	$ 1,220,173
Equipment under capital leases	1,010,769	319,735
Leasehold improvements	207,842	82,084
Total equipment and leasehold improvements	5,520,627	1,621,992
Accumulated depreciation and amortization	(822,011)	(299,355)
Equipment and leasehold improvements, net	$ 4,698,616	$ 1,322,637

Depreciation expense for fiscal 2011, 2010 and 2009 was approximately $523,000, $215,000 and $71,000, respectively.

INVESTMENTS

Fiscal 2011. The Company purchased for $500,000 in cash and a conversion of a $200,000 note a 9.5% interest in a corporation that designs, manufactures, and markets automated optical vision and individual imaging systems for inspection and identification of defects in circuits. The Company accounts for this investment using the equity method of accounting because it can exercise significant influence over the corporation. For fiscal 2011, the Company's proportionate share of this corporation's operations was immaterial.

Flash Technologies, Inc.　　　　**DRAFT**　　　　**For Internal Use Only**

DEBT

Note Payable. The Company maintains a $7,500,000 revolving-line-of-credit agreement with a bank. The Company's credit agreement limits borrowings to a percentage of receivables and inventories and contains certain covenants relating to the Company's net worth and indebtedness, among others. This credit agreement is collateralized by substantially all the assets of the Company. The credit agreement bears interest at the bank's prime interest rate. The agreement expires in April 2012. The Company is currently negotiating a renewal of, and an increase in, its credit agreement with the bank. At December 31, 2011 and 2010, the Company had utilized approximately $4.7 million and $1.2 million, respectively, under this credit agreement.

Capital Leases. The Company leases certain equipment under lease financing agreements with the bank that is currently providing the Company with its line of credit. These lease arrangements have been accounted for as financing transactions. The subject equipment is recorded as an asset for financial statement purposes and is being depreciated accordingly. These loans have terms of three years and bear interest at rates ranging from 7.2% to 9.7% per annum.

Operating Leases. The Company leases its facilities under operating leases with renewal options that expire at various dates through 2015. Under certain leases, the Company is obligated to pay its pro-rata share of operational and maintenance costs. The lease for the Company's principal executive office and manufacturing operations in Binex, MA expires in June 2012. This lease contains an option to renew for an additional five-year period.

At December 31, 2011, the minimum annual rental commitments under non-cancelable lease obligations are as follows:

	Capital Leases	Operating Leases
Years ending December 31:		
2011	$384,022	$299,035
2012	313,171	86,431
2013	74,020	19,589
2014		9,903
2015		1,614
Total minimum lease payments	$771,213	$416,572
Less amounts representing interest	(68,211)	
Present value of future minimum lease payments	703,002	
Less current portion	(336,058)	
	$366,944	

Rental expense totaled approximately $396,000, $330,000, and $229,000 in fiscal 2011, 2010, and 2009, respectively.

RELATED PARTY TRANSACTIONS

During a portion of fiscal 2009 the Company paid the compensation of the Company's Chairman and principal stockholder, through a management corporation. The corporation employed and contracted out his management services to corporations, including the Company. The management corporation, which is not affiliated with the Company, paid the Chairman approximately 70% of the amounts that the Company paid to the management corporation for his services rendered to the Company. During fiscal 2009, the Company paid the management corporation approximately $176,000 under this arrangement.

In January 2011, the Company entered into an agreement with a consulting firm with respect to acquisitions and investments. A nonemployee Director of the Company is a principal of the consulting firm. The Company agreed to pay the consulting firm $3,500 per month and the reimbursement of certain travel expenses related to its consulting services. The Company terminated this agreement in December 2011.

Flash Technologies, Inc.   **DRAFT**   **For Internal Use Only**

LICENSE AGREEMENTS

In December 2009, the Company entered into a license agreement under which the Company licenses from a third party certain patent-pending technology relating to flash memory with a built-in encryption integrated circuit. The initial term of the license was for one year. In December 2010, the Company renewed the license for an additional 15-month period. The license provides for annual license fees that the Company pays quarterly based on the number of units sold. The minimum annual license fee payable by the Company was $100,000 during the first year of the license, and for the 15-month period ending April 30, 2012. Under the current terms of the license the fee will increase by 100% annually for each additional year the license is renewed through September 2014. The Company has the right to terminate this license when the current term expires in April 2012.

COMMITMENTS

In December 2011, the Company entered into an agreement to advance approximately $750,000 to a company in which it has taken a minority equity interest. Such advances are for the purpose of financing the acquisition of inventory components. As of February 1, 2012, the Company has advanced approximately $750,000 under this agreement. In January 2009, the Company purchased additional capital assets, primarily manufacturing equipment, for approximately $1.7 million. The equipment was financed through equipment lease financing. The loan has a term of three years, bears interest at 7.75% per annum and requires minimum annual payments of principal and interest of approximately $618,000.

JOINT VENTURE

In September 2011, the Company entered into an agreement to acquire a 51% interest in a joint venture for $1,250,000 in cash. The joint venture intends to manufacture, in Korea, flash memory and USB flash drive products and related accessories, as well as provide contract-manufacturing services to others. As of December 31, 2011, the Company advanced $25,000 in cash to the joint venture and incurred acquisition costs, which were capitalized, of approximately $37,000. The Company expects the joint venture to begin manufacturing operations by May 2012.

Asher Farms Inc.
Understanding of Client's Business Environment

MARK S. BEASLEY · FRANK A. BUCKLESS · STEVEN M. GLOVER · DOUGLAS F. PRAWITT

LEARNING OBJECTIVES

After completing and discussing this case you should be able to

[1] Describe the implications of an audit client's business environment on the audit engagement strategy

[2] Identify factors affecting an audit client's environment and related business risk

[3] Link business risk factors to the risk of material misstatements in financial statement accounts

INTRODUCTION

Asher Farms, Inc. is a fully-integrated poultry processing company engaged in the production, processing, marketing and distribution of fresh and frozen chicken products. Asher Farms sells ice pack, chill pack and frozen chicken, in whole, cut-up and boneless form to retailers, distributors, and casual dining operators principally in the southeastern and southwestern United States. During its fiscal year ended October 31, 2011 the company processed 343.6 million chickens, or approximately 2.0 billion dressed pounds. According to 2011 industry statistics, Asher Farms is the 4th largest processor of dressed chickens in the United States based on estimated average weekly processing. Asher Farms' common stock is traded on the NASDAQ national market with an aggregate market value of $677 million on October 31, 2011

Asher Farms' chicken operations presently encompass 7 hatcheries, 6 feed mills and 8 processing plants employing 1,059 salaried and 8,646 hourly employees. The company has contracts with operators of approximately 530 broiler farms that provide the company with sufficient housing capacity for its current operations. Asher Farms also has contracts with 173 breeder farm operators and 44 pullet farm operators.

INFORMATION ABOUT THE AUDIT

Asher Farms is required to have an integrated audit of its consolidated financial statements and its internal control over financial reporting in accordance with the standards of the Public Company Accounting Oversight Board (United States). Your firm, Smith and Jones, PA., recently accepted Asher Farms as an audit client and as a staff auditor you have been asked to obtain some preliminary information about the poultry industry to provide a basis for understanding the client's business environment. Background information about the poultry industry from Smith and Jones' industry database is provided for your review.

The case was prepared by Mark S. Beasley, Ph.D. and Frank A. Buckless, Ph.D. of North Carolina State University and Steven M. Glover, Ph.D. and Douglas F. Prawitt, Ph.D. of Brigham Young University, as a basis for class discussion. Asher Farms Inc. is a fictitious company. All characters and names represented are fictitious; any similarity to existing companies or persons is purely conincidental.

REQUIRED

[1] A useful approach for understanding a client's business environment and associated business risks is to perform a PESTLE analysis. PESTLE is an acronym for Political, Economic, Social, Technological, Legal and Environmental factors that are used to asses the client's business environment. A PESTLE analysis focuses on factors that may affect an entity's business model, but are beyond the control or influence of the client. While beyond management's direct influence, such factors may significantly impact an entity's business risk. Read the background information about the poultry industry and conduct additional research on the internet to obtain the latest news and information on the industry. Brainstorm political, economic, social, technological, legal and environmental factors that could affect Asher Farms' business risk. Unless your instructor indicates otherwise, identify at least one business risk factor for each component of the PESTLE acronym.

[2] For each of the business risk factors identified in question 1 above, indicate how each risk factor might impact the risk of material misstatements in specific financial statement accounts or disclosures.

[3] Professional auditing standards provide guidance on the auditor's consideration of an entity's business environment and associated business risks. (a) What is the auditor's objective for understanding an entity's business environment? (b) Why does an auditor not have responsibility to identify or assess all business risks? (c) Provide some examples of business risks associated with an entity that an auditor should consider when performing an audit. (d) Provide some additional examples of business risks that might not lead to a risk of material misstatement in the financial statements.

Smith and Jones, PA.
Background Information: Poultry Industry

Consumption

Over the past decade, both the mix of meat products, which includes beef, pork, chicken, and fish related products, and actual levels of per capita consumption within many nations has changed dramatically. Improved technologies and infrastructure development has expanded production and trade in meat products. At the same time, changing lifestyles, incomes, and a growing awareness of health issues related to meat consumption altered the patterns of meat demand worldwide. The large increase in meat consumption has been largely met by the worldwide growth in intensive livestock production, particularly poultry. This is expected to continue as real income grows in the emerging economies around the world.

The U.S. poultry industry is the world's largest producer and second largest exporter of poultry. U.S. consumption of poultry (broilers, other chicken, and turkey) is the fastest growing segment of all meats. Per capita consumption of meats in the United States from 1988 to 2008 is presented in Figure 1 (Source: U.S. Department of Agriculture).

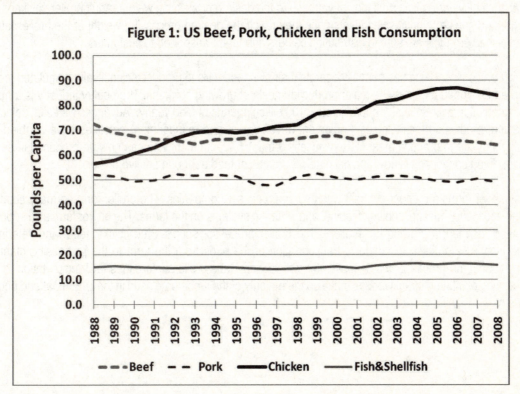

With about 15 percent of total poultry production being exported, the U.S. poultry industry is heavily influenced by currency fluctuations, trade negotiations, and economic growth in its major importing markets.

Production

U.S. broiler chicken production is concentrated in a group of States stretching from Delaware, south along the Atlantic coast to Georgia, then westward through Alabama, Mississippi, and Arkansas. The top broiler-producing State is Georgia, followed by Arkansas, Alabama, Mississippi, and North Carolina. The poultry production industry faces issues common to most businesses, as well as issues that are unique to agriculture and the production of animal-based food products.

There are seven stages involved in getting chicken meat to the consumer:
- Breeder flock
- Pullet farm
- Breeder farm
- Hatchery
- Broiler farm
- Processing
- Distribution

The production of broiler chickens for meat consumption begins with the grandparent breeder flocks. Breeder flock operators specialize in producing the generations of male and female strains that generate the parents that make the broiler chicken. The breeder flocks are raised to maturity in grandparent growing and laying farms where fertile eggs are produced. The fertile eggs are incubated at the grandparent hatchery to produce pullets. Pullets are young female breeder chickens that produce fertile hatching eggs that become broilers for the market. The pullets are sent to breeder farms to produce eggs. The eggs from the pullet breeder farms are sent to hatcheries for incubation. Hatched chicks are sent from the hatcheries to broiler farms. At the broiler farms the chicks are raised until they have reached the desired processing weight. Adult broiler chickens are caught and hauled to processing plants once they reach the desired processing weight at the broiler farms. The finished products are sent to distribution centers and then transported to customers.

Poultry processor companies normally operate their own feed mills to produce scientifically formulated feeds. Corn and soybean meal are the major production costs of growing chickens. The poultry industry is a major feed grain user, accounting for approximately 100 billion pounds of feed yearly. Advances with diet, selective breeding, production technologies, equipment development and management practices have enabled the poultry industry to produce meat faster with less feed. A 5.7 pound chicken can now be produced in seven weeks. Feed conversion is now approximately 2 pounds of feed per pound of live broiler.

Most broiler farms are under contract with poultry processor companies. The broiler farm normally supplies all the necessary heating, cooling, feeding, and watering systems on the farms. The broiler farm also supplies the labor needed in growing the broilers. The broiler processor supplies the chicks, feed, and veterinary medicines. The processor schedules transportation of the birds from the farm to the processing plant. In many cases, the processor also supplies the crews who place broilers into cages for transportation to the processing plant. Immigrant workers make up the majority of the labor force used in the U.S. meat and poultry industry.

Professional and Ethical Issues

CASES INCLUDED IN THIS SECTION

A Day in the Life of Brent Dorsey
Staff Auditor Professional Pressures

MARK S. BEASLEY · FRANK A. BUCKLESS · STEVEN M. GLOVER · DOUGLAS F. PRAWITT

LEARNING OBJECTIVES

After completing and discussing this case you should be able to

[1] Understand the pressures sometimes faced by young professionals in the workplace

[2] Understand more fully the implications of "eating time" and "premature sign-off"

[3] Generate and evaluate alternative courses of action to resolve a difficult workplace issue

[4] More fully appreciate the need to balance professional and personal demands

INTRODUCTION

Brent Dorsey graduated eight months ago with a master's degree in accounting. Immediately after graduation, Brent began working with a large accounting firm in Portland, Oregon. He is now on his second audit engagement—a company called Northwest Steel Producers. Working day-to-day with Brent on the audit are two other staff auditors, Han Choi and Megan Mills, along with the senior auditor, John Peters. Han and Megan are both second-year staff accountants and are anticipating a promotion to senior in the next year.

John Peters has been with the firm for about five years and has been a senior-level auditor for almost three years. Following this busy season, the partners and managers will decide which seniors to promote to manager. The rumor around the office is that only four or five of the seven eligible seniors in the office will be promoted in the Portland office. Those not promoted in Portland will likely be asked to transfer to other offices within the firm that need new managers or be "counseled out" of the firm. John has done a reasonably good job in the audits he has been in charge of, yet he feels he is "on the bubble" as far as the promotion in Portland goes. He has recently received a few performance evaluations that have criticized him for letting his jobs get "out of control" (i.e., over budget and beyond deadline). He believes his performance on the Northwest Steel Producers audit could make a difference in his chances to stay in Portland. John and his wife are both from the Portland area and neither one is ready for a transfer.

Northwest Steel is one of the office's biggest clients. The firm has been auditing Northwest for the past 13 years. Because of the client's reporting deadline, the Northwest Steel audit is notorious for tight deadlines and long hours.

BACKGROUND

With a final click on his laptop, Brent finished his audit work on Northwest's largest cash account. It was 5:45 p.m. on a Friday evening, and Brent was looking forward to a much-needed day off to spend some time with his wife, Katherine, who had a demanding job as a young attorney. They both understood that the degree of tension they had been feeling at home was probably due primarily to their stressful careers, and they felt a need to discuss their relationship in an attempt to "clear the air" and find a workable way forward. It seemed there had been precious little time for any serious discussion these past few weeks.

The case was prepared by Mark S. Beasley, Ph.D. and Frank A. Buckless, Ph.D. of North Carolina State University and Steven M. Glover, Ph.D. and Douglas F. Prawitt, Ph.D. of Brigham Young University, as a basis for class discussion. All characters and names represented are fictitious; any similarity to existing companies or persons is purely coincidental.

Brent started saving files so he could shut down his computer when the door of the small conference room he was using as an office opened a crack. Brent's briefcase partially blocked the door. "Door's open," Brent called out. "Just push a little harder." The door opened wider and Han Choi poked his head in. By the expression on Han's face, Brent had a feeling the news was not going to be good. "Hey Han, what's up?" asked Brent, trying to be upbeat.

"John wants the audit team together for a meeting in 15 minutes," Han said as he pushed his shoulders through the doorway.

Brent glanced quickly at his watch. "It's almost 6:00! What's he doing calling a meeting at this time of the day?"

"I don't know. He just called from his cell phone and said that he was on his way and that it was important that we all meet with him as soon as possible. But I have a feeling it's going to mean more work," Han said as he pulled himself back out the doorway. "I've got to run down a couple of things before the meeting, so I'll see you there." Han disappeared just as quickly as he had appeared.

Brent picked up the phone and called Katherine, who had just arrived home from work. "Hi, Kate. John just called an emergency meeting. I'm going to be late again."

"Brent, this is getting ridiculous. Just because your senior doesn't have a life doesn't mean we can't. I picked up a couple videos and some take-out on the way home. Just leave John a note that you had plans with your wife and come home."

"Katherine, you know I would rather be home with you than in another meeting, but at this stage in my career I don't think blowing off an urgent meeting would be the wise thing to do. I'll get home as soon as I can. Should I invite John over to watch the videos with us?"

"Very funny. Actually, maybe you should bring him along so I can try to talk some sense into him. Our lives seem so crazy. I don't know how much more of this I can take. I see the city bus driver more than I see you."

"It'll get better, Katherine. Once we get through with the Northwest audit, things will lighten up. But for now, this is a good opportunity for me to prove I'm a team player and that I can work as hard as the next guy. I've already seen how important a team-player reputation is in this firm. I've done pretty well so far, and that's why they put me on this audit. If I can prove myself, at some point I'll have more control over my day-to-day schedule. It is just really important that I build a good foundation for my career."

"I know, but I worry that it will never stop. There will always be another client, another promotion. If we don't establish a good pattern now, when will we? Anyway, you do what you've got to do. I'll put your dinner in the fridge, and I'll tell you how the video was." A cold "click" sounded in Brent's ear.

Brent slowly put the receiver back on the hook and stared at the small picture he kept in his briefcase. The picture was taken on Brent and Katherine's wedding day almost ten months ago. They were now expecting their first child, due in another five months. Brent acknowledged he had been working a lot lately, but he felt a need to prove himself in the firm. He felt challenged and fulfilled by his work, and he felt that some sacrifice now would open up more opportunities in the future. He would be able to spend more time with his family sometime down the road. Speaking of family, why did this baby have to come along now, of all times? He and Katherine had wanted children, but not quite this soon. They would soon be facing the difficult issues that come with balancing two careers and a baby.

He realized nearly 15 minutes had passed, and the meeting was about to begin. Jumping up, Brent grabbed his planner and ran out the door, knocking his briefcase to the floor. Han and Megan were already there, looking glum, when Brent arrived at the conference room that John was using as his on-site office. Just as Brent entered the room and shot a questioning look at Han and Megan, John came into the room.

"Sorry to call a meeting so late, but we have something very important to talk over," John said. "So far on this audit we are more than 30 hours over budget." He slumped into his chair. We absolutely have to make some of this time up. We need to come in pretty close to budget on this audit, and we've absolutely got to get it wrapped up in time for the client's scheduled earnings release at the end of next week." John shuffled through some papers on the table. He finally came to the one he was looking for. "I've been looking over the budgeted hours for the remaining segments of the audit. One of the remaining areas is accounts payable. That segment's got a budget of 42 hours, but I'd like to see it completed in no more than 35 hours. We're running out of chances to bring in this audit close to budget. Do a good job, but I really think it should take 35 hours max to do payables and I'd like it wrapped up by Monday afternoon." Megan and Han exchanged a glance.

John stood up and paced around the room. "I know I said I thought we'd be able to take Saturday off. But this is an important engagement and we need to deliver. We all stand to gain on our performance evaluations if we come in looking good on this audit. So let's keep our heads down a few more days. I need your help on this, guys." John stopped pacing and put his hands on his hips. "Han, I want you and Brent to start on payables first thing in the morning. Megan, you make sure you get receivables tied down by the time you go home tomorrow. You're still on track for coming in under budget on receivables, aren't you?" John stared until Megan nodded hesitantly. "Good. Well, that's it. I'll see you all tomorrow morning." John gathered up his things and walked out of the room, looking like he had the weight of the world on his shoulders.

"Great! There goes the weekend," said Megan as soon as John was out of sight. "Yeah, my wife and I had plans, too," muttered Han, glancing down at the stack of folders on his lap. Just then, Han's cell phone went off, playing a few notes from the latest Coldplay CD. "Now what?" said Han as he started for the door. Then he mumbled through a wry smile, "Maybe my house is on fire. At least then maybe I could take the rest of the weekend off."

WHAT ARE THE ALTERNATIVES?

Brent sat slumping in his chair, wondering how on earth he and Han were going to finish accounts payable in 35 hours. Rumor had it that last year's team may have "eaten time" to get some parts of the audit done within budget, and this year's budget was even lower than last years' *reported* time. Brent looked up at Megan, who sat in her chair looking bleary-eyed. "How on earth are Han and I going to get payables tied down in 35 hours, Meg?"

"We've been auditing this firm for years, so you'd think by now we would know how long it takes to audit accounts payable, wouldn't you? Last year it took almost 50 hours. I don't know why we insist on lowering the budget every year," said Megan. "I worked on payables last year and there weren't any problems with them at all. Or the year before, for that matter. In fact, I don't think there has ever been a problem with payables in all the years we've been auditing Northwest. I say if they want to cut the budget they should change the audit plan. Last year we pulled thirty invoices. Maybe this year we only need to pull twenty. That would save a few hours. Maybe that's what you and Han should do. Why invest the extra time when you know there aren't going to be any problems anyway?"

"I see what you mean, but the program step says we have to pull thirty. Can *we* make that decision?" Brent asked.

"I don't see why not. They want us to finish on time and to work another Saturday. What do they expect?" responded Megan.

Brent walked slowly back to his conference room, thinking about what Megan had said. Northwest's people had mostly gone home almost an hour ago. At this time of the evening only the custodial crews were in action. As he reached his office, he saw Han coming down the hall.

"Hey Han, got a minute?"

"Yeah, what's up Brent?"

"I'm wondering what we're going to do to come in under budget on payables—that's not going to be easy.."

"Well, I've found that in times like this, you just have to work until it's done. If we put in a long day tomorrow, we should be about halfway through. Then we can get in here early Monday and get going again. My wife and I were thinking about going to the coast for the weekend but now it's going to be me, you, and piles of invoices, P.O.s, and receiving reports. Romantic, huh?" Han waved a handful of papers at Brent. "And, frankly, given this audit program, not only will we not get payables done in 35 hours, who knows if we can get them done in less than 40 or 45."

"What's John going to say when we come in *over* 35 hours?"

"Nah, you're not getting it. I just work as much as I need to, to get the work done. Then I report that it took me the budgeted amount of hours—in this case 35, I guess. As long as the work gets done and we look good on our performance evals, I figure a few hours won't kill me. I just figure I'm donating a few extra hours to the firm. Plus, the way John is stressing out lately, it is not worth even *thinking* about coming in over 35 hours. Well, I've got to get some hotel reservations cancelled and get home and tell my wife how great the *next* trip is going to be. I'll see you first thing tomorrow morning to get started on those lovely payables."

Brent stepped into the conference room and sat down. He wanted to do the right thing for himself, the client, the firm, and all involved. Megan's and Han's ideas kept going around in his mind. His old auditing professor's sermons about an auditor's duty to the public seemed so long ago and so far removed. "Are there other alternatives?" he asked himself. "On the other hand, maybe I'm being too idealistic." He glanced at the clock and decided he'd better head for home and warm up his dinner. By the time he fought the traffic it was going to be late enough as it was. He gathered up his things and headed out the door and into the parking lot.

On his way home Brent began to think of all the issues he had been putting off. Katherine had not been feeling well lately and he had planned on stopping off to get her a little gift to cheer her up. Suddenly the car made that funny noise again, and Brent remembered for the twentieth time that he needed to get it into the shop before it died completely. Then he thought of his long-abandoned exercise program. "Yeah, right, exercise," thought Brent. "Maybe I'll start doing jumping jacks and push-ups at the office, between audit memos." On top of the long hours and mounting pressures at work, Katherine was insisting that Brent help more around the house and spend more time with her, and he had to admit it was only fair. The traffic didn't bother Brent as much as usual. He had a lot to think about.

REQUIRED

[1] What alternatives are available to Brent in regards to the audit of payables? What are the pros and cons of each alternative?

[2] What consequences for Brent, the auditing firm, and others involved, may arise from "eating time," as Han suggested? Similarly, what consequences for Brent, the auditing firm, and others involved, may arise from not completing audit procedures, as Megan suggested?

[3] In your opinion, which of Brent's alternative courses of action would provide the best outcome and why? What should Brent do? How would you handle the ethical issues involved in this situation?

[4] What could John Peters and the other auditors do to better handle the demands of career and family life?

Nathan Johnson's Rental Car Reimbursement
Should He Pocket the Cash?

MARK S. BEASLEY · FRANK A. BUCKLESS · STEVEN M. GLOVER · DOUGLAS F. PRAWITT

LEARNING OBJECTIVES

After completing and discussing this case you should be able to

[1] Understand ethical considerations that can arise during recruiting and in practice

[2] Reason through alternative courses of action when dealing with these issues

BACKGROUND

Nathan recently interviewed with one of the accounting firms in the city where he wants to live. The firm agreed to cover the expense of a rental car that he used to travel from his university to the firm's office. The rental car agency required that Nathan pay for the car with his credit card and have the firm reimburse Nathan for the expense rather than have the firm pay the expense directly. At the end of his trip, Nathan was supposed to pay the bill and then send the receipt to the firm for reimbursement.

As Nathan prepared to send in the receipt, he noticed that the car rental agency had overbilled him by $75. Nathan called the accounting firm to explain that his reimbursement request would be delayed because he had been overbilled. During his phone conversation with the human resource (HR) manager, Nathan told her he would call the rental agency to have his bill corrected and then would send the firm a copy for reimbursement when the revised bill arrived. The HR manager told Nathan not to bother correcting the overbilling; she suggested that he simply send in the current receipt and the firm would reimburse him for the entire amount. The HR manager was not concerned about paying the higher bill—apparently it did not meet the firm's "materiality threshold."

Before deciding whether to send in the incorrect bill, Nathan called the rental car agency to see why he was overbilled. The agent was quite rude, essentially telling Nathan to "get lost." Now Nathan was determined to get the money back, and after several long-distance phone calls and considerable hassle, the rental car company agreed to credit his card to correct the $75 overbilling. The credit will show up on Nathan's next credit card statement.

The HR manager, however, has already told Nathan that the accounting firm would pay the higher amount and requested that he not worry about the error and just send the bill in for reimbursement. Nathan immediately realized he could have the rental agency credit his card for the $75, but send the current receipt to the accounting firm to get reimbursed for the amount he originally paid. Essentially he would walk away from the deal with $75 in his pocket. Given the two hours he had spent fighting with the rental car company, a little reimbursement for his trouble didn't sound too bad to Nathan.

The case was prepared by Mark S. Beasley, Ph.D. and Frank A. Buckless, Ph.D. of North Carolina State University and Steven M. Glover, Ph.D. and Douglas F. Prawitt, Ph.D. of Brigham Young University, as a basis for class discussion. All characters and names represented are fictitious; any similarity to existing companies or persons is purely coincidental.

REQUIRED

[1] Given that the firm did not have any problem paying the higher bill, would Nathan's planned course of action be ethical? Why or why not?

[2] What other courses of action might be available to Nathan? Which do you think would be the best action for him to take?

The Anonymous Caller
Recognizing It's a Fraud and Evaluating What to Do

Mark S. Beasley · Frank A. Buckless · Steven M. Glover · Douglas F. Prawitt

LEARNING OBJECTIVES

After completing and discussing this case you should be able to

[1] Appreciate real-world pressures for meeting financial expectations

[2] Distinguish financial statement fraud from aggressive accounting

[3] Identify alternative actions when confronted with suspected financial statement fraud

[4] Develop arguments to resist or prevent inappropriate accounting techniques

BACKGROUND

It was 9:30 A.M. on a Monday morning when the call came through. "Hi Dr. Mitchell, do you have a minute?"

"Sure," the professor replied.

"I am one of your former students, but if you don't mind, I would prefer to remain anonymous. I think it is best for both of us if I not reveal my name or company to you. I am concerned that the senior executives of the company where I serve as controller just provided our local bank fraudulently misstated financial statements. I need some fast advice about what to do. Currently, I am on my cell phone and need help evaluating my next step before I head to my office this morning. May I briefly describe what's going on and get some input from you?" she asked.

"Go ahead, let me see if there is some way I can help," responded Dr. Mitchell.

"I am the controller of a privately-held, small, start-up company that I joined three and one-half months ago. On Friday of last week, the company's chief executive officer (CEO), the vice president of operations, and the chief financial officer (CFO) met with representatives of the bank that funds the company's line of credit. One of the purposes of the meeting was to provide our most recent quarterly financial statements. The company is experiencing a severe cash shortage, and the bank recently halted funding the line of credit until we could present our most recent operating results. It was at that meeting, just three days ago, that our senior executive team knowingly submitted financial statements to the bank that overstated sales and receivables accounts."

"Earlier on Friday, prior to the bank meeting, I vehemently refused to sign the commitment letter required by the bank because of my concerns about the inclusion of sales transactions to customers on account that I knew did not meet revenue recognition criteria specified by GAAP. I explained to the CEO and CFO that I believed including those transactions in the quarterly results would constitute fraud. They continued to insist that the financial statements needed to reflect the transactions, because without them, the bank would not continue funding the line of credit. They accused me of living in an "ivory tower" and emphasized that companies booked these kinds of transactions all the time. Although they acted like they appreciated my desires for perfection and exactness, they made me feel like it was my lack of experience in the real world that kept me from having a more practical perspective to a common business practice. Unfortunately, none of the senior executives have accounting-related backgrounds. I am the top-level accounting person at the company."

The case was prepared by Mark S. Beasley, Ph.D. and Frank A. Buckless, Ph.D. of North Carolina State University and Steven M. Glover, Ph.D. and Douglas F. Prawitt, Ph.D. of Brigham Young University, as a basis for class discussion. It is not intended to illustrate either effective or ineffective handling of an administrative situation.

"Over the weekend I had time to think about the situation, and now I am even more convinced that this is clearly fraud. My CEO and CFO have been arm-twisting the accounting staff to book sales transactions before sales occur. They have recorded sales transactions for some of our customers who regularly do business with us. The problem is, however, the customers have not placed any orders with us for those transactions. Rather, the CEO and CFO are anticipating that the orders will be coming in very soon based on the customers' prior ordering history. But, at this point no orders have been received and no goods have been shipped related to the sales included in the financials that have been submitted to the bank. The CEO and CFO noted that booking these kinds of credit sales transactions is a common business practice, even if it isn't technically compliant with GAAP given that the transactions represent sales expected in the very near future, perhaps even next week."

"As it turns out, the CEO even instructed the accounts payable clerk, while I was out of the office for a couple of days, to record entries the CEO had handwritten on a piece of paper. The accounts payable clerk has never worked with sales and receivables. The CEO told the clerk, who works part time while finishing his accounting degree at your university, not to mention the entries to me, unless I specifically asked. In that event, the clerk was supposed to tell me that the entries related to new sales generated by the CEO and that all was under control. Fortunately, the student clerk is currently taking your auditing course, where financial statement fraud is a topic, and he was uncomfortable with what had transpired. He immediately updated me on the day I returned about what had happened. These bizarre entries make up almost half of our first quarter's sales. Of course, given that these are quarterly financial statements, they are unaudited. Because we are not a publicly traded company, our external auditor has not performed any kind of interim review of the interim financial statements."

"Do you think this is limited to just one quarter?" Dr. Mitchell asked.

"I think so," the caller replied. "As I mentioned, I joined the company three and a half months ago. One of my first tasks involved closing out the prior fiscal year and assisting the external auditors with the year-end audit. As best I can tell, these unusual activities began just recently given our poor results in the first quarter of this year. Our company is a start-up enterprise that has been operating at a net loss for a while. Just last week, the bank stopped clearing checks drawn off the company account. They weren't necessarily bouncing them, but they were not funding the line of credit until the first quarter results were presented on Friday. Interestingly, the bank immediately started funding the line late Friday and, I understand based on phone calls with my staff this morning, the bank is continuing to fund the line this morning. I really think the earnings misstatements first occurred this quarter and that the prior year audited financial statements are not misstated. Unfortunately, I had to sign a bank commitment letter only two weeks after joining the company. That commitment letter related to funding the loan right at the close of the last fiscal year. So, my signature is on file at the bank related to prior-year financial results. But, given the current events, I refused to sign the documents delivered to the bank on Friday. One of my accounting clerks resigned last week due to similar concerns. Our vice president of human resources (HR) discussed the resignation with me after learning about the clerk's concern during a final exit interview. I might add, however, that the HR vice president is the wife of the CEO."

"Anyway, I'm just not sure what responsibilities I have to disclose the earnings misstatements to outside parties. I am considering all sorts of options and thought I would see what advice you could offer. What do you think I should do, Dr. Mitchell?"

REQUIRED

[1] (a) What would you recommend to the caller if you were Dr. Mitchell? (b) What are the risks of continuing to work with the company? (c) What are the risks of resigning immediately? (d) Could the state board of accountancy be a source of advice?

[2] What responsibility, if any, does the caller have to report this situation directly to the bank involved? Before you respond, think about the risks present if the caller does inform the bank and it later turns out that the caller's assessment of the situation was inaccurate, i.e., there was no fraud.

[3] (a) What other parties, if any, should be notified in addition to the bank? (b) What concerns do you have about notifying the external auditors?

[4] (a) Do you think situations like this (i.e., aggressive accounting or even financial statement fraud) are common in practice? (b) What pressures or factors will executives use to encourage accounting managers and staff to go along? (c) What arguments can you use to resist those pressures? (d) How does one determine whether a company is aggressively reporting, but still in the guidelines of GAAP, versus fraudulently reporting financial information?

[5] People who study instances of financial statement fraud often note that three conditions are generally present for fraud to occur. First, the person perpetrating the fraud has an *incentive* or pressure to engage in fraud. Second, there is an *opportunity* for that person to carry out the fraud. Third, the person's *attitude* or ethical values allows the perpetrator to rationalize the unethical behavior. Describe examples of incentive, opportunity, and attitude conditions that were present in this situation.

[6] The Securities and Exchange Commission (SEC) issued Staff Accounting Bulletin No. 101, *Revenue Recognition in Financial Statements*, to provide guidance for publicly traded companies. Review SAB No. 101, which is available on the SEC's website (www.sec.gov) and determine how the company violated revenue recognition criteria.

[7] (a) Which financial statement assertion related to sales transactions did management violate when it issued the falsified financial statements? (b) What types of audit procedures could an external auditor perform that might help the auditor detect this fraudulent activity?

WorldCom
The Story of a Whistleblower

MARK S. BEASLEY · FRANK A. BUCKLESS · STEVEN M. GLOVER · DOUGLAS F. PRAWITT

LEARNING OBJECTIVES

After completing and discussing this case you should be able to

[1] Understand the pressures a person faces when he or she becomes aware of an accounting fraud

[2] Describe possible actions a person can take when he or she suspects fraud may exist

[3] Recommend characteristics of an effective corporate whistleblower program

[4] Describe key requirements in the Sarbanes–Oxley Act related to whistleblower and code of ethics processes for public companies

BACKGROUND[1]

Don't ever tell yourself, "that won't happen to me." Just ask Cynthia Cooper, former Vice President of Internal Audit at WorldCom.

Cynthia Cooper was a typical accounting student as an undergrad at Mississippi State University. Raised in Clinton, Mississippi, Cynthia was "the girl next door." Growing up in a family with a modest income, she attended the local high school, worked as a waitress at the local Golden Corral, and headed off to one of the state's well-known universities.

After graduating from college, she later completed her Master of Accounting degree at the University of Alabama and became a certified public accountant. Her career began like most accounting graduates in the field of public accounting, working with one of the major accounting firms in Atlanta.

Most likely, she never thought she would face the challenge of her lifetime before reaching the age of 40. However, a few short weeks in May and June of 2002 changed her life forever. This case summarizes how she unraveled a $3.8 billion fraud that ultimately grew to over $11 billion and sent one of the country's largest and most visible companies to its knees in bankruptcy. Consider how you would have handled the situation if you had been in her shoes.

WORKING FOR WORLDCOM

Cynthia Cooper joined the company that eventually became WorldCom after returning from Atlanta to her hometown of Clinton, Mississippi in the early 1990s. Following a recent divorce, she moved with her two-year-old daughter to be closer to family. She first joined Long Distance Discount Service (LDDS), which later became known as WorldCom, as a consultant in the finance department earning $12 an hour. She left LDDS for a short stint to join SkyTel, a paging company, but later returned to LDDS to head up its internal audit department in the mid-1990s.

---

1   Amanda Ripley, "The Night Detective;" Ricardo Lacayo and Amanda Ripley, "Persons of the Year," *Time*, New York, December 30, 2002-January 6, 2003, Volume 160, Issue 27/1 pp. 32 and 45. Gary Perilloux, "WorldCom Whistleblower Speaks to Mississippi State University Students," *Northeast Mississippi Daily Journal*, November 18, 2003. Kurt Eichenwald and Simon Romero, "Inquiry Finds Effort at Delay at WorldCom," *The New York Times*, July 4, 2002, pg C-1.

The case was prepared by Mark S. Beasley, Ph.D. and Frank A. Buckless, Ph.D. of North Carolina State University and Steven M. Glover, Ph.D. and Douglas F. Prawitt, Ph.D. of Brigham Young University, as a basis for class discussion. It is not intended to illustrate either effective or ineffective handling of an administrative situation.

WorldCom started as a small "mom and pop" company in the early 1980s. Bernie Ebbers moved the WorldCom headquarters to Clinton, Mississippi, because it was the college town of his alma mater, Mississippi College. By 1997, the company had emerged within the telecom industry and caught the eye of many on Wall Street when it issued a bid to acquire the much larger and better known company, MCI.

Cynthia Cooper enjoyed the rising status of WorldCom's growth in the business community. She was promoted to Vice President of Internal Audit in 1999, leading the internal audit function in what became the 25th largest company in the United States. WorldCom's stock price continued to rise through 2000, and she and her colleagues dreamed of retiring early and starting their own businesses. Cynthia dreamed of opening a bead shop and actually purchased a couple hundred thousand beads that she stored in her garage.

Establishing internal audit's role in the company wasn't easy. WorldCom's CEO, Bernie Ebbers, was forceful about his distaste for the term "internal controls" and allegedly banned the use of the term in his presence. At one point, Cynthia called a meeting with her boss, WorldCom CFO Scott Sullivan, Bernie Ebbers, and a few others to help them see how an internal audit department could help the company's bottom line. Despite being almost 30 minutes late to the meeting, Ebbers was the last person to leave the meeting. At that point, internal audit's focus on efficiency of operations became its primary charge, leaving the financial audit-related tasks in the hands of the external auditor, Arthur Andersen, LLP. Cynthia, as Vice President of Internal Audit, would report to the CFO, Scott Sullivan.

While WorldCom's growth skyrocketed throughout the 1990s, the telecom market was saturated by 2001 and WorldCom's earnings began to fall. WorldCom executives began to feel tremendous pressure to maintain their stellar track record of financial performance.

UNRAVELING OF A FRAUD

According to press reports, Cynthia Cooper and her internal audit team didn't know about any unusual accounting manipulations until March 2002. It wasn't until a worried executive in a division of WorldCom told Cynthia about the handling of certain expenses in his division. At that point, Cynthia learned that the corporate office accounting team had taken $400 million out of the division's reserve account to boost WorldCom's consolidated income.

As Cynthia and her team pursued the matter with WorldCom's CFO, Scott Sullivan, she immediately faced tremendous resistance and pressure. In fact, Sullivan informed Cynthia that there was no problem and that internal audit shouldn't be focused on the issue. She received a similar reaction when she approached the external auditors at Arthur Andersen, who told Cynthia there was no problem at all with the accounting treatment.

Fortunately, Cynthia did not let the intimidation of her boss or the opposition of a major national accounting firm dampen her concerns about getting to the truth. In fact, Sullivan's harsh reaction only increased her skepticism surrounding the matter. She and others within the internal audit team began to secretly work on the project late at night. At one point, they began making backup copies of their files in response to fears that if their investigation was revealed, files might be destroyed.

Within two months—at the end of May 2002—Cynthia and her team had unraveled the key aspects of the fraud. They discovered that the company had erroneously capitalized billions of dollars of network lease expenses as assets on WorldCom's books. The accounting gimmickry allowed the company to report a profit of $2.4 billion instead of a $662 million loss.

In some ways the fraud was simple. The corporate accounting team led by Sullivan had merely transferred normal operating lease expenses to the balance sheet as an asset. The expenses were for normal fees WorldCom paid to local telephone companies for use of their telephone networks and were not capital outlays.

On June 11, 2002 Scott Sullivan summoned Cynthia to his office demanding to know what was going on with her investigation. At that meeting, Sullivan asked Cynthia to delay her audit investigation until later in the year. Cynthia stood her ground and told him at that meeting the investigation would continue. Imagine the pressure Cynthia felt as she faced her boss, believing he was covering-up the large accounting fraud.

Cynthia decided to go over Sullivan's head, which was a huge gamble for her. She would not only be risking her career, but she would also personally suffer following any devaluation of her investment in WorldCom stock. Furthermore, it was likely she would experience rejection from others around town for upsetting a good thing. In any event, on the very next day, June 12, 2002, Cynthia contacted Max Bobbit, chairman of WorldCom's audit committee. Feeling tremendous pressure from the encounter, Cynthia cleaned the personal items out of her desk that day in anticipation of the backlash she might face.

At first, Cynthia was disappointed to see the audit committee chairman delay taking action based on her report. However, he soon passed her report along to the company's newly appointed external auditors, KPMG LLP. WorldCom had replaced its former auditor, Arthur Andersen, due to Andersen's quick demise following the firm's guilty verdict related to the Enron debacle. This occurred about the same time Cynthia and her team were investigating the WorldCom fraud.

Later that week, Max Bobbit and the KPMG lead partner, Farrell Malone, went to Clinton, Mississippi to meet with Cynthia face-to-face. Over the next several days, Cynthia and the KPMG partner began interviewing numerous people in the corporate office, including Scott Sullivan. Following each interview, they would keep the audit committee chairman informed of their findings. Soon, the audit committee chairman decided it was time to inform the rest of the audit committee of their discoveries.

Bobbitt presented information to the audit committee at a June 20, 2002 meeting in Washington. Scott Sullivan was instructed to attend, along with Cynthia Cooper and key members of her internal audit team, to discuss the matter. At that meeting, Scott Sullivan made every attempt to justify the accounting treatment claiming that certain SEC staff accounting bulletins supported his handling of the expenses as assets. Despite his reasoning, WorldCom's new auditors, KPMG, tactfully offered the firm's view that the treatment didn't meet generally accepted accounting principles.

The audit committee instructed Scott Sullivan to document his position in writing. Four days later, on June 24, 2002, Sullivan submitted a three-page memo justifying his accounting treatment. The main theme of his argument was that WorldCom was justified in classifying the lease expenses as assets. The expenses, in his view, related to payments for network capacity that would be used in future years as business demand increased and new customers were added to the WorldCom network. In essence, he argued that the company needed to spend money on additional network capacity to entice new customers to come on board.

Most experts agreed that his justification was a "stretch" at best. Other companies in the industry did not take a similar approach to accounting and instead expensed network lease costs as incurred. The audit committee didn't buy Sullivan's arguments. Later that day, the audit committee informed Sullivan and the WorldCom controller, David Myers, that they would be terminated if they didn't resign before the board meeting the next day. Myers resigned, but Sullivan refused, and was fired. By August 2002, Sullivan had been indicted by a grand jury.

The next day WorldCom announced the fraud to the public and the unraveling of Mississippi's largest public company began. Soon the company would be in bankruptcy.

THE AFTERMATH

The nightmare for Cynthia Cooper didn't end following Sullivan's termination. For the next several days, Cynthia and her team worked around the clock trying to gather more evidence about the underlying fraud and to help KPMG redo the previous financial statement audits conducted by Andersen. She moved to her parents' home because it was close to the WorldCom headquarters.

In spite of incredible hours and effort required by Cynthia to uncover and expose the fraud, Cynthia was now a key person in the massive federal investigation; both as a source of information and even as a potential suspect. At one point she returned to her office only to find eight federal investigators going through her files. Copies of her phone and email messages were being captured, which likely created concerns for her about personal legal risk exposure as well. She was even asked to appear before a Congressional investigations committee. She quickly realized she needed to have her own attorney to help guide her steps through the maze of events.

Like most whistleblowers, Cynthia was facing the crisis of a lifetime. Friends noticed the toll the stress was taking on Cynthia. In a few short months, she had lost close to 30 pounds. At times she couldn't stop crying. Looking back on this time period, she later stated that she felt like she was in a "very dark place." She repeatedly reread Psalm 23, "Yea, though I walk through the valley of the shadow of death, I will fear no evil, for thou art with me."

Imagine the reaction she faced from the 50,000 or so employees working for the defunct WorldCom. To some, she was a hero. To others, she was a villain. Asked by one interviewer if she had been publicly thanked for her actions, all she could do was laugh.

Fortunately, Cynthia had a tremendous support network of family and close friends. Despite the trend for most whistleblowers to be isolated and suffer from depression and alcoholism, Cynthia has managed to keep her head above it all. She continued to head up the internal audit department at WorldCom (now MCI) for a couple more years before deciding to pursue another career path. Now she has her own consulting firm and frequently travels around the U.S. speaking to corporations, associations, and universities about her experience and the need for ethical and leadership reform. In 2008, she released her book, *Extraordinary Circumstances: The Journey of a Corporate Whistleblower*, summarizing her experience.

In December 2002, *Time* magazine named Cynthia Cooper as one of its "Persons of the Year" along with two other whistleblowers: Sherron Watkins of Enron and Coleen Rowley of the FBI. She has received notes and emails from hundreds of strangers thanking her for her actions. She is now widely known across the country as the key whistleblower of the WorldCom fraud.

Cynthia does not feel like her actions warrant hero status. She has noted that she was merely doing her job. Cynthia attributes her actions to the guidance and leadership she received as a child at home. She has quoted her mother as saying "Never allow yourself to be intimidated; always think about the consequences of your actions." Fortunately for Cynthia, she heeded her mother's advice. It most likely saved her career and family.

REQUIRED

[1] At the time Cynthia Cooper discovered the accounting fraud, WorldCom did not have a whistleblower hotline process in place. Instead, Cynthia took on significant risks when she stepped over Scott Sullivan's head and notified the audit committee chairman of her findings. Conduct an Internet search to locate a copy of the Sarbanes–Oxley Act of 2002. Summarize the requirements of Section 301.4 of the Act.

[2] Use the Internet to conduct research related to whistleblower processes. Prepare a report summarizing key characteristics for the operation of an effective corporate whistleblower hotline. Be sure to highlight potential pitfalls that should be avoided.

[3] As Vice President of Internal Audit, Cynthia Cooper reported directly to WorldCom's CFO, Scott Sullivan, and not to the CEO or audit committee. Research professional standards of the Institute of Internal Auditors to identity recommendations for the organizational reporting lines of authority appropriate for an effective internal audit function within an organization.

[4] Conduct an Internet search to locate a copy of the Sarbanes–Oxley Act of 2002 and summarize the requirements of Section 406 of the Act. Then, search the SEC's website (www.sec.gov) to locate the SEC's Final Rule: "Disclosure Required by Sections 406 and 407 of the Sarbanes–Oxley Act of 2002 [Release No. 33-8177]. Summarize the SEC's rule related to implementation of the Section 406 requirements.

[5] Often the life of a whistleblower involves tremendous ridicule and scrutiny from others, despite doing the "right thing." Describe your views as to why whistleblowers face tremendous obstacles as a result of bringing the inappropriate actions of others to light.

[6] Describe the personal characteristics a person should possess to be an effective whistleblower. As you prepare your list, consider whether you think you've got what it takes to be a whistleblower.

[7] Assume that a close family member came to you with information about a potential fraud at his or her employer. Prepare a summary of the advice you would offer as he or she considers taking the information forward.

[8] Conduct an Internet search to locate a copy of the Sarbanes–Oxley Act of 2002. Read and summarize the requirements of Section 302 of the Act. Discuss how those provisions would or would not have deterred the actions of Scott Sullivan, CFO at WorldCom.

[9] Document your views about the effectiveness of regulatory reforms, such as the Sarbanes–Oxley Act of 2002, in preventing and deterring financial reporting fraud and other unethical actions. Discuss whether you believe the solution for preventing and deterring such acts is more effective through regulation and other legal reforms or through teaching and instruction about moral and ethical values conducted in school, at home, in church, or through other avenues outside legislation.

Hollinger International
Realities of Audit-Related Litigation

MARK S. BEASLEY · FRANK A. BUCKLESS · STEVEN M. GLOVER · DOUGLAS F. PRAWITT

LEARNING OBJECTIVES

After completing and discussing this case you should be able to

[1] Appreciate the nature and significance of testimony in an alleged financial statement fraud case

[2] Understand the importance of audit documentation

[3] Outline GAAP requirements with respect to related party transactions

[4] Describe auditor responsibilities for identifying related party transactions

[5] Understand required auditor communications with those charged with governance

BACKGROUND

On November 15, 2004, the Securities and Exchange Commission (SEC) filed an enforcement action in the Northern Illinois U.S. District Court against Hollinger Inc., a Toronto-based company, and its former Chairman and CEO, Conrad Black, and the company's former chief operating officer, David Radler.[1] In the SEC's Civil Action Complaint, the SEC alleged that during the period 1999 to at least 2003, Black and Radler engaged in a fraudulent scheme to divert cash and assets from Hollinger International, Inc., a Chicago-based company that owned newspapers such as the *Chicago-Sun Times*, *The Daily Telegraph* in London, and *The Jerusalem Post*, among others. Hollinger International's Class A common stock shares were publicly traded on the New York Stock Exchange under the symbol "HLR" while its Class B common shares were owned by Toronto-based Hollinger Inc.

The SEC alleged in its complaint that Black and Radler diverted millions of dollars for personal use by misrepresenting and omitting material facts from communications with Hollinger International's Audit Committee and Board of Directors regarding a series of related party transactions. These men diverted cash by issuing "non-competition" payments to themselves by including disguised clauses in contracts they negotiated as part of several transactions involving Hollinger International's sale of several of its U.S. and Canadian newspaper properties. In total, at least $85 million was diverted as disguised non-compete payments, which constituted about 14 percent of Hollinger International's total pretax income and 340 percent of its net earnings for the three-year period from 1999 through 2001.

The fraud was fairly simple. As Black and Radler negotiated contracts for the sale of selected newspaper subsidiaries, they included a clause in each sales contract stating that neither they nor Hollinger Inc. (the Toronto owner of the Class B shares) would compete against the new owner of the newspaper for a period of time. When each transaction was settled, portions of the sales transaction proceeds were allocated to Black, Radler, and Hollinger Inc. as compensation for their willingness to not compete with the new owners of the newspaper. Thus, Black and Radler were able to take advantage of their positions within Hollinger to benefit personally at the expense of Hollinger International and its Class A common shareholders.

---

1 Civil Action Complaint, *United States Securities and Exchange Commission, Plaintiff, vs. Conrad M. Black, F. David Radler, and Hollinger, Inc., Defendants.* November 15, 2004 (see www.sec.gov).

The case was prepared by Mark S. Beasley, Ph.D. and Frank A. Buckless, Ph.D. of North Carolina State University and Steven M. Glover, Ph.D. and Douglas F. Prawitt, Ph.D. of Brigham Young University, as a basis for class discussion. It is not intended to illustrate either effective or ineffective handling of an administrative situation.

Because of Black's and Radler's positions, these non-compete transactions constituted "related party transactions." Hollinger International's internal policies required that all related party transactions be reviewed and approved by the Audit Committee of Hollinger International's Board of Directors. However, Black and Radler failed to disclose and they misled the Audit Committee of Hollinger International about the non-competition agreements they negotiated on behalf of Hollinger International. In addition to their misrepresentations and failure to disclose these related-party transactions to the company's Audit Committee for approval, Black and Radler omitted these transactions from the financial statements and proxy documents filed with the SEC. Black and Radler also attempted to disguise these payments from their auditors at KPMG, LLP.

In the SEC's complaint, Stephen M. Cutler, Director of the SEC's Division of Enforcement said, *"Black and Radler abused their control of a public company and treated it as their personal piggy bank. Instead of carrying out their responsibilities to protect the interest of public shareholders, the defendants cheated and defrauded these shareholders through a series of deceptive schemes and misstatements."*

THE TRIAL

The trial began in March 2007 in a Chicago federal courtroom, more than two years after the filing of the SEC's complaint. After months of testimony, which included a damaging confession from Black's closest business associate, David Radler, the jury returned to the courtroom hopelessly deadlocked. Instructed by the judge to continue deliberations, the jury returned 12 days later with its verdict. Black was found guilty on four of the 13 charges against him, including obstruction of justice and mail fraud. In December 2007, Black was sentenced to 6.5 years in jail and ordered to report to prison in 12 weeks.

As part of the trial deliberations, representatives from KPMG, LLP were required to testify regarding numerous aspects of their financial statement audits of Hollinger Inc. and Hollinger International. The testimony provided by KPMG partner Marilyn Stitt includes information regarding KPMG's role in performing an audit, detecting fraud, examining related party transactions, and communicating with Hollinger International's Audit Committee.

TRANSCRIPTS OF MS. STITT'S TESTIMONY

In the text boxes that follow you will find selected excerpts of Ms. Stitt's testimony on the morning of April 23, 2007. Each excerpt is presented verbatim from transcripts of the trial testimony. Different sections of testimony are separated by either a series of asterisks (***) or by bold headings indicating a different topic of discussion in the transcript. In the text that follows, "Q" represents the question asked of Ms. Stitt and "A" represents the response. "Witness" refers to Ms. Stitt and "The Court" refers to the judge in the trial. When reading the transcripts, keep in mind that the testimony is captured verbatim. Thus, grammatical errors made by the witness or examiner are captured word-for-word.

As you read the transcripts, pay particular attention to the testimony about KPMG's discussions with some of the members of management about the related party transactions, including discussions with the Hollinger International Audit Committee. One can begin to see examples of how management failed to be forthcoming with details about these transactions in their effort to conceal their fraud and in their attempt to mislead the Audit Committee into thinking these transactions were approved by the Audit Committee when they were not.

While KPMG was not a defendant in this particular trial, imagine the stress felt by Ms. Stitt as she was required to respond under oath in the spring of 2007 to voluminous and incredibly detailed questions regarding audits of Hollinger financial statements dating back to 1999 – 2001. In two days of back-to-back testimony on April 23-24, 2007, Ms. Stitt had to recall events and discussions between KPMG personnel and client personnel and respond to numerous specific questions about detailed working papers prepared by KPMG colleagues not only in Chicago, but also in Toronto and other KPMG offices involved in the engagement.

As you read the trial transcripts, picture yourself in Ms. Stitt's shoes as she sat on the witness stand in a Chicago courtroom. Imagine the difficulty of accurately testifying about events that may have occurred as far back as seven years earlier. Also, think about how important clear, specific audit working papers would be in terms of her ability to testify and respond to cross-examination. You can imagine that Ms. Stitt might have wished that the working paper documentation had been more exact regarding the procedures performed during the 1999-2001 audits.

APRIL 23, 2007 – AM
SELECTED TESTIMONY ABOUT CONCEPT OF "REASONABLE ASSURANCE"[2]

[Q] Would you state your name, please?

[A] Mailyn Stitt.

[Q] How do you spell your last name?

[A] S-t-i-t-t.

[Q] What's your line of work, Ms. Stitt?

[A] I'm a Chartered Accountant.

[Q] Are you with a firm?

[A] Yes, I'm a partner with KPMG Canada.

[Q] And tell the members of the jury what KPMG is, please.

[A] KPMG is a professional services firm. We provide services in accounting, auditing, taxation and a variety of business advisory services.

* * *

[Q] Describe for us what this concept of "reasonable assurance" means, as it's articulated here, and as you applied it in your conduct for audits of KPMG.

[A] All right. So, "reasonable assurance" isn't necessarily, to the best of my recollection, defined in the standard, but it certainly distinguishes it from "absolute assurance" and says that it is a lower — a lower — level than "absolute assurance." It's being reasonably comfortable that the financial statements are free of material misstatement. There's a — I think the reasons why it's, you know, distinguished — or, sorry, why we cannot provide absolute assurance or a guarantee — is articulated in the second bullet, which is, "because of a nature of audit evidence and the characteristics of fraud."

[Q] We're going to come to the characteristics of fraud, again, from an audit perspective in just a moment; but, as for the first part — the nature of audit evidence — tell us why the nature of doing an audit prevents you from giving an absolute assurance or guarantee about the financial statements?

[A] Sure. So, to be able to give absolute assurance, you would need to sort of look at every transaction; every balance that a company would be involved with. And for a company, they may have millions of transactions, millions of sales, millions of receivables. And the whole concept of an audit, as I explained a little bit earlier, is on the premise of selective testing. So, there's a huge amount of judgment that goes in to decide sort of, "What are the areas that we're going to focus on when we're doing our audit?" And even within those we make judgments about, "Well, what kinds of tests are we going to be performing? How much work are we going to do? When are we going to do those tests?" So, there's a lot of judgment. And, then, even when you get audit evidence, there's a fair amount of judgment involved as to, you know, what conclusion you can draw from that audit evidence. So, as an example, if you were going to rely on a particular control in a company, you might test 30 items and go, "It would appear

---

2   Trial transcripts of the April 23, 2007 – AM – Testimony of Marilyn Stitts in the federal trial, *United States Securities and Exchange Commission, Plaintiff, vs. Conrad M. Black, F. David Radler, and Hollinger, Inc., Defendants.*

that that control is working." And you could draw a reasonable conclusion that the control seems to be effective and perhaps could reduce your testing. Well, you may have selected 30 items where it did work, but that's not to say for the other millions of transactions that the company's undertaken, that that control has always operated effectively. So –

* * *

[Q] Now, you mentioned that the second reason has to do with characteristics of fraud, again, from an audit perspective. If we continue looking at the reasonable assurance standard, it states, "Because of the characteristics of fraud, a properly planned and performed audit may not detect a material misstatement." Can you explain that for us?

[A] Generally, a fraud is an intentional act to deceive. And, so, as a result of that, it may not be apparent to us, because a fraud may involve collusion amongst individuals, concealment of information; it may involve falsification of documentation that we receive; it may involve overriding of internal controls that, based on the testing we did, it appeared as though it was operating effectively, but perhaps there was somebody specifically asking someone to override that control.

* * *

[Q] And if we look at the audit description in Auditing Standard 230, Paragraph 12, it states, "Characteristics of fraud include: A, concealment through collusion among management, employees or third parties; B, withheld, misrepresented or falsified documentation; and, C, the ability of management to override or instruct others to override what otherwise appears to be effective controls." In the course of conducting your financial audits at KPMG, are you trying to detect fraud as it's described in the auditing standards?

[A] An audit requires us to make assessments up front in that planning stage as to where there may be a risk of fraud. We engage in discussions with the client around those. Make — you know, use professional judgment in understanding how those risks may have been mitigated. And we determine from that, you know, "Is there any adjustments that are needed to sort of the planned procedures that we would carry out?" So, we're generally not necessarily out doing a whole bunch of procedures to find, you know, necessarily fraud or illegal activity; but, we become — keep our radar up, in terms of if there's something that comes to our attention; and, this general risk assessment upfront as to where the risk of fraud may occur.

APRIL 23, 2007 – AM
SELECTED TESTIMONY ABOUT CANWEST NON-COMPETE PAYMENTS[3]

[Q] In early 2002, did you become aware of these CanWest non-compete payments to individuals?

[A] Yes.

[Q] In particular, the $11.9 million to Mr. Black and Mr. Radler; and, also, the payments to Mr. Boultbee, Mr. Atkinson and Ravelston?

[A] Yes.

[Q] Now, as of early 2002, at the time that you were working on this 10-K, had these CanWest non-compete payments then been disclosed in any 10-Ks that had been audited by KPMG?

[A] No, they had not.

[Q] Were they included in that 2000 10-K that we were just looking at, Government Exhibit Filing 9-C?

[A] No, they were not.

---

3   The CanWest transaction represented one of the several sale transactions that triggered non-compete payments to Black and Radler. CanWest represents "CanWest Global Communications Corporation," a former subsidiary of Hollinger International.

[Q] Were you planning to include them in the 2001 10-K?

[A] Yes, when we became aware of them, we had concluded in our view they were material-related party transactions and needed to be disclosed in the company's 2001 financial statements.

[Q] Did you discuss that at the time with anyone from Hollinger's management?

[A] Yes.

[Q] And who did you talk to first?

[A] The first I spoke to was Jack Boultbee.[4]

[Q] Approximately when was your discussion with Mr. Boultbee?

[A] I believe it was early the first week of February —

[Q] And where?

[A] — of 2002.

[Q] Where did this conversation take place, Ms. Stitt?

[A] I met with Jack Boultbee in his offices at 10 Toronto Street.

[Q] Was anyone else present besides you and Mr. Boultbee?

[A] No, it was just the two of us.

[Q] What did Mr. Boultbee say to you and what did you say to him?

[A] I started the conversation by indicating that I had become aware of the CanWest non-compete payments.

[Q] Keep your voice up, Ms. Stitt.

[A] Sorry. I had become aware of the 2000 payments – the CanWest non-compete payments — to the Ravelston and to the executives that, in my view, they were material-related party transaction; and, that I was of the view that it needed to be disclosed in 2001, and was concerned that it had not been disclosed in the 2000 financial statements.

[Q] And, again, you're having this conversation with Mr. Boultbee in early '02?

[A] Early February. So, February 5th or 6th of 2002.

[Q] When you made these statements to Mr. Boultbee, how did he respond?

[A] I don't remember his exact words, but I do remember Jack indicated that these were not related-party transactions under generally accepted accounting principles; they did not need to be disclosed. I do recall Jack indicating to me that CanWest had demanded the non-compete payments — or, sorry, the Non-Compete Agreements — and that Hollinger International was really acting as an agent in receiving the funds. They were just acting as an agent to take the funds from CanWest and make those payments to the individuals; and, that it was not a related-party transaction that needed to be disclosed under GAAP.

[Q] What was your response?

[A] I said I didn't — didn't — didn't agree with him on his conclusion that he had reached; that, in my view, the company was not acting as an agent; that the company — it was the company, not CanWest, who had concluded that the payments would be made to the individuals.

[Q] Which company are you referring to?

[A] Sorry, Hollinger International was the company who had decided that the payments would be made to the individuals; that that was not — that was not — CanWest. So, I didn't accept the argument that the company was simply acting as an agent between CanWest and the employees. That it was my view that it was a material related-party transaction; that if it wasn't disclosed, we would probably be in a position where we would need to qualify our audit report; and, that while I couldn't necessarily speak for my U.S. colleagues who issued the opinion on the Hollinger International statements, I was reasonably comfortable that they would reach the same conclusion or be of the same view.

[Q] Is this what you communicated to Mr. Boultbee that day?

[A] Yes.

---

4   From 1995 through 2002, Jack Boultbee served as Hollinger International's chief financial officer, and in 1998 he became Executive Vice President of Hollinger International.

APRIL 23, 2007 – AM
TESTIMONY ABOUT AUDIT COMMITTEE PRESENTATION

[Q] Ms. Stitt, I'd like you to turn forward with me and focus on February 20, 2002. So, a couple weeks after these conversations you had with Mr. Boultbee and Mr. Kipnis. Okay?[5]

[A] Yes.

[Q] Was there a meeting of Hollinger International's Audit Committee that day?

[A] Yes, there was.

[Q] Did you attend the meeting?

[A] Yes.

[Q] Where did the meeting take place?

[A] It took place in Hollinger International's offices in New York City.

[Q] And who else from KPMG was there besides you?

[A] Pat Ryan, who is a partner with KPMG in Toronto; Jim Winikates, who is the Lead Engagement Partner from Chicago on the Hollinger International audit; and, another partner from KPMG Chicago by the name of Leslie Coolidge, who was the SEC Concurring Review Partner working with Jim on the Hollinger International audit.

[Q] Were there any members of the Audit Committee present?

[A] Yes. Governor Thompson was president — sorry, was present.

[Q] He was present in person?

[A] Yes.

[Q] And do you remember if anybody was on the phone from the Audit Committee?

[A] I know one member of the Audit Committee participated by phone. I don't recall which — whether it was Mr. Burt or Ms. Kravis.

[Q] And in terms of Hollinger International's management, were any representatives of management present?

[A] Yes.

[Q] Do you recall who was there?

[A] Mark Kipnis was there, Jack Boultbee, Fred Creasey, David Radler.

[Q] And might there have been others present, as well?

[A] Yeah, there may — Linda Loye may have been present, as well.

[Q] Now, in terms of getting ready for this meeting, Ms. Stitt, what did you understand would be the purpose of the meeting?

[A] At the conclusion of every audit, before we issue our audit report, we would generally meet with — for a public company with — the company's Audit Committee. And in that meeting, our professional standards — so, the book that was shown, one of the standards in there are some required communications. So, there's some things that we mandatorily need to communicate to the Audit Committee. But, in addition to that, we generally outline sort of the scope of the work that we've done; what areas we have focused on; you know, the — our findings; if we had any significant concerns; and, we talk about independence and unrecorded adjustments.

[Q] And this was a meeting that you had annually with the Audit Committee?

[A] Yes.

* * *

[Q] Approximately how long did the meeting last all together?

[A] Hour, hour and ten minutes is what I would recall.

---

5 Mr. Kipnis served as Secretary and Vice President – Law for Hollinger International from 1998 through 2003.

[Q] And in terms of the talking points that you had prepared on the related-party transactions in particular, did you, in fact, speak to those items at the meeting?

[A] No, I did not.

[Q] Who did?

[A] Pat Ryan.

* * *

[Q] Once the group reached this portion of the presentation that Mr. Ryan was walking through, did any of the members of management have anything to say on the topic of non-compete agreements?

[A] I recall management sort of interjecting into the Minutes on —

[MR. NEWMAN]

Objection to the form of that response. Management interjecting, Judge.

[THE COURT]

Sustained.

[MS. RUDER]

[Q] Did it — first "Yes" or "No," did anyone from management make any comments during this portion of the presentation?

[A] Yes.

[Q] Who from management made comments?

[A] Mark Kipnis and Jack Boultbee.

* * *

[Q] And when you reached that portion of the presentation, what in particular did Mr. Kipnis say?

[A] I remember Mr. Kipnis leaning over to Governor Thompson going — "You — that is on the agenda for this afternoon's meeting or the meeting later to formally ratify that."

[Q] Now, at some other point in the presentation, you said Mr. Boultbee made a comment?

* * *

[Q] What did Mr. Boultbee say?

[A] I recall Mr. Boultbee interjecting into the meeting and saying, "Governor Thompson, you will recall when the CanWest non-compete payments were approved, there was an error in the minutes and that was subsequently rectified."

[Q] And was Mr. Ryan, in fact, talking about the company's Minutes with respect to non-compete payments in general, as far as the presentation?

[A] Yes. I mean, we're — we're talking about the fact that we were looking for approval of these various payments.

[Q] All right. So, Mr. Kipnis mentioned Osprey and Mr. Boultbee mentioned CanWest; is that correct?

[A] That is correct.

[Q] What, if anything, did Mr. Kipnis or Mr. Boultbee say during the portion of the comments concerning the U.S. Community non-competes?

[A] Don't recall them saying anything.

[Q] What, if anything, did Mr. Radler say during that portion of the discussion?

[A] Nothing.

[Q] Did anyone on the Audit Committee speak to any of these issues?

[A] No.

[Q] Were they listening — or only Mr. Thompson was in front of you; is that correct?

[A] Yeah. Mr. Thompson was sitting at the head of the table, yes.

[Q] And did Mr. Thompson say anything during this portion of Mr. Ryan's presentation?

[A] No.

[Q] Now, in terms of the context, I'm putting next to each other Government Exhibit KPMG 19 and Government Exhibit KPMG 5. Before we leave this meeting, I want to understand a little better from you, Ms. Stitt, the context of where the "related-party transactions" discussion fits into the overall meeting. You mentioned that the overall meeting was around an hour, hour and ten minutes?

[A] That — that — is my recollection, yes.

[Q] It could have been a little longer or a little shorter?

[A] Yeah.

[Q] In terms of this discussion on related-party transactions, approximately how long did that portion of the discussion take?

[A] I would estimate it was somewhere between five to ten minutes.

* * *

[Q] Coming away from the meeting — well, before we go away from the meeting, during the meeting was there some – was there anything — different or especially significant about your discussion about the U.S. Community non-competes, as opposed to any of the other topics that were covered during the session?

[A] No. We — we — wanted to make sure that the Audit Committee were aware of them. And we wanted — although it's not necessarily required under our auditing standards, we wanted — to ensure — because we thought it was the appropriate thing to do, to make sure — that they had previously been approved and that — and, so, we were there looking for confirmation that there was perhaps some lack of clarity in the original Minutes; and, we were just looking for clarification that, in fact, they had been previously approved.

[Q] And coming out of the meeting, what was your understanding of the status of that issue concerning the U.S. Community non-competes?

[A] Although they didn't say anything explicit, they didn't — they didn't — raise any concerns; they didn't object; they didn't ask any questions in the general session, in the private session. I — I — took the — you know, there was a pregnant pause as we were sort of waiting for a reaction, and there was none. And we proceeded with the rest of it. And I took away from that meeting that they, basically, confirmed to us that they had previously been approved.

* * *

[Q] Why was it, coming away from the meeting — with the interaction that you've described, why were you satisfied coming away from that meeting with the status of the issue?

[A] Because nobody objected at the meeting to say these hadn't previously been approved. I mean, I took their silence as meaning that they had — they had — considered them before and they had been approved.

APRIL 23, 2007 – AM
SELECTED TESTIMONY ABOUT AUDIT WORKING PAPERS

[Q] Now, I want to switch topics for a second and just focus on work papers. You mentioned work papers previously?

[A] Correct.

[Q] Work papers are the — and we're going to talk about them a lot later, but work papers are the documentation of the work of the auditors, right?

[A] It's what we've performed and what we found, yeah. The results of our tests.

[Q] And work papers provide support for the auditor's ultimate conclusion as your evidential matter?

[A] Yes, that is correct.

[Q] And work papers are the official records of the audit, right?

[A] That is correct.

[Q] And they get prepared by auditors reviewing the records?

[A] Yes. They're prepared by whoever is performing the test, yeah.

[Q] And sometimes the work papers include discussions with clients?

[A] Yes.

[Q] And they reflect confirmation from outside sources when that's done?

[A] Yeah. When that's done, yeah.

[Q] But the work papers don't necessarily record all of the work or considerations that go into the audit, right?

[A] I mean, generally, we try to document all of the items that we think are significant and perform a foundation for us expressing our opinion.

[Q] You do your best, but not everything makes it into the work papers, right?

[A] That's — that could be a fair comment, yeah.

[Q] But, like you said, it records many important considerations and what you're focusing on as material, right?

[A] That's correct.

* * *

[Q] And when you initial a work paper, it means that, basically, you've reviewed it and you signed off on it subject to any comments you might have written onto the document, right?

[A] Practice is somewhat mixed. I mean, sometimes you may review a document and have a question and you've prepared what we refer to as review notes. And you would sort of separately track your outstanding items with respect to review of a document.

[Q] But it's — the typical practice is when you initial it, you're signing — is it called "signing off on the document"?

[A] Generally, that is the practice. You shouldn't sign off on it until you have cleared your review notes.

[Q] And, then, after the audit's completed, the work papers are all filed in a central place that KPMG keeps, right?

[A] That is correct.

REQUIRED

[1] The following requirements relate to Ms. Stitt's testimony about the concept of reasonable assurance:

[a] Research the auditing standards for "reasonable assurance" and provide your assessment as to the accuracy of Ms. Stitt's description of that concept in her testimony.

[b] Ms. Stitt testified that audit evidence is often not conclusive. Describe professional standards requirements related to the need to collect audit evidence and provide a summary of what is meant by "sufficient appropriate audit evidence."

[c] As part of Ms. Stitt's testimony, she describes auditor responsibility for detecting material misstatements due to fraud. Review auditing standards requirements related to auditor responsibilities for detecting material misstatements due to fraud and assess whether her testimony is consistent with auditing standards.

[2] The following requirements relate to Ms. Stitt's testimony about the CanWest non-compete payments:

[a] The concept of a "related party" is defined by generally accepted accounting principles (GAAP). Provide a brief overview of the concept of "related party transactions."

[b] Based on your understanding of the concept of "related party transactions," why would the non-compete payments described in this case be considered a "related party transaction?"

[c] Summarize what the auditing standards say regarding auditor's responsibilities with respect to identifying related party relationships and transactions.

[d] What financial statement disclosures are required by generally accepted accounting principles (GAAP) for related party transactions?

[3] The following requirements relate to Ms. Stitt's testimony about the audit committee presentation:

[a] Provide a brief overview of the requirements in auditing standards about the auditor's communications with those charged with governance. Be sure to describe the overall purpose of this required communication.

[b] Based on your overview of the auditor's communication responsibilities, why was it appropriate for KPMG to discuss the related party transactions with Hollinger International's Audit Committee?

[c] Based on your review of the transcript about the audit committee meeting, describe whether you believe KPMG exercised due professional care in pursuing this issue with Hollinger International's Audit Committee. Did KPMG accomplish the intent of auditing standards? What could KPMG have done differently with respect to this issue during this meeting?

[4] The following requirements relate to Ms. Stitt's testimony about the audit working papers:

[a] Based on your review of requirements in auditing standards related to auditor documentation, why must auditors prepare audit documentation?

[b] Discuss the concept of "experienced auditors" as described in auditing standards and highlight how that concept relates to the form, content, and extent of audit documentation.

[c] Summarize the requirements for identifying the preparer and reviewer of audit documentation. Is Ms. Stitt's testimony consistent with those requirements? Briefly explain.

[d] Summarize the responsibilities for reviewing audit documentation as described in auditing standards.

Accounting Fraud and Auditor Legal Liability

CASES INCLUDED IN THIS SECTION

Enron Corporation and Andersen, LLP
Analyzing the Fall of Two Giants

MARK S. BEASLEY · FRANK A. BUCKLESS · STEVEN M. GLOVER · DOUGLAS F. PRAWITT

LEARNING OBJECTIVES

After completing and discussing this case you should be able to

[1] Understand the events leading to Enron's bankruptcy and Andersen's downfall

[2] Appreciate the importance of understanding an audit client's core business strategies

[3] Recognize potential conflicts arising from auditor relationships with their clients

[4] Understand how accounting standards may have contributed to the Enron debacle and describe how some in the accounting profession are seeking to change the fundamental nature of those standards

[5] Understand the difference between "rule-based" and "principle-based" accounting standards to better appreciate some of the issues involved in the movement toward international financial reporting standards (IFRS).

[6] Consider challenges facing the accounting profession and evaluate alternative courses of action for overcoming these obstacles

INTRODUCTION

Enron Corporation entered 2001 as the seventh largest public company in the United States, only to later exit the year as the largest company to ever declare bankruptcy in U.S history. Investors who lost millions and lawmakers seeking to prevent similar reoccurrences were shocked by these unbelievable events. The following testimony of Rep. Richard H. Baker, chair of the House Capital Markets Subcommittee, exemplified these feelings:

> We are here today to examine and begin the process of understanding the most stunning business reversal in recent history. One moment an international corporation with a diversified portfolio enjoying an incredible run-up of stock prices, the darling of financial press and analysts, which, by the way, contributed to the view that Enron had indeed become the new model for business of the future, indeed, a new paradigm. One edition of Fortune magazine called it the best place in America for an employee to work. Analysts gave increasingly creative praise, while stock prices soared…. Now in retrospect, it is clear, at least to me, that while Enron executives were having fun, it actually became a very large hedge fund, which just happened to own a power company. While that in itself does not warrant criticism, it was the extraordinary risk-taking by powerful executives which rarely added value but simply accelerated the cash burn-off rate. Executives having Enron fun are apparently very costly and, all the while, they were aggressive in the exercise of their own [Enron] stock options, flipping acquisitions for quick sale. One executive sold a total of $353 million in the 3-year period preceding the failure. What did he know? When did he know it? And why didn't we?[1]

---

1 Rep. Richard H. Baker (R-LA), December 12, 2001 Hearing of the Capital Markets, Insurance, and Government sponsored enterprises subcommittee and oversight and investigations subcommittee of the House Financial Services Committee, "The Enron Collapse: Impact on Investors and Financial Markets."

The case was prepared by Mark S. Beasley, Ph.D. and Frank A. Buckless, Ph.D. of North Carolina State University and Steven M. Glover, Ph.D. and Douglas F. Prawitt, Ph.D. of Brigham Young University, as a basis for class discussion. It is not intended to illustrate either effective or ineffective handling of an administrative situation.

Although company executives were involved in questionable business practices and even fraud, Enron's failure was ultimately due to a collapse of investor, customer, and trading partner confidence. In the boom years of the late 1990's, Enron entered into a number of aggressive transactions involving "special purpose entities" (SPEs) for which the underlying accounting was questionable or fraudulent. Some of these transactions essentially involved Enron receiving borrowed funds without recording liabilities on the company's balance sheet. Instead, the inflow of funds was made to look like it came from the sale of assets. The "loans" were guaranteed with Enron stock, trading at over $100 per share at the time. The company found itself in real trouble when, simultaneously, the business deals underlying these transactions went sour and Enron's stock price plummeted. Debt holders began to call the loans due to Enron's diminished stock price, and the company found its accounting positions increasingly problematic to maintain.

The August 2001 resignation of Enron's chief executive officer (CEO), Jeffrey Skilling, only six months after beginning his "dream job" further fueled Wall Street skepticism and scrutiny over company operations. Shortly thereafter, The Wall Street Journal's "Heard on the Street" column of August 28, 2001 drew further attention to the company, igniting a public firestorm of controversy that quickly undermined the company's reputation. The subsequent loss of confidence by trading partners and customers quickly dried up Enron's trading volume, and the company found itself facing a liquidity crisis by late 2001.

Skilling summed it up this way when he testified before the House Energy Commerce Committee on February 7, 2002:

> It is my belief that Enron's failure was due to a classic 'run on the bank:' a liquidity crisis spurred by a lack of confidence in the company. At the time of Enron's collapse, the company was solvent and highly profitable - but, apparently, not liquid enough. That is my view of the principal cause of its failure.[2]

Public disclosure of diminishing liquidity and questionable management decisions and practices destroyed the trust Enron had established within the business community. This caused hundreds of trading partners, clients, and suppliers to suspend doing business with the company—ultimately leading to its downfall.

Enron's collapse, along with events related to the audits of Enron's financial statements, caused a similar loss of reputation, trust, and confidence in Big-5 accounting firm, Andersen, LLP. Enron's collapse and the associated revelations of alleged aggressive and inappropriate accounting practices caused major damage for this previously acclaimed firm. News about charges of inappropriate destruction of documents at the Andersen office in Houston, which housed the Enron audit, and the subsequent unprecedented federal indictment was the kiss of death. Andersen's clients quickly lost confidence in the firm, and by June 2002, more than 400 of its largest clients had fired the firm as their auditor, leading to the sale or desertion of various pieces of Andersen's U.S. and international practices. On June 15th, a federal jury in Houston convicted Andersen on one felony count of obstructing the SEC's investigation into Enron's collapse. Although the Supreme Court later overturned the decision in May 2005, the reversal came nearly three years after Andersen was essentially dead. Soon after the June 15, 2002 verdict, Andersen announced it would cease auditing publicly owned clients by August 31. Thus, like Enron, in an astonishingly short period of time Andersen went from being one of the world's largest and most respected business organizations into oblivion.

Because of the Congressional hearings and intense media coverage, along with the tremendous impact the company's collapse had on the corporate community and on the accounting profession, the name "Enron" will reverberate for decades to come. Here is a brief analysis of the fall of these two giants.

---

2   Skilling, Jeffrey, "Prepared Witness Testimony: Skilling, Jeffrey, K." House Energy Subcommittee. See the following website: http://energycommerce.house.gov/107/hearings/ 02072002Hearing485/Skilling797.htm

ENRON IN THE BEGINNING

Enron Corporation, based in Houston, Texas, was formed as the result of the July 1985 merger of Houston Natural Gas and InterNorth of Omaha, Nebraska. In its early years, Enron was a natural gas pipeline company whose primary business strategy involved entering into contracts to deliver specified amounts of natural gas to businesses or utilities over a given period of time. In 1989, Enron began trading natural gas commodities. After the deregulation of the electrical power markets in the early 1990s—a change for which senior Enron officials lobbied heavily—Enron swiftly evolved from a conventional business that simply delivered energy, into a "new economy" business heavily involved in the brokerage of speculative energy futures. Enron acted as an intermediary by entering into contracts with buyers and sellers of energy, profiting by arbitraging price differences. Enron began marketing electricity in the U.S. in 1994, and entered the European energy market in 1995.

In 1999, at the height of the Internet boom, Enron furthered its transformation into a "new economy" company by launching Enron Online, a Web-based commodity trading site. Enron also broadened its technological reach by entering the business of buying and selling access to high-speed Internet bandwidth. At its peak, Enron owned a stake in nearly 30,000 miles of gas pipelines, owned or had access to a 15,000-mile fiber optic network, and had a stake in several electricity-generating operations around the world. In 2000, the company reported gross revenues of $101 billion.

Enron continued to expand its business into extremely complex ventures by offering a wide variety of financial hedges and contracts to customers. These financial instruments were designed to protect customers against a variety of risks, including events such as changes in interest rates and variations in weather patterns. The volume of transactions involving these "new economy" type instruments grew rapidly and actually surpassed the volume of Enron's traditional contracts involving delivery of physical commodities (such as natural gas) to customers. To ensure that Enron managed the risks related to these "new economy" instruments, the company hired a large number of experts in the fields of actuarial science, mathematics, physics, meteorology, and economics.[3]

Within a year of its launch, Enron Online was handling more than $1 billion in transactions daily. The website was much more than a place for buyers and sellers of various commodities to meet. *Internetweek* reported that, *"It was the market, a place where everyone in the gas and power industries gathered pricing data for virtually every deal they made, regardless of whether they executed them on the site."*[4] The site's success depended on cutting-edge technology and more importantly on the trust the company developed with its customers and partners who expected Enron to follow through on its price and delivery promises.

When the company's accounting shenanigans were brought to light, customers, investors, and other partners ceased trading through the energy giant when they lost confidence in Enron's ability to fulfill its obligations and act with integrity in the marketplace.[5]

ENRON'S COLLAPSE

On August 14, 2001, Kenneth Lay was reinstated as Enron's CEO after Jeffrey Skilling resigned for "purely personal" reasons after having served for only a six-month period as CEO. Skilling joined Enron in 1990 after leading McKinsey & Company's energy and chemical consulting practice and became Enron's president and chief operating officer in 1996. Skilling was appointed CEO in early 2001 to replace Lay, who had served as chairman and CEO since 1986.[6]

---

3 "Understanding Enron: Rising Power." *The Washington Post.* May 11, 2002. See the following website: http://www.washingtonpost.com/wp-srv/business/enron/front.html

4 Preston, Robert. "Enron's Demise Doesn't Devalue Model It Created." *Internetweek.* December 10, 2001.

5 Ibid.

6 "The Rise and Fall of Enron: The Financial Players." *The Washington Post.* May 11, 2002. See the following website: http://www.washingtonpost.com/wp-srv/business/daily/articles/ keyplayers_financial.htm

Skilling's resignation proved to be the beginning of Enron's collapse. The day after Skilling resigned, Enron's vice president of corporate development, Sherron Watkins, sent an anonymous letter to Kenneth Lay (see Exhibit 1). In the letter, Ms. Watkins detailed her fears that Enron "might implode in a wave of accounting scandals." When the letter later became public, Ms. Watkins was celebrated as an honest and loyal employee who tried to save the company through her whistle-blowing efforts.

EXHIBIT 1: SHERRON WATKINS LETTER TO ENRON CEO, KENNETH LAY

Dear Mr. Lay,

Has Enron become a risky place to work? For those of us who didn't get rich over the last few years, can we afford to stay?

Skilling's abrupt departure will raise suspicions of accounting improprieties and valuation issues. Enron has been very aggressive in its accounting - most notably the Raptor transactions and the Condor vehicle. We do have valuation issues with our international assets and possibly some of our EES MTM positions.

The spotlight will be on us, the market just can't accept that Skilling is leaving his dream job. I think that the valuation issues can be fixed and reported with other goodwill write-downs to occur in 2002. How do we fix the Raptor and Condor deals? They unwind in 2002 and 2003, we will have to pony up Enron stock and that won't go unnoticed.

To the layman on the street, it will look like we recognized funds flow of $800 mm from merchant asset sales in 1999 by selling to a vehicle (Condor) that we capitalized with a promise of Enron stock in later years. Is that really funds flow or is it cash from equity issuance?

We have recognized over $550 million of fair value gains on stocks via our swaps with Raptor, much of that stock has declined significantly - Avici by 98%, from $178 mm to $5 mm, The New Power Co by 70%, from $20/share to $6/share. The value in the swaps won't be there for Raptor, so once again Enron will issue stock to offset these losses. Raptor is an LJM entity. It sure looks to the layman on the street that we are hiding losses in a related company and will compensate that company with Enron stock in the future.

I am incredibly nervous that we will implode in a wave of accounting scandals. My 8 years of Enron work history will be worth nothing on my resume, the business world will consider the past successes as nothing but an elaborate accounting hoax. Skilling is resigning now for 'personal reasons' but I think he wasn't having fun, looked down the road and knew this stuff was unfixable and would rather abandon ship now than resign in shame in 2 years.

Is there a way our accounting gurus can unwind these deals now? I have thought and thought about how to do this, but I keep bumping into one big problem - we booked the Condor and Raptor deals in 1999 and 2000, we enjoyed a wonderfully high stock price, many executives sold stock, we then try and reverse or fix the deals in 2001 and it's a bit like robbing the bank in one year and trying to pay it back 2 years later. Nice try, but investors were hurt, they bought at $70 and $80/share looking for $120/share and now they're at $38 or worse. We are under too much scrutiny and there are probably one or two disgruntled 'redeployed' employees who know enough about the 'funny' accounting to get us in trouble.

What do we do? I know this question cannot be addressed in the all-employee meeting, but can you give some assurances that you and Causey will sit down and take a good hard objective look at what is going to happen to Condor and Raptor in 2002 and 2003?

Watkins, Sherron. Letter to Kenneth Lay, CEO. 15 Aug. 2001 (1st page only)

Two months later, Enron reported a 2001 third quarter loss of $618 million and a reduction of $1.2 billion in shareholder equity related to partnerships run by chief financial officer (CFO), Andrew Fastow. Fastow had created and managed numerous off-balance-sheet partnerships for Enron, which also benefited him personally. In fact, during his tenure at Enron, Fastow collected approximately $30 million in management fees from various partnerships related to Enron.

News of the company's third quarter losses resulted in a sharp decline in Enron's stock value. Lay even called U.S. Treasury Secretary, Paul O'Neill, on October 28 to inform him of the company's financial difficulties. Those events were then followed by a November 8th company announcement of even worse news—Enron had overstated earnings over the previous four years by $586 million and owed up to $3 billion for previously unreported obligations to various partnerships. This news sent the stock price further on its downward slide.

Despite these developments, Lay continued to tell employees that Enron's stock was undervalued. Ironically, he was also allegedly selling portions of his own stake in the company for millions of dollars. Lay was one of the few Enron employees who managed to sell a significant portion of his stock before the stock price collapsed completely. In August 2001, he sold 93,000 shares for a personal gain of over $2 million.

Sadly, most Enron employees did not have the same chance to liquidate their Enron investments. Most of the company employees' personal 401(k) accounts included large amounts of Enron stock. When Enron changed 401(k) administrators at the end of October 2001, employee retirement plans were temporarily frozen. Unfortunately, the November 8th announcement of prior period financial statement misstatements occurred during the freeze, paralyzing company employee 401(k) plans. When employees were finally allowed access to their plans, the stock had fallen below $10 per share from earlier highs exceeding $100 per share.

Corporate "white knights" appeared shortly thereafter, spurring hopes of a rescue. Dynegy Inc. and ChevronTexaco Corp. (a major Dynegy shareholder) almost spared Enron from bankruptcy when they announced a tentative agreement to buy the company for $8 billion in cash and stock. Unfortunately, Dynegy and ChevronTexaco later withdrew their offer after Enron's credit rating was downgraded to "junk" status in late November. Enron tried unsuccessfully to prevent the downgrade, and allegedly asked the Bush administration for help in the process.

After Dynegy formally rescinded its purchase offer, Enron filed for Chapter 11 bankruptcy on December 2, 2001. This announcement pushed the company's stock price down to $0.40 per share. On January 15, 2002, the New York Stock Exchange suspended trading in Enron's stock and began the process to formally de-list it.

It is important to understand that a large portion of the earnings restatements may not *technically* have been attributable to improper accounting treatment. So, what made these enormous restatements necessary? In the end, the decline in Enron's stock price triggered contractual obligations that were never reported on the balance sheet, in some cases due to "loopholes" in accounting standards, which Enron exploited. An analysis of the nuances of Enron's partnership accounting provides some insight into the unraveling of this corporate giant.

Unraveling the "Special Purpose Entity" Web

The term "special purpose entity" (SPE) has become synonymous with the Enron collapse because these entities were at the center of Enron's aggressive business and accounting practices. SPEs are separate legal entities set up to accomplish specific company objectives. For example, SPEs are sometimes created to help a company sell off assets. After identifying which assets to sell to the SPE, under the rules existing in 2001, the selling company would secure an outside investment of at least three percent of the value of the assets to be sold to the SPE.[7] The company would then transfer the identified assets to the SPE. The SPE would pay for the contributed assets through a new debt or equity issuance. The selling company could then recognize the sale of the assets to the SPE and thereby remove the assets and any related debts from its balance sheet. The validity of such an arrangement is, of course, contingent on the outside investors bearing the risk of their investment. In other words, the investors are not permitted to finance their interest through a note payable or other type of guarantee that might absolve them from accepting responsibility if the SPE suffers losses or fails.[8]

---

7   Since the collapse of Enron, the FASB has changed the requirements for consolidations and now requires a ten percent minimum outside investment among other requirements designed to prevent abuses (See the FASB's Accounting Standard Codification (ASC) 805 and ASC 810)

8   The FEI Research Foundation. 2002. *Special Purpose Entities: Understanding the Guidelines*. Accessed at http://www.fei.org/download/SPEIssuesAlert.pdf

While SPEs are fairly common in corporate America, they have been controversial. Some argued at the time that SPEs represented a "gaping loophole in accounting practice."[9] Accounting rules dictate that once a company owns 50% or more of another, the company must consolidate, thus including the related entity in its own financial statements. However, as the following quote from *BusinessWeek* demonstrates, such was not the case with SPEs in 2001:

> *The controversial exception that outsiders need invest only three percent of an SPE's capital for it to be independent and off the balance sheet came about through fumbles by the Securities & Exchange Commission and the Financial Accounting Standards Board. In 1990, accounting firms asked the SEC to endorse the three percent rule that had become a common, though unofficial, practice in the '80s. The SEC didn't like the idea, but it didn't stomp on it, either. It asked the FASB to set tighter rules to force consolidation of entities that were effectively controlled by companies. FASB drafted two overhauls of the rules but never finished the job, and (as of May 2002) the SEC is still waiting.[10]*

While SPEs can serve legitimate business purposes, it is now apparent that Enron used an intricate network of SPEs, along with complicated speculations and hedges—all couched in dense legal language—to keep an enormous amount of debt off the company's balance sheet. Enron had literally hundreds of SPEs. Through careful structuring of these SPEs that took into account the complex accounting rules governing their required financial statement treatment, Enron was able to avoid consolidating the SPEs on its balance sheet. Three of the Enron SPEs have been made prominent throughout the congressional hearings and litigation proceedings. These SPEs were widely known as "Chewco," "LJM2," and "Whitewing."

Chewco was established in 1997 by Enron executives in connection with a complex investment in another Enron partnership with interests in natural gas pipelines. Enron's CFO, Andrew Fastow, was charged with managing the partnership. However, to prevent required disclosure of a potential conflict of interest between Fastow's roles at Enron and Chewco, Fastow employed Michael Kopper, managing director of Enron Global Finance, to "officially" manage Chewco. In connection with the Chewco partnership, Fastow and Kopper appointed Fastow relatives to the board of directors of the partnership. Then, in a set of complicated transactions, another layer of partnerships was established to disguise Kopper's invested interest in Chewco. Kopper originally invested $125,000 in Chewco and was later paid $10.5 million when Enron bought Chewco in March 2001.[11] Surprisingly, Kopper remained relatively unknown throughout the subsequent investigations. In fact, Ken Lay told investigators that he did not know Kopper. Kopper was able to continue in his management roles through January 2002.[12]

The LJM2 partnership was formed in October 1999 with the goal of acquiring assets chiefly owned by Enron. Like Chewco, LJM2 was managed by Fastow and Kopper. To assist with the technicalities of this partnership, LJM2 engaged PricewaterhouseCoopers, LLP and the Chicago-based law firm, Kirkland & Ellis. Enron used the LJM2 partnership to deconsolidate its less-productive assets. These actions generated a 30 percent average annual return for the LJM2 limited-partner investors.

The Whitewing partnership, another significant SPE established by Enron, purchased an assortment of power plants, pipelines, and water projects originally purchased by Enron in the mid-1990s that were located in India, Turkey, Spain, and Latin America. The Whitewing partnership was crucial to Enron's move from being an energy provider to becoming a trader of energy contracts. Whitewing was the vehicle through which Enron sold many of its physical energy production assets.

---

9   Henry, David, "Who Else is Hiding Debt?" *BusinessWeek*. May 11, 2002. See the following website: http://www.businessweek.com/magazine/content/02_04/b3767704.htm

10   Ibid.

11   The Fall of Enron; Enron Lawyer's Qualms Detailed in New Memos. *The Los Angeles Times*. February 7, 2002. Richard Simon, Edmund Sanders, Walter Hamilton.

12   Fry, Jennifer. "Low-Profile Partnership Head Stayed on Job until Judge's Order." *The Washington Post*. February 7, 2002.

In creating this partnership, Enron quietly guaranteed investors in Whitewing that if Whitewing's assets (transferred from Enron) were sold at a loss, Enron would compensate the investors with shares of Enron common stock. This obligation—unknown to Enron's shareholders—totaled $2 billion as of November 2001. Part of the secret guarantee to Whitewing investors surfaced in October 2001, when Enron's credit rating was downgraded by credit agencies. The credit downgrade triggered a requirement that Enron immediately pay $690 million to Whitewing investors. It was when this obligation surfaced that Enron's talks with Dynegy failed. Enron was unable to delay the payment and was forced to disclose the problem, stunning investors and fueling the fire that led to the company's bankruptcy filing only two months later.

In addition to these partnerships, Enron created financial instruments called "Raptors," which were backed by Enron stock and were designed to reduce the risks associated with Enron's own investment portfolio. In essence, the Raptors covered potential losses on Enron investments as long as Enron's stock market price continued to do well. Enron also masked debt using complex financial derivative transactions. Taking advantage of accounting rules to account for large loans from Wall Street firms as financial hedges, Enron hid $3.9 billion in debt from 1992 through 2001. At least $2.5 billion of those transactions arose in the three years prior to the Chapter 11 bankruptcy filing. These loans were in addition to the $8 to $10 billion in long and short-term debt that Enron disclosed in its financial reports in the three years leading up to its bankruptcy. Because the loans were accounted for as a hedging activity, Enron was able to explain away what looked like an increase in borrowings, (which would raise red flags for creditors), as hedges for commodity trades, rather than as new debt financing.[13]

The Complicity of Accounting Standards.

Limitations in generally accepted accounting principles (GAAP) are at least partly to blame for Enron executives' ability to hide debt, keeping it off the company's financial statements. These technical accounting standards lay out specific "bright-line" rules that read much like the tax or criminal law codes. Some observers of the profession argue that by attempting to outline every accounting situation in detail, standard-setters are trying to create a specific decision model for every imaginable situation. However, very specific rules create an opportunity for clever lawyers, investment bankers, and accountants to create entities and transactions that circumvent the intent of the rules while still conforming to the "letter of the law."

In his congressional testimony, Robert K. Herdman, SEC Chief Accountant at the time, discussed the difference between rule and principle-based accounting standards:

> *Rule-based accounting standards provide extremely detailed rules that attempt to contemplate virtually every application of the standard. This encourages a check-the-box mentality to financial reporting that eliminates judgments from the application of the reporting. Examples of rule-based accounting guidance include the accounting for derivatives, employee stock options, and leasing. And, of course, questions keep coming. Rule-based standards make it more difficult for preparers and auditors to step back and evaluate whether the overall impact is consistent with the objectives of the standard.[14]*

In some cases it is clear that Enron neither abode by the spirit nor the letter of these accounting rules (for example, by securing outside SPE investors against possible losses). It also appears that the company's lack of disclosure regarding Fastow's involvement in the SPEs fell short of accounting rule compliance.

---

13 Altman Daniel. "Enron Had More Than One Way to Disguise Rapid Rise in Debt," *The New York Times*, February 17, 2002
14 Herdman, Robert K. "Prepared Witness Testimony: Herdman, Robert K., US House of Representatives. See the following website: http://energycommerce.house.gov/107/hearings/ 02142002Hearing490/Herdman802.htm

These "loopholes" allowed Enron executives to keep many of the company's liabilities off the financial statements being audited by Andersen, LLP, as highlighted by the *BusinessWeek* article summarized in Exhibit 2. Given the alleged abuse of the accounting rules, many asked, "Where was Andersen, the accounting firm that was to serve as Enron's public 'watchdog,' while Enron allegedly betrayed and misled its shareholders?"

EXHIBIT 2: THE ENRON/ANDERSEN TUG-OF-WAR

In the memos that have poured out of federal investigations, the tug-of-war between Arthur Andersen LLP and Enron Corp. is clear. Time after time, Enron would seek creative accounting for some joint venture or special-purpose entity. Some Andersen accountants would resist, arguing in many cases that the deal didn't serve any legitimate business purpose: "In effect, nothing was accomplished in this transaction but a sale of future revenues," Andersen partner Carl E. Bass wrote in a Mar. 4, 2001, e-mail.

But the bottom line was always clear: If Andersen couldn't show Enron a specific rule prohibiting what it wanted to do, Enron would do it.

Now the mandarins who write accounting rules want to change that dynamic. The idea: slash the 100,000-plus pages of rules that define "generally accepted accounting principles" in favor of broader, simpler statements of what accountants are supposed to look for when they review, say, a lease or a hedging transaction.

Advocates—led by Securities & Exchange Commission Chairman Harvey L. Pitt—say a return to simpler standards will paint a clearer picture for investors. The move will allow auditors to focus on whether the bookkeeping for a deal makes good business sense. It also will put the burden on corporate clients to prove that their aggressive accounting meets the standards. "What we've got now," says Robert K. Herdman, the SEC's chief accountant, "invites Wall Street and others to create transactions that dot every 'i' and cross every 't,' but violate the intent of the rules and fuzz up what's really going on."

Source: *BusinessWeek*, May 20, 2002, p. 123. Used with permission.

THE ROLE OF ANDERSEN

It is clear that investors and the public believed that Enron executives were not the only parties responsible for the company's collapse. Many fingers also pointed to Enron's auditor, Andersen, LLP, which issued "clean" audit opinions on Enron's financial statements from 1997 to 2000 but later agreed that a massive earnings restatement was warranted. Andersen's involvement with Enron ultimately destroyed the accounting firm—something the global business community would have thought next to impossible prior to 2001. Ironically, Andersen ceased to exist for the same essential reasons Enron failed–the company lost the trust of its clients and other business partners.

Andersen in the Beginning

Andersen was originally founded as Andersen, Delaney & Co. in 1913 by Arthur Andersen, an accounting professor at Northwestern University in Chicago. By taking tough stands against clients' aggressive accounting treatments, Andersen quickly gained a national reputation as a reliable keeper of the public's trust:

> In 1915, Andersen took the position that the balance sheet of a steamship-company client had to reflect the costs associated with the sinking of a freighter, even though the sinking occurred after the company's fiscal year had ended but before Andersen had signed off on its financial statements. This marked the first time an auditor had demanded such a degree of disclosure to ensure accurate reporting.[15]

Although Andersen's storied reputation began with its founder, the accounting firm continued the tradition for years. An oft-repeated phrase at Andersen was, "*there's the Andersen*

---

15 Brown, K., et al., "Andersen Indictment in Shredding Case Puts Its Future in Doubt as Clients Bolt," *The Wall Street Journal*, March 15, 2000.

way and the wrong way." Another was "do the right thing." Andersen was the only one of the major accounting firms to back reforms in the accounting for pensions in the 1980s, a move opposed by many corporations, including some of its own clients.[16] Ironically, prior to the Enron debacle, Andersen had also previously taken an unpopular public stand to toughen the very accounting standards that Enron exploited in using SPEs to keep debt off its balance sheets.

Andersen's Loss of Reputation

While Andersen previously had been considered the cream of the crop of accounting firms, just prior to the Enron disaster Andersen's reputation suffered from a number of high profile SEC investigations launched against the firm. The firm was investigated for its role in the financial statement audits of Waste Management, Global Crossing, Sunbeam, Qwest Communications, Baptist Foundation of Arizona, and WorldCom. In May 2001, Andersen paid $110 million to settle securities fraud charges stemming from its work at Sunbeam. In June 2001, Andersen entered a no-fault, no-admission-of-guilt plea bargain with the SEC to settle charges of Andersen's audit work on Waste Management, Inc. for $7 million. Andersen later settled with investors of the Baptist Foundation of Arizona for $217 million without admitting fault or guilt (the firm subsequently reneged on the agreement because the firm was in liquidation). Due to this string of negative events and associated publicity, Andersen found its once-applauded reputation for impeccable integrity questioned by a market where integrity, independence, and reputation are the primary attributes affecting demand for a firm's services.

Andersen at Enron

By 2001, Enron had become one of Andersen's largest clients. Despite the firm's recognition that Enron was a high-risk client, Andersen apparently had difficulty sticking to its guns at Enron:

> *[Andersen had] found $51 million of problems in the company's books – and decided to let them go uncorrected. While auditing Enron's 1997 financial results, Andersen proposed that the energy company make 'adjustments' that would have cut its annual income by almost 50 percent, to $54 million from $105 million.....Enron chose not to make those adjustments and Andersen put its stamp of approval on the company's financial report anyway.*[17]

Andersen's chief executive, Joseph F. Berardino, testified before the U.S. Congress that, after proposing the $51 million of adjustments to Enron's 1997 results, the accounting firm decided that those adjustments were not material.[18] Congressional hearings and the business press allege that Andersen was unable to stand up to Enron because of the conflicts of interest that existed due to large fees and the mix of services Andersen provided to Enron.

In 2000, Enron reported that it paid Andersen $52 million—$25 million for the financial statement audit work and $27 million for consulting services. Andersen not only performed the external financial statement audit, but also carried out Enron's internal audit function, a relatively common practice in the accounting profession before the Sarbanes-Oxley Act of 2002. Ironically, Enron's 2000 annual report disclosed that one of the major projects Andersen performed in 2000 was to examine and report on management's assertion about the effectiveness of Enron's system of internal controls.

Comments by investment billionaire, Warren E. Buffett, summarize the perceived conflict that often arises when auditors receive significant fees from clients: *"Though auditors should regard the investing public as their client, they tend to kowtow instead to the managers who choose them and dole out their pay."* Buffett continued by quoting an old saying: *"Whose bread I eat, his song I sing."* [19]

---

16 Ibid

17 Hilzenrath, David S., "Early Warnings of Trouble at Enron." *The Washington Post.* December 30, 2001 See the following website: http://www.washingtonpost.com/wp-dyn/articles/A40094-2001Dec29.html

18 Ibid

19 Hilzenrath, David S., "Early Warnings of Trouble at Enron." *The Washington Post.* December 30, 2001. See the following website: http://www.washingtonpost.com/wp-dyn/articles/A40094-2001Dec29.html

It also appears that Andersen knew about Enron's problems nearly a year before the downfall. According to a February 6, 2001 internal firm e-mail, Andersen considered dropping Enron as a client. The e-mail, which was written by an Andersen partner to David Duncan, partner in charge of the Enron audit, detailed the discussion at an Andersen meeting about the future of the Enron engagement. The essential text of that email is reproduced in Exhibit 3.

The Andersen Indictment

Although the massive restatements of Enron's financial statements cast serious doubt on Andersen's professional conduct and audit opinions, ultimately it was the destruction of Enron-related documents in October and November 2001 and the March 2002 federal indictment of Andersen that led to the firm's rapid downward spiral. The criminal charge against Andersen related to the obstruction of justice for destroying documents after the federal investigation had begun into the Enron collapse. According to the indictment, Andersen allegedly eliminated potentially incriminating evidence by shredding massive amounts of Enron-related audit workpapers and documents. The government alleged that Andersen partners in Houston were directed by the firm's national office legal counsel in Chicago to shred the documents. The U.S. Justice Department contended that Andersen continued to shred Enron documents after it knew of the SEC investigation, but before a formal subpoena was received by Andersen. The shredding stopped on November 8th when Andersen received the SEC's subpoena for all Enron-related documents.

Andersen denied that its corporate counsel recommended such a course of action and assigned the blame for the document destruction to a group of rogue employees in its Houston office seeking to save their own reputations. The evidence is unclear as to exactly who ordered the shredding of the Enron documents or even what documents were shredded.

However, central to the Justice Department's indictment was an email forwarded from Nancy Temple, Andersen's corporate counsel in Chicago, to David Duncan, the Houston-based Enron engagement partner. The body of the email states, *"It might be useful to consider reminding the engagement team of our documentation and retention policy. It will be helpful to make sure that we have complied with the policy. Let me know if you have any questions."*[20]

The Justice Department argued that Andersen's general counsel's email was a thinly veiled directive from Andersen headquarters to ensure that all Enron-related documents that *should* have previously been destroyed according to the firm's policy *were* destroyed. Andersen contended that the infamous Nancy Temple memo simply encouraged adherence to normal engagement documentation policy, including the explicit need to retain documents in certain situations and was never intended to obstruct the government's investigation. However, it is important to understand that once an individual or a firm has reason to believe that a federal investigation is forthcoming, it is considered "obstruction of justice" to destroy documents that might serve as evidence, even before an official subpoena is filed.

In January 2002, Andersen fired Enron engagement partner David Duncan, for his role in the document shredding activities. Duncan later testified that he did not initially think that what he did was wrong and initially maintained his innocence in interviews with government prosecutors. He even signed a joint defense agreement with Andersen on March 20, 2002. Shortly thereafter, Duncan decided to plead guilty to obstruction of justice charges after *"a lot of soul searching about my intent and what was in my head at the time."* [21]

In the obstruction of justice trial against Andersen, Duncan testified for the Federal prosecution, admitting that he ordered the destruction of documents because of the email he received from Andersen's counsel reminding him of the company's document retention policy. He also testified that he wanted to get rid of documents that could be used by prosecuting attorneys and SEC investigators.[22]

---

20 Temple, Nancy A. Email to Michael C. Odom, "Document Retention Policy" October 12, 2001.

21 Beltran, Luisa, Jennifer Rogers, and Brett Gering. "Duncan: I Changed My Mind." cnnfn.com. May 15, 2002. See the following website: http://money.cnn.com/2002/05/15 /news/companies/andersen/index.htm

22 Weil, Jonathan, Alexei Barrionuevo. "Duncan Says Fears of Lawsuits Drove Shredding." *The Wall Street Journal*. New York.

EXHIBIT 3: INTERNAL ANDERSEN EMAIL ON ENRON

From:	Michael D. Jones, Houston, 2541
Sent:	Tuesday, February 6, 2001 08:24 AM
To:	David B. Duncan@ANDERSEN WO, Thomas H. Bauer@ANDERSEN WO
Subject:	Enron retention meeting

Dave, I was not sure whether you were planning on documenting the meeting yesterday. My significant notes were as follows (these were not very detailed, but I was not sure how detailed you wanted to get, assuming that you were going to document the meeting). Let me know if you want me to take a stab at it first (if so we should probably get together for a few minutes to discuss your documentation ideas).

Attendees:
By Phone: Samek, Swanson, Jeneaux, Jonas, Kutsenda, Stewart
In Houston: Bennett, Goddard, Goolsby, Odom, Lowther, Duncan, Bauer, Jones

Significant discussion was held regarding the related party transactions with LJM including the materiality of such amounts to Enron's income statement and the amount retained "off balance sheet." The discussion focused on Fastow's conflicts of interest in his capacity as CFO and the LJM fund manager, the amount of earnings that Fastow receives for his services and participation in LJM, the disclosures of the transactions in the financial footnotes, Enron's BOD's views regarding the transactions and our and management's communication of such transactions to the BOD and our testing of such transactions to ensure that we fully understand the economics and substance of the transactions.

The question was raised as whether the BOD gets any competing bids when the company executes transactions with LJM. DBD replied that he did not believe so, but explained their transaction approval process generally and specifically related to LJM transactions.

A significant discussion was also held regarding Enron's MTM earnings and the fact that it was "intelligent gambling." We discussed Enron's risk management activities including authority limits, valuation and position monitoring.

We discussed Enron's reliance on its current credit rating to maintain itself as a high credit rated transaction party.

We discussed Enron's dependence on transaction execution to meet financial objectives, the fact that Enron often is creating industries and markets and transactions for which there are no specific rules which requires significant judgement and that Enron is aggressive in its transaction structuring. We discussed consultation among the engagement team, with Houston management, practice management and the PSG to ensure that we are not making decisions in isolation.

Ultimately the conclusion was reached to retain Enron as a client citing that it appeared that we had the appropriate people and processes in place to serve Enron and manage our engagement risks. We discussed whether there would be a perceived independence issue solely considering our level of fees. We discussed that the concerns should not be on the magnitude of fees but on the nature of fees. We arbitrarily discussed that it would not be unforseeable that fees could reach a $100 million per year amount considering the multi-disciplinary services being provided. Such amount did not trouble the participants as long as the nature of the services was not an issue.

In addition to the above, discussions were held to varying degrees on each page of the presentation materials.

Take away To Do's:
Inquire as to whether Andy Fastow and / or LJM would be viewed as an "affiliate" from an SEC perspective which would require looking through the transactions and treating them as within the consolidated group.

Suggest that a special committee of the BOD be established to review the fairness of LJM transactions (or alternative comfort that the transactions are fair to Enron, e.g., competitive bidding).

Why did Andy not select AA as auditors, including when PWC was replaced with KPMG. Discussions concluded that we would likely not want to be LJM's financial advisors given potential conflicts of interest with Enron.

Focus on Enron preparing their own documentation and conclusions to issues and transactions.

AA to focus on timely documentation of final transaction structures to ensure consensus is reached on the final structure.

Although convicted of obstruction of justice, Andersen continued to pursue legal recourse by appealing the verdict to the Fifth U.S. Circuit Court of Appeals in New Orleans. The Fifth Court refused to overturn the verdict, so Andersen appealed to the U.S. Supreme Court. The firm claimed that the trial judge "gave jurors poor guidelines for determining the company's wrongdoing in shredding documents related to Enron Corp."[23] The Supreme Court agreed with Andersen and on May 31, 2005, the Court overturned the lower court's decision.

Sadly, the Supreme Court's decision had little effect on the future of Arthur Andersen. By 2005, Andersen employed only 200 people, most of whom were involved in fighting the remaining lawsuits against the firm and managing its few remaining assets. However, the ruling may have helped individual Arthur Andersen partners in civil suits named against them. The ruling also may have made it more difficult for the government to pursue future cases alleging obstruction of justice against individuals and companies.

The End of Andersen

In the early months of 2002, Andersen pursued the possibility of being acquired by one of the other four Big-5 accounting firms: PricewaterhouseCoopers, Ernst & Young, KPMG, and Deloitte & Touche. The most seriously considered possibility was an acquisition of the entire collection of Andersen partnerships by Deloitte & Touche, but the talks fell through only hours before an official announcement of the acquisition was scheduled to take place. The biggest barrier to an acquisition of Andersen apparently centered around fears that an acquirer would assume Andersen's liabilities and responsibility for settling future Enron-related lawsuits.

In the aftermath of Enron's collapse, Andersen began to unravel quickly, losing over 400 publicly traded clients by June 2002—including many high-profile clients with which Andersen had enjoyed long relationships.[24] The list of former clients includes Delta Air Lines, FedEx, Merck, SunTrust Banks, Abbott Laboratories, Freddie Mac, and Valero Energy Corp. In addition to losing clients, Andersen lost many of its global practice units to rival accounting and consulting firms, and agreed to sell a major portion of its consulting business to KPMG consulting for $284 million as well as most of its tax advisory practice to Deloitte & Touche.

On March 26, 2002, Joseph Berardino, CEO of Andersen Worldwide, resigned as CEO, but remained with the firm. In an attempt to salvage the firm, Andersen hired former Federal Reserve chairman, Paul Volcker, to head an oversight board to make recommendations to rebuild Andersen. Mr. Volcker and the board recommended that Andersen split its consulting and auditing businesses and that Volcker and the seven-member board take over Andersen in order to realign firm management and to implement reforms. The success of the oversight board depended on Andersen's ability to stave off criminal charges and settle lawsuits related to its work on Enron. Because Andersen failed to persuade the justice department to withdraw its charges, Mr. Volcker suspended the board's efforts to rebuild the firm in April 2002.

Andersen faced an uphill battle in its fight against the federal prosecutors' charges of a felony count for obstruction of justice, regardless of the trial's outcome. Never in the 215-year history of the U.S. financial system has a major financial-services firm survived a criminal indictment, and Andersen would not likely have been the first, even had the firm not actually been convicted of a single count of obstruction of justice on June 15, 2002. Andersen, along with many others, accused the justice department of a gross abuse of governmental power, and announced that it would appeal the conviction. However, the firm ceased to audit publicly held clients by August 31, 2002.

May 15, 2002.

23 Bravin, Jess. "Justices Overturn Criminal Verdict in Andersen Case." *The Wall Street Journal*. New York. May 31, 2005.

24 Luke, Robert. "Andersen Explores Office Shifts in Atlanta." *The Atlanta Journal - Constitution*, May 18, 2002.

REQUIRED

[1] What were the business risks Enron faced, and how did those risks increase the likelihood of material misstatements in Enron's financial statements?

[2] (a) What are the responsibilities of a company's board of directors? (b) Could the board of directors at Enron—especially the audit committee—have prevented the fall of Enron? (c) Should they have known about the risks and apparent lack of independence with Enron's SPEs? What should they have done about it?

[3] In your own words, summarize how Enron used SPEs to hide large amounts of company debt.

[4] What are the auditor independence issues surrounding the provision of external auditing services, internal auditing services, and management consulting services for the same client? Develop arguments for why auditors should be allowed to perform these services for the same client. Develop separate arguments for why auditors should not be allowed to perform non-audit services for their audit clients. What is your view, and why?

[5] Explain how "rule-based" accounting standards differ from "principle-based" standards. How might fundamentally changing accounting standards from "bright-line" rules to principle-based standards help prevent another Enron-like fiasco in the future? Some argue that the trend toward adoption of international accounting standards represents a move toward more "principle-based" standards. Are there dangers in removing "bright-line" rules? What difficulties might be associated with such a change?

[6] Enron and Andersen suffered severe consequences because of their perceived lack of integrity and damaged reputations. In fact, some people believe the fall of Enron occurred because of a form of "run on the bank." Some argue that Andersen experienced a similar "run on the bank" as many top clients quickly dropped the firm in the wake of Enron's collapse. Is the "run on the bank" analogy valid for both firms? Why or why not?

[7] A perceived lack of integrity caused irreparable damage to both Andersen and Enron. How can you apply the principles learned in this case personally? Generate an example of how involvement in unethical or illegal activities, or even the appearance of such involvement, might affect your career. What are the possible consequences when others question your integrity? What can you do to preserve your reputation throughout your career?

[8] Why do audit partners struggle with making tough accounting decisions that may be contrary to their client's position on an issue? What changes should the profession make to eliminate these obstacles?

[9] What has been done, and what more do you believe should be done to restore the public trust in the auditing profession and in the nation's financial reporting system?

Comptronix Corporation
Identifying Inherent Risk and Control Risk Factors

MARK S. BEASLEY · FRANK A. BUCKLESS · STEVEN M. GLOVER · DOUGLAS F. PRAWITT

LEARNING OBJECTIVES

After completing and discussing this case you should be able to

[1] Understand how managers can fraudulently manipulate financial statements

[2] Recognize key inherent risk factors that increase the potential for financial reporting fraud

[3] Recognize key control risk factors that increase the potential for financial reporting fraud

[4] Understand the importance of effective corporate governance for overseeing the actions of top executives

[5] Identify auditor responsibilities for addressing the risk of management override of internal control

INTRODUCTION

All appeared well at Comptronix Corporation, a Guntersville, Alabama based electronics company, until word hit the streets November 25, 1992 that there had been a fraud. When reports surfaced that three of the company's top executives had inflated company earnings for the past three years, the company's stock price plummeted 72% in one day, closing at $6^{1/8}$ a share down from the previous day's closing at $22 a share.[1]

The Securities and Exchange Commission's (SEC) subsequent investigation determined that Comptronix's chief executive officer (CEO), chief operating officer (COO), and controller/ treasurer all colluded to overstate assets and profits by recording fictitious transactions. The three executives overrode existing internal controls so that others at Comptronix would not discover the scheme. All this unraveled when the executives surprisingly confessed to the company's board that they had improperly valued assets, overstated sales, and understated expenses. The three were immediately suspended from their duties.

Within days, class action lawsuits were filed against the company and the three executives. Immediately, the company's board of directors formed a special committee to investigate the alleged financial reporting fraud, an interim executive team stepped in to take charge, and Arthur Andersen, LLP was hired to conduct a detailed fraud investigation.

Residents of the small Alabama town were stunned. How could a fraud occur so close to home? Were there any signs of trouble that were ignored?

BACKGROUND

Comptronix based its principal operations in Guntersville, a town of approximately 7,000 residents located about 35 miles southeast of Huntsville, Alabama. The company provided contract manufacturing services to original equipment manufacturers in the electronics industry. Its primary product was circuit boards for personal computers and medical equipment. Neighboring Huntsville's heavy presence in the electronics industry provided Comptronix a local base of customers for its

---

1 "Company's profit data were false," *The New York Times*, November 26, 1992, D:1.

The case was prepared by Mark S. Beasley, Ph.D. and Frank A. Buckless, Ph.D. of North Carolina State University and Steven M. Glover, Ph.D. and Douglas F. Prawitt, Ph.D. of Brigham Young University, as a basis for class discussion. It is not intended to illustrate either effective or ineffective handling of an administrative situation.

circuit boards. In addition to the Alabama facility, the company also maintained manufacturing facilities in San Jose, California, and Colorado Springs, Colorado. In total, Comptronix employed about 1800 people at the three locations and was one of the largest employers in Guntersville.

The company was formed in the early 1980s by individuals who met while working in the electronics industry in nearby Huntsville. Three of those founders became senior officers of the company. William J. Hebding became Comptronix's chairman and CEO, Allen L. Shifflet became Comptronix's president and COO, and J. Paul Medlin served as the controller and treasurer. Prior to creating Comptronix, all three men worked at SCI Systems, a booming electronics maker. Mr. Hebding joined SCI Systems in the mid-1970s to assist the chief financial officer (CFO). While in that role, he met Mr. Shifflet, the SCI Systems operations manager. Later, when Mr. Hebding become SCI Systems' CFO, he hired Mr. Medlin to assist him. Along with a few other individuals working at SCI Systems, these three men together formed Comptronix in late 1983 and early 1984.[2]

The local townspeople in Guntersville were excited to attract the startup company to the local area. The city enticed Comptronix by providing it with an empty knitting mill in town. As an additional incentive, a local bank offered Comptronix an attractive credit arrangement. Comptronix in turn appointed the local banker to its board of directors. Town business leaders were excited to have new employment opportunities and looked forward to a boost to the local economy.

The early years were difficult, with Comptronix suffering losses through 1986. Local enthusiasm for the company attracted investments from venture capitalists. One of those investors included a partner in the Massey Burch Investment Group, a venture capital firm located in Nashville, Tennessee, just more than 100 miles to the north. The infusion of venture capital allowed Comptronix to generate strong sales and profit growth during 1987 and 1988. Based on this strong performance, senior management took the company's stock public in 1989, initially selling Comptronix stock at $5 a share in the over-the-counter markets.[3]

THE ACCOUNTING SCHEME[4]

According to the SEC's investigation, the fraud began soon after the company went public in 1989 and was directed by top company executives. Mr. Hebding as chairman and CEO, Mr. Shifflett as president and COO, and Mr. Medlin as controller and treasurer used their positions of power and influence to manipulate the financial statements issued from early 1989 through November 1992.

They began their fraud scheme by first manipulating the quarterly statements filed with the SEC during 1989. They misstated those statements by inappropriately transferring certain costs from cost of goods sold into inventory accounts. This technique allowed them to overstate inventory and understate quarterly costs of goods sold, which in turn overstated gross margin and net income for the period. The three executives made monthly manual journal entries, with the largest adjustments occurring just at quarter's end. Some allege that the fraud was motivated by the loss of a key customer in 1989 to the three executives' former employer, SCI.

The executives were successful in manipulating quarterly financial statements partially because their quarterly filings were unaudited. However, as fiscal year 1989 came to a close, the executives grew wary that the company's external auditors might discover the fraud when auditing the December 31, 1989, year-end financial statements. To hide the manipulations from their auditors, they devised a plan to cover up the inappropriate transfer of costs. They decided to remove the transferred costs from the inventory account just before year-end, because they feared the auditors would closely examine the inventory account as of December 31, 1989, as part of their year-end testing. Thus, they transferred the costs back to cost of goods sold. However, for each transfer back to cost of goods sold, the fraud team booked a fictitious sale of products and a related fictitious accounts receivable. That, in turn, overstated revenues and receivables.

---

2 "Comptronix fall from grace: Clues were there, Alabama locals saw lavish spending, feud," *The Atlanta Journal and Constitution*, December 5, 1992, D:1.

3 See footnote 2.

4 Accounting and Auditing Enforcement Release No. 543, Commerce Clearing House, Inc., Chicago.

The net effect of these activities was that interim financial statements included understated cost of goods sold and overstated inventories, while the annual financial statements contained overstated sales and receivables. Once they had tasted success in their manipulations of year-end sales and receivables, they later began recording fictitious quarterly sales in a similar fashion.

To convince the auditors that the fictitious sales and receivables were legitimate, the three company executives recorded cash payments to Comptronix from the bogus customer accounts. In order to do this, they developed a relatively complex fraud scheme. First, they recorded fictitious purchases of equipment on account. That, in turn, overstated equipment and accounts payable. Then, Hebding, the chairman and CEO, and Medlin, the controller and treasurer, cut checks to the bogus accounts payable vendors associated with the fake purchases of equipment. But they did not mail the checks. Rather, they deposited them in Comptronix's disbursement checking account and recorded the phony payments as debits against the bogus accounts payable and credits against the bogus receivables. This accounting scheme allowed the company to eliminate the bogus payables and receivables, while still retaining the fictitious sales and equipment on the income statement and balance sheet, respectively.

This scheme continued over four years, stretching from the beginning of 1989 to November 1992, when the three executives confessed to their manipulations. The SEC investigation noted that the Form 10-K filings for the years ended December 31, 1989, 1990, and 1991 were materially misstated as follows:

	1989	1990	1991
Sales (in 000's)			
Reported Sales	$ 42,420	$ 70,229	$102,026
Restated Sales	37,275	63,444	88,754
Overstatement of Sales	5,145	6,785	13,272
Percentage Overstatement	13.8%	10.7%	14.9%
Net Income (in 000's)			
Reported Net Income	$ 1,470	$ 3,028	$ 5,071
Restated Net Income	(3,524)	(3,647)	(3,225)
Overstatement of Net Income	4,994	6,675	8,296
Earnings Per Share (EPS)			
Reported EPS	$ .19	$ .35	$ .51
Restated EPS (loss)	(.47)	(.43)	(.34)
Overstatement of EPS	.66	.78	.85
Property, Plant, & Equipment (in 000's)			
Reported PP&E	$ 18,804	$ 26,627	$ 38,720
Restated PP&E	13,856	15,846	20,303
Overstatement of PP&E	4,948	10,781	18,417
Percentage Overstatement	35.7%	68.0%	90.7%
Stockholders' Equity (in 000's)			
Reported Stockholders' Equity	$ 19,145	$ 22,237	$ 39,676
Restated Stockholders' Equity	14,151	10,568	18,778
Overstatement of Stockholders' Equity	4,994	11,669	20,898
Percentage Overstatement	35.3%	110.4%	111.3%

The executives' fraud scheme helped the company avoid reporting net losses in each of the three years, with the amount of the fraud increasing in each of the three years affected.[5] The fraud scheme also inflated the balance sheet by overstating property, plant, and equipment and stockholders' equity. By the end of 1991, property, plant, and equipment was overstated by over 90%, with stockholders' equity overstated by 111%.

---

5 Information about fiscal year 1992 was not reported because the fraud was disclosed before that fiscal year ended.

THE COMPANY'S INTERNAL CONTROLS[6]

The three executives were able to perpetrate the fraud by bypassing the existing accounting system. They avoided making the standard entries in the sales and purchases journals as required by the existing internal control, and recorded the fictitious entries manually. Other employees were excluded from the manipulations to minimize the likelihood of the fraud being discovered.

According to the SEC's summary of the investigation, Comptronix employees normally created a fairly extensive paper trail for equipment purchases, including purchase orders and receiving reports. However, none of these documents were created for the bogus purchases. Approval for cash disbursements was typically granted once the related purchase order, receiving report, and vendor invoice had been matched. Unfortunately, Mr. Shifflett or Mr. Medlin could approve payments based solely on an invoice. As a result, the fraud team was able to bypass internal controls over cash disbursements. They simply showed a fictitious vendor invoice to an accounts payable clerk, who in turn prepared a check for the amount indicated on the invoice.

Internal controls were also insufficient to detect the manipulation of sales and accounts receivable. Typically, a shipping department clerk would enter the customer order number and the quantity to be shipped to the customer into the computerized accounting system. The accounting system then automatically produced a shipping document and a sales invoice. The merchandise was shipped to the customer, along with the invoice and shipping document. Once again, Mr. Medlin, as controller and treasurer, had the ability to access the shipping department system. This allowed him to enter bogus sales into the accounting system. He then made sure to destroy all shipping documents and sales invoices generated by the accounting system to keep them from being mailed to the related customers. The subsequent posting of bogus payments on the customers' accounts was posted personally by Mr. Medlin to the cash receipts journal and the accounts receivable subsidiary ledger.

The fraud scheme was obviously directed from the top ranks of the organization. Like most companies, the senior executives at Comptronix directed company operations on a day-to-day basis, with only periodic oversight from the company's board of directors.

The March 1992 proxy statement to shareholders noted that the Comptronix board of directors consisted of seven individuals, including Mr. Hebding who served as board chairman. Of those seven individuals serving on the board, two individuals, Mr. Hebding, chairman and CEO and Mr. Shifflett, president and COO, represented management on the board. Thus, 28.6% of the board consisted of inside directors. The remaining five directors were not employed by Comptronix. However, two of those five directors had close affiliations with management. One served as the company's outside general legal counsel and the other served as vice president of manufacturing for a significant customer of Comptronix. Directors with these kinds of close affiliations with company management are frequently referred to as "gray" directors due to their perceived lack of objectivity.

The three remaining "outside" directors had no apparent affiliations with company management. One of the remaining outside directors was a partner in the venture capital firm that owned 574,978 shares (5.3%) of Comptronix's common stock. That director was previously a partner in a Nashville law firm and was currently serving on two other corporate boards. A second outside director was the vice chairman and CEO of the local bank originally loaning money to the company. He also served as chairman of the board of another local bank in a nearby town. The third outside director was president of an international components supplier based in Taiwan. All of the board members had served on the Comptronix board since 1984, except for the venture capital partner who joined the board in 1988 and the president of the key customer who joined the board in 1990.

Each director received an annual retainer of $3,000 plus a fee of $750 for each meeting attended. The company also granted each director an option to purchase 5,000 shares of common stock at an exercise price that equaled the market price of the stock on the date that the option was granted.

---

6   See footnote 4.

The board met four times during 1991. The board had an audit committee that was charged with recommending outside auditors, reviewing the scope of the audit engagement, consulting with the external auditors, reviewing the results of the audit examination, and acting as a liaison between the board and the internal auditors. The audit committee was also charged with reviewing various company policies, including those related to accounting and internal control matters. Two outside directors and one gray director made up the three-member audit committee. One of those members was an attorney, and the other two served as president and CEO of the companies where they were employed. There was no indication of whether any of these individuals had accounting or financial reporting backgrounds. The audit committee met twice during 1991.

MANAGEMENT BACKGROUND

The March 1992 proxy statement provided the following background information about the three executives committing the fraud: Mr. Hedding, Mr. Shifflett, and Mr. Medlin.

William J. Hebding served as the Comptronix Chairman and CEO. He was responsible for sales and marketing, finance, and general management of the company. He also served as a director from 1984 until 1992 when the fraud was disclosed. He was the single largest shareholder of Comptronix common stock by beneficially owning 6.7% (720,438 shares) of Comptronix common stock as of March 2, 1992. Before joining Comptronix, Mr. Hebding worked for SCI Systems Inc. from 1974 until October 1983. He held the title of treasurer and CFO at SCI from December 1976 to October 1983. In October 1983, Mr. Hebding left SCI to form Comptronix. He graduated from the University of North Alabama with a degree in accounting and was a certified public accountant. Mr. Hebding's 1991 cash compensation totaled $187,996.

Allen L. Shifflett served as Comptronix's president and COO, and was responsible for manufacturing, engineering, and programs operations. He also served as a director from 1984 until 1992 when the fraud unfolded. He owned 4% (433,496 shares) of Comptronix common stock as of March 2, 1992. Like Mr. Hebding, he joined the company after previously being employed at SCI as a plant manager and manufacturing manager from October 1981 until April 1984 when he left to help form Comptronix. Mr. Shifflett obtained his B.S. degree in industrial engineering from Virginia Polytechnic Institute. Mr. Shifflett's 1991 cash compensation totaled $162,996.

Paul Medlin served as Comptronix's controller and treasurer. He also previously worked at SCI, as Mr. Hebding's assistant after graduating from the University of Alabama. Mr. Medlin did not serve on the Comptronix board. The 1992 proxy noted that the board of directors approved a company loan to him for $79,250 on November 1, 1989, to provide funds for him to repurchase certain shares of common stock. The loan, which was repaid on May 7, 1991, bore interest at an annual rate equal to one percentage point in excess of the interest rate designated by the company's bank as that bank's "Index Rate." The 1992 proxy did not disclose Mr. Medlin's 1991 cash compensation.

The company had employment agreements with Mr. Hebding and Mr. Shifflett, which expired in April 1992. Those agreements provided that if the company terminated employment with them prior to the expiration of the agreement for any reason other than cause or disability, they would each receive their base salary for the remaining term of the agreement. If terminated for cause or disability, each would receive their base salary for one year following the date of such termination.

The company had an Employee Stock Incentive Plan and an Employee Stock Option Plan that the compensation committee of the board of directors administered. The committee made awards to key employees at its discretion. The compensation committee consisted of three nonemployee directors. One of these directors was an attorney who served as Comptronix's outside counsel on certain legal matters. Another served as an officer of a significant Comptronix customer. The third member of the committee was a partner in the venture capital firm providing capital for Comptronix.

The SEC's investigation noted that during the period of the fraud, the three men each sold thousands of shares of Comptronix common stock. Their knowledge of material, non-public information about Comptronix's actual financial position allowed them to avoid trading losses in excess of $500,000 for Mr. Hebding and Mr. Shifflett, and over $90,000 for Mr. Medlin. Each also received bonuses: $198,000 for Mr. Hebding, $148,000 for Mr. Shifflett, and $46,075 for Mr. Medlin. These bonuses were granted during the fraud years as a reward for the supposed strong financial performance.

After the fraud was revealed, newspaper accounts reported that red flags had been present. *The New York Times* reported that Mr. Hebding and Mr. Shifflett created reputations in the local community that contrasted with their conservative professional reputations. Mr. Hebding purchased a home worth over $1 million, often described as a mansion, with two boathouses, a pool, a wrought-iron fence with electric gate, and a red Jaguar in the driveway. *The Atlanta Journal and Constitution* reported that Mr. Hebding's marriage had failed, and that he had led an active bachelor's life that led to some problems in town. He also had a major dispute with another company founder who was serving as executive vice president. That individual was suddenly fired from Comptronix in 1989. Later it was revealed that he was allegedly demoted and fired for trying to investigate possible wrongdoing at Comptronix.[7]

Mr. Shifflett, too, had divorced and remarried. He and his second wife purchased an expensive scenic lot in an exclusive country club community in a neighboring town. Mr. Shifflett reportedly had acquired extensive real estate holdings in recent years.[8]

Others were shocked, noting that they would be the last to be suspected of any kind of fraud. In the end, it was unclear why the three stunned the board with news of the fraud. There was some speculation that an on-going IRS tax audit triggered their disclosure of the shenanigans.

EPILOGUE

After the fraud was revealed, all three men were suspended and the board appointed an interim CEO and an interim president to take over the reins. The SEC's investigation led to charges being filed against all three men for violating the antifraud provisions of the Securities Act of 1933 and the Securities and Exchange Act of 1934, in addition to other violations of those securities acts. None of the men admitted or denied the allegations against them. However, all three men agreed to avoid any future violations of the securities acts. They also consented to being permanently prohibited from serving as officers or directors of any public company. The SEC ordered them to pay back trading losses avoided and bonuses paid to them by Comptronix during the fraud period, and it directed Mr. Hebding and Mr. Shifflett to pay civil penalties of $100,000 and $50,000, respectively. The SEC did not impose civil penalties against Mr. Medlin due to his inability to pay.

The company struggled financially. It sold its San Jose operations in 1994 to Sanmina Corporation, a California-based electronics manufacturer. Comptronix eventually filed for Chapter 11 bankruptcy protection in August 1996, which allowed the company to continue operating while it developed a restructuring plan. In September 1996, the company announced that it had sold substantially all of its remaining assets to Sanmina Corp. As a result of the sale, the secured creditors of Comptronix were fully repaid; however, the unsecured creditors received less than 10 cents on the dollar.

---

7   "A Comptronix founder, in 1989 suit, says he flagged misdeeds," *The Wall Street Journal*, December 7, 1992, A:3.

8   See footnote 2 and "In town, neighbors saw it coming," *The New York Times*, December 4, 1992, D:1.

REQUIRED

[1] Professional auditing standards present the audit risk model, which is used to determine the nature, timing, and extent of audit procedures. Describe the components of the model and discuss how changes in each component affect the auditor's need for evidence.

[2] One of the components of the audit risk model is inherent risk. Describe typical factors that auditors evaluate when assessing inherent risk. With the benefit of hindsight, what inherent risk factors were present during the audits of the 1989 through 1992 Comptronix financial statements?

[3] Another component of the audit risk model is control risk. Describe the five components of internal control. What characteristics of Comptronix's internal control increased control risk for the audits of the 1989 – 1992 year-end financial statements?

[4] The board of directors, and its audit committee, can be an effective corporate governance mechanism.

   [a] Discuss the pros and cons of allowing inside directors to serve on the board. Describe typical responsibilities of audit committees.

   [b] What strengths or weaknesses were present related to Comptronix's board of directors and audit committee?

[5] Public companies must file quarterly financial statements in Form 10-Qs that have been reviewed by the company's external auditor. The PCAOB embraced existing auditing standards in place at April 2003 as its Interim Standards. Guidance for auditors of public companies in regards to reviews of public company interim statements is contained in the Interim Standards (AU) Section 722, *Interim Financial Information*, which is available online at the PCAOB's website (www.pcaob.org) under the Standards link. Research the content in that Interim Standard and briefly describe the key requirements for reviews of interim financial information of a public company. Why wouldn't all companies (public and private) engage their auditors to perform timely reviews of interim financial statements?

[6] Describe whether you think Comptronix's executive team was inherently dishonest from the beginning. How is it possible for otherwise honest people to become involved in frauds like the one at Comptronix?

[7] Auditing standards note that three conditions are generally present when fraud occurs. Research the authoritative standards for auditors and provide a brief summary of each of the three fraud conditions. Additionally, provide an example from the Comptronix fraud of each of the three fraud conditions.

[8] Auditing standards note that there is a possibility that management override of controls could occur in every audit and accordingly, the auditor should include audit procedures in every audit to address that risk.

   [a] What do you think is meant by the term "management override"?

   [b] Provide two examples of where management override of controls occurred in the Comptronix fraud.

   [c] Research auditing standards to identify the three required auditor responses to further address the risk of management override of internal controls.

Cendant Corporation
Assessing the Control Environment and Evaluating Risk of Financial Statement Fraud

Mark S. Beasley · Frank A. Buckless · Steven M. Glover · Douglas F. Prawitt

LEARNING OBJECTIVES

After completing and discussing this case you should be able to

[1] Describe the auditor's responsibility for considering a client's internal controls

[2] Describe the auditor's responsibility to detect material misstatements due to fraud

[3] Identify red flags present during the audits of CUC International, Inc.'s financial statements, which suggest weaknesses in the company's control environment (CUC International, Inc. was the predecessor company to Cendant Corporation)

[4] Identify red flags present during the audits of CUC International, Inc.'s financial statements suggesting a higher likelihood of financial statement fraud

[5] Identify management assertions violated as a result of the misstatements included in CUC International, Inc.'s 1995 through 1997 financial statements (prior to its merger with HFS, Inc.)

[6] Identify audit procedures that could have been performed to detect misstatements that occurred

INTRODUCTION

One can only imagine the high expectations of investors when the boards of directors of CUC International, Inc. (CUC) and HFS, Inc. (HFS) agreed to merge in May 1997 to form Cendant Corporation. The $14 billion stock merger of HFS and CUC, considered a marriage of equals, united two large service organizations. CUC was a direct marketing giant with shopping, travel, automobile, and entertainment clubs serving over 68 million members worldwide while HFS was a franchisor of brand-name chains such as Ramada, Days Inn, Avis, and Century 21, with over 100 million consumers worldwide. The cross-marketing opportunities between CUC and HFS were expected to create synergies that would further increase the revenue and profit growth of the newly formed entity, Cendant.[1]

Henry R. Silverman, chairman and chief executive officer (CEO) of HFS, noted in the joint press release announcing the merger that:

This transaction creates a world-class consumer services company with extraordinary revenue and profit growth potential. By combining HFS's brands and our consumer reach of more than 100 million customers annually with CUC's direct marketing expertise, powerful club membership delivery system, and 68 million memberships worldwide, we will create tremendous new opportunities that are not available to either company on its own. In so doing, we have the combined potential for exceptional earnings and shareholder value creation for two companies that have already established excellent records in this regard. Walter Forbes and his management team have created one of the most innovative and successful companies

---

1   The background information about Cendant Corporation was predominantly taken from 8-Ks filed by the company (and its predecessor CUC International, Inc.) with the Securities and Exchange Commission from May 1997 to December 1999 and Accounting and Auditing Enforcement Release Nos. 1272, 1273, 1274, 1275, 1276, 1372, 2014, 2600 issued by the Securities and Exchange Commission.

The case was prepared by Mark S. Beasley, Ph.D. and Frank A. Buckless, Ph.D. of North Carolina State University and Steven M. Glover, Ph.D. and Douglas F. Prawitt, Ph.D. of Brigham Young University, as a basis for class discussion. It is not intended to illustrate either effective or ineffective handling of an administrative situation.

in the history of the services industry. We are confident that by combining our operating, financial and management strengths, we will create one of the foremost consumer and business services companies in the world. (Form 8-K, CUC International, Inc., May 27, 1997)

Walter A. Forbes, chairman and CEO of CUC, expressed similar views:

Together, we will benefit from this unique franchise: providing value-added services to consumers and businesses while substantially enhancing growth opportunities. With similar business models, both companies have pursued two sides of the same high growth businesses, to compete in a global, information-intensive and increasingly competitive economy. The combined company will have increased purchasing power and other advantages associated with greater scale. (Form 8-K, CUC International, Inc., May 27, 1997)

THE NEW COMPANY: CENDANT CORPORATION

The merger of CUC and HFS was finalized in December 1997. Henry Silverman was named CEO, and Walter Forbes was named chairman of the board. The positions of the two officers were scheduled to switch on January 1, 2000, with Henry Silverman assuming the role of chairman of the board and Walter Forbes assuming the role of CEO. The merger created a service company headquartered in Parsippany, New Jersey with operations in more than 100 countries involving over 30,000 employees. The market value of Cendant's approximately 900 million shares of outstanding common stock at the time of the merger was estimated to be $29 billion, making it one of the 100 largest U. S. corporations. Cendant, a global service provider, was positioned to provide superior growth and value opportunities for its owners. As Henry Silverman noted when the merger was finalized:

Cendant arrives at the global market place as the world's premier consumer and business services company, with strong growth prospects. (Form 8-K, CUC International, Inc., December 18, 1997)

Initially, Ernst & Young, LLP, CUC's auditor, was retained to complete the audit of CUC's 1997 financial statements, and Deloitte & Touche, LLP, HFS's auditor, was retained to complete the audit of HFS's 1997 financial statements. Deloitte & Touche, LLP was selected as the successor auditor for the newly formed company. Cendant's 8-K filing with the Securities and Exchange Commission announcing the selection of Deloitte & Touche, LLP as the successor auditor noted that during the past two years there were no material disagreements between the company and Ernst & Young, LLP on accounting principles or practices, financial statement disclosures, auditing scope, or procedures.

Management organized Cendant's operations around three business segments: travel services, real estate services, and alliance marketing. The travel services segment facilitated vacation timeshare exchanges, manages corporate and government vehicle fleets, and franchises car rental and hotel businesses. Franchise systems operated by Cendant in this business segment included: Days Inn, Ramada, Howard Johnson, Super 8, Travelodge, Villager Lodge, Knights Inn, Wingate Inn, Avis, and Resort Condominiums International, LLC.

The real estate services segment assisted with employee relocation, provides homebuyers with mortgages, and franchises real estate brokerage offices. Franchise systems operated by Cendant in this business segment included: Century 21, Caldwell Banker, and ERA. The origination, sale, and service of residential mortgage loans were handled by the company through Cendant Mortgage Corporation.

The alliance marketing segment provided an array of value-driven products and services through more than 20 membership clubs and client relationships. Cendant's alliance marketing activities were conducted through subsidiaries such as FISI Madison Financial Corporation, Benefits Consultants, Inc., and Entertainment Publications, Inc. Individual membership programs included Shoppers Advantage, Travelers Advantage, Auto Advantage, Credit Card Guardian, and PrivacyGuard.

As a franchisor of hotels, residential real estate, brokerage offices, and car rental operations, Cendant licensed the owners and operators of independent businesses to use the Company's brand names. At that time, Cendant did not own or operate these businesses. Rather, the company provided its franchisee customers with services designed to increase their revenue and profitability.

ANNOUNCEMENT OF FRAUD

The high expectations of management and investors were severely deflated in April 1998, when Cendant announced a massive financial reporting fraud affecting CUC's 1997 financial statements, which were issued prior to the merger with HFS. The fraud was discovered when responsibility for Cendant's accounting functions was transferred from former CUC personnel to former HFS personnel. Initial estimates provided by senior Cendant management were that CUC's 1997 earnings would need to be reduced by between $100 and $115 million.

To minimize the fallout from the fraud, Cendant quickly hired special legal counsel who in turn hired Arthur Andersen, LLP, to perform an independent investigation. Cendant then fired Cosmo Corigliano, former chief financial officer (CFO) of CUC, and dismissed Ernst & Young, LLP, which was serving as the auditor for Cendant's CUC business units. The staff of the Securities and Exchange Commission and the United States Attorney for the District of New Jersey also initiated investigations relating to the accounting fraud.

Unfortunately, the bad news did not stop for Cendant. In July 1998, Cendant announced that the fraud was more widespread than initially believed and affected the accounting records of all major CUC business units. Cendant revised its earlier announcement by noting that CUC's 1997, 1996, and 1995 financial statements would all be restated. The total cumulative overstatement of pretax quarterly earnings over the three-year period totaled approximately $300 million.

CUC's management allegedly inflated earnings by recording fictitious revenues and reducing expenses to meet Wall Street analysts' earnings expectations. CUC managers simply looked at the analysts' earnings estimates and fictitiously increased revenues and/or reduced expenses to meet those expectations. Meeting analysts' expectations artificially inflated CUC's stock prices thereby providing it with more opportunities to merge or acquire other companies in the future through stock issuances. The pretax operating earnings were inflated by $176 million, $87 million, and $31 million for the first three quarters of 1997, 1996, and 1995, respectively.

The misstatements reflected in CUC's quarterly reports filed with the Securities and Exchange Commission were not recorded in the general ledger. However, for year-end reporting purposes, CUC made various year-end adjustments to incorporate the misstatements into the general ledger. Some of the most significant misstatement techniques used by CUC to adjust its general ledger included the following:

- *Irregular charges against merger reserves.* In its earlier acquisitions of other companies, CUC would record a one-time expense and establish a reserve (liability) for restructuring costs expected as a result of the merger. CUC would later artificially inflate earnings by fictitiously recording revenues or reducing expenses and reducing the merger reserve (liability) account. The reserve was used as a cushion to offset poor future performance.

- *False coding of services sold to customers.* CUC would falsely classify amounts received from customers for deferred revenue recognition programs as amounts received from customers for immediate revenue recognition programs. For example, CUC would improperly record amounts received for the Shoppers Advantage program (which required revenues to be recognized over 12 to 15 months) to amounts received from the Creditline program (which allowed revenues to be recognized immediately). This misclassification of purchased benefits allowed CUC to immediately recognize revenues and profits instead of deferring them over the benefit period.

- *Delayed recognition of membership cancellations and bank rejection of charges made to members' credit card accounts.* Customers were assessed an annual fee to be a member of the benefit programs, such as Auto Advantage. CUC would delay recognizing customer cancellations of benefit programs and bank rejections of credit card charges to inflate revenues and profits during the current reporting period.

The final results of the fraud investigation were announced to the public in August 1998. In the end, pretax annual operating earnings were overstated by $262 million, $122 million, and $127 million for 1997, 1996, and 1995, respectively. All told, more than one-third of CUC's reported earnings during the fraud period were deliberately and fictitiously manufactured.

MARKET REACTION TO THE FRAUD

Prior to the announcement of the fraud, Cendant's stock was trading at a 52-week high of approximately $42 per share. After the second announcement that the fraud was more widespread than initially believed, Cendant's stock dropped to a 52-week low of approximately $16 per share, a 62 percent drop, causing a total market value decline of over $20 billion. The resulting drop in Cendant's stock price squelched the company's planned $3.1 billion cash and stock acquisition of American Bankers Insurance. Additionally, numerous class action lawsuits were filed against the company and the current and former company officers and directors. On March 17, 1999, Cendant reached an agreement on one class action lawsuit that resulted in a $351 million pretax charge to the 1999 financial statements and on December 7, 1999, Cendant reached an agreement on the principal class action lawsuit that resulted in a $2.83 billion pretax charge to the 1999 financial statements.

ASSIGNING BLAME

Many questions remain in the aftermath of the CUC fraud. How could CUC's senior management and the board of directors not be aware of the fraud? Where was CUC's audit committee? How could Ernst & Young, LLP, not have detected the fraud?

Walter Forbes, chairman and CEO of CUC, and Kirk Shelton, chief operating officer (COO) of CUC, denied any involvement or knowledge of the alleged fraud. Cendant's audit committee, which oversaw the fraud investigation, concluded that:

> *Walter Forbes and Kirk Shelton because of their positions, had responsibility to create an environment in which it was clear to all employees at all levels that inaccurate financial reporting would not be tolerated. The fact that there is evidence that many of the senior accounting and financial personnel participated in irregular activities and that personnel at many of the business units acquiesced in practices which they believed were questionable suggests that an appropriate environment to ensure accurate financial reporting did not exist.* (Form 8-K, Cendant Corporation, August 28, 1998)

Cosmo Corigliano, CFO of CUC, in court testimony regarding the fraud noted:

> *It was ingrained in all of us, ingrained in us by our superiors, over a long period of time, that that was what we did.*[2]

Casper Sabatino, CUC's accountant, in response to the judge's question on why he went along with the fraud noted:

> *Honestly, your honor, I just thought I was doing my job.*[3]

---

[2] "3 Admit Guilt in Falsifying CUC's Books," by Floyd Norris and Diana B. Henriques. *The New York Times*, June 15, 2000, p. C:1.

[3] Ibid.

Finally, Cendant's audit committee also noted in its report of the fraud investigation that:

Senior management failed to have in place appropriate controls and procedures that might have enabled them to detect the irregularities in the absence of actual knowledge of those irregularities. (Form 8-K, Cendant Corporation, August 28, 1998)

Information obtained during the fraud investigation suggests that Cosmo Corigliano, CFO of CUC, directed or was aware of several of the irregular activities noted during the investigation. Evidence also suggests that Anne Pember, the controller of CUC, who reported directly to Corigliano, directed individuals to carry out some of the irregular activities noted. All told, more than twenty CUC employees were identified as participating in the fraud.

Why did CUC's board of directors and audit committee not ferret out the fraud? The board of directors for CUC met several times during the year and reviewed financial reports that contained the fraudulent information. Were the outside directors too cozy with senior management? Four of CUC's directors were noted as having personal ties with Walter Forbes through other joint investments in startup companies.[4]

Did Ernst & Young, LLP, exercise the professional skepticism required of an external auditor? Were the auditors inappropriately swayed by CUC employees who were formerly employed by Ernst & Young, LLP? Two alleged leaders in the fraud, Cosmo Corigliano and Anne Pember, along with two other financial managers of CUC, were previously employed by Ernst & Young, LLP. Moreover, Cosmo Corigliano was an auditor on the CUC engagement prior to being employed by CUC. The audit committee report on the fraud investigation notes several instances in which Ernst & Young, LLP did not substantiate or question fraudulent transactions. However, the report also shows that the senior management of CUC encouraged subordinates not to show certain information to the auditors. Additionally, the report notes instances in which the auditors accepted incomplete answers from management regarding CUC's financial performance.

During the late 1980's and early 1990's, CUC was required to amend its financial statements filed with the Securities and Exchange Commission several times for using aggressive accounting practices, such as capitalizing marketing costs in place of using the standard practice of expensing them as incurred.[5] Why didn't these problems sensitize the auditors to the potential for problems with financial reporting?

EPILOGUE

Walter Forbes, chairman of the board of Cendant and former chairman and CEO of CUC, and ten other members of Cendant's board of directors formerly associated with CUC tendered their resignations shortly after it was announced that the fraud was more widespread than initially believed. Cendant's board of directors, after reviewing the fraud investigation report, dismissed Kirk Shelton, COO of CUC, for cause, eliminating the company's obligation to fulfill his previously negotiated severance package. Walter Forbes was allowed to receive a severance package totaling $47.5 million since he was not directly linked to the fraud; however, Cendant attempted to recover the severance payment Walter Forbes received.

In January 1999, Cendant Corporation filed a lawsuit against Ernst & Young, LLP, for allegedly violating professional standards. No resolution of this lawsuit has been made public. Ernst & Young, LLP did settle the principal shareholder class action lawsuit for $335 million. Additionally, investigations by the Securities and Exchange Commission and the United States Attorney for the District of New Jersey found that CUC and its predecessors were issuing fraudulently prepared financial reports beginning as early as 1985. Two Ernst & Young, LLP partners involved with the audit engagement during the fraud period agreed to suspensions from practice before the SEC with rights to reapply in four years.[6]

---

4   "Cendant Audit Panel's Ties Are in Question," by Joann S. Lublin and Emily Nelson, *The Wall Street Journal*, July 24, 1998, p. A:3.

5   "Hear No See No Speak No Fraud," by Ronald Fink, *CFO*, October 1998, pp. 37-44.

6   "SEC to Suspend Two Auditors of Cendant Corporation and CUC International from Practicing before the Commission," United States Securities and Exchange Commission Litigation Release No. 18102, April 23, 2003. See the following website: http://www.sec.gov/litigation/litreleases/lr18102.htm.

In January 2005, a federal jury convicted Kirk Shelton on federal conspiracy and fraud charges.[7] Kirk Shelton was sentenced to 10 years in prison and ordered to pay $3.275 billion in restitution to Cendant.[8] The fine covers settlements paid by Cendant for shareholder class action lawsuits and $25 million in legal fees paid by Cendant for Shelton's legal defense. After two mistrials in October 2006, a federal jury convicted Walter A. Forbes on federal conspiracy and false statement charges.[9] Walter Forbes was sentenced to 12 years, seven months in prison and also ordered to pay $3.275 billion in restitution to Cendant.[10] Cosmo Corigliano, Anne Pember, and Casper Sabatino pleaded guilty to federal conspiracy and fraud charges. Cosmo Corigliano was sentenced to 6 months house arrest and 3 years probation while Anne Pember and Casper Sabatino were sentenced to two years probation.[11] These three individuals were given reduced sentences as a result of cooperating with authorities related to the fraud investigation. Cosmo Corigliano agreed to pay civil penalties in excess of $14 million and Anne Pember agreed to pay civil penalties of $100,000.

REQUIRED

[1] Professional auditing standards outline the auditor's consideration of material misstatements due to errors and fraud. (a) What responsibility does an auditor have to detect material misstatements due to errors and fraud? (b) What two main categories of fraud affect financial reporting? (c) What types of factors should auditors consider when assessing the likelihood of material misstatements due to fraud? (d) Which factors existed during the 1995 through 1997 audits of CUC that created an environment conducive for fraud?

[2] Professional auditing standards indicate that an entity's internal controls consist of five interrelated components. (a) What responsibility does an auditor have related to each of these five components? (b) One component of internal control is the entity's control environment. What factors should an auditor consider when evaluating the control environment? (c) What red flags were present during the 1995 through 1997 audits of CUC that may have suggested weaknesses in CUC's control environment?

[3] Professional auditing standards recognize there is a possibility that management may override internal controls. (a) Provide an example where management override occurred in the Cendant fraud. (b) What are the required auditor responses to further address the risk of management override of internal controls?

[4] Several misstatements were identified as a result of the fraud perpetrated by CUC management. (a) For each misstatement identified, indicate one management assertion that was violated. (b) For each misstatement identified, indicate one audit procedure the auditor could have used to detect the misstatement.

[5] Some of the members of CUC's financial management team were former auditors for Ernst & Young, LLP. (a) Why would a company want to hire a member of its external audit team? (b) If the client has hired former auditors, how might this affect the independence of the existing external auditors?

7   "Former Cendant Vice Chairman E. Kirk Shelton Guilty on All Counts of Massive Accounting Fraud," United States Department of Justice News Release, January 4, 2005. See the following website: http://www.usdoj.gov/usao/nj/press/files/cend0104_r.htm.

8   "Former Cendant Vice Chairman E. Kirk Shelton Sentenced to 10 years in Massive Accounting Scandal," United States Department of Justice News Release, August 3, 2005. See the following website: http://www.usdoj.gov/usao/nj/press/files/cend0803_r.htm

9   "Former Cendant Chairman Walter Forbes Convicted of Conspiracy to Commit Securities Fraud and False Statements to SEC," United States Department of Justice News Release, October 31, 2005. See the following website: http://www.usdoj.gov/usao/nj/press/ files/pdffiles/forb1031rel.pdf.

10   "Former Cendant Chairman Walter Forbes Sentenced to 151 Months in Prison for Lead Role in Massive Accounting Fraud," United States Department of Justice News Release, January 17, 2007. See the following website: http://www.usdoj.gov/usao/nj/press/files/ pdffiles/forb0117rel.pdf.

11   "Chief Cooperating Witness in Cendant Accounting Fraud Sentenced to Three Years of Probation, Six Months House Arrest," United States Department of Justice News Release, January 30, 2007. See the following website: http://www.usdoj.gov/usao/nj/press/files/ pdffiles/cori0130rel.pdf.

Waste Management, Inc.
Manipulating Accounting Estimates

MARK S. BEASLEY · FRANK A. BUCKLESS · STEVEN M. GLOVER · DOUGLAS F. PRAWITT

LEARNING OBJECTIVES

After completing and discussing this case you should be able to

[1] Recognize risk factors suggesting the presence of the three conditions of fraud

[2] Identify financial statement accounts that are based on subjective management estimates

[3] Recognize inherent risks associated with accounting estimates

[4] Describe auditor responsibilities for assessing the reasonableness of management's estimates

BACKGROUND

Waste Management, Inc.'s Form 10-K filed with the Securities and Exchange Commission (SEC) on March 28, 1997 described the company at that time as a leading international provider of waste management services. According to disclosures in the Form 10-K, the primary source of its business involved providing solid waste management services consisting of collection, transfer, resource recovery, and disposal services for commercial, industrial, municipal, and residential customers, as well as other waste management companies. As part of these services, the company provided paper, glass, plastic, and metal recycling services to commercial and industrial operations and curbside collection of such materials from residences. The company also provided services involving the removal of methane gas from sanitary landfill facilities for use in electricity generation and provided Port-O-Let portable sanitation services to municipalities, commercial businesses, and special event customers. In addition to solid waste management services, the company provided hazardous waste and other chemical removal, treatment, storage, and disposal services.

According to information in the Form 10-K, the Oak Brook, Illinois based company was incorporated in 1968. In 28 years of operations, the company had grown to be a leader in waste management services. For the year ended December 31, 1996, the company reported consolidated revenues of $9.19 billion, net income of $192 million, and total assets of $18.4 billion. The company's stock, which traded around $36 per share in 1996, was listed on the New York Stock Exchange (NYSE), in addition to being listed on the Frankfurt, London, Chicago, and Swiss stock exchanges.

Despite being a leader in the industry, the 1996 financial statements revealed that the company was feeling pressures from the effects of changes that were occurring in its markets and in the environmental industry. Although consolidated revenues were increasing, the 1996 Consolidated Statement of Income showed decreasing net income, as summarized on the next page.

The case was prepared by Mark S. Beasley, Ph.D. and Frank A. Buckless, Ph.D. of North Carolina State University and Steven M. Glover, Ph.D. and Douglas F. Prawitt, Ph.D. of Brigham Young University, as a basis for class discussion. It is not intended to illustrate either effective or ineffective handling of an administrative situation.

	For the Years Ended December 31 (in millions)		
	1994	1995	1996
Revenues	$ 8,483	$ 9,053	$ 9,187
Operating expenses	$ 5,828	$ 6,221	$ 6,373
Special charges	—	335	472
Selling and administrative expenses	997	1,005	979
Interest expense	333	421	376
Interest income	(33)	(37)	(28)
Minority interest	127	82	57
Sundry income, net	(64)	(76)	(85)
Income from operations before income taxes	$ 1,295	$ 1,102	$ 1,043
Provision for income taxes	553	484	565
Income from continuing operations	742	618	478
Discontinued operations			
Income from operations	42	49	15
Provision for loss on disposal	—	(63)	(301)
Net Income	$ 784	$ 604	$ 192

According to management's disclosures in the 1996 Form 10-K, Waste Management, Inc. was encountering intense competition, primarily in the pricing and rendering of services, from various sources in all phases of its waste management and related operations. In the solid waste collection phase, competition was being felt from national, regional, and local collection companies. In addition, the company was competing with municipalities and counties, which through the use of tax revenues were able to provide such services at lower direct charges to the customer than could Waste Management. Also, the company faced competition from some large commercial and industrial companies, which handled their own waste collection. In addition, the company encountered intense competition in pricing and rendering of services in its portable sanitation services business and its on-site industrial cleaning services business.

Management noted that the pricing, quality, and reliability of services and the type of equipment utilized were the primary methods of competition in the industry. Over half of the company's assets as of December 31, 1995 and 1996 involved property and equipment, consisting of land (primarily disposal sites), buildings, vehicles and equipment, and leasehold improvements, with land and vehicles and equipment representing 20% and 27%, respectively, of the company's total consolidated assets. Disposal sites included approximately 66,400 total acres, which had estimated remaining lives ranging from one to over 100 years based upon management's site plans and estimated annual volumes of waste. The vehicles and equipment included approximately 21,400 collection and transfer vehicles, 1.6 million containers, and 25,100 stationary compactors. In addition, the Form 10-K stated that the company owned, operated or leased 16 trash-to-energy facilities, eight cogeneration and small power production facilities, two coal handling facilities, three biosolids drying, pelletizing and composting facilities, one wastewater treatment plant and various other manufacturing, office and warehouse facilities.

The accounting policies footnote in the 1996 financial statements disclosed that the cost of property and equipment, less estimated salvage value, was being depreciated over the estimated useful lives on the straight-line method as follows:

Buildings	10 to 40 years
Vehicles and equipment	3 to 20 years
Leasehold improvements	Over the life of the lease

Other information about the company's financial position as of December 31, 1996 is shown below in the Consolidated Balance Sheet:

As of December 31
(in millions)

Assets	1995	1996	Liabilities	1995	1996
Cash and cash equivalents	$ 170	$ 323	Current portion of LTD	$ 1,088	$ 554
Short-term investments	34	341	Accounts payable	994	948
Accounts receivable, net	1,656	1,682	Accrued expenses	906	1,324
Employee receivables	8	10	Unearned revenue	204	213
Parts and supplies	150	142	Total Current Liabilities	$ 3,192	$ 3,039
Costs + estimated earnings in excess of billings	243	241			
Prepaid expenses	347	354	Deferrals	$ 2,102	$ 2,197
Total Current Assets	$ 2,608	$ 3,093			
			Long-term debt	$ 6,390	$ 6,972
Property & equipment					
Land – disposal sites	4,554	5,019	Minority Interest in Subs	$ 1,385	$ 1,187
Buildings	1,532	1,495			
Vehicles and equipment	7,165	7,521	Put Options	$ 262	$ 96
Leasehold improvements	84	86			
Total property & equipment	13,335	14,121	**Stockholder Equity**		
Less accumulated depr.	(3,829)	(4,399)	Common stock	499	507
Property & equip., net	$ 9,506	$ 9,722	Additional paid-in	423	865
			Cumulative translation adjustment	(103)	(79)
Other assets			Retained earnings	4,487	4,364
Intangibles - goodwill, net	3,823	3,885	Less Treasury stock	(363)	(360)
Sundry assets	1,551	1,452	Total Stockholder Equity	$ 4,942	$ 4,876
Net assets of discontinued operations	876	214			
Total Other Assets	$ 6,250	$ 5,552			
			Total Liabilities and		
Total Assets	$ 18,364	$ 18,367	**Stockholder Equity**	$ 18,364	$ 18,367

FRAUD REVEALED

Before the 1997 annual financial statements were released, the company issued a press release on January 5, 1998 announcing that it would file amended reports on Form 10-K and 10-Q for the year ended December 31, 1996 and for the three-month periods ended March 31, 1997 and June 30, 1997. The press release also disclosed management's plans to revise certain previously reported financial data and to issue revised financial statements for 1994 and 1995 to reflect various revisions of various items of income and expense.

The revisions were prompted by a request by the SEC's Division of Corporation Finance. The January 5th press release noted that the Waste Management board of directors and audit committee were engaged in an extensive examination of its North American operations, assets, and investments as well as a review of certain of its accounting methods and estimates. The company stated further that it was continuing to carefully examine the company's accounting estimates and methods in several areas, including the areas of vehicle and equipment depreciation and landfill cost accounting. The company also disclosed that it had named a new acting chief executive officer (CEO) and an acting chief financial officer (CFO) to replace the former CEO and CFO, both of whom resigned in 1997.

On January 28, 1998, the company issued another press release reporting that the company would restate prior period financial results including earnings for 1992 through 1997 to reflect revisions in various items of expense, including those in the areas of vehicle and equipment depreciation and landfill cost accounting. The January 28, 1998 press release also noted that the restatement would not affect revenues for these periods.

Finally, on February 24, 1998, the company publicly reported restated earnings for 1992 through 1996, in addition to reporting its financial results for the year ended December 31, 1997. The press release noted that the 1997 fourth quarter results included a special charge and adjustments to expenses related to the company's comprehensive examination of its operations and accounting practices. The cumulative charge totaled $2.9 billion after-tax and $3.5 billion pre-tax, which reduced stockholders' equity to $1.3 billion as of December 31, 1997. The restatement of the 1996 financial results alone took the company from a previously reported net income of $192 million to a restated 1996 net loss of $39 million.

The February press release further disclosed that certain items of expense were incorrectly reported in prior year financial statements. According to the release, the restatements principally related to the calculation of vehicle, equipment, and container depreciation expense and capitalized interest costs related to landfills. The company admitted to the use of incorrect vehicle and container salvage values and useful lives assumptions. In response, the company disclosed that it had implemented new, more conservative accounting policies and practices including those related to landfill cost accounting and had adopted a new fleet management strategy impacting vehicle and equipment depreciation and amortization. In particular, the company disclosed that it was adopting new policies that included shortening the depreciable lives for certain categories of assets to reflect their current anticipated useful lives and had eliminated salvage values for trucks and waste containers. Additionally, the company revealed that it had revised certain components of the landfill cost accounting process by adopting more specific criteria to determine whether currently unpermitted expansions to existing landfills should be included in the estimated capacity of sites for depreciation purposes.

The financial community responded immediately to the news. On February 25, 1998, Standard & Poor's lowered its rating on Waste Management, Inc. to "BBB" from "A-". As news of the company's overstatements of earnings became public, Waste Management's shareholders lost more than $6 billion in the market value of their investments when the stock price plummeted by more than 33%. In March 1998, the SEC announced a formal investigation into the company's bookkeeping.

SEC INVESTIGATION FINDINGS

By March 2002, the SEC announced it had completed its investigation of the accounting practices at Waste Management, Inc. and announced that it had filed suit against the founder and five other top officers of the company, charging them with perpetrating a massive financial fraud lasting more than five years. The complaint filed in the U.S. District Court in Chicago, charged that the defendants engaged in a systematic scheme to falsify and misrepresent Waste Management's financial results between 1992 and 1997. According to Thomas C. Newkirk, associate director of the SEC's Division of Enforcement, *"Our complaint describes one of the most egregious accounting frauds we have seen. For years, these defendants cooked the books, enriched themselves, preserved their jobs, and duped unsuspecting shareholders."*[1]

The SEC's complaint alleges that company management fraudulently manipulated the company's financial results to meet predetermined earnings targets. The company's revenues were not growing fast enough to meet those targets, so the defendants resorted to improperly eliminating and deferring current period expenses to inflate earnings. They employed a multitude of improper accounting practices to achieve this objective. Among other things, the SEC noted that the defendants:

---

1   Press release issued by the SEC on March 26, 2002 (see www.sec.gov).

- Avoided depreciation expenses on their garbage trucks by both assigning unsupported and inflated salvage values and extending their useful lives,
- Assigned arbitrary salvage values to other assets that previously had no salvage value,
- Failed to record expenses for decreases in the value of landfills as they were filled with waste,
- Refused to record expenses necessary to write off the costs of unsuccessful and abandoned landfill development projects,
- Established inflated environmental reserves (liabilities) in connection with acquisitions so that the excess reserves could be used to avoid recording unrelated operating expenses,
- Improperly capitalized a variety of expenses, and
- Failed to establish sufficient reserves (liabilities) to pay for income taxes and other expenses.

The SEC alleged that the improper accounting practices were centralized at corporate headquarters, with Dean L. Buntrock, founder, chairman, and CEO as the driving force behind the fraud. Allegedly, Buntrock set the earnings targets, fostered a culture of fraudulent accounting, personally directed certain of the accounting changes to make the targeted earnings, and was the spokesperson who announced the company's phony numbers. During the year, Buntrock and other corporate officers monitored the company's actual operating results and compared them to the quarterly targets set in the budget. To reduce expenses and inflate earnings artificially, the officers used "top-level adjustments" to conform the company's actual results to the predetermined earnings targets. The inflated earnings of one period became the floor for future manipulations. To sustain the scheme, earnings fraudulently achieved in one period had to be replaced in the next period.

According to the SEC, the defendants allegedly concealed their scheme by using accounting manipulations known as "netting" and "geography" to make reported results appear better than they actually were and to avoid public scrutiny. The netting activities allowed them to eliminate approximately $490 million in current period accounting misstatements by offsetting them against unrelated one-time gains on the sale or exchange of assets. The geography entries allowed them to move tens of millions of dollars between various line items on the company's income statement to make the financial statements appear as management wanted.

In addition to Buntrock, the SEC complaint named other Waste Management officers as participants in the fraud. Phillip B. Rooney, president and chief operating officer (COO), and James Koenig, executive vice president CFO, were among the six officers named in the complaint. According to the SEC, Rooney was in charge of building the profitability of the company's core solid waste operations and at all times exercised overall control over the company's largest subsidiary. He ensured that required write-offs were not recorded and, in some instances, overruled accounting decisions that would have a negative impact on operations. Koenig was primarily responsible for executing the scheme. He ordered the destruction of damaging evidence, misled the audit committee and internal accountants, and withheld information from the outside auditors.

According to the SEC staff, the defendants' fraudulent conduct was driven by greed and a desire to retain their corporate positions and status in the business and social communities. Buntrock posed as a successful entrepreneur. With charitable contributions made with the fruits of the ill-gotten gains or money taken from the company, Buntrock presented himself as a pillar of the community. According to the SEC, just 10 days before certain of the accounting irregularities first became public, he enriched himself with a tax benefit by donating inflated company stock to his college alma mater to fund a building in his name. He was the primary beneficiary of the fraud and allegedly reaped more than $16.9 million in ill-gotten gains from, among other things, performance-based bonuses, retirement benefits, charitable giving, and selling company stock while the fraud was ongoing. Rooney allegedly reaped more than $9.2 million in ill-gotten gains from, among other things, performance-based bonuses, retirement benefits, and selling company stock while the fraud was ongoing. Koenig profited by more than $900,000 from his fraudulent acts.

According to the SEC, the defendants were allegedly aided in their fraud by the company's long-time auditor, Arthur Andersen, LLP, which had served as Waste Management's auditor since before the company became a public company in 1971. Andersen regarded Waste Management as a "crown jewel" client. Until 1997, every CFO and chief accounting officer (CAO) in Waste Management's history as a public company had previously worked as an auditor at Andersen.

During the 1990s, approximately 14 former Andersen employees worked for Waste Management, most often in key financial and accounting positions. During the period 1991 through 1997, Andersen billed Waste Management approximately $7.5 million in audit fees and $11.8 million in other fees related to tax, attest work, regulatory issues, and consulting services. A related entity, Andersen Consulting (now Accenture) also billed Waste Management corporate headquarters approximately $6 million in additional non-audit fees.

The SEC alleged that at the outset of the fraud, Waste Management executives capped Andersen's audit fees and advised the Andersen engagement partner that the firm could earn additional fees through "special work." Andersen nevertheless identified the company's improper accounting practices and quantified much of the impact of those practices on the company's financial statements. Andersen annually presented company management with what it called Proposed Adjusting Journal Entries (PAJEs) to correct errors that understated expenses and overstated earnings in the company's financial statements.

Management consistently refused to make the adjustments called for by the PAJEs, according to the SEC's complaint. Instead, the defendants secretly entered into an agreement with Andersen to write off the accumulated errors over periods up to ten years and to change the underlying accounting practices in future periods. The signed, four-page agreement, known as the Summary of Action Steps, identified improper accounting practices that went to the core of the company's operations and prescribed 32 "must do" steps for the company to follow to change those practices. The Action Steps thus constituted an agreement between the company and its outside auditor to cover up past frauds by committing additional frauds in the future, according to the SEC complaint.

As time progressed, the defendants did not comply with the Action Steps agreement. Writing off the errors and changing the underlying accounting practices as prescribed in the agreement would have prevented the company from meeting earnings targets, and the defendants from enriching themselves.

The fraud scheme eventually unraveled. In mid-July 1997, a new CEO ordered a review of the company's accounting practices. That review ultimately led to the restatement of the company's financial statements for 1992 through the third quarter of 1997.

EPILOGUE

In addition to the fraudulent activities related to the 1992 through 1997 financial statements, Waste Management's fraudulent activities continued. In July 1999 the SEC issued a cease and desist order alleging that management violated U.S. securities laws when they publicly projected results for the company's 1999 second quarter. According to the SEC, in June 1999 management continued to reiterate projected results for the quarter ended June 30, 1999, despite being aware of significant adverse trends in its business which made continued public support of its announced forecasts unreasonable. Apparently, Waste Management's information system failures made June's earnings forecast even more unreasonable since the company could not generate information from which reliable forecasts could be made.

The SEC's order was triggered by a July 6, 1999 company announcement of revenue shortfalls versus its internal budget of approximately $250 million for the second quarter. This news sent the share prices falling. On July 7, 1999, share prices went from $53.56 to $33.94 per share, and by August 4, 1999, share prices were down to $22.25 per share. *The Wall Street Journal* subsequently reported that the company evidentially settled a class action suit related to these 1999 charges for $457 million.[2] Despite these negative events, the company continues to operate.

As for Arthur Andersen, the SEC eventually settled charges with Andersen and four of its partners related to the 1992 through 1996 audited financial statements. Andersen agreed to pay a penalty of $7 million, the largest ever assessed against an accounting firm at that time. The SEC's complaint against Andersen said that the firm knew Waste Management was exaggerating its profits throughout the early and mid-1990s, and repeatedly pleaded with the company to make changes. Each year Andersen gave in, certifying the company's annual financial statements conformed to generally accepted accounting principles. According to Richard Walker, SEC Director of Enforcement, *"Arthur Andersen and its partners failed to stand up to company management and thereby betrayed their ultimate allegiance to Waste Management's shareholders and the investing public. Given the positions held by these partners and the duration and gravity of the misconduct, the firm itself must be held responsible for the false and misleading audit reports."* The SEC filed a civil fraud complaint against three Andersen partners who were involved in the audit, all of whom settled without admitting or denying the allegations. The three partners agreed to pay fines of $30,000 to $50,000 each and agreed to be banned from auditing public companies for up to five years. A fourth partner was barred from auditing for one year.

These charges against Andersen related to the Waste Management fraud and other high profile frauds, including the fraud at Sunbeam Corporation, provided a significant backdrop for all the allegations against Andersen in 2001 and 2002 for its role in the audits of Enron Corporation and the accounting firm's ultimate demise.

---

2   Coleman, Calmetta, "Waste Management to Pay $457 Million to Settle Suit, Posts Profit in 3rd Quarter," *The Wall Street Journal*, November 8, 2001, page A4.

REQUIRED

[1] Three conditions are often present when fraud exists. First, management or employees have an *incentive* or are under pressure, which provides them a reason to commit the fraud act. Second, circumstances exist – for example, absent or ineffective internal controls or the ability for management to override controls – that provide an *opportunity* for the fraud to be perpetrated. Third, those involved are able to rationalize the fraud as being consistent with their personal code of ethics. Some individuals possess an *attitude*, character, or set of ethical values that allows them to knowingly commit a fraudulent act. Using hindsight, identify factors present at Waste Management that are indicative of each of the three fraud conditions: incentives, opportunities, and attitudes.

[2] Review Waste Management's Consolidated Balance Sheet as of December 31, 1996. Identify accounts whose balances were likely based on significant management estimation techniques. Describe the reasons why estimates were required for each of the accounts identified.

[3] Describe why accounts involving significant management estimation are generally viewed as inherently risky.

[4] Review professional auditing standards to describe the auditor's responsibilities for examining management-generated estimates. Also, describe the techniques commonly used by auditors to evaluate the reasonableness of management's estimates.

[5] The Waste Management fraud primarily centered on inappropriate estimates of salvage values and useful lives for property and equipment. Describe techniques Andersen auditors could have used to assess the reasonableness of those estimates used to create Waste Management's financial statements.

[6] Several of the Waste Management accounting personnel were formerly employed by the company's auditor, Arthur Andersen. What are the risks associated with allowing former auditors to work for a client in key accounting positions? Research Section 206 of the Sarbanes–Oxley Act of 2002 and provide a brief summary of the restrictions related to the ability of a public company to hire accounting personnel who were formerly employed by the company's audit firm.

[7] Discuss possible reasons why the Andersen partners allegedly allowed Waste Management executives to avoid recording the identified accounting errors. How could accounting firms ensure that auditors do not succumb to similar pressures on other audit engagements?

Xerox Corporation
Evaluating Risk of Financial Statement Fraud

Mark S. Beasley · Frank A. Buckless · Steven M. Glover · Douglas F. Prawitt

LEARNING OBJECTIVES

After completing and discussing this case you should be able to

[1] Describe the auditor's responsibility to detect material misstatements due to fraud

[2] Recognize risk factors suggesting the presence of fraud

[3] Describe auditor responsibilities for assessing the reasonableness of management's estimates

[4] Describe processes that can be used by audit firms to reduce the likelihood that auditors will subordinate their judgments to client preferences

[5] Identify audit procedures that could have been performed to assess the appropriateness of questionable accounting manipulations used by Xerox

INTRODUCTION

Xerox Corporation (Xerox), once a star in the technology sector of the economy, found itself engulfed in an accounting scandal alleging that it was too aggressive in recognizing equipment revenue.[1] The complaint filed by the Securities and Exchange Commission (SEC) alleged that Xerox used a variety of accounting manipulations over the period 1997 through 2000 to meet Wall Street expectations and disguise its true operating performance. The SEC alleged that between 1997 and 2000 Xerox overstated revenues by $3 billion and pre-tax earnings by $1.5 billion. Also engulfed in this scandal was KPMG, Xerox's auditor, whose actions were also investigated by the SEC for its possible involvement with the alleged accounting manipulations.

BACKGROUND

Xerox, a Stamford, Connecticut-based company, described itself as "the document company." At that time, Xerox focused on developing, manufacturing, marketing, servicing, and financing a complete range of document processing products and services to enhance its customers' productivity. It sold and leased document imaging products, services, and supplies to customers in the United States and 130 other countries. In 2000, Xerox had reported revenues of $18.7 billion (restated) and employed approximately 92,000 people worldwide. Xerox's stock trades on the New York and Chicago Stock Exchanges.

Fundamental changes have affected the document industry. The industry has steadily transitioned from black and white to color capable devices, from light-lens and analog technology to digital technology, from stand alone to network-connected devices, and from paper to electronic documents. Xerox's product revenues for 1997 through 1999 are shown on the next page.

---

1   The background information about this case was primarily obtained from 8-K's and 10-K's filed by Xerox with the Securities and Exchange Commission and Accounting and Auditing Enforcement Release Nos. 1542, 1796, 2235, 2333, 2379 issued by the Securities and Exchange Commission.

The case was prepared by Mark S. Beasley, Ph.D. and Frank A. Buckless, Ph.D. of North Carolina State University and Steven M. Glover, Ph.D. and Douglas F. Prawitt, Ph.D. of Brigham Young University, as a basis for class discussion. It is not intended to illustrate either effective or ineffective handling of an administrative situation.

	1999	1998	1997
	(in billions)		
Digital products	$ 10.2	$ 8.6	$ 6.3
Light-lens copiers	5.8	7.4	8.3
Paper, Other products, currency	3.2	3.4	3.5
Total revenues	$ 19.2	$ 19.4	$ 18.1

Intense price competition from its overseas rivals during the late 1990s compounded the problems stemming from a changing business environment. Foreign competitors became more sophisticated and beat Xerox to the market with advanced color and digital copying technology. The intense competition and changing business environment made it difficult for Xerox to generate increased revenues and earnings in the late 1990s.

Unfortunately, several factors put pressure on Xerox to report continued revenue and earnings growth during this challenging period. The investment climate of the 1990s created high expectations for companies to report revenue and earnings growth. Companies that failed to meet Wall Street's earnings projections by even a penny often found themselves punished with significant declines in stock price. Xerox management also felt pressure to maintain its strong credit rating so it could continue to internally finance the majority of its customers' sales, by gaining access to the necessary credit markets. Finally, Xerox's compensation system put pressure on management to report revenue and earnings growth. Compensation of senior management was directly linked to Xerox's ability to report increasing revenues and earnings.

In 1998, management announced a restructuring program to address the emerging business challenges Xerox faced. Chairman and chief executive office (CEO) Paul A. Allaire, noted:

> *The markets we serve are growing strongly and transitioning rapidly to digital technologies. In the digital world, profitable revenue growth can only be assured by continuous significant productivity improvements in all operations and functions worldwide and we are determined to deliver these improvements. This restructuring is an important and integral part of implementing our strategy and ensuring that we maintain our leadership in the digital world. The continued adverse currency and pricing climate underscores the importance of continuous and, in certain areas, dramatic productivity improvements.*

> *This repositioning will strengthen us financially and enable strong cash generation. We have strong business momentum. We have exciting market opportunities and excellent customer acceptance of our broad product line. These initiatives will underpin the consistent delivery of double-digit revenue growth and mid- to high-teens earnings-per-share growth. This restructuring is another step in our sustained strategy to lead the digital document world and provide superior customer and shareholder value (Form 8-K, Xerox Corporation, April 8, 1998).*

Chief operating officer (COO), G. Richard Thoman, noted:

> *Xerox has accomplished what few other companies have — foreseen, adapted to and led a major transformation in its market. As our markets and customer needs continue to change, Xerox will continue to anticipate and lead. We are focused on being the best in class in the digital world in all respects. To enhance our competitive position, we must be competitive in terms of the cost of our products and infrastructure, the speed of our response to the marketplace, the service we provide our customers and the breadth and depth of our distribution channels (Form 8-K, Xerox Corporation, April 8, 1998).*

Selected financial information from Xerox's 1997 through 2000 financial statements is presented on the opposing page (before restatement).

	For the Year Ended December 31			
	2000	**1999**	**1998**	**1997**
	(in millions)			
Revenues	$ 18,632	$ 19,228	$ 19,447	$ 18,144
Cost and expenses (excluding income taxes)	19,188	17,192	18,684	16,003
Income/(loss) from continuing operations	(384)	1,424	585	1,452
Net income/(loss)	(384)	1,424	395	1,452
Cash flows from operating activities	(827)	1,224	(1,165)	472

	As of December 31			
	2000	**1999**	**1998**	**1997**
Assets	(in millions)			
Cash	$ 1,741	$ 126	$ 79	$ 75
Accounts receivable, net	2,281	2,622	2,671	2,145
Finance receivables, net	5,141	5,115	5,220	4,599
Inventory	1,930	2,961	3,269	2,792
Other current assets	2,001	1,161	1,236	1,155
Total current assets	13,094	11,985	12,475	10,766
Finance receivables	8,035	8,203	9,093	7,754
Land, building, and equipment, net	2,495	2,456	2,366	2,377
Investments in affiliates	1,362	1,615	1,456	1,332
Goodwill, net	1,639	1,724	1,731	1,375
Other assets	3,062	1,701	1,233	1,103
Investment in discontinued operations	—	1,130	1,670	3,025
Total assets	$ 29,687	$ 28,814	$ 30,024	$ 27,732
Liabilities and Equity				
Short-term and current portion of long-term debt	$ 2,693	$ 3,957	$ 4,104	$ 3,707
Accounts payable	1,033	1,016	948	776
Accrued compensation and benefit costs	662	630	722	811
Unearned income	250	186	210	205
Other current liabilities	1,648	2,161	2,523	2,193
Total current liabilities	6,286	7,950	8,507	7,692
Long-term debt	15,404	10,994	10,867	8,779
Postretirement medical benefits	1,197	1,133	1,092	1,079
Deferred taxes and other liabilities	1,933	2,263	2,711	2,469
Discontinued operations, liabilities, policyholders' deposits and other	—	428	911	1,693
Deferred ESOP benefits	(221)	(299)	(370)	(434)
Minorities' interests in equity subsidiaries	141	127	124	127
Obligation for equity put options	32	—	—	—
Company-obligated, mandatorily redeemable preferred securities of subsidiary trust holding solely subordinated debentures of the Company	638	638	638	637
Preferred stock	647	669	687	705
Common shareholders' equity	3,630	4,911	4,857	4,985
Total liabilities and equity	$ 29,687	$ 28,814	$ 30,024	$ 27,732

The desired turnaround did not materialize in 1999. The worsening business environment had a negative affect on 1999 results. Revenues and earnings (before the restructuring charge) were down. Management's letter to shareholders in the 1999 annual report stated:

> Our 1999 results were clearly a major disappointment. A number of factors contributed, some largely beyond our control. And the changes we're making to exploit the opportunities in the digital marketplace are taking longer and proving more disruptive than we anticipated. We remain confident, however, that these changes are the right ones to spur growth, reduce costs and improve shareholder value.
>
> We also saw intensifying pressure in the marketplace in 1999, as our competitors announced new products and attractive pricing. We're prepared to beat back this challenge and mount our own challenge from a position of strength (1999 Xerox Annual Report).

ACCOUNTING MANIPULATIONS UNRAVELED

The SEC initiated an investigation in June 2000 when Xerox notified that agency of potential accounting irregularities occurring in its Mexico unit. After completing its investigation, the SEC alleged that Xerox used several accounting manipulations to inflate earnings from 1997 through 1999 including:

- **Acceleration of Lease Revenue Recognition from Bundled Leases.** The majority of Xerox's equipment sales revenues were generated from long-term lease agreements where customers paid a single negotiated monthly fee in return for equipment, service, supplies and financing (called bundled leases). Xerox accelerated the lease revenue recognition by allocating a higher portion of the lease payment to the equipment, instead of the service or financing activity. Generally accepted accounting principles (GAAP) allow most of the fair market value of a leased product to be recognized as revenue immediately if the lease meets the requirements for a sales-type lease. Non-equipment revenues such as service and financing are required to be recognized over the term of the lease. By reallocating revenues from the finance and service activities to the equipment, Xerox was able to recognize greater revenues in the current reporting period instead of deferring revenue recognition to future periods. The approach Xerox used to allocate a higher portion of the lease payment from the finance activity to equipment was called "return on equity." With this approach Xerox argued that its finance operation should obtain approximately a 15 percent return on equity. By periodically changing the assumptions used to calculate the return on equity, Xerox was able to reduce the interest rates used to discount the leases thereby increasing the allocation of the lease payment to equipment (and thus increasing the equipment sales revenue). The approach Xerox used to allocate a higher portion of the lease payment from services to equipment was called "margin normalization." With this approach Xerox allocated a higher portion of the lease payment to equipment in foreign countries where the equipment gross margins would otherwise be below gross margins reported in the United States due to foreign competition in those overseas markets. In essence, Xerox adjusted the lease payment allocations for bundled leases in foreign countries to achieve service and equipment margins consistent with those reported in the United States where competition was not as fierce.
- **Acceleration of Lease Revenue from Lease Price Increases and Extensions.** In some countries Xerox regularly renegotiated the terms of lease contracts. Xerox elected to recognize the revenues from lease price increases and extensions immediately instead of recognizing the revenues over the remaining lives of the leases. GAAP requires that increases in the price or length of a lease be recognized over the remaining life of the lease.
- **Increases in the Residual Values of Leased Equipment.** Cost of sales for leased equipment is derived by taking the equipment cost and subtracting the expected residual value of

the leased equipment at the time the lease is signed. Periodically Xerox would increase the expected residual value of previously recorded leased equipment. The write-up of the residual value was reflected as a reduction to cost of sales in the period the residual value was increased. GAAP does not allow upward adjustment of estimated residual values after lease inception.

- *Acceleration of Revenues from Portfolio Asset Strategy Transactions.* Xerox was having difficulty using sales-type lease agreements in Brazil, so it switched to rental contracts. Because revenues from these rental contracts could not be recognized immediately, Xerox packaged and sold these lease revenue streams to investors to allow immediate revenue recognition. No disclosure of the change in business approach was made in any of Xerox's reports filed with the SEC.

- *Manipulation of Reserves.* GAAP requires the establishment of reserves for identifiable, probable, and estimable loss contingencies. Xerox established an acquisition reserve for unknown business risks and then recorded unrelated business expenses to the reserve account to inflate earnings. In other words, Xerox debited the reserve account for unrelated business expenses thereby reducing operating expenses and increasing net income. Additionally, Xerox tracked reserve accounts to identify excess reserves that could be used to inflate earnings in future periods as needed using similar techniques.

- *Manipulation of Other Incomes.* Xerox successfully resolved a tax dispute that required the Internal Revenue Service to refund taxes along with paying interest on the disputed amounts. Instead of recognizing the interest income during the periods 1995 and 1996, when the tax dispute was finalized and the interest was due, Xerox elected to recognize most of the interest income during the periods 1997 through 2000.

- *Failure to Disclose Factoring Transactions.* Analysts were raising concerns about Xerox's cash position. The accounting manipulations discussed above did nothing to improve Xerox's cash position. In an effort to improve its cash position, Xerox sold future cash streams from receivables to local banks for immediate cash (factoring transactions). No disclosure of these factoring transactions was made in any of the reports Xerox filed with the SEC.

Senior management allegedly directed or approved the above accounting manipulations frequently under protest from field managers who believed the actions distorted their operational results. Senior management viewed these accounting manipulations as "accounting opportunities." KPMG, Xerox's outside auditor, also questioned the appropriateness of many of the accounting manipulations used by Xerox. Discussions between KPMG personnel and senior management did not persuade management to change its accounting practices. Eventually KPMG allowed Xerox to continue using the questionable practices (with minor exceptions). The SEC noted in its complaint that:

> *Xerox's reliance on these accounting actions was so important to the company that when the engagement partner for the outside auditor [KPMG] challenged several of Xerox's non-GAAP accounting practices, Xerox's senior management told the audit firm that they wanted a new engagement partner assigned to its account. The audit firm complied* (Compliant: Securities and Exchange Commission v. Xerox Corporation, Civil Action No. 02-272789).

The aggregate impact of the previously listed accounting manipulations was to increase pretax earnings from 1997 to 1999 by the following amounts:

	For the Year Ended December 31				
	1997	1998	1999	2000	Total
			(in millions)		
The Total Net Impact to Pretax Earnings	$ 405	$ 656	$ 511	$ (55)	$ 1,517

Xerox's accounting manipulations enabled the company to meet Wall Street earnings expectations during the 1997 through 1999 reporting periods. Without the accounting manipulations, Xerox would have failed to meet Wall Street earnings expectations for 11 of 12 quarters from 1997 through 1999. Unfortunately, the prior years accounting manipulations and a deteriorating business environment caught up with Xerox in 2000. Xerox could no longer hide its declining business performance. There were not enough revenue inflating adjustments that could be made in 2000 to offset the lost revenues due to premature recognition in preceding years.

During the 1997 through 1999 reporting periods, Xerox publicly announced that it was an "earnings success story" and that it expected revenue and earnings growth to continue each quarter and year. The reported revenue and earnings growth allowed senior management to receive over $5 million in performance-based compensation and over $30 million in profits from the sale of stock. The SEC complaint also noted that Xerox did not properly disclose policies and risks associated with some of its unusual leasing practices and that it did not maintain adequate accounting controls at its Mexico unit. Xerox Mexico, pressured to meet financial targets established by corporate headquarters, relaxed its credit standards and leased equipment to high risk customers. This practice improved short-term earnings but quickly resulted in a large pool of uncollectible receivables. Xerox Mexico also improperly handled transactions with third-party resellers and government agencies to inflate earnings.

EPILOGUE

Xerox's stock, which traded at over $60 per share prior to the announcement of the accounting problems, dropped to less than $5 per share in 2000 after the questionable accounting practices were made public. In April 2002, Xerox reached an agreement to settle its lawsuit with the SEC. Under the Consent Decree, Xerox agreed to restate its 1997 through 2000 financial statements. Xerox also agreed to pay a $10 million fine and create a committee of outside directors to review the company's material accounting controls and policies. In June 2003, six senior executives of Xerox agreed to pay over $22 million to settle their lawsuit with the SEC related to the alleged fraud. The six executives were Paul A. Allaire, chairman and CEO; Barry B. Romeril, chief financial officer (CFO); G. Richard Thoman, president and COO; Philip D. Fishback, controller; and two other financial executives: Daniel S. Marchibroda and Gregory B. Tayler. Because the executives were not found guilty Xerox agreed to pay all but $3 million of the fines. All of these executives resigned their positions at Xerox.

PricewaterhouseCoopers replaced KPMG as Xerox's auditor on October 4, 2001. In April 2005, KPMG agreed to pay $22 million to the SEC to settle its lawsuit with the SEC in connection with the alleged fraud. KPMG also agreed to undertake reforms designed to improve its audit practice. In October of 2005 and February of 2006, four former KPMG partners involved with the Xerox engagement during the alleged fraud period each agreed to pay civil penalties from $100,000 to $150,000 and agreed to suspensions from practice before the SEC with rights to reapply from within one to three years. A fifth KPMG partner agreed to be censured by the SEC.

The alleged inappropriate accounting manipulations used in Xerox's financial statements resulted in multiple class action lawsuits against Xerox, management, and KPMG. In March 2008, Xerox agreed to pay $670 million and KPMG agreed to pay $80 million to settle a shareholder lawsuit related to the alleged fraud.[2]

---

2 "Xerox Settles Securities Lawsuit," News release issued by Xerox on March 27, 2008. See the following website: http://www.xerox.com.

REQUIRED (CONTINUED ON NEXT PAGE)

[1] Financial information was provided for Xerox for the period 1997 through 2000. Go to the SEC website (www.sec.gov) and obtain financial information for Hewlett Packard Company for the same reporting periods. How were Xerox's and Hewlett Packard's businesses similar and dissimilar during the relevant time periods? Using the financial information, perform some basic ratio analyses for the two companies. How did the two companies financial performance compare? Explain your answers.

[2] Professional standards outline the auditor's consideration of material misstatements due to errors and fraud. (a) What responsibility does an auditor have to detect material misstatements due to errors and fraud? (b) What two main categories of fraud affect financial reporting? (c) What types of factors should auditors consider when assessing the likelihood of material misstatements due to fraud? (d) Which factors existed during the 1997 through 2000 audits of Xerox that created an environment conducive for fraud?

[3] Three conditions are often present when fraud exists. First, management or employees have an *incentive* or are under pressure, which provides them a reason to commit the fraud act. Second, circumstances exist – for example, absent or ineffective internal controls or the ability for management to override controls – that provide an *opportunity* for the fraud to be perpetrated. Third, those involved are able to rationalize the fraud as being consistent with their personal code of ethics. Some individuals possess an *attitude*, character, or set of ethical values that allows them to knowingly commit a fraudulent act. Using hindsight, identify factors present at Xerox that are indicative of each of the three fraud conditions: incentives, opportunities, and attitudes.

[4] KPMG has publicly stated that the main accounting issues raised in the Xerox case do not involve fraud, as suggested by the SEC, rather they involve differences in judgment.[3] (a) Which of the questionable accounting manipulations used by Xerox involved estimates? (b) Refer to professional auditing standards and describe the auditor's responsibilities for examining management-generated estimates.

[5] Some will argue that KPMG inappropriately subordinated its judgments to Xerox preferences. How could accounting firms ensure that auditors do not subordinate their judgments to client preferences on other audit engagements?

[6] Several questionable accounting manipulations were identified by the SEC. (a) For each accounting manipulation identified, indicate the financial statement accounts affected. (b) For each accounting manipulation identified, indicate one audit procedure the auditor could have used to assess the appropriateness of the practice.

[7] In its complaint, the SEC indicated that Xerox inappropriately used accounting reserves to inflate earnings. Walter P. Schuetze noted in a 1999 speech:

> One of the accounting "hot spots" that we are considering this morning is accounting for restructuring charges and restructuring reserves. A better title would be accounting for general reserves, contingency reserves, rainy day reserves, or cookie jar reserves. Accounting for so-called restructurings has become an art form. Some companies like the idea so much that they establish restructuring reserves every year. Why not? Analysts seem to like the idea of recognizing as a liability today, a budget of expenditures planned for the next year or next several years in down-sizing, right-sizing, or improving operations, and portraying that amount as a special, below-the-line charge in the current period's income statement. This year's earnings are happily

---

3 "After Andersen KPMG's Work With Xerox Sets New Test for SEC," by James Bandler and Mark Maremont, *The Wall Street Journal*, May 6, 2002, pp. A:1 and A:10.

reported in press releases as "before charges." CNBC analysts and commentators talk about earnings "before charges." The financial press talks about earnings before "special charges." (Funny, no one talks about earnings before credits—only charges.) It's as if special charges aren't real. Out of sight, out of mind (Speech by SEC Staff: Cookie Jar Reserves, April 22, 1999).

What responsibility do auditors have regarding accounting reserves established by company management? How should auditors test the reasonableness of accounting reserves established by company management?

[8] In 2002 Andersen was convicted for one felony count of obstructing justice related to its involvement with the Enron Corporation scandal (this conviction was later overturned by the United States Supreme Court). Read the "Enron Corporation and Andersen, LLP" case included in this casebook. (a) Based on your reading of that case and this case, how was Enron Corporation's situation similar or dissimilar to Xerox's situation? (b) How did the financial and business sectors react to the two situations when the accounting issues became public? (c) If the financial or business sectors reacted differently, why did they react differently? (d) How was KPMG's situation similar or dissimilar to Andersen's situation?

[9] On April 19, 2005, KPMG agreed to pay $22 million to the SEC to settle its lawsuit with the SEC in connection with the alleged fraud. Go to the SEC's website to read about the settlement of this lawsuit with the SEC (try, "http:// www.sec.gov/news/press/2005-59.htm"). Do you agree or disagree with the findings? Explain your answer.

[10] The SEC outlines in Accounting and Auditing Enforcement Release No. 2234 its assessment of the Xerox fraud. Obtain and read a copy of the enforcement release (try http://www.sec.gov/litigation/admin/34-51574.pdf). Compared to the information presented in this case would your opinion of KPMG's audit performance change after reading the enforcement release. Explain your answer.

[11] The SEC outlines in Accounting and Auditing Enforcement Release No. 2234 five "undertakings" for KPMG to alter or amend its audit practices. Obtain a copy of the enforcement release (try http://www.sec.gov/litigation/admin/34-51574.pdf) and read the five "undertakings." Based on your reading of the five "undertakings," which elements of a system of quality control did KPMG have weaknesses? Explain your answer.

[12] A 2002 editorial in *BusinessWeek* raised issues with compensation received by corporate executives even when the company does not perform well. In 1980 corporate executive compensation was 42 times the average worker compensation while in 2000 it was 531 times the average worker compensation.[4] (a) Do you believe executive compensation levels are reasonable? (b) Explain your answer. (c) What type of procedures could corporations establish to help ensure the reasonableness of executive compensation?

---

4 "CEOs: Why They're So Unloved," *BusinessWeek*, April 22, 2002, p. 118.

Phar-Mor, Inc.
Accounting Fraud, Litigation, and Auditor Liability

Mark S. Beasley · Frank A. Buckless · Steven M. Glover · Douglas F. Prawitt

LEARNING OBJECTIVES

After completing and discussing this case you should be able to

[1] Identify factors contributing to an environment conducive to accounting fraud

[2] Understand what factors may inappropriately influence the client-auditor relationship and auditor independence

[3] Understand auditor legal liability issues related to suits brought by plaintiffs under both statutory and common law

INTRODUCTION

In December 1995, the flamboyant entrepreneur, Michael "Mickey" Monus, formerly president and chief operating officer (COO) of the deep-discount retail chain Phar-Mor, Inc., was sentenced to 19 years and seven months in prison. Monus was convicted for the accounting fraud that inflated Phar-Mor's shareholder equity by $500 million, resulted in over $1 billion in losses, and caused the bankruptcy of the twenty-eighth largest private company in the United States. The massive accounting fraud went largely undetected for nearly six years. Several members of top management confessed to, and were convicted of, financial-statement fraud. Former members of Phar-Mor management were collectively fined over $1 million, and two former Phar-Mor management employees received prison sentences. Phar-Mor's management, as well as Phar-Mor creditors and investors, subsequently brought suit against Phar-Mor's independent auditors, Coopers & Lybrand LLP (Coopers), alleging Coopers was reckless in performing its audits. At the time the suits were filed, Coopers faced claims in excess of $1 billion. Even though there were never allegations that the auditors knowingly participated in the Phar-Mor fraud, on February 14, 1996, a jury found Coopers liable under both state and federal laws. Ultimately, Coopers settled the claims for an undisclosed amount.

PHAR-MOR STORES[1]

Between 1985 and 1992, Phar-Mor grew from 15 stores to 310 stores in 32 states, posting sales of more than $3 billion. By seemingly all standards, Phar-Mor was a rising star touted by some retail experts as the next Wal-Mart. In fact, Sam Walton once announced that the only company he feared at all in the expansion of Wal-Mart was Phar-Mor.

Mickey Monus, Phar-Mor's president, COO and founder, was a local hero in his hometown of Youngstown, Ohio. As demonstration of his loyalty, Monus put Phar-Mor's headquarters in a deserted department store in downtown Youngstown. Monus—known as shy and introverted to friends, cold and aloof to others—became quite flashy as Phar-Mor grew. Before the fall of his Phar-Mor empire, Monus was known for buying his friends expensive gifts and he was building an extravagant personal residence, complete with an indoor basketball court. He was also an initial

---

1 Unless otherwise noted, the facts and statements included in this case are based on actual trial transcripts.

The case was prepared by Mark S. Beasley, Ph.D. and Frank A. Buckless, Ph.D. of North Carolina State University and Steven M. Glover, Ph.D. and Douglas F. Prawitt, Ph.D. of Brigham Young University, as a basis for class discussion. It is not intended to illustrate either effective or ineffective handling of an administrative situation.

equity investor in the Colorado Rockies major league baseball franchise. This affiliation with the Colorado Rockies and other high profile sporting events sponsored by Phar-Mor fed Monus' love for the high life and fast action. He frequently flew to Las Vegas, where a suite was always available for him at Caesar's Palace. Mickey would often impress his traveling companions by giving them thousands of dollars for gambling.

Phar-Mor was a deep-discount retail chain selling a variety of household products and prescription drugs at substantially lower prices than other discount stores. The key to the low prices was "power buying," the phrase Monus used to describe his strategy of loading up on products when suppliers were offering rock-bottom prices. The strategy of deep-discount retailing is to beat competitors' prices, thereby attracting cost-conscious consumers. Phar-Mor's prices were so low that competitors wondered how Phar-Mor could turn a profit. Monus' strategy was to undersell Wal-Mart in each market where the two retailers directly competed.

Unfortunately, Phar-Mor's prices were so low that Phar-Mor began losing money. Unwilling to allow these shortfalls to damage Phar-Mor's appearance of success, Monus and his team began to engage in creative accounting so that Phar-Mor never reported these losses in its financial statements. Federal fraud examiners discerned later that 1987 was the last year Phar-Mor actually made a profit.

Investors, relying upon these erroneous financial statements, saw Phar-Mor as an opportunity to cash in on the retailing craze. Among the big investors were Westinghouse Credit Corp., Sears Roebuck & Co., mall developer Edward J. de Bartolo, and the prestigious Lazard Freres & Co. Corporate Partners Investment Fund. Prosecutors say banks and investors put $1.14 billion into Phar-Mor based on the phony records.

The fraud was ultimately uncovered when a travel agent received a Phar-Mor check signed by Monus paying for expenses that were unrelated to Phar-Mor. The agent showed the check to her landlord, who happened to be a Phar-Mor investor, and he contacted Phar-Mor's chief executive officer (CEO), David Shapira. On August 4, 1992, David Shapira announced to the business community that Phar-Mor had discovered a massive fraud perpetrated primarily by Michael Monus, former president and COO, and Patrick Finn, former chief financial officer (CFO). In order to hide Phar-Mor's cash flow problems, attract investors, and make the company look profitable, Monus and Finn altered Phar-Mor's accounting records to understate costs of goods sold and overstate inventory and income. In addition to the financial statement fraud, internal investigations by the company estimated an embezzlement in excess of $10 million.[2]

Phar-Mor's executives had cooked the books, and the magnitude of the collusive management fraud was almost inconceivable. The fraud was carefully carried out over several years by persons at many organizational layers, including the president and COO, CFO, vice president of marketing, director of accounting, controller, and a host of others.

The following list outlines seven key factors contributing to the fraud and the ability to cover it up for so long.

[1] *The lack of adequate management information systems (MIS).* According to the federal fraud examiner's report, Phar-Mor's MIS was inadequate on many levels. At one point, a Phar-Mor vice president raised concerns about the company's MIS and organized a committee to address the problem. However, senior officials involved in the scheme to defraud Phar-Mor dismissed the vice president's concerns and ordered the committee disbanded.

[2] *Poor internal controls.* For example, Phar-Mor's accounting department was able to bypass normal accounts payable controls by maintaining a supply of blank checks on two different bank accounts and by using them to make disbursements. Only those involved in the fraud were authorized to approve the use of these checks.

[3] *The hands-off management style of David Shapira, CEO.* For example, in at least two instances Shapira was made aware of potential problems with Monus' behavior and Phar-Mor's financial information. In both cases Shapira chose to distance himself from the knowledge.

---

2   Stern, Gabriella, "Phar-Mor Vendors Halt Deliveries; More Layoffs Made," *The Wall Street Journal,* August 10, 1992.

[4] *Inadequate internal audit function.* Ironically, Michael Monus was appointed a member of the audit committee. When the internal auditor reported that he wanted to investigate certain payroll irregularities associated with some of the Phar-Mor related parties, Monus and CFO Finn forestalled these activities and then eliminated the internal audit function altogether.

[5] *Collusion among upper management.* At least six members of Phar-Mor's upper management, as well as other employees in the accounting department, were involved in the fraud.

[6] *Phar-Mor's knowledge of audit procedures and objectives.* Phar-Mor's fraud team was made up of several former auditors, including at least one former auditor who had worked for Coopers on the Phar-Mor audit. The fraud team indicated that one reason they were successful in hiding the fraud from the auditors was because they knew what the auditors were looking for.

[7] *Related parties.* Coopers & Lybrand, in a countersuit, stated that Shapira and Monus set up a web of companies to do business with Phar-Mor. Coopers contended that the companies formed by Shapira and Monus received millions in payments from Phar-Mor. The federal fraud examiner's report confirms Coopers' allegations. The complexity of the related parties involved with Phar-Mor made detection of improprieties and fraudulent activity difficult. During its investigation, the federal fraud examiner identified 91 related parties.

ALLEGATIONS AGAINST COOPERS

Attorneys representing creditors and investors pointed out that every year from 1987 to 1992, Coopers & Lybrand acted as Phar-Mor's auditor and declared the retailer's books in order. At the same time, Coopers repeatedly expressed concerns in its annual audit reports and letters to management that Phar-Mor was engaged in hard-to-reconcile accounting practices and called for improvements. Coopers identified Phar-Mor as a "high risk" audit client and Coopers documented that Phar-Mor appeared to be systematically exaggerating its accounts receivables and inventory, its primary assets. Phar-Mor's bankruptcy examiner would later note that the retailer said its inventory jumped from $11 million in 1989 to $36 million in 1990 to a whopping $153 million in 1991.

Creditors suggested that the audit partner's judgment was clouded by his desire to sell additional services to Phar-Mor and other related parties. Such "cross-selling" was common, and it was not against professional standards; however, the creditors claimed Coopers put extraordinary pressure on its auditors to get more business.[3] The audit partner was said to be hungry for new business because he had been passed over for additional profit sharing for failing to sell enough of the firm's services. The following year, the audit partner began acquiring clients connected to Mickey Monus and eventually sold over $900,000 worth of services to 23 persons who were either Monus' relatives or friends.

INVESTORS AND CREDITORS—WHAT COURSE OF ACTION TO TAKE?

After the fraud was uncovered, investors and creditors sued Phar-Mor and individual executives. These lawsuits were settled for undisclosed terms. Although many of the investors were large corporations like Sears and Westinghouse, representatives from these companies were quick to point out that their stockholders, many of whom were pension funds and individual investors, were the ultimate losers. These investors claimed they were willing to accept the business risk associated with Phar-Mor; however, they did not feel they should have had to bear the information risk associated with fraudulent financial statements. One course of action was to sue Phar-Mor's external auditors,

---

3   Subsequent to Coopers & Lybrand's audits of Phar-Mor, cross selling of certain services (e.g., information systems implementation, aggressive tax strategies) was prohibited for public company auditors by the Sarbanes-Oxley Act of 2002 and related rulings of the PCAOB, SEC and AICPA.

Coopers & Lybrand. However, although the investors and creditors were provided with copies of the audited financial statements, they did not have a written agreement with the auditor outlining the auditor's duty of care. As is common with many audits, the only written contract was between Coopers and Phar-Mor.

Thirty-eight investors and creditors filed suit against Coopers, under Section 10(b) of the Federal Securities Exchange Act of 1934 and under Pennsylvania common law. All but eight plaintiffs settled their claims with Coopers without going to trial. However, the remaining plaintiffs chose to take their cases to a jury trial.

COURTROOM STRATEGIES

The Defense

Attorneys for Coopers continually impressed upon the jury that this was a massive fraud perpetrated by Phar-Mor's management. They clearly illustrated the fraud was a collusive effort by multiple individuals within the upper management at Phar-Mor who continually worked to hide evidence from the auditors. The auditors were portrayed as victims of a fraud team at Phar-Mor that would do, and did, whatever it took to cover up the fraud. After the verdict the defense attorney said:

> The jury [rightly] saw that a corporate fraud had been committed, but it mistakenly blamed the outside auditor for not uncovering something no one but the perpetrators could have known about... It's a first...that effectively turns outside auditors into insurers against crooked management. (Robert J. Sisk, chairman of New York's Hughes Hubbard & Reed)

The Plaintiffs

The plaintiffs opened their case by acknowledging the incidence of fraud does not, by itself, prove there was an audit failure. Moreover, they did not allege that Coopers knowingly participated in the Phar-Mor fraud; nor did they allege Coopers was liable because it did not find the fraud. Rather, plaintiffs alleged Coopers made misrepresentations in its audit opinions. The following quotes from plaintiff attorneys' statements to the jury illustrate the plaintiffs' strategy:

> ... [W]e're not going to try to prove in this case what happened at Coopers & Lybrand. That's not our burden. We don't know what happened. We do know that we invested in Phar-Mor on the basis of the financials of Phar-Mor, with the clean opinions of Coopers & Lybrand. We've now lost our investment, and it's a very simple case. We just want our money back...[I]f Coopers can demonstrate to you that they performed a GAAS audit in the relevant time periods, then you should find for them. But if you find based upon the testimony of our experts and our witnesses that Coopers never, ever conducted a GAAS audit...then I submit you should ultimately find for the [plaintiffs]. (Ed Klett, attorney for Westinghouse)

> So the question, ladies and gentlemen, is not whether Coopers could have discovered the fraud. The question is whether Coopers falsely and misleadingly stated that it conducted a GAAS audit and falsely and misleadingly told [plaintiffs] that Phar-Mor's worthless financial statements were fairly presented. And the answer to that question is yes. (Sarah Wolff, attorney for Sears)

Throughout the five-month trial, the plaintiffs continually emphasized the following facts in an effort to have the jury believe the auditors were motivated to overlook any problems that might have been apparent to a diligent auditor:

- The fraud went on for a period of six years, and, therefore, should have become apparent to a diligent auditor.
- Coopers was aware that Phar-Mor's internal accountants never provided the auditors with requested documents or data without first carefully reviewing them.
- Greg Finnerty, the Coopers partner in-charge of the Phar-Mor audit, had previously been criticized for exceeding audit budgets and, therefore, was under pressure to carefully control audit costs.

- Mickey Monus, Phar-Mor's president, was viewed by Finnerty as a constant source of new business.

The areas where the plaintiffs alleged the auditors were reckless and did not perform an audit in accordance with GAAS centered around the accounting for inventory and its corresponding effects on both the balance sheet and the income statement. The plaintiffs' allegations centered on the five major issues detailed below.

EARLY WARNING SIGNS—THE TAMCO SETTLEMENT

The Fact Pattern

In 1988, internal gross profit reports at Phar-Mor indicated serious deterioration in margins. Phar-Mor was facing an unexpected $5 million pretax loss. It was determined, with the assistance of a specialist from Coopers, that the drop in margins was due mainly to inventory shortages from one of Phar-Mor's primary suppliers, Tamco. Tamco, a subsidiary of Giant Eagle, Phar-Mor's principal shareholder, had been shipping partial orders, but billing Phar-Mor for full orders. Unfortunately, Tamco's records were so poor that it could not calculate the amount of the shortage. Likewise, Phar-Mor had no way to determine the exact amount of the shortage because during this time period Phar-Mor was not logging in shipments from Tamco.

A Phar-Mor accountant performed the only formal analysis of the shortage, which he estimated at $4 million. However, negotiations between Phar-Mor and Tamco (along with its parent company Giant Eagle) resulted in a $7 million settlement. Phar-Mor recorded the $7 million as a reduction to purchases, resulting in a pretax profit of approximately $2 million in 1988. Because Tamco and Phar-Mor were both subsidiaries of Giant Eagle, the settlement was disclosed in a related-party footnote to the financial statements.

Trial evidence indicates the final settlement amount was determined, in part, by looking at Phar-Mor's profitability in prior years. After the settlement, Phar-Mor's gross margin was nearly identical to the prior year. After the fraud was uncovered, it was determined there were signals that Phar-Mor's profitability had slipped in 1988.

Plaintiff Allegations

The plaintiffs claimed the settlement was a disguised capital contribution and thus simply a vehicle to artificially inflate Phar-Mor's earnings. The plaintiffs alleged Coopers acted recklessly by not obtaining sufficient persuasive evidence to support this highly material transaction. The following excerpts are from testimony given (in a deposition) by Pat Finn, former CFO of Phar-Mor, and Charles Drott, an expert witness for the plaintiffs:

> There was really no way to support the amount of the settlement. We did a number of tests, but based on our in-house review, we didn't think that we could support $7 million. Mickey [Monus] did an excellent job of negotiating with David [Shapira] and he got us $7 million. (Pat Finn, former CFO of Phar-Mor)

> What Mr. Finn is basically describing is that, although there may well have been some shortages, that what Phar-Mor was really doing was entering into a transaction, which would enable them to manipulate its profit to overcome losses, to hide losses. So, essentially what he's describing is fraudulent financial reporting...[T]he Coopers & Lybrand workpapers contain no independent verification, nor was there any attempt by Coopers & Lybrand to determine the actual amount of the shortages. It simply just was not done. (Charles Drott, expert witness for the plaintiffs)

Plaintiffs also alleged the footnote documenting the receipt and the accounting treatment of the settlement was misleading. Although the footnote disclosed the nature and amount of the related-party transaction, the plaintiffs argued the footnote should have more clearly indicated the uncertainty in the settlement estimate. And plaintiffs felt the footnote should have explicitly stated that without the settlement, Phar-Mor would have shown a loss.

Defense Response

A copy of the analysis conducted by the Phar-Mor accountant indicating a $4 million shortage was included in Coopers' workpapers. However, Coopers considered the analysis very crude and included it only as support for the existence of a shortage, not the dollar amount. Although the workpapers contained relatively little documentation specifically supporting a $7 million settlement, Coopers, who audited all three companies party to the negotiation, did perform a number of procedures to satisfy themselves of the propriety of the settlement. After the internal investigation pointed to Tamco, Phar-Mor began to maintain a log of Tamco shipments. Coopers tracked the results of the log and in every subsequent Tamco shipment shortages were found. Coopers also contacted another company that had received Tamco shipments during this time period and learned that retailer was also experiencing shortages from Tamco.

Coopers' experts examined Tamco's operations and confirmed the shortages were due to a new computer inventory system at Tamco. Greg Finnerty, Coopers' partner in charge of the audit, explained the auditors' position as follows:

> ...[I]t's a related-party transaction, and we don't have the responsibility to validate the amount. The responsibilities in accordance with GAAS standards are twofold. One, in any related-party transaction, is to understand the business purpose of the transaction; and two, to agree to the disclosure of the transaction...[W]e understood the business transaction, and the disclosure was adequate. It talked about the $7 million transaction; and we saw a check, not just an intercompany account. We did a lot of those transactions, so we fulfilled our two responsibilities that are the standards for related-party transactions. I was not in that settlement session, nor should I have been. That was between the two related parties. When the discussions were over with, I talked to both parties separately, myself, and talked to them about the settlement, the reasonableness of that settlement. I, in fact, asked David Shapira—and I specifically recall asking David Shapira—of the $7 million, is that all merchandise or is there any sense that you are—you or the board of directors of Giant Eagle—passing additional capital into Phar-Mor through this transaction? And I was given absolute assurance that he was satisfied that the $7 million was a reasonable number; and, in fact, he indicated that this was a number much lower than what Phar-Mor thought it should have been. So it seemed to me that there was a reasonable negotiation that went on between these parties. (Greg Finnerty, engagement partner for the Phar-Mor audit)

Regarding the footnote disclosure, Coopers pointed out the footnote was typical of related-party footnotes, and that it was rather obvious that without the $7 million settlement, Phar-Mor would have reported a loss. Evidence also showed that, prior to the release of the financial statements, Phar-Mor met with investors and creditors to cover the terms and significance of the settlement. Finally, to this day, none of the parties involved—not Tamco, Phar-Mor, or Giant Eagle—have suggested the settlement was part of the fraud. Further testimony in the trial suggested the Tamco settlement was not an issue of concern with investors and creditors until their attorneys made it an issue years later in the litigation.

THE PRICE TEST

The Fact Pattern

Inventory at Phar-Mor increased rapidly from $11 million in 1989 to $36 million in 1990 to $153 million in 1991. Phar-Mor's inventory system did not include a perpetual inventory record. Therefore, Phar-Mor used the retail method for valuing inventory. Phar-Mor contracted with an outside firm to physically count and provide the retail price of each item in inventory twice per year. Phar-Mor would then apply a cost complement to determine the cost of inventory. Phar-Mor's initial strategy was to mark all merchandise up 20%, resulting in a gross margin of 16.7% and a cost complement of 83.3%. However, to be competitive, Phar-Mor lowered the margins on certain "price sensitive" items to get customers in the door. As a result, Phar-Mor's overall budgeted gross margin fell to 15.5%, resulting in a cost complement of 84.5%.

Coopers identified inventory valuation as a high-risk area in its workpapers. As a detailed test of Phar-Mor's inventory costing, Coopers annually attended the physical inventory count at four stores and selected from 25 to 30 items per store to perform price testing. Sample items were selected by the attending auditor in a haphazard fashion. Purchase invoices were examined for the items selected and an overall gross margin for the sample was determined. In the years 1988 through 1991, Coopers' sample gross margins averaged from 16.1% to 17.7%. Coopers explained the difference between the expected 15.5% gross margin and the sample gross margin resulted because the sample taken did not include many price sensitive items, and, therefore, the sample gross margin was higher than Phar-Mor's overall margin. Coopers concluded the difference noted was reasonable and consistent with expectations.

After the fraud was uncovered, it was determined that Phar-Mor's actual margins were really much lower than the budgeted 15.5%, because the price sensitive items made up a relatively large percentage of sales. When Phar-Mor's management saw the fiscal 1989 gross profit reports were coming in below historical levels, it started changing the gross margin reports because it feared Giant Eagle would want back some of the $7 million paid in Tamco settlement money. Management continued to alter the gross profit reports from that time until the fraud was uncovered.

Plaintiff Allegations

The plaintiffs argued that had the Coopers auditors employed a more extensive and representative price test, they would have known what Phar-Mor's gross margins actually were, no matter what the fraud team was doing to the gross profit reports. Plaintiffs alleged the way the auditors conducted their price test and the way they interpreted the results, were both woefully inadequate and unreliable due to the sample size and acknowledged lack of representativeness.

> ...[T]he attitudes of the people involved in this were simply that even though there was clear recognition in the workpapers that this test was so flawed that it was virtually worthless, did not produce anything to them that they could use in their audit, yet they still concluded year after year that everything was reasonable, and that's—that defies my imagination. I don't understand how that conclusion can come from their own recognition of that, the test was so severely flawed. Also, they gave consideration to doing a better price test, but in fact never made any attempt to do so because in each of the four years they did the same exact kind of test, year after year after year, even though they knew the test produced unreliable results. (Charles Drott, expert witness for the plaintiffs)

The plaintiffs also pointed to Coopers' workpapers where the auditors had indicated that even a one-half percent misstatement in gross margin would result in a material misstatement. Plaintiffs argued the auditors recklessly ignored the sample results indicating a material misstatement.

The plaintiffs also argued the gross profit schedules could not be used to independently test the cost complement because the calculated profit margin and ending inventory were a function of the standard cost complement that was applied to the retail inventory balance derived from the physical inventory.

> So, what we have here is a daisy chain...the price test is the basis for the gross margin test. The price test is reasonable because the gross margins are reasonable. But, the only reason the gross margins are reasonable is because they are based on the price test. It keeps ping-ponging back and forth. And the problem is, none of this was tested. And when it was tested...the price tests [and] the cost complement did not meet Coopers' expectations. It was not what it was supposed to be. (Sarah Wolff, attorney for Sears)

Defense Response

Coopers explained to the jury that the price test was simply a reasonableness test intended to provide limited assurance that Phar-Mor was properly applying its methodology for pricing and costing inventory.

...[I]n the context of all our inventory testing and testing the gross profit, which is a continuous testing of the pricing philosophy, we felt it was adequate testing for our purposes...[T]he price test is just one element of what we did to confirm our understanding and the representation of management as to their pricing philosophy. The primary test of all that is the continuation of taking the physical inventories that they did throughout the year, reconciling that through the compilation and determining the gross profit. If [Phar-Mor is] receiving the gross profit that [they] expected, that is the truest indication and the most valid indication that the pricing philosophy is, in fact, working. It was a valid test, it still is a valid test after reviewing it time and time again. And the staff person suggesting we drop it was just not...right. And throughout the whole time that we audited Phar-Mor, we continued to do the price test. It was a valid test, and it still is. (Greg Finnerty, engagement partner for the Phar-Mor audit)

Further, Coopers pointed out that differences are expected in reasonableness tests and those differences do not represent actual misstatements. It was obvious to Coopers that while Phar-Mor's costing method was applying one standard cost factor, Phar-Mor was applying a variety of pricing strategies. Coopers' price tests on the individual items selected resulted in a wide range of gross margins from items sold below cost to margins of 30% or higher.

Coopers also pointed out that the auditors performed a number of other procedures that compensated for the weaknesses in the price tests. The primary testing was performed on Phar-Mor's gross profit reports. For a sample of gross profit schedules, Coopers recalculated percentages and traced inventory balances back to the physical inventory report submitted by the independent count firm. This was an important procedure for Coopers because, if the margins were consistent, this indicated that the controls over purchases and sales were operating properly. In addition to these procedures, the control environment over purchases and inventory was documented, and certain controls were tested. Individual store and overall company inventory levels and gross margins were compared to prior years. Analytics, such as inventory turnover and days in inventory, were also examined.

INVENTORY COMPILATIONS

The Fact Pattern

After the outside inventory service submitted a report of its physical count, Phar-Mor accountants would prepare an inventory compilation packet. The package included the physical counts, retail pricing, Phar-Mor's calculations of inventory at cost, and cost of goods sold. Based on the compilation, a series of journal entries were prepared and recorded in the operating general ledger to adjust inventory per books to the physical count. Each year, the auditors randomly selected 1 compilation packet for extensive testing and 14 other packets for limited testing. The auditors reviewed journal entries for reasonableness for all 15 packets.

The postfraud examination determined that many of Phar-Mor's inventory compilations packets contained fraudulent journal entries. The entries were often large, in even dollar amounts, did not have journal entry numbers, had no explanation or supporting documentation, and contained suspicious account names like "Accounts Receivable Inventory Contra" or "Cookies." Phar-Mor's fraud team used these entries to inflate inventory and earnings. Based on the physical count and results of the compilation, an appropriate entry was made to reduce (credit) inventory. However, rather than record the offsetting debit to cost of goods sold, a debit entry was recorded to a "bucket" account. The bucket accounts accumulated the fraudulent entries during the year. At year-end, to avoid auditor detection, the bucket accounts were emptied by allocating a portion back to the individual stores as inventory or some other asset.

Plaintiff Allegations

The plaintiffs alleged that some of the compilations reviewed by the auditors contained fraudulent entries. Plaintiffs' experts claimed Coopers should have noticed these unusual entries.

Coopers' audit work in this inventory compilation area, because of its failure to investigate all of these fraudulent entries which were obvious, suspicious entries on their face, their failure to do this is a failure, in my opinion, that is reckless professional conduct, meaning that it is an extreme departure from the standard of care. They had the entries in front of them, and they chose to do nothing whatsoever to investigate. Had they done so, they would have found the fraud right then and there. (Charles Drott, expert witness for the plaintiffs)

Defense Response

Coopers was able to prove with its workpapers that none of the compilations selected by the auditors for extensive review over the years contained fraudulent entries. Although Coopers did retain an entire copy of the extensively tested compilation packet in its workpapers, it noted only key information from the packets on which it performed limited testing.

In preparation for the trial, the packets that had been subjected to only limited testing were pulled from Phar-Mor's files, many of them containing fraudulent journal entries. However, there was evidence suggesting these compilations may have been altered after Coopers reviewed them. For instance, in many cases even the key information Coopers had noted in its workpapers no longer agreed to the file copies. Mark Kirsten, a Coopers audit manager who was the staff and senior auditor on the Phar-Mor engagement, testified why he believes the compilations retrieved from Phar-Mor's files were altered after Coopers performed its audit work:

I never saw this entry or any other fraudulent entries. When we got these packages, we got them from John Anderson who was part of this fraud. And I refuse to agree that John Anderson walked into my audit room, and we are poring over these for a couple days at a time, and says, here, if you happen to turn to the third page, you are going to find a fraudulent entry that has no support. That's unimaginable...we know there is a fraud. That's why we are here. I know I did my job. My job was to review the packages. These packages went through extensive reviews. So, I am saying when you show me a package that has on one page something that...is fraud, I can't imagine that I saw that. We didn't see these packages for ten seconds during the audit. We spent days with these. I am a staff accountant who is doing my job, and I am poring through these and asking questions. We don't audit in a box. (Mark Kirsten, engagement senior for the Phar-Mor audit)

GENERAL LEDGER

The Fact Pattern

A monthly operating general ledger (GL) was prepared and printed for each store and for corporate headquarters. The plaintiffs argued that not only could the fraud have been uncovered by examining the journal entries proposed on the inventory compilations, but also by scanning the GL. Post-fraud reviews of the GLs revealed the fraudulent entries from the compilation reports were posted directly to the GLs. The GLs contained other fraudulent entries as well. Because the fraud team was aware that zero balance accounts typically draw little attention from the auditor, they recorded numerous "blow-out" entries in the last monthly corporate GL to empty the bucket accounts that had fraudulently accumulated during the year. The bucket accounts were emptied by allocating a portion, usually in equal dollar amounts, back to the stores as inventory or other assets. These entries were typically very large. For example, in 1991, there was an entry labeled "Accrued Inventory" for $9,999,999.99. Also, in 1991, there was an entry labeled "Alloc Inv" (Allocate Inventory) for $139 million.

Plaintiff Allegations

The plaintiffs pointed out that scanning the GL, which was a recognized procedure in Coopers' audit manual and training materials, would certainly and easily have uncovered the fraud. Further, plaintiffs pointed to Coopers' inventory audit program for Phar-Mor that included procedures requiring the examination of large and unusual entries. The following comments from plaintiff attorney, Sarah Wolff, to the jury illustrate the plaintiffs' allegations.

I want to talk about the issue of general ledger...All we ask you to do in this issue is, don't listen to what the lawyers have told you...what we ask you to do is look at Coopers' own words. Look at Coopers' training materials. The auditor must also review for large or unusual nonstandard adjustments to inventory accounts. Read Coopers & Lybrand's own audit program for this particular engagement that has steps nine and steps eleven that say look for fourth quarter large and unusual adjustments. Those are their words, ladies and gentlemen. That's their audit program, and you have seen witness after witness run from those words. (Sarah Wolff, attorney for Sears)

Although a witness for the plaintiffs agreed it would not have been practical to carefully scan all the operating GLs, (which would have been a pile of computer paper 300 hundred feet tall), they felt it was reckless, and a failure to comply with GAAS, to not carefully scan at least the last month of the corporate office GL.

The plaintiffs repeatedly played a video clip of one of the chief perpetrators of the Phar-Mor fraud, the former CFO, saying that if Coopers had asked for the backup to any one of the fraudulent journal entries, *"It [the fraud] would have been all over."*

Defense Response

Coopers' audit program did have a step to obtain selected nonstandard adjusting journal entries so that any large and unusual items could be further examined. The step was signed-off by staff auditors without further explanation. Coopers witnesses testified that the fact that the step was signed-off indicated that either the step was performed or was considered not necessary. Trial testimony indicated Coopers auditors asked Phar-Mor accountants if there were any large and unusual adjusting entries and the auditors were told there were none. Coopers pointed out it is normal for the client to provide the auditor with an audit packet including lead schedules that agree to the GL and tie to the financial statements. None of the lead schedules contained fraudulent or "bucket" accounts. When it was suggested by plaintiff attorneys that if the auditors had reviewed the operating general ledgers, there would have been a high probability that they would have discovered the fraud, the partner responded:

No. I would say that it wouldn't be a high probability of that because we are doing a GAAS audit. A GAAS audit requires us to do the procedures that we did. There is no requirement in GAAS—none of my partners or I have ever followed a procedure that says you review operating general ledgers line by line, or whatever, unless you are doing a fraud audit. In the course of doing our GAAS audit, we would look to the general ledgers to the extent necessary in order to do our work on the account balances. We don't audit all the various ways that the balances are arrived at....We don't look at day-to-day activity. This is not what we do as accountants, not only at Phar-Mor, but in every audit we do. We look at the ending balances and audit the ending balances. (Greg Finnerty, engagement partner for the Phar-Mor audit)

Although Coopers was aware of the operating GLs, it worked primarily with the consolidated GL, which combined all the operating GLs and included only ending balances and not transaction details. In the consolidated GL, the "bucket" or fraud accounts were either completely absent or had zero balances. To counter the plaintiffs' video clip of the CFO saying the auditors never asked for backup to the blowout entries, the defense played its own video clip of this same CFO (who was a former Big Six auditor), testifying he and his fraud team went to great lengths to prepare for the audit. On this same video clip, the former CFO also testified that if Coopers had asked for the closing journal entry binder, he would have removed the journal entries that emptied the fraud bucket before giving it to the auditors. Members of the fraud team also testified that had Coopers changed its approach to more carefully scrutinize the operating GLs, they would have changed their approach to cover up the fraud.

ROLL FORWARD

The Fact Pattern

Because the physical inventories were completed during the fiscal year, it was necessary to roll forward or account for the inventory purchase and sales transactions between the inventory count date and the balance sheet date. Coopers' roll-forward examinations always revealed there was a large increase in the ending book inventory balance. Phar-Mor explained to the auditors that the "spike" was due to two factors. First, inventory levels at the physical count date were always lower than normal because a store would reduce inventory shipments in the weeks prior to the physical inventory to prepare for the physical count. Second, since the fiscal year-end was June 30, there was always a buildup of inventory to handle the big July 4th holiday demand. The drop-off in inventory just after year-end was attributed mainly to the large amounts of inventory sold over July 4th. Although the client's explanation did account for a portion of the spike, investigations performed subsequent to the discovery of the fraud indicate that a large portion of the spike was due to the fraud.

Plaintiff Allegations

Plaintiffs claimed the spike was a big red flag that Coopers recklessly overlooked.

> And what this is simply showing is that the increase is a sharp spike upward at fiscal year-end. Interestingly, also, is that subsequent to the fiscal year, just a short time thereafter—the inventory levels drop off. Now, that is a very interesting red flag as to why would that be. If I were an auditor, I'd certainly want to know why the inventories increase sharply, reaching its crest right at the fiscal year-end date. In other words, when the financial statements were prepared, and why they drop off again after fiscal year-end, just two weeks later, as a matter of fact, and go down that much. It's what I call the spike. Clearly the spike, in my opinion, was caused in large part by the actual fraud at Phar-Mor, because if you recall, these fraudulent entries, these blow-out entries that I described, were these very large journal entries that were adding false inventory to each of the stores, and it was done at fiscal year-end; so if you're adding—and we're talking like entries as high as $139 million of false inventory being added in one journal entry to these stores. When you have that, being false inventory, added to the stores at fiscal year-end, that's obviously going to spike up the books at year-end. And then subsequent to year-end, many of these entries are what we call reversed or taken out of the stores, which would cause some of that spike, if not all of it, to come down. (Charles Drott, expert witness for the plaintiffs)

The plaintiffs also argued that auditing texts and an AICPA practice guide describe tests of controls and tests of detail that must be performed for the interim period. In addition, plaintiffs pointed to a procedure described as scrutinizing the books of original entry to identify unusual transactions during the roll-forward period.

Defense Response

When asked if the spike would cause an experienced retail auditor to have suspicions about inventory at Phar-Mor, the audit partner responded:

> Well, no, it wouldn't. But, let me give you an example. At Christmastime, it's the same concept. There is a tremendous spike in inventory of retailers at Christmastime, and then after that, after Christmas, sales go down. That is, you are going to see a natural decline in the inventory levels of a retailer after Christmas. So, it so happens in this analysis, this has to do with the year-end of Phar-Mor, June 30. (Greg Finnerty, engagement partner for the Phar-Mor audit)

Given that this sort of spike was not unusual, Coopers expected the inventory roll forward comparisons to result in differences. Coopers explained the difference noted in its reasonableness test comparing year-end inventory and the previous physical inventory was within expectations and differences in reasonableness tests do not represent known, actual misstatements.

Coopers elected not to test specific purchases or sales transactions during the roll-forward period. Rather, it relied on its tests of the gross profit schedules both before and after year-end, which suggested that controls over purchases and sales were functioning properly. Coopers contended that if any large or unusual journal entries were recorded after the last physical inventory and before year-end, they should affect the gross profit of the general ledger, which was one of the comparisons made on the gross profit reports. Unfortunately, the fraud team was falsifying the gross profit reports.

VERDICT

On February 14, 1996, a federal jury found Coopers & Lybrand, LLP guilty of fraud under both state and federal law. Even though neither Phar-Mor's management, the plaintiffs' attorneys, or anyone else associated with the case ever alleged the auditors knowingly participated in the Phar-Mor fraud, Coopers was liable under a fraud claim. The crux of this fraud charge was the plaintiffs' allegation that Coopers made representations recklessly without regard to whether they were true or false, which legally enabled plaintiffs to sue the auditors for fraud. After the verdict, plaintiff attorney Sarah Wolff indicated this case could prove to be the model for getting a jury to find a respected accounting firm behaved recklessly. Ultimately, Coopers settled the claims for an undisclosed amount.

POSTFRAUD PHAR-MOR

Discovery of the fraud resulted in immediate layoffs of over 16,000 people and the closure of 200 stores. In September of 1995, after over three years of turmoil, Phar-Mor emerged from Chapter 11 bankruptcy. Phar-Mor's CEO at that time, Robert Half, was optimistic about the company's future: "You can make money in this business. It's our job to prove it."[4]

In September 2001, Phar-Mor operated 139 stores in 24 states under the names of Phar-Mor, Rx Place, and Pharmhouse. However, on September 24, 2001, Phar-Mor and certain of its affiliates filed voluntary petitions under Chapter 11 of the United States Bankruptcy Code to restructure their operations in an effort to return to profitability. Management determined that the reorganization was necessary to address operational and liquidity difficulties resulting from factors such as the slowing economy, increased competition from larger retail chains, the reduction of credit terms by vendors and the service of high-cost debt. Phar-Mor was not able to recover from these problems and liquidated the last of its assets in 2002.

In 1998, Mickey Monus was back in court to hear another jury's decision. Monus was charged with obstruction of justice related to a jury tampering charge from his first trial. One of Monus' friends did plead guilty to offering a $50,000 bribe to a juror. Monus was sentenced to 19 ½ years in federal prison for his involvement in the corporate fraud, he denied any knowledge of the bribery and cried when a U.S. District Court jury acquitted him on the jury tampering charges. His sentence was later reduced when Mickey and wife Mary Ciferno cooperated with the FBI in a case against another Youngstown fraudster. Mickey and Mary were married at the Elkton, Ohio prison camp in 1998. Mary served as a paralegal on Mickey's defense team.[5]

---

4   "Our Destiny is in Our Hands," *Drug Store News*, October 9, 1995, p. 3.
5   Bill Moushey, "No Deal for Monus, Bad Deal for Fraud Victims," *The Pittsburgh Post-Gazette*, September 17, 2000, and Gene Wojciechowski, "Rockies born of Monus' work, but he never saw his baby grow up", *ESPN.com*, October 23, 2007.

REQUIRED

[1] Some of the members of Phar-Mor's financial management team were former auditors for Coopers & Lybrand. (a) Why would a company want to hire a member of its external audit team? (b) If the client has hired former auditors, would this affect the independence of the existing external auditors? (c) How did the Sarbanes-Oxley Act of 2002 and related rulings by the PCAOB, SEC or AICPA affect a public company's ability to hire members of its external audit team? (d) Is it appropriate for auditors to trust executives of a client?

[2] (a) What factors in the auditor-client relationship can put the client in a more powerful position than the auditor? (b) What measures has and/or can the profession take to reduce the potential consequences of this power imbalance?

[3] (a) Assuming you were an equity investor, would you pursue legal action against the auditor? Assuming the answer is yes, under what law(s) would you bring suit and what would be the basis of your claim? (b) Define negligence as it is used in legal cases involving independent auditors. (c) What is the primary difference between negligence and fraud; between fraud and recklessness?

[4] Coopers & Lybrand was sued under both federal statutory and state common law. The judge ruled that under Pennsylvania law the plaintiffs were not primary beneficiaries. Pennsylvania follows the legal precedent inherent in the Ultramares Case. (a) In jurisdictions following the Ultramares doctrine, under what conditions can auditors be held liable under common law to third parties who are not primary beneficiaries? (b) How do jurisdictions that follow the legal precedent inherent in the Rusch Factors case differ from jurisdictions following Ultramares?

[5] Coopers was also sued under the Securities Exchange Act of 1934. The burden of proof is not the same under the Securities Acts of 1933 and 1934. Identify the important differences and discuss the primary objective behind the differences in the laws (1933 and 1934) as they relate to auditor liability?

[6] The popular press has indicated that inventory fraud is one of the biggest reasons for the proliferation of accounting scandals. (a) Name two other high profile cases where a company has committed fraud by misstating inventory. (b) What makes the intentional misstatement of inventory difficult to detect? How was Phar-Mor successful in fooling Coopers & Lybrand for several years with overstated inventory? (c) To help prevent or detect the overstatement of inventory, what are some audit procedures that could be effectively employed?

[7] (a) The auditors considered Phar-Mor to be an inherently "high risk" client. List several factors at Phar-Mor that would have contributed to a high inherent risk assessment. (b) Should auditors have equal responsibility to detect material misstatements due to errors and fraud? (c) Which conditions, attitudes, and motivations at Phar-Mor created an environment conducive for fraud could have been identified as red flags by the external auditors?

Satyam Computer Services Limited
Controlling the Confirmation Process

MARK S. BEASLEY · FRANK A. BUCKLESS · STEVEN M. GLOVER · DOUGLAS F. PRAWITT

LEARNING OBJECTIVES

After completing and discussing this case you should be able to

[1] Understand common procedures used to audit cash, including proper confirmation procedures.

[2] Identify audit documentation requirements, especially once an audit is complete.

[3] Recognize consequences that can be imposed on an audit firm subsequent to a PCAOB enforcement action.

[4] Understand the SEC's oversight authority for companies that trade shares on U.S. stock exchanges as American Depositary Shares (ADS).

[5] Recognize how membership in a network of firms might impact a member accounting firm.

INTRODUCTION[1]

"It was like riding a tiger, not knowing how to get off without being eaten," according to Satyam Computer Services Limited (Satyam) former Chairman, B. Ramalinga Raju, soon after massive fraud involving the company's financial statements was revealed. For over five years, Raju was at the top of a massive fraud scheme orchestrated by senior executives at the Hyderabad, India information technology services company that falsely inflated its cash and cash-related balances by over $1 billion. In an amazing fraud scheme that went undetected by the company's external auditors, senior executives directed the creation of over 6,000 false invoices and manufactured numerous false bank statements to create over $1 billion in fictitious cash balances and other interest bearing deposits.

Just before the fraud was revealed in January 2009, Satyam's shares traded on the New York Stock Exchange (NYSE) at a price of $9.35. When trading resumed the next day, those shares dropped nearly 85 percent to close at $1.46. Institutional investors who owned those shares realized losses of over $450 million.

The audit of cash is often viewed as a fairly simple and straightforward set of procedures. Frequently, responsibility for verification of cash balances is assigned to newer, experienced members of the audit engagement team because of the relative low risk nature of cash related assertions and the objective versus subjective types of audit evidence typically examined. So, when the fraud was revealed, many were left wondering how such a massive fraud involving overstatement of cash balances went undetected by auditors for several years.

---

1   The information in this case is based on the SEC Litigation Release No. 21915/Accounting and Auditing Enforcement Release No. 3258, U.S. Securities and Exchange Commission v. Satyam Computer Services Limited d/b/a Mahindra Satyam, Civil Action No. 1:11-CV-00672 (D.D.C.), and PCAOB Release No. 105-2011-002, Order Instituting Disciplinary Proceedings, Making Findings, and Imposing Sanctions, In the Matter of Price Waterhouse, Bangalore, Lovelack & Lewes, Price Waterhouse & Co., Bangalore, Price Waterhouse, Calcutta, and Price Waterhouse & Co., Calcutta (April 5, 2011).

The case was prepared by Mark S. Beasley, Ph.D. and Frank A. Buckless, Ph.D. of North Carolina State University and Steven M. Glover, Ph.D. and Douglas F. Prawitt, Ph.D. of Brigham Young University, as a basis for class discussion. It is not intended to illustrate either effective or ineffective handling of an administrative situation.

SATYAM COMPUTER SERVICES LIMITED

Satyam was a large information technology services company with principal executive offices in Hyderabad, India. At the time of the fraud, the company employed over 50,000 individuals worldwide and maintained offices around the globe, including several in the United States. Company shares traded on the Bombay Stock Exchange, the National Stock Exchange of India, and 65 million of its American Depositary Shares (ADS) traded on the New York Stock Exchange. The ADS shares represented between 11 and 20 percent of the company's total shares outstanding. As an ADS registrant, the company filed its financial statements with the United States Securities and Exchange Commission (SEC).

The main line of business for Satyam was information technology services that it provides to a variety of customers worldwide. The company prepared and submitted invoices for the services performed to its customers and recorded those invoices in its invoice management system. Data from that system was then exported into Satyam's financial accounting system, which management used to prepare the financial statements for its March 31 fiscal year ends.

FALSIFICATION OF REVENUES AND CASH

On January 7, 2009, Satyam submitted a Form 6-K to the SEC that included a letter prepared by then-Satyam Chairman Raju admitting that the company had been engaged in a billion dollar financial fraud involving the overstatement of more than $1 billion in cash and bank balances when the actual amounts were $66 million. The overstatement of cash was tied to a fraud scheme senior management had used to overstate company revenues over the past five fiscal years ending in 2004-2008.

During that period, senior management falsified the company's reported revenues by creating false invoices for services never performed and for customers who never existed. To orchestrate the falsification of invoices, senior management provided certain employees with "super-user" login identification and password access to the invoice management system. The "super-user" login allowed the inclusion of false invoices to overstate revenues while also enabling the concealment of those invoices from lower-level members of management who might recognize the invoices as fake. Employees in on the fraud generated between 100 to 200 fake invoices a month, which ultimately led to the recording of over 6,600 false invoices in the invoice management system and the company's quarter and annual financial statements.

The chart below summarizes the impact of the falsification of the fictitious invoices for five and one-half years ending in 2009:

Fiscal Year	Number of False Invoices	Recorded Revenues	False Revenues
2004	267	$ 566,370,000	$ 46,410,000
2005	451	793,600,000	68,860,000
2006	1,180	1,096,300,000	149,500,000
2007	654	1,461,400,000	151,650,000
2008	2,483	2,138,100,000	430,390,000
2009	1,568	1,289,500,000	275,860,000
Total	**6,603**	**$7,345,270,000**	**$1,122,670,000**

Note: Because the fraud was revealed in the middle of 2009, the amounts reflected above for 2009 only represent misstatements for the first two quarters of the fiscal year.

As can be seen in the table above, the fraud enabled the company to overstate its revenues on a cumulative basis over the five plus years in excess of $1.1 billion, enabling the company to report net profits in periods where net income was actually less than zero. To compensate for their recording of false revenues, management buried the false entries in numerous cash accounts linked to bank accounts at six banks. Senior management concealed the scheme by preparing false bank statements to reflect cash deposits that it did not have in the company's bank accounts. As shown below, cash-related balances reported on the balance sheets at each fiscal year end were massively overstated.

Balance Sheet Date	Reported Cash and Interest	Actual Cash and Interest	Amount of Overstatement
March 31, 2004	$252,022,199	$ 4,369,680	$ 247,652,519
March 31, 2005	417,067,645	260,436	416,807,209
March 31, 2006	432,722,174	26,511,770	406,210,404
March 31, 2007	780,756,619	13,365,348	767,391,271
March 31, 2008	912,660,956	2,210,812	910,450,144
September 30, 2008	784,605,511	2,177,546	782,427,965

In addition to overstating the cash balance, management also overstated its accounts receivable balances.

THE AUDIT OF SATYAM'S FINANCIAL STATEMENTS

Price Waterhouse, Bangalore (PW Bangalore) based in Bangalore, Karnataka, India served as Satyam's independent auditor, signing the audit opinions on the financial statements of Satyam from 2000 through 2009. PW Bangalore was one of five India firms that worked closely together as part of a larger network of accounting firms known as PW India. The other four firms linked with PW Bangalore in the PW India network were: Lovelock & Lewes, Price Waterhouse & Co., Bangalore, Price Waterhouse, Calcutta, and Price Waterhouse & Co., Calcutta.[2] This network of firms shared resources under a common leadership that included the sharing of engagement personnel, office space, and telephone numbers.

While Lovelock & Lewes participated in the audits of Satyam's financial statements for the years ended 2005 through 2008, the remaining three firms in the network did not participate in any of the audits. PW Bangalore was engaged to perform the audits of the financial statements and issued unqualified audit opinions on the Satyam annual financial statements based on audits performed in accordance with PCAOB auditing standards for each of the fiscal years 2005 through 2008.

AUDIT OF CASH AND RECEIVABLES

Because reported cash represented between 50 and 60 percent of total reported assets on the balance sheets during the years 2004 through 2008, the audit engagement team sought to verify the existence and accuracy of the recorded cash balances. As part of the audit team's procedures, the engagement team signed the auditor's confirmation requests and gave the requests to employees of Satyam, who were responsible for sending the confirmation requests to the banks.

Later, Satyam employees returned the alleged completed confirmation responses from the six banks to the audit engagement team. These responses covered approximately 93 percent of Satyam's reported cash for each year end. At the same time, the engagement team separately received confirmation responses directly from other branches of the same banks. Interestingly, the bank-supplied confirmation responses reflected significantly smaller cash balances than Satyam

---

2 Despite having very similar names, each of these four firms are distinct firms. That is, Price Waterhouse, Calcutta, and Price Waterhouse and Co., Calcutta are different firms.

management asserted were held in fixed deposits at the same banks and significantly lower than the amounts reported on the "confirmation responses" provided to the engagement team by Satyam management. For example, in the 2008 audit, Satyam management provided a confirmation response supposedly from the Mumbai branch of a bank that indicated the company held approximately $176 million of fixed deposits with the bank. At the same time, the auditors received directly from the Hyderabad branch of the same bank a confirmation response indicating that Satyam had no fixed assets with the bank. Unfortunately, the engagement team did not perform procedures to reconcile these kinds of differences in responses.

The approach the auditors took in their audit of accounts receivable was similar to the approach the auditors took in the audit of cash. For the 2006 and 2007 audits, the engagement team relied on Satyam management to send confirmation requests for accounts receivable. Despite never receiving any responses to these confirmation requests, the engagement team made no attempt to follow-up on the non-responses with second confirmation requests.

At one point, the auditors did perform alternative procedures by verifying subsequent cash receipts. However, they never ensured that the cash received after year end related to individual invoices outstanding at year end. And, in some cases, the subsequent cash receipts testing was performed as of a date that differed from the fiscal year end date.

These audit responses also failed to take into account deficiencies they noted in Satyam controls. As part of the firm's testing of IT controls in 2007 and 2008 required by Section 404 of the Sarbanes-Oxley Act, the firm noted over 170 deficiencies in internal control, including eight significant deficiencies that indicated a heightened risk related to accounts receivable. Unfortunately, the audit firm failed to adjust its audit plan in response to these findings.

AUDIT DOCUMENTATION

To make matters worse, in November 2007, PW Bangalore and Lovelock & Lewes learned that the 2007 Satyam audit engagement would be inspected by the PCAOB in February 2008. PW Bangalore issued its audit opinion on the March 31, 2007 financial statements on April 27, 2007. Between November 2007 and the arrival of the inspectors in early 2008, members of the audit engagement team created new documents that were added to the audit working papers; however, none of the documents disclosed the dates the documents were added, the persons preparing the documents, or the reasons for adding those documents.

CHARGES AND SANCTIONS

Shortly after the fraud was revealed, the Government of India assumed control of the company and dissolved the existing board of directors, replacing them with new government-nominated directors. In February 2009, the Company Law Board of India authorized the new board of directors to seek a strategic investor for Satyam. By May 2009, an Indian information technology company, Tech Mahindra Limited, a subsidiary of Venturbay Consultants Private Limited, was selected. The new board of directors had installed new senior management team, which included executives from Tech Mahindra Limited, and announced its new brand identity as "Mahindra Satyam" by the end of June 2009. Additionally, Indian authorities filed criminal charges against several former officers.

In April 2011 the SEC announced that it had settled a civil action against the company and that the company had agreed to pay a $10 million penalty. The SEC's enforcement action also noted that Satyam must require specific training of officers and employees concerning securities laws and accounting principles and improve its internal audit function. In addition, the company agreed to hire an independent consultant to evaluate the internal controls at Satyam.

As for the auditors, the PCAOB censured all five audit firms included in the PW India network. The PCAOB also temporarily limited the activities and operations of PW India, including a prohibition from accepting SEC issuer referred engagement work for new clients for a period of six months. In addition, the PCAOB required PW India to engage an independent monitor, adopt and implement certain changes to the network of firm's quality control, and provide additional professional education and training to its personnel. Finally, the PCAOB imposed a civil monetary penalty in the amount of $1.5 million on PW Bangalore and Lovelock & Lowes.

REQUIRED

[1] Research the difference between American Depositary Shares and American Depositary Receipts. Then, visit the SEC's website (www.sec.gov) to locate the final SEC rule Release No. 33-8879 issued on December 21, 2007 and research whether foreign issuers must file with the SEC financial statements in conformity with generally accepted accounting principles (GAAP).

[2] Research PCAOB auditing standards (which can be found on the PCAOB's website – www.pcaob.org) related to the use of confirmations and document the specific requirements related to maintaining control of the confirmation process.

   [a] Based on what you learn, provide an assessment of deficiencies in the confirmation approach Satyam's auditors took related to cash and accounts receivable.

   [b] Do auditing standards require the use of confirmations in the audits of cash balances and accounts receivable balances?

[3] The Satyam auditors attempted to confirm both cash and accounts receivable balances with external parties. Which of the audit assertions for cash and accounts receivable would confirmations be most relevant?

[4] Research PCAOB auditing standards (which can be found on the PCAOB's website – www.pcaob.org) related to the use of audit documentation and identify specific requirements related to deadlines for including audit documentation in the engagement workpapers, such as the documentation completion date. Also, identify requirements related to what must be documented on the workpaper, including the date of preparation of audit documentation and the identification of the preparers of the documentation. Based on your findings, provide your assessment of how PW Bangalore violated these requirements.

[5] Research the AICPA's Code of Professional Conduct (which is available on the AICPA's website – www.aicpa.org) to research what it means to be in a "network" of firms. How might the actions of one of the accounting firms in the network impact other members of the network?

[6] Locate the PCAOB's Settled Disciplinary Order against the auditors of the Satyam financial statements, which can be found on the PCAOB's website under the link for "Enforcement" (see PCAOB Release No. 105-2011-002 dated April 5, 2011), and review the sanctions imposed on the audit firms within the PW India network. You will see that the PCAOB censured all five firms in the PW India network, even though three of those firms did not participate in the audit of Satyam's financial statements. Discuss why the PCAOB charged all five firms rather than only charge PW Bangalore and Lovelock & Lewes?

Internal Control Over Financial Reporting

CASES INCLUDED IN THIS SECTION

Simply Steam, Co.
Evaluation of Internal Control Environment

MARK S. BEASLEY · FRANK A. BUCKLESS · STEVEN M. GLOVER · DOUGLAS F. PRAWITT

LEARNING OBJECTIVES

After completing and discussing this case you should be able to

[1] Evaluate a new audit client's control environment

[2] Appreciate the judgment involved in evaluating the overall internal control environment based on interview data

[3] Provide an initial evaluation of certain components of the client's control environment

[4] Provide support for your internal control assessments

INTRODUCTION

Tina is an audit manager with a national public accounting firm and one of her clients is Simply Steam, Co. Simply Steam provides industrial and domestic carpet steam-cleaning services. This is the first time Simply Steam has been audited. Thus, Tina does not have any prior-year audit files to review. Tina recently conducted a preliminary interview with Doug Dosio, who along with his brother, Phil, owns Simply Steam. Tina's objective for the interview was to establish an understanding of the control environment.

To prepare for her interview, Tina reviewed professional auditing standards. Auditing standards indicate that the control environment sets the tone of an organization, influencing the control consciousness of its people. It is the foundation for all other components of internal control, providing discipline and structure. Control environment factors include the following:

- Integrity and ethical values
- Board of directors
- Management's philosophy and operating style
- Organizational structure

- Financial reporting competencies
- Authority and responsibility
- Human resources

REQUIRED

Using the interview dialogue provided below, you will be evaluating the seven components of the client's control environment in order to make an evaluation of the overall internal control environment. To assist you in making this overall assessment, an evaluation form follows this dialogue that provides detailed descriptions of factors that may weaken or strengthen each of the seven components comprising the overall control environment. Before reading the interview information, please spend a couple of minutes reviewing the assessments you will make.

After reading the dialogue, you will make the overall assessment labeled, "Overall Evaluation of the Control Environment." Unless otherwise notified by your instructor, please rate the effect each of the seven components has on the control environment at Simply Steam. When making your judgments, please circle the appropriate number according to the scales provided.

The case was prepared by Mark S. Beasley, Ph.D. and Frank A. Buckless, Ph.D. of North Carolina State University and Steven M. Glover, Ph.D. and Douglas F. Prawitt, Ph.D. of Brigham Young University, as a basis for class discussion. Simply Steam is a fictitious company. All characters and names represented are fictitious; any similarity to existing companies or persons is purely coincidental.

INTERVIEW WITH CLIENT

[TINA] Doug, can you give me a little information on the background of Simply Steam?

[DOUG] Simply Steam provides both a domestic and industrial carpet steam-cleaning service and sells a relatively small amount of inventory, such as spot removers and carpet fresheners. Our company provides this service throughout three counties, which cover over 40 townships in a densely populated area. Simply Steam is completely owned by Phil and me.

Our business has grown rapidly from one car-pulled trailer to 12 fully equipped vans, worth about $30,000 each, in less than six years. After the second van was purchased, we just figured the idea was to go "full steam ahead" by anticipating the continuing and, quite frankly, totally unexpected surge of business. We like the idea of purchasing a new van each year until we just can't keep them all busy. The company grossed just over $1,650,000 in revenues last year, about half of which was collected in cash. We feel our continuing success is due in large part to "word of mouth."

[TINA] Can you tell me something about the day-to-day operations?

[DOUG] Well, Mr. Day, our office manager, and I are in charge of a small sales force that goes out on leads to give estimates for new jobs. Mr. Day is paid a salary plus a percentage of the total sales each month. My brother, Phil, is usually out in the field managing the 20 employees who work as cleaners for Simply Steam. Phil is the only other person who helps me with managerial and operating decisions, and is in charge if Mr. Day or I are not available.

Salespeople are paid on a commission basis, selling both the domestic and industrial jobs based on standard prices established by the owners. Salespeople may sometimes negotiate special cut rates during the slow spring and fall seasons. However, these are usually subject to approval by Mr. Day or me. Large industrial jobs are typically booked well in advance of the actual work.

The job commitments obtained by the salespeople are normally submitted to Mr. Day, who signs them to indicate his approval and then returns them to the salespeople. Salespeople then forward job commitments to one of the two data input clerks for processing.

The computer processes each commitment by extending the number of jobs by the standard price stored on the pricing file, or in specially negotiated situations, by the price on the input document. The sales, accounts receivable, and commitment files are updated and invoices are produced. An exception report of special prices is produced and sent to the salespeople to ensure that the specially negotiated commitments to jobs were processed correctly.

Mr. Day pieced together this sales system himself, and so far it's working fairly well. He hasn't had a chance to finish a user manual for the system yet. I've also discovered that he sometimes alters the system. He says he does this to make the accounting process more efficient. I've told him to reevaluate the process at least once every couple of months.

[TINA] And how about your accounting department? How big is it, and who oversees the accounting process?

[DOUG] The accounting department of Simply Steam consists of seven part-time clerks, including the two data input clerks, who are all paid an hourly wage. None of our clerks has an accounting degree, but all, except one, are college students majoring in accounting. Mr. Day trains all new accounting help when they are first hired. They're only with us a couple of years and generally leave as soon as they graduate. We keep them pretty busy around here, but despite the heavy workload, everyone helps each other when necessary and somehow the job always seems to get done.

[TINA]   What are your brother Phil's responsibilities?

[DOUG]   Phil takes care of the cleaning end of the business. He usually trains all newly hired cleaning employees and explains what they need to know and how to do the job. When he feels the time is right, the new hire is teamed with a more experienced worker and assigned to a truck unit. When additional help is needed, Phil places ads in the local newspaper. Phil is pretty good at running that part of the business.

[TINA]   What about employee turnover?

[DOUG]   It happens all the time in this business, but Phil deals with it. We try to prevent any concerns or other problems with the help by having an open door policy so that if any of the employees have questions about what they are supposed to be doing they can let us know or ask for help without feeling awkward about it. If something comes up that affects everyone, Phil and I will bring the problem up at the next monthly office meeting to be certain everyone knows about it. Phil and I make sure the problem gets straightened out one way or the other.

Doug leaves to give an estimate and Tina continues her observations of the business.

Later that day, after spending time with the accounting staff, Tina has a moment to ask Mr. Day, the office manager, a few questions.

[TINA]   Mr. Day, I'm wondering if you could help me clarify some things regarding my brief observations of the accounting staff?

[MR. DAY]   Sure, I'd be glad to. What can I do for you?

[TINA]   I got the impression from the staff that they're not always certain about their assigned functions. Are job responsibilities clearly defined?

[MR. DAY]   In assigning office responsibilities, Doug says that one of the main considerations is that the work should be done by the people who are available when it has to be done, assuming they're familiar with a task and capable of doing it. This does lead to an overlap between one person's job and another's. But the actual assigning of daily duties and overview of each day's accounting records are left to me and I don't feel there's any confusion.

[TINA]   The staff mentioned that they've occasionally had problems processing collections of trade receivables. Do you prelist cash receipts before they're recorded?

[MR. DAY]   Well, actually we don't. The way the system is set up, we collect all of the checks at the end of the day and record them all at one time, so we don't need to write them down twice. Besides, we always find a way to resolve any collection processing problems that arise.

[TINA]   Do you ever run into accounting policy problems?

[MR. DAY]   Not very often. I usually handle any accounting policy problems that arise, although Doug will handle the situation if he feels strongly about the issue.

[TINA]   Well, thank you Mr. Day. I need to talk to Doug before he leaves for the day.

A few moments later, in Doug's office . . .

[TINA]   Are you satisfied with the processing of trade receivables?

[DOUG]   You don't need to worry about that. Mr. Day prides himself on being meticulous in clerical operations, being well systematized and having excellent control over the trade receivables. Besides, the receivables are pledged as security for a continually renewable bank loan. The bank has been lending us money for the past year and a half based on a list of pledged receivables we furnish them each week. The loan is relatively small, and the contract allows the bank to access Simply Steam's checking account if collection of the loan seems doubtful.

Phil and I don't know much about accounting and trust Mr. Day completely with all the accounting duties, but Phil and I are the only people allowed to sign company checks.

[TINA]   One of the accounting clerks mentioned that you're thinking about making a change in the accounting system.

[DOUG]   As a matter of fact, Mr. Day has been looking into using a new accounting software package that should make the bookkeeping process an easier task for the clerks. This package will include a budgeting system that Mr. Day believes will help control costs and identify those areas that need attention. Up to now, I've always monitored the company's expenses on an intuitive basis and I just never saw the need for a formal budget. If something didn't seem right, Phil or I would bring the problem up at the informal monthly office meeting between all the employees to resolve the issue. Since our business has been getting bigger, maybe we'll have to give in, spend the money and get some kind of sophisticated budgeting system.

[TINA]   I'm also interested in your security measures. How do you protect your accounting records and physical assets?

[DOUG]   After hours, the office door and windows are heavily bolted. All three of us—Phil, Mr. Day, and I—have keys to open the office. To tell you the truth, none of the file cabinets used to store the hard copies of the accounting records and data disks is locked up at night. We don't have the computers bolted down to the desks, either. It's occurred to us that maybe we should lock everything up, but we've never had any problems.

As for the vans, they're kept in a fenced-in lot behind our office. We give each driver a key to the gate lock so they can let themselves in or out for work. We have to do this because a lot of the commercial cleaning is done after hours, when the office is closed. To avoid any mischief, we change the lock every once in a while.

[TINA]   That should about do it for now, until I can get in to do some preliminary audit investigation. But before I leave, I'd like to ask you a few more general questions. To start with, can you tell me what you feel is responsible for Simply Steam's recent success?

[DOUG]   Well, Tina, because Simply Steam is using the newest steam-cleaning procedure, we provide a much better result than the traditional rotary shampoo methods used by our competitors. And our customers can tell. Plus, Phil and I understand the business well, we are very personable and we pride ourselves on doing good work.

[TINA]   Having an audit performed by our firm is a big step. Why did you decide to have an audit now? Have you ever been audited before?

[DOUG]   Both Phil and I are excited about the success of our company because it will allow us to pursue other business endeavors in the future. We realize that the bigger the company grows and the better it looks, the more outside opportunities we will have. In order to meet this objective, we've asked your firm to not only provide an opinion on our financial statements, but also to make the financial statements take on a professional lookputting us in the best light possible. We feel that audited financial statements will establish Simply Steam as a truly viable concern and lend credibility to the company with the local business and banking community.

We've never been audited before, although we have used a local tax preparer to fill out our tax returns ever since Simply Steam has been in business. Incidentally, we did ask another firm, about two years ago, to come in to do an audit. But the audit never took place. Although I can't remember the audit firm's name, Phil and I just decided that Simply Steam could not afford the fees at that time. Hopefully, we're ready for the audit now.

[TINA]   Are there any issues of concern that you have regarding the audit?

[DOUG]   Not really. I'm proud of Simply Steam. The company, to date, has had no record of fraud and has rarely had a problem with bad debts, since most of our receivable balances are collected within two to three weeks.

[TINA]   I understand that Simply Steam does not have an audit committee, which is typical of an organization this size. Can you tell me if Simply Steam has a board of directors and, if so, who serves on the board and how active the board is in overseeing important issues at Simply Steam?

[DOUG]   We do have a board of directors of sorts. It isn't really all that formal, but Phil, I, and our wives function as directors. We do have at least one regularly scheduled meeting each year, and we have met on other occasions as necessary. Obviously, Phil and I have a pretty good idea of what is happening at Simply Steam on a daily basis. We don't believe it makes sense at this point to try to include any outsiders on the board. Maybe we'll do that in a couple of years, if we keep growing.

[TINA]   One final thing I'd like to ask—have you and your brother Phil set out any goals for the future?

[DOUG]   Well, although we've never actually written down any goals or objectives for Simply Steam, I do agree with Phil that future plans would include covering a larger sales territory, increasing advertising, investing in more help and additional equipment, and taking a well-deserved vacation in Hawaii. We're not certain about our long-term goals, but the possibility of making a fortune and retiring early sounds pretty good.

Simply Steam, Co.
Control Environment Evaluation Form
December 31, 2011

Reference:	CE 1a
Prepared by:	
Date:	
Reviewed by:	

	Greatly Weakens Control		Neither Weakens nor Strengthens			Greatly Strengthens Control	

1. Integrity and Ethical Values   1   2   3   4   5   6   7

In evaluating this component, consider whether:
- there appears to be sufficient integrity on the part of management and employees
- management articulates ethical values to all levels of the organization, processes are in place to monitor adherence to ethical values, and deviations from ethical values are identified and addressed in an appropriate and timely manner

2. Board of Directors   1   2   3   4   5   6   7

In evaluating this component, consider whether:
- a board of directors and audit committee exists and is sufficient in membership to deal with important issues adequately
- directors or audit committee members have sufficient knowledge, industry experience and time to serve effectively
- some directors or audit committee members are independent of management
- frequency and timeliness with which meetings are held with accounting officers and external auditors
- the board oversees and takes action as needed

3. Management's Philosophy and Operating Style   1   2   3   4   5   6   7

In evaluating this component, consider whether:
- business risks are adequately monitored
- management is willing to undertake relatively low levels of business risk
- management places a high priority on internal control
- management explicitly attempts to reduce the risk of misstatements

4. Organizational Structure   1   2   3   4   5   6   7

In evaluating this component, consider whether:
- the organization's lines of authority and responsibility are clearly defined
- operating policies are determined centrally by senior management
- transaction policies and procedures are clearly established and strictly followed
- the organization is adequately structured given its complexity and size
- management is actively involved in the supervision of data processing
- job descriptions and organizational charts are maintained and periodically updated

Simply Steam, Co.
Control Environment Evaluation Form
December 31, 2011

Reference: _CE 1b_
Prepared by: _____
Date: _____
Reviewed by: _____

	Greatly Weakens Control		Neither Weakens nor Strengthens			Greatly Strengthens Control	

5. Financial Reporting Competencies   1   2   3   4   5   6   7

In evaluating this component, consider whether:
- *management has specified the competence level needed for particular skills and translated the desired levels of competence into requisite knowledge and skills*
- *evidence exists indicating that employees appear to have the requisite knowledge and skills*
- *management provides training for employees to review and improve competencies*

6. Authority and Responsibility   1   2   3   4   5   6   7

In evaluating this component, consider whether:
- *appropriate policies for acceptable business practices, conflicts of interest, and codes of conduct have been established and have been communicated to employees*
- *there is a clear assignment of responsibility and delegation of authority for goals and objectives, operating functions, and regulatory requirements*
- *employee job responsibilities and specific duties are clearly established and communicated*
- *computer system documentation clearly indicates the procedures for authorizing transactions and for approving system changes*
- *data processing policies and procedures are adequately documented*

7. Human Resources   1   2   3   4   5   6   7

In evaluating this component, consider whether:
- *employees have the background and experience necessary for their job duties*
- *employees understand the duties and procedures applicable to their jobs*
- *the organization provides for adequate training of new personnel*
- *the workloads of accounting personnel permit them to adequately control the quality of their work*
- *the turnover rate of accounting personnel is low*
- *the turnover rate of non-accounting personnel is low*
- *organization maintains and periodically updates position descriptions as well as policies and procedures*

Simply Steam, Co.
Control Environment Evaluation Form
December 31, 2011

Reference: _CE 1c_
Prepared by: _____
Date: _____
Reviewed by: _____

Overall Evaluation of the Control Environment: Based on all of the evidence gathered in the interview, please circle the number which best represents your assessment of the control environment at Simply Steam:

Very Weak Control Environment	*Weak Control Environment*	*Intermediate Control Environment*	*Strong Control Environment*	*Very Strong Control Environment*

1	2	3	4	5	6	7	8	9	10

Please list a few of the key pieces of information that influenced your decision:

Easy Clean, Co.
Evaluation of Internal Control Environment

MARK S. BEASLEY · FRANK A. BUCKLESS · STEVEN M. GLOVER · DOUGLAS F. PRAWITT

LEARNING OBJECTIVES

After completing and discussing this case you should be able to

[1] Evaluate a new audit client's control environment

[2] Appreciate the judgment involved in evaluating the overall internal control environment based on interview data

[3] Provide an initial evaluation of certain components of the client's control environment

[4] Provide support for your internal control assessments

INTRODUCTION

Ted is an audit manager with a national public accounting firm and one of his clients is Easy Clean, Co. Easy Clean provides industrial and domestic carpet steam-cleaning services. This is the first time Easy Clean has been audited. Thus, Ted does not have any prior-year audit files to review. Ted recently conducted a preliminary interview with Doug Dosio, who along with his brother, Phil, owns Easy Clean. Ted's objective for the interview was to establish an understanding of the control environment.

To prepare for his interview, Ted reviewed professional auditing standards. Auditing standards indicate that the control environment sets the tone of an organization, influencing the control consciousness of its people. It is the foundation for all other components of internal control, providing discipline and structure. Control environment factors include the following:

- Integrity and ethical values
- Board of directors
- Management's philosophy and operating style
- Organizational structure
- Financial reporting competencies
- Authority and responsibility
- Human resources

REQUIRED

Using the interview dialogue provided below, you will be evaluating the seven components of the client's control environment in order to make an evaluation of the overall internal control environment. To assist you in making this overall assessment, an evaluation form follows this dialogue that provides detailed descriptions of factors that may weaken or strengthen each of the seven components comprising the overall control environment. Before reading the interview information, please spend a couple of minutes reviewing the assessments you will make.

After reading the dialogue, you will make the overall assessment labeled, "Overall Evaluation of the Control Environment." Unless otherwise notified by your instructor, please rate the effect each of the seven components has on the control environment at Easy Clean. When making your judgments, please circle the appropriate number according to the scales provided.

The case was prepared by Mark S. Beasley, Ph.D. and Frank A. Buckless, Ph.D. of North Carolina State University and Steven M. Glover, Ph.D. and Douglas F. Prawitt, Ph.D. of Brigham Young University, as a basis for class discussion. Easy Clean is a fictitious company. All characters and names represented are fictitious; any similarity to existing companies or persons is purely coincidental.

INTERVIEW WITH CLIENT

[TED]   Doug, can you give me a little information on the background of Easy Clean?

[DOUG]   Easy Clean provides both a domestic and industrial carpet steam-cleaning service and sells a relatively small amount of inventory, such as spot removers and carpet fresheners. Our company provides this service throughout three counties, which cover over 40 townships in a densely populated area. Easy Clean is completely owned by Phil and me.

Our business has grown steadily over the course of several years after starting out with just one car-pulled trailer over five years ago. Over the years, the business has gradually added 12 fully equipped vans, worth about $30,000 each. Now in our sixth year of business, we plan to purchase approximately one new van each year to meet the growing demand for our services. The company grossed just over $1,650,000 in revenues last year, about half of which was collected in cash. We feel our continuing success is due in large part to "word of mouth."

[TED]   Can you tell me something about the day-to-day operations?

[DOUG]   Well, Mr. Day, our office manager, and I are in charge of a small sales force that goes out on leads to give estimates for new jobs. Mr. Day is paid a salary plus a percentage of the total sales each month. My brother, Phil, is usually out in the field managing the 20 employees who work as cleaners for Easy Clean. Phil also helps with managerial and operating decisions.

Salespeople are paid on a commission basis, selling both the domestic and industrial jobs based on standard prices established by the owners. Salespeople may sometimes negotiate special cut rates during the slower spring and fall seasons. Of course, these are almost always subject to approval by Mr. Day or me. Large industrial jobs are typically booked well in advance of the actual work.

The job commitments obtained by the salespeople are normally submitted to Mr. Day, who signs them to indicate his approval and then returns them to the salespeople. Sales people then forward job commitments to one of the two data input clerks for processing.

The computer processes each commitment by extending the number of jobs by the standard price stored on the pricing file, or in specially negotiated situations, by the price on the input document. The sales, accounts receivable, and commitment files are updated and invoices are produced. An exception report of special prices is produced and sent to the salespeople to ensure that the specially negotiated commitments to jobs were processed correctly.

Mr. Day developed this sales system himself and it's working rather well. He's currently in the process of creating the user manual for the system. I've also noticed that he sometimes makes adjustments to improve the system, which makes the accounting process more efficient. We've agreed that he'll reevaluate the process at least once every eight weeks.

[TED]   And how about your accounting department? How big is it, and who oversees the accounting process?

[DOUG]   The accounting department of Easy Clean consists of seven part-time clerks, including the two data input clerks, who are all paid an hourly wage. All, except one, are college students working towards their accounting degrees. Mr. Day trains all new accounting help when they are first hired. Typically, they stay on with us until they graduate, which usually covers two full years. We keep them pretty busy around here, but everyone helps each other out and they always get the job done.

[TED]   What are your brother Phil's responsibilities?

[DOUG] Phil manages the service component of the business. He usually trains all newly hired cleaning employees and explains their specific duties and responsibilities. When he feels sure that the employee is ready, the new hire is teamed with a more experienced worker and assigned to a truck unit. When additional help is needed, Phil places ads in the local newspaper. Phil is the expert at running that end of the business.

[TED]   What about employee turnover?

[DOUG] We haven't had a problem with employee turnover. Phil expects some turnover in this type of business and knows how to deal with it. We try to prevent any employee concerns by maintaining an open door policy and encouraging employees who have questions or concerns about their responsibilities to ask for help or to come talk with us. If a problem should arise that might affect others, Phil or I will immediately address the problem at the monthly office meeting, making all employees aware of the issue. Both Phil and I work hard to ensure that any problem is resolved promptly.

Doug leaves to give an estimate and Ted continues his observations of the business.

Later that day, after spending time with the accounting staff, Ted has a moment to ask Mr. Day, the office manager, a few questions.

[TED]   Mr. Day, I'm wondering if you could help me clarify some things regarding my brief observations of the accounting staff?

[MR. DAY]   Sure, I'd be glad to. What can I do for you?

[TED]   I got the impression from the staff that they're not always certain about their assigned functions. Are job responsibilities clearly defined?

[MR. DAY]   In assigning office responsibilities, Doug says the main considerations are that work should be done by the people who are familiar with a task and who are capable of doing it. But, he also admits that availability has to be a consideration. Although this does lead to some overlap in duties, it doesn't create any confusion in responsibilities. I carefully assign the daily duties and overview each day's accounting records. This keeps the office running smoothly and in a well-organized manner.

[TED]   The staff mentioned that they've occasionally had problems processing collections of trade receivables. Do you prelist cash receipts before they're recorded?

[MR. DAY]   Well, we haven't really experienced any need to. The system is set up so that we collect all of the checks at the end of the day, making it possible to record them all at one time. This way, we can be more efficient by avoiding the need to write them down twice. On those rare occasions when there is a collection processing problem, we resolve it immediately.

[TED]   Do you ever run into accounting policy problems?

[MR. DAY]   Not very often. I usually handle any policy problems that do arise, although Doug will handle the situation if he feels strongly about the issue.

[TED]   Well, thank you Mr. Day. I need to talk to Doug before he leaves for the day.

A few moments later, in Doug's office . . .

[TED]   Are you satisfied with the processing of trade receivables?

[DOUG] Yes, definitely. Mr. Day is meticulous in his clerical operations, which is well systematized. He has excellent control over the trade receivables. In fact, it's been over a year and a half since the bank accepted a list of pledged receivables as security for a loan. From then on, we've had access to a continually renewable loan based on a list that's updated weekly. The loan is relatively small, and the contract allows the bank to access Easy Clean's checking account in the unlikely event that collection of the loan seems doubtful.

Perhaps I should add that although Phil and I have no formal accounting training and we have given Mr. Day full responsibility for the accounting duties, Phil and I are the only people allowed to sign company checks.

[TED]   One of the accounting clerks mentioned that you're thinking about making a change in the accounting system.

[DOUG] As a matter of fact, Mr. Day has been looking into using a new accounting software package that should make the bookkeeping process an easier task for the clerks. This package includes a budgeting system that should help control costs and identify those areas that need attention.

Because I've always monitored the company's expenses, I didn't previously see the need for a formal budgeting system. If something didn't seem right, Phil or I would bring the problem up at the informal monthly office meeting between all the employees and try to resolve the issue. Given our current success, the implementation of a more sophisticated budgeting system seems like a wise investment.

[TED]   I'm also interested in your security measures. How do you protect your accounting records and physical assets?

[DOUG] After hours, the office door and windows are heavily bolted. Only Phil, Mr. Day and I have keys to open the office. Although there haven't been any problems, we're considering locking up the file cabinets where the hard copies of the accounting records and data disks are stored at night. I've also been meaning to see about having the computers bolted down to the desks.

As for the vans, they're kept in a fenced-in lot behind our office. Each driver gets a key to the gate lock so they can let themselves in or out for work. We have to do this because a lot of the commercial cleaning is done after hours, when the office is closed. As a precautionary measure, we change the lock regularly.

[TED]   That should about do it for now, until I can get in to do some preliminary audit work. But before I leave, I'd like to ask you a few more general questions. To start with, can you tell me what you feel is responsible for Easy Clean's recent success?

[DOUG] Well, Ted, because Easy Clean is using the newest steam-cleaning procedure, we provide a much better result than the traditional rotary shampoo methods used by our competitors. And, our customers can tell. Plus, Phil and I understand the business well, we are personable and we pride ourselves on doing good work.

[TED]   Having an audit performed by our firm is a big step. Why did you decide to have an audit now? Have you ever been audited before?

[DOUG] Phil and I are confident that Easy Clean is a truly viable concern. We feel that audited financial statements will corroborate our claim. We're eager to learn what suggestions your firm can give us regarding the most professional way to record and present our financial statements. We also have an interest in learning how to increase the company's credibility with the local business and banking community. Both Phil and I are excited about the success of our company, and we're motivated to continue strengthening the organization with the eventual goal of pursuing additional business opportunities and endeavors.

We've never been audited before, although we have used a local tax preparer to fill out our tax returns ever since Easy Clean has been in business. We did ask another firm, about two years ago, to come in to do an audit. We decided not to have the audit performed, though, because the company's fees were too high. Although I'd have to look up the audit firm's name, Phil and I decided that Easy Clean would have to wait for an audit until we could reasonably afford the fees. We've come to the decision that now is the time.

[TED]   Are there any issues of concern that you have regarding the audit?

[DOUG]   Not really. I'm proud of Easy Clean. The company has had no record of serious problems and has rarely had a problem with bad debts, since most of our receivable balances are collected within two to three weeks.

[TED]   I understand that Easy Clean does not have an audit committee, which is typical of an organization this size. Can you tell me if Easy Clean has a board of directors and, if so, who serves on the board and how active the board is in overseeing important issues at Easy Clean?

[DOUG]   We do have a board of directors. It is somewhat informal, but Phil, I, and our wives function as directors. We do have at least one regularly scheduled meeting each year and we have met on other occasions as necessary. Obviously, Phil and I have a pretty good idea of what is happening at Easy Clean on a daily basis. We do not believe our company is yet at a stage that could effectively support a separate board comprised of outside directors. Maybe we'll do that in a couple of years, if we keep growing.

[TED]   One final thing I'd like to ask—have you and your brother Phil set out any goals for the future?

[DOUG]   Phil and I have spent a lot of time talking about our goals and objectives, but we've never formally recorded them anywhere. Our long-term goals are fairly uncertain, but we're hoping to build our nest egg to the point where we can potentially retire early. We both agree that our future plans include expanding our sales territory, increasing advertising, investing in more help and additional equipment; and, I have to admit, taking a well-deserved vacation in Hawaii.

	Reference:	CE 1a
Easy Clean, Co.	Prepared by:	
Control Environment Evaluation Form	Date:	
December 31, 2011	Reviewed by:	

	Greatly Weakens Control		Neither Weakens nor Strengthens			Greatly Strengthens Control	

1.   Integrity and Ethical Values

1	2	3	4	5	6	7

In evaluating this component, consider whether:
- *there appears to be sufficient integrity on the part of management and employees*
- *management articulates ethical values to all levels of the organization, processes are in place to monitor adherence to ethical values, and deviations from ethical values are identified and addressed in an appropriate and timely manner*

2.   Board of Directors

1	2	3	4	5	6	7

In evaluating this component, consider whether:
- *a board of directors and audit committee exists and is sufficient in membership to deal with important issues adequately*
- *directors or audit committee members have sufficient knowledge, industry experience and time to serve effectively*
- *some directors or audit committee members are independent of management*
- *frequency and timeliness with which meetings are held with accounting officers and external auditors*
- *the board oversees and takes action as needed*

3.   Management's Philosophy and Operating Style

1	2	3	4	5	6	7

In evaluating this component, consider whether:
- *business risks are adequately monitored*
- *management is willing to undertake relatively low levels of business risk*
- *management places a high priority on internal control*
- *management explicitly attempts to reduce the risk of misstatements*

4.   Organizational Structure

1	2	3	4	5	6	7

In evaluating this component, consider whether:
- *the organization's lines of authority and responsibility are clearly defined*
- *operating policies are determined centrally by senior management*
- *transaction policies and procedures are clearly established and strictly followed*
- *the organization is adequately structured given its complexity and size*
- *management is actively involved in the supervision of data processing*
- *job descriptions and organizational charts are maintained and periodically updated*

Easy Clean, Co.
Control Environment Evaluation Form
December 31, 2011

Reference: _CE 1b_
Prepared by: _____
Date: _____
Reviewed by: _____

	Greatly Weakens Control		Neither Weakens nor Strengthens		Greatly Strengthens Control	

5. Financial Reporting Competencies   1   2   3   4   5   6   7

In evaluating this component, consider whether:
- *management has specified the competence level needed for particular skills and translated the desired levels of competence into requisite knowledge and skills*
- *evidence exists indicating that employees appear to have the requisite knowledge and skills*
- *management provides training for employees to review and improve competencies*

6. Authority and Responsibility   1   2   3   4   5   6   7

In evaluating this component, consider whether:
- *appropriate policies for acceptable business practices, conflicts of interest, and codes of conduct have been established and have been communicated to employees*
- *there is a clear assignment of responsibility and delegation of authority for goals and objectives, operating functions, and regulatory requirements*
- *employee job responsibilities and specific duties are clearly established and communicated*
- *computer system documentation clearly indicates the procedures for authorizing transactions and for approving system changes*
- *data processing policies and procedures are adequately documented*

7. Human Resources   1   2   3   4   5   6   7

In evaluating this component, consider whether:
- *employees have the background and experience necessary for their job duties*
- *employees understand the duties and procedures applicable to their jobs*
- *the organization provides for adequate training of new personnel*
- *the workloads of accounting personnel permit them to adequately control the quality of their work*
- *the turnover rate of accounting personnel is low*
- *the turnover rate of non-accounting personnel is low*
- *organization maintains and periodically updates position descriptions as well as policies and procedures*

Easy Clean, Co.
Control Environment Evaluation Form
December 31, 2011

Reference:	*CE 1c*
Prepared by:	
Date:	
Reviewed by:	

Overall Evaluation of the Control Environment: Based on all of the evidence gathered in the interview, please circle the number which best represents your assessment of the control environment at Simply Steam:

Very Weak Control Environment		Weak Control Environment		Intermediate Control Environment		Strong Control Environment		Very Strong Control Environment	
1	2	3	4	5	6	7	8	9	10

Please list a few of the key pieces of information that influenced your decision:

Red Bluff Inn & Café
Establishing Effective Internal Control in a Small Business

MARK S. BEASLEY · FRANK A. BUCKLESS · STEVEN M. GLOVER · DOUGLAS F. PRAWITT

LEARNING OBJECTIVES

After completing and discussing this case you should be able to

[1] Assess how the absence of effective internal controls in a small business operation increases the likelihood of fraud

[2] Use common sense and creativity to generate internal control suggestions that will effectively and efficiently reduce the potential for fraud

BACKGROUND

An entrepreneur by the name of Francisco Fernandez recently entered into a new venture involving ownership and operation of a small, 26-room motel and café. The motel is located in a remote area of southern Utah. The area is popular for tourists, who come to hike and mountain bike through the area's unique red rock terrain. Francisco has hired you to provide advice.

Francisco hired a young couple to run the motel and café on a day-to-day basis and plans to pay them a monthly salary. They will live for free in a small apartment behind the motel office. The couple will also be responsible for hiring and supervising the four or five part-time personnel who will help with cleaning the rooms, cooking, and waiting on customers in the café, etc. The couple will maintain records of rooms rented, meals served, and payments received (whether by cash, check, or credit card). They will make weekly deposits of the business's proceeds at the local bank.

As the time approaches for the business to open, Francisco is concerned that he will have little control over the operations or records relating to the motel and café, given that the day-to-day control is fully in the hands of the couple. He lives almost five hours away, in northern Utah, and will only be able to visit periodically. The distance is beginning to make Francisco a bit nervous. He trusts the couple he has hired, but has been around long enough to know that it is unwise to place employees in situations where they might be tempted.

Francisco needs your help to identify possible ways his motel and café could be defrauded. He especially wants your assistance to devise creative internal controls to help prevent or detect fraud.

REQUIRED (CONTINUED ON NEXT PAGE)

[1] What are your two biggest concerns relating to possible fraud for the motel part of the business? For each concern, generate two or three controls that could effectively reduce risk related to your concerns. Use common sense and be creative!

[2] What are your two biggest concerns relating to possible fraud for the café part of the business? For each concern, generate two or three controls that could effectively reduce risk related to your concerns. Use common sense and be creative!

The case was prepared by Mark S. Beasley, Ph.D. and Frank A. Buckless, Ph.D. of North Carolina State University and Steven M. Glover, Ph.D. and Douglas F. Prawitt, Ph.D. of Brigham Young University, as a basis for class discussion. Red Bluff is a fictitious company. All characters and names represented are fictitious; any similarity to existing companies or persons is purely coincidental.

[3] Briefly describe the impact each proposed control would have on the efficiency of running the business. Are the controls you generated both effective and efficient?

[4] Describe the potential impact of your proposed controls on the morale of the couple in charge of the day-to-day operations. How might Francisco deal with these concerns?

St. James Clothiers
Evaluation of Manual and IT-Based Sales Accounting System Risks

MARK S. BEASLEY · FRANK A. BUCKLESS · STEVEN M. GLOVER · DOUGLAS F. PRAWITT

LEARNING OBJECTIVES

After completing and discussing this case you should be able to

[1] Recognize risks in a manual-based accounting sales system

[2] Explain how an information technology (IT)-based accounting system can reduce manual system risks

[3] Identify new risks potentially arising from the use of an IT-based accounting system

[4] Recognize issues associated with the process of converting from a manual to an IT-based accounting system

INTRODUCTION

St. James Clothiers is a high-end clothing store located in a small Tennessee town. St. James has only one store, which is located in the shopping district by the town square. St. James enjoys the reputation of being the place to buy nice clothing in the local area. The store is in its twentieth year of operation.

The owner, Sally St. James, recently decided to convert from a relatively simple manual sales system to an IT-based sales application package. The sales application software will be purchased from a software vendor. As the audit senior on the St. James engagement, you recently asked one of your staff auditors, Joe McSweeney, to visit with the client more formally to learn more about the proposed accounting system change. You asked Joe to review the narrative in last year's audit files that he prepared, which describes the existing manual sales accounting system, and update it for any current-year changes. You also asked him to prepare a second narrative describing the proposed IT-based sales accounting system, using information he obtained in his discussions with St. James personnel. The narrative from last year's audit files and the narrative Joe recently prepared are provided in the pages that follow.

The case was prepared by Mark S. Beasley, Ph.D. and Frank A. Buckless, Ph.D. of North Carolina State University and Steven M. Glover, Ph.D. and Douglas F. Prawitt, Ph.D. of Brigham Young University, as a basis for class discussion. St. James is a fictitious company. All characters and names represented are fictitious; any similarity to existing companies or persons is purely coincidental.

REQUIRED

The audit partner on the St. James engagement, Betty Watergate, has asked you to review the narratives prepared by Joe as part of your audit planning procedures for the current year's December 31, 2012 financial statement audit. Betty wants you to prepare a memorandum for her that addresses these questions:

[1] What aspects of the current manual sales accounting system create risks that increase the likelihood of material misstatements in the financial statements? Specifically identify each risk and how it might lead to a misstatement. For example, don't just put "**Risk:** *Sales tickets are manually prepared by the cashier.*" Rather, you should state why this increases risks of material misstatements by adding "*This increases the risk of material misstatements because it increases the risk of random mathematical errors by the cashier.*"

[2] What features, if any, of the proposed IT-based sales accounting system will help minimize the risks identified in question 1? If a deficiency exists that is expected to persist under the new system, indicate that "*no computer controls reduce this risk.*"

[3] How does the IT-based sales system create new risks for material misstatements?

[4] What recommendations do you have related to plans for the actual conversion to this new system?

Prepare a memorandum containing your responses to Betty's questions. You may find it helpful to combine your responses to questions 1 and 2. For example, you might present your answers to questions 1 and 2 using the worksheet format on the next page (Note: You can download an electronic version of the worksheet at www.pearsonhighered.com/beasley5e).

Student Name: _____

Worksheet for Answering Questions 1 and 2

Risks of Manual System	How Risks Impact Financial Statements	New IT System Features that Mitigate Manual System Risks

Reference:	*P 1-1*
Prepared by:	*JMc*
Date:	*6/29/2011 Updated: 7/10/2012*
Reviewed by:	

St. James Clothiers
Narrative Description of Manual-Based Sales Accounting System
For the Year Ended December 31, 2011

This narrative is based on discussions with client personnel at St. James Clothiers on June 29, 2011, in conjunction with the audit of the December 31, 2011 financial statements. This narrative describes the manual sales system in place during the year ended December 31, 2011.

Description of the Existing Sales Accounting System

St. James has several salespeople who work with customers. Sales personnel are compensated based on an hourly rate plus a bonus for sales they generate by assisting customers. When the customer is ready to purchase the goods, the salesclerk directs the customer to the store cashier for payment.

To process a sale, the cashier manually records the salesclerk's name, the product number, quantity sold, and sales price on a pre-numbered sales ticket using information on the clothing price tag. The sales ticket is in duplicate form. For special sale items, the cashier refers to newspaper clippings of advertisements or in-store sales signs. Occasionally, the cashier has to rely on the salesperson to determine the sales price. The cashier manually extends the price times quantity to compute the sales amount and then adds the sales tax to arrive at the total sale amount. Once the sales ticket is computed, the pre-tax sales total and the sales tax amount are entered into the cash register, and the cash register records these amounts plus computes and records the total sales amount on a duplicate cash register tape. The cashier staples the customer copy of the cash register tape receipt to a copy of the manually prepared sales ticket and gives that to the customer.

The other copy of the cash register tape is maintained inside the locked cash register. No one except the store accountant, Meredith McGlomm, can unlock the tape from the register. The cash register is a relatively simple machine – it is basically used to generate the sales ticket and to provide a locked drawer for cash collected. The cash drawer is generally only opened when a sale is entered; however, the drawer can also be opened by pressing the "Total" button.

The original sales ticket is retained in a file box beside the cash register. Salesclerks assist the cashier during breaks and busy peaks (Saturdays particularly). St. James will accept customer returns only if the customer can provide his/her copy of the sales ticket. The cashier processes sales returns by completing a sales ticket using negative amounts.

John Thornberg, the store's manager, counts the cash in the cash register each night and prepares the deposit slip. He takes the cash to the local bank each night and drops it in the overnight depository. On the next day, the bank processes the deposit and sends the validated deposit slip directly to the store accountant (Meredith McGlomm).

At the end of each day, Meredith collects all the sales tickets from the cashier and also takes the cash register tape that is locked inside the cash register. Those are stored in a safe located in the accounting office. On the next day, Meredith groups all sales tickets by salesclerk number and records sales by salesclerk in separate columns of a spreadsheet. Meredith accumulates the subtotals of sales by salesclerk to determine the total sales amount for that day for the store.

Reference:	P 1-2
Prepared by:	JMc
Date:	6/29/2011 Updated: 7/10/2012
Reviewed by:	

Meredith manually enters the daily total into the Sales Journal. She compares the daily sales total in the Sales Journal to the cash register tape total for that day. When the validated deposit slip arrives from the bank, Meredith compares the deposited amount to the Sales Journal for that day noting agreement. The store owner, Sally St. James, periodically compares the daily deposit slip to the Sales Journal recorded amounts. At the end of each month, the store accountant foots the Sales Journal columns and posts account totals to the General Ledger. She uses the monthly sales by salesclerk totals to calculate salesclerk bonuses for the month. Because of the volume of sales transactions that occur, the store is unable to maintain a perpetual inventory system. Thus, at month end, the store performs an inventory count to establish ending inventory for the month. This is used to compute Cost of Goods Sold for the month.

Update for Year Ended December 31, 2012 Audit:

Based on my review and discussions with St. James Clothiers personnel on July 10, 2012, the above narrative description of the manual-based sales accounting system accurately describes the sales accounting system currently in place.

Joe McSweeney

July 10, 2012

Reference:	P 1-3
Prepared by:	JMc
Date:	7/10/2012
Reviewed by:	

St. James Clothiers
Narrative Description of the Proposed IT-Based Sales Accounting System
For the Year Ended December 31, 2012

This narrative is based on discussions I had with client personnel at St. James Clothiers on July 10, 2012. The narrative describes the key components of the proposed new IT-based sales accounting system, which St. James plans to install in the fourth quarter of the current year.

Description of the Proposed IT-Based Sales Accounting System

The new IT-based sales system that St. James is planning to implement later this year is an externally developed sales accounting software package that will be purchased from Olive States Software. Sally St. James learned about this software package while attending an industry meeting several months ago. From talking with several store owners, Sally is convinced that this software package would be great for St. James Clothiers.

Sally talked with some local friends who recommended a Nashville-based computer consultant to assist with the implementation. The consultant has met with Sally on five different occasions to discuss their plans for installation. The installation is scheduled for the last two weeks of November 2012. St. James will begin using the new system effective December 1.

Although the system will come ready to install, there are numerous features associated with the system that St. James will have the option of activating. Sally has asked the consultant to be responsible for setting those features, given that Sally and the rest of the store staff have no experience with computer programming or software installation.

When the new system is implemented, the old cash registers will be removed, and a new computer will be used by the cashier to process sales. The computer ("PC") has a special cash drawer attachment that can only be opened after a sale is entered into the PC. To open the drawer any other time requires a special password code, which will be maintained by the store manager. Thus, if the cashier makes a mistake while entering a sale, the store's manager will have to enter a password to void the sale.

To operate the new PC cash register, the cashier must input a three-digit password prior to processing each sale. Salesclerks will continue to fill in for the cashier, but each clerk will have a unique password to operate the PC. The PC will record the operator's password for each sale on an internal storage device that can only be accessed by the store manager. The store manager will be able to generate reports by password number for review. Sales tickets will no longer be prepared. Instead, the cashier will input the product number, quantity sold, and salesclerk number. The PC will extend price times quantity and compute the pre-tax sales amount, sales tax amount, and total sale amount. The PC will pull the unit price from a Price List master file based on the product number entered. As a result, sales cannot be processed for invalid product numbers or for product numbers with no price in the Price List master file.

The PC generates a receipt, which will be given to the customer. The receipt will indicate the product number, quantity, extended transaction amounts, and salesclerk number. The PC does not generate a separate cash register tape. Instead, the daily sales figures are stored internally on a hard drive. At the end of each day, the cashier selects the "daily closing procedure" menu option, which automatically updates the Sales Journal and Perpetual Inventory master file maintained on a hard drive. Sales returns can only be processed by the store manager using a special password option.

Reference:	P 1-4
Prepared by:	JMc
Date:	7/10/2012
Reviewed by:	

A maintenance application that comes with the new computerized sales system must be used to input changes to the Price List master file. The application will be loaded on a different machine where access to the application can be protected by requiring the use of a password to access the master file. Sally and the consultant have decided to load this price list maintenance application on the store manager's PC for the manager to update as price changes occur. The store manager's PC will be network connected to the cashier's and accountant's PCs.

The store manager will continue to make the nightly deposits in a manner consistent with the manual system procedures.

The new system will dramatically change the store accountant's responsibilities. Given that the computer automatically posts individual transactions to the Sales Journal by salesclerk, the store accountant will no longer prepare the Sales Journal. As a matter of fact, a Daily Sales Journal will not be produced in hardcopy form. Instead, the store accountant will be able to READ ONLY the daily sales figures from a PC in the accounting office. READ ONLY means the accountant can only view the contents of the file.

When the validated deposit slip arrives from the bank each day, the store accountant will enter the deposit-slip total into the accounting system, and the system will then compare the deposit amount to the daily recorded sales totals. Any differences will be listed on an exception report forwarded via email to Sally St. James each day. In addition, the nightly posting will also update the Perpetual Inventory master file. Because the store accountant's daily procedures will change significantly, she will be able to test the perpetual inventory records on a daily basis by physically counting selected inventory items for comparison to the perpetual inventory records, which can be printed daily in the accounting office. Discrepancies will be reviewed by the store manager daily and by the owner on a test basis.

As part of the monthly closing procedures, the computer will automatically post sales and inventory transactions to the General Ledger accounts. The store accountant will print the General Ledger Trial Balance to prepare monthly financial statement reports. No other hardcopy reports or journals will be generated.

Joe McSweeney
July 10, 2012

Collins Harp Enterprises
Recommending IT Systems Development Controls

MARK S. BEASLEY · FRANK A. BUCKLESS · STEVEN M. GLOVER · DOUGLAS F. PRAWITT

LEARNING OBJECTIVES

After completing and discussing this case you should be able to

[1] Recognize risks associated with the IT organizational structure and systems development
processes at a potential audit client

[2] Identify general IT-related controls that, if
implemented, could reduce risks associated with
IT systems development

[3] Communicate negative information to a potential new audit client in a way that might lead to
new audit services for that company

BACKGROUND

You are the new information technology (IT) audit specialist at the accounting firm of Townsend and
Townsend, LLP. One of the audit partners, Harold Mobley, asked you to evaluate the effectiveness of general
and application IT-related controls for a potential new audit client, Collins Harp Enterprises, which is a
privately-held business. During a round of golf last week, an executive of Collins Harp Enterprises asked
Harold to have someone with good IT training look at the company's IT systems development process.
Harold recently summarized the following information about Collins Harp's IT systems development
process based on his recent conversation with Linda Seth, IT Vice President at Collins Harp.

IT SUMMARY

Because of the company's unique business processes, Collins Harp Enterprises develops most of
its computer software applications in-house. Over the past several years, Linda Seth has been able
to hire several good software programmers with relatively strong programming experience. She has
assembled a team of five programmers who handle most of the application and systems programming
needs. Because of their strong backgrounds, Ms. Seth involves all five programmers in new application
developments or modifications to existing applications and also involves all of them in operating,
security, utility, and other system software programming and maintenance tasks. The staff is relatively
versatile, and any one of them is able to handle the programming demands of most changes.

Linda notes that because the programmers are typically more "free-spirited," she prefers to
give the programmers relatively free latitude in the development of new applications or modifications
to existing applications. She comments that the programmers like to view their work as a form
of art. As a result, she notes that the programmers "attack" the programming logic development
using their own, unique programming style and approach. She believes that such "freedom" for the
programming staff enhances the quality of the application development.

New applications are generally initiated by Linda after she identifies suggestions for changes
to existing applications based on conversations with similar IT personnel at other companies.
Because she regularly attends IT development conferences, she believes that she is in the best

The case was prepared by Mark S. Beasley, Ph.D. and Frank A. Buckless, Ph.D. of North Carolina State University and Steven M. Glover, Ph.D.
and Douglas F. Prawitt, Ph.D. of Brigham Young University, as a basis for class discussion. Collins Harp is a fictitious company. All characters and
names represented are fictitious; any similarity to existing companies or persons is purely coincidental.

position to identify ways to improve current application procedures. Occasionally, non-IT personnel (like accounting department personnel who work with the accounting systems) identify suggested changes. Linda notes that she generally hears about application changes or new application ideas from non-IT personnel in informal settings such as over lunch in the company cafeteria or when bumping into people in the office hallways. When that occurs, she makes a mental note to take back to her programming staff.

When applications are developed or changes are made, the assigned programmer generally telephones or emails the non-IT personnel primarily responsible for the application to discuss the programmer's suggested modification and to get their unofficial "blessing" to proceed. Occasionally, the programmer meets with the respective personnel, if requested. However, the programmers generally feel that such meetings have limited benefit because users have very little understanding of the programming logic used.

If the programmer is making a modification to an existing application, he or she makes a copy of the current version of the software program being used so that they don't have to reprogram the entire application. Before beginning, the programmer generally tries to meet with the programmer who was previously involved with any programming associated with this application to get a "big picture feel" for the application. Given the small size of the programming staff, the programmer can generally identify the person last involved with this application by talking with the other programmers. The programmer locates documents related to the programming logic maintained in the programming department's files. Generally, this documentation includes electronic files and memos that contain the programmer's notes about his or her programming logic used to program the software application. The newly assigned programmer is able to recreate a trail of the most recent modifications to the application from these notes.

Programmers test all application developments and modifications. To increase the independence of the testing, Linda assigns a different programmer to perform the testing of the application before implementation. The test programmer creates a fictitious data set by copying one of the actual data sets used in the relevant application. The test programmer performs a test of the new application or modification and documents the results. Linda says that there are tight controls over program testing because of her detailed reviews of all program test results and personal approval of each program before implementation into live production. And, she adds that copies of all test results are maintained in the files for subsequent review.

Once Linda believes that the program is accurately processing the test data, she approves the program for implementation into live production. Linda notes that it is a big event for the programmers when their application is ready for implementation. She comments that the programmers take pride in the completion of the project and that all the programmers celebrate once the project programmer announces that he or she has compiled the final version into object code and forwarded the object code version to the IT Librarian.

REQUIRED

Harold would like you to prepare a draft letter to Linda Seth that

[1] Describes deficiencies in the Collins Harp IT system development and program change process.

[2] Provides a brief description explaining your primary concern for each deficiency noted in question 1.

[3] Includes a recommendation of an IT system development control that could be implemented to minimize your concern for each deficiency described in question 1.

Remember you are writing to Linda Seth at Collins Harp. Therefore, prepare your response in a letter (not memo) format. Be sure to be professional in your response. You want to pinpoint obvious deficiencies without being offensive, given that Collins Harp could become a new client.

As an alternative to preparing a draft letter, your instructor may ask you to complete the worksheet on the following page (Note: You can download an electronic version of the worksheet at www.pearsonhighered.com/beasley5e).

Worksheet for Answering Questions 1, 2 and 3

Student Name: _____

Deficiencies in IT Systems Development and Program Change Process	Description of the Noted Deficiency	Recommendation to Mitigate Noted Deficiency

Sarbox Scooter, Inc.
Scoping and Evaluation Judgments in the Audit of Internal Control over Financial Reporting

Mark S. Beasley · Frank A. Buckless · Steven M. Glover · Douglas F. Prawitt

LEARNING OBJECTIVES

After completing and discussing this case you should be able to

[1] Understand the complexities of auditing internal control over financial reporting in an integrated audit required by PCAOB Auditing Standard No. 5

[2] Identify significant accounts for an integrated audit

[3] Identify significant locations or business units for an integrated audit

[4] Apply an evaluation methodology to determine the likelihood and magnitude of control deficiencies

[5] Appreciate the judgment needed to evaluate control deficiencies

INTRODUCTION

Section 404 of the Sarbanes-Oxley Act of 2002 requires public companies to report on the effectiveness of their internal control over financial reporting. Section 404 also requires companies to hire an auditor to perform an "integrated audit" involving both a traditional financial statement audit and an audit of internal control over financial reporting. PCAOB Audit Standard No. 5, *An Audit of Internal Control Over Financial Reporting That Is Integrated with An Audit of Financial Statements* (AS5), provides guidance for the audit of internal control and requires the auditor to obtain sufficient competent[1] evidence about the effectiveness of controls for all relevant assertions related to all significant accounts in the financial statements. Before an auditor can identify which controls to test, some important audit decisions need to be made. Some of these decisions are listed below.

- *Identify Significant Accounts.* Significance is determined by applying quantitative and qualitative measures of materiality to the consolidated financial statements.

- *Identify Relevant Financial Statement Assertions.* For each significant account, relevant assertions are identified by considering the assertions that have a meaningful bearing on whether the account is fairly stated. Relevant assertions are those assertions (one or more) related to significant accounts that, if inaccurate, present a reasonable possibility of containing a misstatement or misstatements that would cause the financial statements to be materially misstated.

- *Identify Significant Processes and Major Classes of Transactions.* The auditor must understand relevant processing procedures involved in the flow of transactions for significant accounts. The controls auditors will test reside within the significant transaction processes (e.g., sales and collection cycle, period-end financial reporting process).

---

1 PCAOB Auditing Standards refer to sufficient "competent" evidence, while AICPA Auditing Standards refer to sufficient "appropriate" evidence.

The case was prepared by Mark S. Beasley, Ph.D. and Frank A. Buckless, Ph.D. of North Carolina State University and Steven M. Glover, Ph.D. and Douglas F. Prawitt, Ph.D. of Brigham Young University, as a basis for class discussion. Sarbox is a fictitious company. All characters and names represented are fictitious; any similarity to existing companies or persons is purely coincidental.

Once significant accounts, relevant assertions, and significant processes have been identified, the auditor identifies the controls to test. Determining the location where testing will occur is not always a simple decision. Significant accounts at the consolidated company level are an aggregation of the accounts at the company's various business units, which may be geographically dispersed across several locations. For example, consolidated accounts receivable is the aggregation of the accounts receivable balances at each of the company's individual business units (i.e., locations, divisions, or subsidiaries). Thus, another important logistical decision the auditor must make for each significant account is to determine which business units to visit in order to test the controls pertaining to the account.

AS5 does not require the auditor to visit all of a company's business units or locations. Rather, AS5 requires the auditor to gather sufficient competent evidence for each significant account at the consolidated level in order to support his or her opinion regarding management's assertion about the effectiveness of internal control over financial reporting. To illustrate, suppose a company has ten different business units, each of which has accounts receivable. Assuming accounts receivable is deemed to be a significant account at the consolidated company level, the auditor might appropriately decide to test controls over accounts receivable at the company's six largest locations, representing 75 percent of the total consolidated receivables balance.

Part A of this case asks you to identify significant accounts and to determine which locations you would visit to perform tests of controls for Sarbox Scooter, Inc., a hypothetical manufacturer of scooters and mini-motorcycles. Completing the requirements of Part A will require you to exercise judgment to determine which accounts would be considered significant.

Part B of this case, which can be completed independently of Part A, asks you to evaluate the likelihood and magnitude of control deficiencies as defined and required by AS5. When a deficiency is deemed to be a material weakness, the auditor issues an adverse opinion with respect to the effectiveness of a company's controls over financial reporting. Approximately 17 percent of the first wave of companies required to comply with Section 404 (known as "accelerated filers") received an adverse audit opinion in early 2005 due to material weaknesses. That number has dropped to less than 5 percent in recent years.

BACKGROUND

Sarbox Scooter, Inc. manufactures and distributes pocket bikes and scooters internationally. Sarbox Scooter has operations in the U.S., Mexico, and Europe. Pocket bikes (also known as "minimotos," "mini GP's" or "pocket rockets") are miniature GP "Grand Prix" racing motorcycles. Approximately one-fourth the size of a regular motorcycle, pocket bikes are accurate in detail and proportion to world-class GP bikes. Common features include the following: small two-stroke gas engines (between 40 – 50 cubic centimeters in size), front/rear disc brakes, racing tires, a sturdy light weight aluminum or aluminum alloy frame, and the look and feel of a real GP racing motorcycle. Pocket bikes are built for racing and intended for use on speedways, go-kart tracks, or closed parking lots. Pocket bike racing is very popular in Europe and Japan and is becoming increasingly popular in the U.S.

Traditional scooters have been a kid favorite for many years. However, the craze for motorized scooters took off in the early 2000's and is spreading worldwide. While Sarbox Scooters carries a line of traditional non-motorized scooters, the company specializes in gas and electric powered scooters.

Sarbox Scooter was founded in 2002 and is headquartered in Basking Bridge, New Jersey. The company is one of the leading manufacturers of pocket bikes and motorized scooters. Sarbox Scooter's vision is to be the world's premier pocket bike and motorized scooter manufacturer and distributor. In line with this vision, Sarbox Scooter is striving to increase brand share by 1% each year for the next five years, to 30% of the market for motorized scooters. However, competition in the industry is intense and is based on price, quality, and aesthetics. In the last year, several competitors with strong brand recognition (e.g., Schwinn) have demonstrated renewed interest in the motorized scooter market with expensive ad campaigns.

Sarbox Scooter's customer base consists primarily of dealerships both domestically and internationally. Sales to the dealerships account for approximately 90% of Sarbox Scooter's annual sales. The remaining 10% of sales come from bulk orders sold directly to rental agencies and vacation resorts.

Sarbox Scooter's business units are divided by geographical region into the U.S., Mexico and Europe. The U.S. region is further sub-divided into five business units: Northeast, Southeast, Central, Southwest and Northwest. The international business units have individual finance directors who report to Warwick Schawb (CFO) at the Basking Bridge headquarters. The Mexico Finance Director recently resigned following deep scrutiny from Sarbox Scooter's internal audit team of his control, monitoring, and reporting practices. All of the individual business units have sales directors and manufacturing plant managers.

Sarbox Scooter's computer systems are located within data centers at each regional business unit. All financial statement consolidations and "roll ups" from the business units are performed at headquarters. The company was able to synchronize revenue recording and reporting for all of its business units on the same accounting software systems for the first time in 2009.

The company continued to progress in the areas of corporate governance and social responsibility by strengthening the Board of Directors via the addition of a highly respected business leader, Morris Graybeard, Chairman and Chief Executive Officer of the Rubio Company. Sarbox Scooter has also bolstered its internal audit function by hiring Jenna Jaynes, formerly the head of internal audit at a large international food distributor.

You are an auditor with Sarbox Scooter's external audit firm, Delmoss Watergrant LLP. Sarbox Scooter has been an audit client since it went public in 2004. Because Sarbox Scooter's corporate shares are publicly traded, the audit will be an integrated audit in accordance with AS5, including both an audit of internal control over financial reporting and a financial statement audit. Section 404 of the Sarbanes-Oxley Act of 2002 and related rulings of the Securities and Exchange Commission (SEC) require management to assess and evaluate the effectiveness of its internal control over financial reporting. Management must identify significant accounts and locations for testing. While management will provide the auditors with documentation of its risk assessment, controls, and testing, auditing standards require the auditor to independently evaluate the design and operating effectiveness of controls for each of the components of internal control that relate to relevant assertions for all significant accounts and disclosures in the financial statements. Furthermore, the auditors must independently identify each significant process over each major class of transactions and test controls at enough significant locations to obtain sufficient competent evidence regarding the effectiveness of internal controls over financial reporting. In forming your judgments, you will consider the background information above, Sarbox Scooter's financial statements, and Delmoss Watergrant's audit policies.

REQUIRED – PART A

[1] According to AS5:

[a] What should the auditor consider when determining whether an account should be considered significant?

[b] What qualitative factors might cause an account that is otherwise relatively small quantitatively to be considered significant?

[c] What qualitative factors might cause an account that is greater than materiality to be considered not significant?

[2] Referring to Delmoss Watergrant's policy for identifying significant accounts (see Appendix A) as well as Sarbox Scooter's consolidated balance sheet and income statement, answer the following questions:

[a] Determine a planning materiality threshold to use to identify significant accounts for Sarbox Scooter. Please show your work and justify judgments.

[b] At a consolidated financial statement level, are there accounts on Sarbox Scooter's financial statements that are greater than planning materiality that should not be considered significant? Please justify your response.

[c] Identify two accounts, at the consolidated level, that are not quantitatively significant, but that should be deemed significant due to qualitative factors. Provide the qualitative factors you considered.

[d] Which Sarbox Scooter business units (geographic locations), if any, would not be considered quantitatively significant? Which business units (locations) have specific risks that would render the unit significant regardless of its quantitative size?

[e] If you had to eliminate or scope out one entire business unit (geographic location), which unit would it be? Please justify your response and include both quantitative and qualitative reasons for doing so.

[3] Auditing standards require the identification and testing of entity-level controls. What are examples of entity-level controls? What are the auditor's responsibilities with respect to evaluating and testing a client's period-end financial reporting process?

REQUIRED – PART B (CAN BE COMPLETED INDEPENDENTLY OF PART A)

[1] What are the definitions of a control deficiency, significant deficiency, and material weakness as contained in AS5? Which, if any, of these deficiency categories must the external auditor include in the audit report?

[2] Referring to Delmoss Watergrant's policy for evaluating control deficiencies (see Appendix B), determine if the following three deficiencies represent a control deficiency, a significant deficiency, or a material weakness. Please consider each case separately and justify your answers.

[a] While examining Sarbox's period-end financial reporting process, you discover that revenue has been recognized on orders that were received and completed, but not yet shipped to the customer. No specific goods were set aside for these orders; however, there is sufficient inventory on hand to fill them. Also, you observe that some orders were shipped before being recorded as sales, so that your best estimate of total revenue cutoff error at year-end was approximately $2.3 million.

[b] Sarbox's revenue recognition policy requires that all nonroutine sales (i.e. sales to clients other than dealerships) receive authorization from management in order to verify proper pricing and terms of sale. However, after examining a sample of nonroutine sales records you find that this control is not closely adhered to and that sales representatives offered discounts or altered sales terms that were not properly recorded in Sarbox's records. As a result, in instances when the control is not followed the recorded sales prices tend to be too high and/or terms are not correctly reflected in the sales invoice and the customers complain. In some situations, customers have cancelled orders due to the over-billing or changed sales terms. Nonroutine sales represent about 10% of Sarbox's sales revenue. From your sample testing of the authorization control, you find that the control doesn't operate 4% of the time, with an upper bound of 9% (i.e., based on your sample, you can be 95% confident that the exception rate does not exceed 9%).

[c] Sarbox Scooter requires that all credit sales to new customers or to customers with a current balance over their pre-approved credit limit be approved by the credit manager prior to shipment. However, during peak seasons this policy is not strictly followed in order to accommodate the need of both the company and its customers to have orders processed rapidly. Because of these findings, you estimate that the allowance for doubtful accounts is materially understated. While the client does not dispute that the authorization control was not operating effectively during peak seasons, the client has pointed out compensating controls that it feels should reduce the magnitude of the deficiency below a material weakness. The first compensating control is that an accounts receivable aging schedule is reviewed each quarter by management and accounts that are older than 180 days are written-off. Also, management distributes a list of companies that default or fail to pay on time to all sales staff on a monthly basis to prohibit such companies from making additional purchases on credit.

Sarbox Scooters, Inc.
Consolidating Income Statement

December 31, 2011 (In Thousands)

	Consolidated	US Northeast	US Southeast	US Central	US Southwest	US Northwest	Mexico	Europe
Sales Revenue	1,987,174	59,615	298,076	208,653	317,948	218,589	89,423	794,870
Other Revenue	435,548	13,066	65,332	45,733	69,688	47,910	19,600	174,219
Total Revenue	2,422,722	72,681	363,408	254,386	387,636	266,499	109,023	969,089
Assembly Cost	1,091,939	32,758	163,791	114,654	174,710	120,113	49,137	436,776
Maintenance Cost	344,037	10,321	51,605	36,125	55,046	37,844	15,482	137,614
Impairment of Acquired Intangible Assets	44,875	1,346	6,731	4,713	7,180	4,936	2,019	17,950
Severance Charges	14,958	449	2,244	1,571	2,393	1,645	673	5,983
Total Cost of Goods Sold	1,495,809	44,874	224,371	157,063	239,329	164,538	67,311	598,323
Gross profit	926,913	27,807	139,037	97,323	148,307	101,961	41,712	370,766
Sales Expense	88,200	2,645	13,230	9,261	14,112	9,702	3,969	35,281
Marketing Expense	84,744	2,542	12,712	8,898	13,559	9,322	3,813	33,898
Research and Development	51,785	1,557	7,783	5,448	8,301	5,707	2,235	20,754
General and Administrative	50,155	1,505	7,523	5,266	8,025	5,517	2,257	20,062
Depreciation	46,694	1,401	7,004	4,903	7,471	5,136	2,101	18,678
Amortization	24,212	726	3,632	2,542	3,874	2,663	1,090	9,685
Total Operating Expenses	345,790	10,376	51,884	36,318	55,342	38,047	15,465	138,358
Income from operations	581,123	17,431	87,153	61,005	92,965	63,914	26,247	232,408
Interest income, net	11,673	350	1,751	1,226	1,868	1,284	525	4,669
Other, net	(3,194)	(96)	(479)	(335)	(511)	(351)	(144)	(1,278)
Suspense	—	—	—	(600)	(700)		1,300	
Income before Income Taxes	589,602	17,685	88,425	61,296	93,622	64,847	27,928	235,799
Provision for income taxes	204,806	6,144	30,721	21,505	32,769	22,529	9,216	81,922
Net income	384,796	11,541	57,704	39,791	60,853	42,318	18,712	153,877

Sarbox Scooters, Inc.
Consolidating Balance Sheet

December 31, 2011 (In Thousands)

	Consolidated	US Northeast	US Southeast	US Central	US Southwest	US Northwest	Mexico	Europe
ASSETS								
Current assets:								
Cash and cash equivalents	10,236	2,607	1,535	1,075	1,638	1,126	461	1,794
Marketable securities	423,474	10,704	63,521	44,465	67,756	46,582	19,056	171,390
Receivables								
Accounts receivable, net	93,199	2,796	13,980	9,786	14,912	10,252	4,194	37,279
Current portion of finance receivables, net	820,652	24,620	123,098	86,168	131,304	90,272	36,929	328,261
Miscellaneous receivables	3,208	96	481	337	513	353	144	1,284
Notes receivables	7,892	237	1,184	829	1,263	868	355	3,156
Inventories								
Raw Materials	81,035	2,431	12,155	8,509	12,965	8,914	3,647	32,414
Work in Progress	15,518	466	2,328	1,629	2,483	1,707	698	6,207
Finished Goods	75,861	2,276	11,379	7,965	12,138	8,345	3,414	30,344
Deferred income taxes	42,459	1,204	6,369	4,458	6,793	4,670	1,911	17,054
Prepaid expenses & other current assets	27,544	14,896	2,132	1,891	2,409	2,029	1,240	2,947
Total current assets	1,601,078	62,333	238,162	167,112	254,174	175,118	72,049	632,130
Long Term Assets:								
Finance receivables, net	610,762	18,023	91,614	64,130	97,722	67,184	27,484	244,605
Property, plant, and equipment, net	868,438	20,053	130,266	91,186	138,950	95,528	39,080	353,375
Goodwill	44,553	1,337	6,683	4,678	7,128	4,901	2,005	17,821
Other assets	297,236	8,917	44,585	31,210	47,558	32,696	13,376	118,894
Total Assets	3,422,067	110,663	511,310	358,316	545,532	375,427	153,994	1,366,825

Sarbox Scooters, Inc.
Consolidating Balance Sheet (Continued)

December 31, 2011

	Consolidated	US Northeast	US Southeast	US Central	US Southwest	US Northwest	Mexico	Europe
LIABILITIES AND SHAREHOLDERS' EQUITY								
Current liabilities:								
Accounts payable	182,828	13,078	25,019	17,609	27,215	19,211	8,363	72,333
Payroll and related	65,734	1,972	9,857	6,904	10,519	7,231	2,960	26,291
Accrued expenses and other liabilities	277,057	9,176	41,742	29,519	44,125	31,211	12,263	109,021
Current portion of finance debt	267,673	7,575	40,376	28,263	43,068	28,609	12,113	107,669
Total current liabilities	793,292	31,801	116,994	82,295	124,927	86,262	35,699	315,314
Finance debt	556,901	16,707	83,535	58,475	89,104	61,259	25,061	222,760
Other long-term liabilities	7,562	227	1,134	794	1,210	832	340	3,025
Postretirement health care benefits	195,780	5,873	29,367	20,557	31,325	21,536	8,810	78,312
Deferred income taxes	108,448	3,253	16,267	11,387	17,352	11,929	4,880	43,380
Shareholders' equity:								
Common Stock	1,153,004	34,590	172,951	121,065	184,481	126,830	51,885	461,202
Retained earnings	607,080	18,212	91,062	63,743	97,133	66,779	27,319	242,832
Total Liabilities and Shareholder's Equity	3,422,067	110,663	511,310	358,316	545,532	375,427	153,994	1,366,825

Appendix A: Excerpts from the Audit Policy of Delmoss Watergrant LLP to Identify Significant Accounts and Locations
(For use with Part A of the case)

Identifying Significant Accounts and Assertions

For purposes of scoping the audit of internal controls over financial reporting, we consider planning materiality[1] when identifying significant accounts from a quantitative standpoint. Generally, financial statement line items and/or accounts that exceed planning materiality should be considered for designation as significant accounts for both the audits of internal control over financial reporting (ICFR) and the financial statements. Further disaggregation of each financial statement line item may be necessary to determine which component account balances are significant or, alternatively, insignificant. For example, "other assets" may include several component account balances, some of which are individually significant and others that are not individually significant. The more an account exceeds planning materiality, the greater the likelihood it should be considered a significant account, even when the qualitative risk factors are low. However, an account that exceeds planning materiality is not automatically a significant account as qualitative factors may also be considered. Qualitative factors may also lead us to consider an account or disclosure less than planning materiality to be significant.

Qualitatively, we deem accounts to be significant if they are impacted by inherent and fraud risks that have a reasonable possibility of resulting in a material misstatement, either on an individual or an aggregate basis. Relevant qualitative factors include the following:

- Susceptibility of loss due to errors or fraud;
- Volume of activity, complexity, and homogeneity of the individual transactions processed through the account;
- Nature of the account;
- Accounting and reporting complexities associated with the account;
- Exposures to losses represented by the account;
- Likelihood of significant contingent liabilities arising from the activities represented by the account;
- Existence of related party transactions in the account, and
- Changes in account characteristics from the prior period.

For example, accounts that may not be quantitatively significant at any point in time, but include significant activity (e.g., cash, work in process, suspense accounts) should be considered significant accounts.

Similarly, some accounts that are quantitatively significant may not require testing for qualitative reasons. Accounts that have low susceptibility to error or fraud, have a low volume of activity, and that are not complex in nature, may not require testing—especially if the area has been thoroughly tested in the recent past. For example, while fixed assets in a service organization may be a large account, it may have very little change from year to year and may present low inherent and fraud risk. For such an account we may rotate our testing and/or rely more on the work of others to evaluate the related controls.

In addition, the qualitative factors of separate account components should be considered when determining which components of an account should be tested. For example, the petty cash component of the cash account rarely poses more than a remote risk that the financial statements are materially misstated.

After identifying significant accounts we should consider relevant assertions. Relevant assertions are those that present risks that result in a reasonable possibility of a material misstatement and as a result, only controls over those assertions need be tested to assess ICFR. For example, if we determine payroll expense

---

1   Delmoss Watergrant's policy on materiality indicates that from a quantitative perspective planning materiality will generally fall in the range of 3-5% of pretax earnings or 1-2% of sales, whichever is less so long as both bases are an accurate reflection of the company's size, past performance, and complexity (i.e., when income is near zero or negative, it is not typically considered representative).

is a significant account, we may determine that only the completeness and valuation assertions present risks that result in a reasonable possibility of materiality misstatement, and as a result we would obtain evidence of design and operating effectiveness of ICFR from walkthroughs and tests of controls associated with these two assertions.

As part of identifying significant accounts and their relevant assertions, we should determine the likely sources of potential misstatements that would cause the financial statements to be materially misstated. We might determine the likely sources of potential misstatements by asking ourselves "what could go wrong?" within a given significant account or disclosure.

Identifying Significant Business Units or Locations

Determining the business units/locations for audit testing requires us to evaluate factors such as the relative financial significance of the business unit/location and the risk of material misstatement arising from the business unit/location. In making this determination we should categorize business units/locations into the following categories:

1. Individually important.

2. Contain specific risks that by themselves could create a material misstatement in the consolidated financial statements.

3. Business units/locations that should not be able, individually or in the aggregate, to create a material misstatement in the financial statements (those at which we will perform no or very limited testing).

4. When aggregated, could represent a level of financial significance that could create a material misstatement in the consolidated financial statements.

In identifying business units/locations at which to perform testing (item 1 above), we expect that a large portion of our audit assurance will be derived from testing individually important business units/locations.

Determining Individually Important Business Units/Locations

Individually important business units/locations are those that are financially significant to the entity as a whole. From a quantitative perspective we determine individually significant accounts by selecting business units/locations that exceed either of the following metrics:

Business Unit/Location's Net Income Greater than 10% of Total Consolidated Net Income	**OR**	**Business Unit/Location's Assets Greater than 10% of Total Consolidated Assets**

Determining Business Units/Locations That Have Specific Risks

Even after considering the quantitative factors above, the engagement team will need to use significant judgment when determining the individually important business unit's/location's qualitative or specific risks. A location or business unit might present specific risks that, by themselves, could create a material misstatement in the company's financial statements, even though the unit might not be individually financially significant. For example, a business unit responsible for foreign exchange trading could expose the company to the risk of material misstatement, even though the relative financial significance of individual transactions is low.

A detailed consideration of inherent and fraud risks of material misstatement should be made for those locations that were not initially selected as an individually important location. A high degree of auditor judgment must be applied by the engagement leader in assessing whether certain locations have specific risks that make them important. The engagement team would normally only obtain evidence about the effectiveness of controls over specific risks that could lead to material misstatements.

Appendix B: Excerpts from the Audit Policy of Delmoss Watergrant LLP on Evaluating Control Deficiencies (For use with Part B of the case)

Evaluating Control Deficiencies

Auditing Standard 5 (AS5) requires that all control deficiencies be evaluated and included individually and in combination with other deficiencies to be either:

- Internal control deficiencies that do not rise to the level of significant deficiencies,
- Significant deficiencies, or
- Material weaknesses.

AS5 defines these categories as control deficiency, significant deficiency, and material weakness, and the three categories are not mutually exclusive. Control deficiencies encompass all deficiencies, including those evaluated as significant deficiencies and material weaknesses. Thus, we first identify control deficiencies and then consider, individually and in the aggregate, by significant account balance, disclosure, relevant assertion or component of internal control (i.e., the COSO components) to determine whether they result in significant deficiencies or material weaknesses. Multiple control deficiencies that affect the same financial statement account or disclosure increase the likelihood of misstatement and may, in combination, constitute a material weakness, even though such deficiencies may individually be less severe.

AS5 requires that we evaluate the significance of a deficiency in internal control by determining:

- the **likelihood** (reasonable possibility or probable, or remote) that the deficiency, individually or in combination with other deficiencies, could result in a misstatement of an account balance or disclosure, and
- the **magnitude** (not material or significant, not material but significant, or material) of the potential misstatement resulting from the deficiency or deficiencies.

The term "reasonable possibility" and "probable" as used in the definitions of significant deficiency and material weakness are to be interpreted using the guidance in Financial Accounting Standards Board Statement No. 5, *Accounting for Contingencies*. Delmoss Watergrant has interpreted reasonable possibility to mean more than a 5% likelihood.

A misstatement is not "significant" if a reasonable person would conclude, after considering the possibility of further undetected misstatements, that the misstatement, either individually or when aggregated with other misstatements, would clearly be immaterial to the financial statements. Delmoss Watergrant has interpreted "not significant" to mean anything less than 10% of planning materiality.

In evaluating deficiencies we typically first consider likelihood and then magnitude because under the PCAOB definitions, only control deficiencies with at least a "reasonable possibility" likelihood can rise to the level of a significant deficiency or a material weakness.

The joint consideration of likelihood and magnitude becomes more important as the *potential* magnitude of misstatements becomes higher. For example, where any misstatement from the failure of a control is likely to be material, judgments as to whether the deficiency has a reasonable possibility or probable likelihood of misstatement becomes critical. Whether a control deficiency is determined to be a significant deficiency or a material weakness does not depend on the size of detected misstatements related to the deficiency. Rather, we must evaluate the *potential* likelihood and *potential* magnitude of a misstatement resulting from the deficiency.

If we find effective complementary or redundant controls that achieve the same control objective we may conclude that there is a control deficiency or no deficiency at all. We should gather evidence of the operating effectiveness of complementary or redundant controls.

Section 5: Internal Control over Financial Reporting

The following chart illustrates the interplay between the likelihood of misstatement and the potential magnitude of misstatement.

Potential Amount	Likelihood	
	Remote	Reasonable Possibility or Probable
Material amount	Internal control deficiency but not significant deficiency	Material weakness
Significant (i.e., more than 10% of overall materiality) but less than a material amount	Internal control deficiency but not significant deficiency	Significant deficiency but not material weakness
Not material or significant amount (i.e., less than 10% of overall materiality)	Internal control deficiency but not significant deficiency	Internal control deficiency but not significant deficiency

AS5 paragraph 69 lists certain deficiencies that are indicators of material weakness in internal control over financial reporting. We should carefully consider this list as we evaluate deficiencies. There may be rare situations where indicators of a material weakness do not result in a control deficiency. For example, if a company had to restate previously issued financial statements we would need to carefully understand the cause of the restatement. If the company had a reasonable position for the application of generally accepted accounting principles and its controls for making such a determination were properly designed and effective, we may conclude that the restatement did not result from a control deficiency.

When evaluating and classifying process/transaction-level control deficiencies, we use the decision tree that follows. The decision tree assumes the auditor has determined that an exception discovered in testing represents a control deficiency.

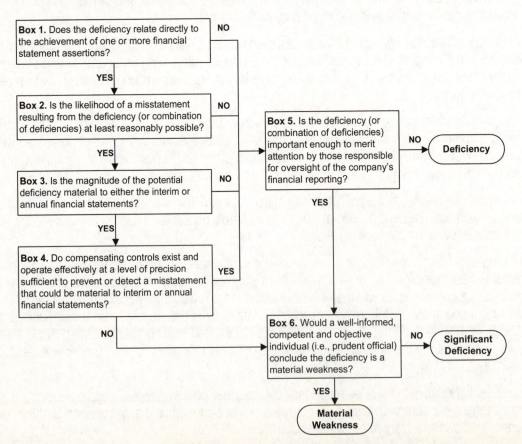

Decision Tree for Evaluating Process/Transaction-Level Control Deficiencies

The decision tree is used to evaluate the classification of control deficiencies from the following sources:
- Design effectiveness evaluation,
- Operating effectiveness testing,
- Deficiencies that resulted in a financial statement misstatement detected by management or the auditor in performing substantive test work.

Guidance for using the Decision Tree *(see diagram on previous page)*

Box 1 Consider whether the deficiency identified relates directly to the achievement of financial statement assertions. Some controls relate only indirectly (e.g., entity-level controls related to the control environment, information technology general controls). Evaluating the severity of deficiencies in controls that contribute only indirectly to the achievement of financial statement assertions should take into account the likelihood and significance of other control deficiencies that may occur or have occurred as a result of the indirect control's deficiency.

Box 2 Determine if it is reasonably possible that the failure of the control or combination of controls will fail to prevent or detect a misstatement of an account balance. At this point, we are only concerned with the likelihood of a misstatement, regardless of size (i.e., we do not limit our evaluation to the likelihood of a material misstatement—the magnitude evaluation is performed separately).

Certain risk factors affect whether there is a reasonable possibility that a deficiency, or combination of deficiencies, will result in a misstatement of an account balance or disclosure. AS5.65 provides examples, which include, but are not limited to:
- The nature of the financial statement accounts, disclosures, and assertions involved.
- The susceptibility of the related assets or liability to loss or fraud; that is, greater susceptibility increases risk.
- The subjectivity, complexity, or extent of judgment required to determine the amount involved; that is, greater subjectivity, complexity, or judgment, like that related to an accounting estimate, increases risk.
- The interaction or relationship with other controls, including whether they are interdependent or redundant.
- The interaction of deficiencies.
- The possible future consequences of the deficiency.

Box 3 When evaluating deficiencies, factors that affect the potential magnitude in controls include, but are not limited to, the following (AS5.66):
- Financial statement amounts or total of transactions exposed to the deficiency
- Volume of activity in the account balance or class of transactions exposed to the deficiency that has occurred in the current period or that is expected in the future.

Evaluation of the magnitude of a deficiency includes the impact of actual and/or potential misstatements on both annual and interim financial statements. In considering potential magnitude, it may be useful to consider a "gross exposure," or in other words the total dollars exposed to the identified deficiency. For example if the total dollars exposed is less than materiality, then the deficiency would not likely rise to the level of a material weakness. After considering the "gross exposure," it may be useful to consider the "likely exposure" based on the results of the testing performed. For example, if a sampling technique indicates an upper exception limit of 12 percent, then 12 percent of the "gross exposure" would be an estimate of the "likely exposure."

In considering materiality, we consider both quantitative and qualitative considerations as outlined in SEC's Staff Accounting Bulletin 99.

Box 4   If we find effective complementary or redundant controls that achieve the same control objective we would only have a control deficiency or no deficiency at all. If there are no effective complementary or redundant controls, we should evaluate compensating controls to determine if there is a reasonable possibility that a material misstatement will go undetected. We must obtain evidence that the compensating controls are operating effectively. Effective compensating controls will operate at a level of precision that would result in the prevention or detection of a material misstatement, thereby mitigating or reducing the magnitude of the potential misstatements resulting from the identified control deficiency. Compensating controls that operate at a level of precision that would result in the prevention or detection of a material misstatement of the annual or interim financial statements may support a conclusion that the deficiency is not a significant deficiency or a material weakness.

Box 5   The evaluation of whether a deficiency is important enough to merit the attention of those responsible for oversight of the company's financial reporting requires the use of professional judgment and is dependent on the facts and circumstances.

When evaluating the significance of a deficiency in internal control over financial reporting, the auditor determines the level of detail and degree of assurance that would satisfy prudent officials in the conduct of their own affairs that they have reasonable assurance that transactions are recorded as necessary to permit the preparation of financial statements in conformity with generally accepted accounting principles. If the auditor determines that the deficiency would prevent prudent officials in the conduct of their own affairs from concluding that they have reasonable assurance, then the auditor should deem the deficiency to be at least a significant deficiency. Having determined in this manner that a deficiency represents a significant deficiency, the auditor must further evaluate the deficiency to determine whether individually, or in combination with other deficiencies, the deficiency is a material weakness.

Box 6   The evaluation of the severity of a control deficiency, or combination of control deficiencies, involves the consideration of whether a well-informed, competent and objective individual (i.e., prudent official) would conclude that the control deficiency represents a material weakness because the risk of material misstatement is unacceptably high.

Société Générale
How a Low-Risk Trading Area Caused a $7.2 Billion Loss

MARK S. BEASLEY · FRANK A. BUCKLESS · STEVEN M. GLOVER · DOUGLAS F. PRAWITT

LEARNING OBJECTIVES

After completing and discussing this case you should be able to

[1] Understand the importance of effective risk assessment and risk management

[2] Understand the difference between effective design and operation of controls

[3] Understand the importance of proper controls and the potential magnitude of loss associated with poor controls

[4] Evaluate control deficiencies and consider how the controls could have been improved

[5] Understand the conditions necessary to commit fraud

INTRODUCTION

On January 24, 2008, Société Générale, France's second largest bank announced the largest trading loss in history, a staggering 4.9 billion Euro ($7.2 billion U.S.), which it blamed on a single rogue trader. The trader, Jérôme Kerviel, worked at what Société Générale considered a low-level, low-risk trading desk. The announcement sent a shock wave through the global financial services community and immediately triggered memories of a another rogue trader, Nick Leeson, who, 13 years earlier, single-handedly bankrupted the 233-year old Barings Bank of London.

LESSON FROM THE PAST

Nick Leeson was seemingly infallible. In 1993, his already legendary trading prowess was responsible for approximately 10% of Barings Bank's bottom line. Barings Bank, headquartered in London, was one of the world's oldest and most respected banks. What the bank's leadership did not realize was that Leeson, stationed in Singapore, was trading outside of established company policies. Rather than seeking gains via futures contract arbitrage (his assigned job), he was engaging in extremely risky speculation without any offsetting hedge to protect against massive loss.

By early 1995 Leeson had lost $512 million. Rather than admit his mistakes, Leeson gambled bank resources in a vain attempt to overcome the loss. Essentially, Leeson "doubled-down" by betting big that Japan's main stock index would not fall below 19,000. This seemed like a relatively safe gamble as Japan had been rebounding off a thirty-month recession. However, on January 17, 1995, a devastating earthquake hit the city of Kobe, Japan. The tragedy caused the Japanese stock index to tumble. When Leeson realized his gamble had failed, he attempted to move the market by placing orders to sell 20,000 contracts, each worth approximately $180,000. Ultimately, Leeson's gambling cost the bank $1.3 billion.

In analyzing what went wrong, the bank discovered that Leeson had been hiding his massive losses in a secret account. In the process, the bank identified serious control deficiencies that allowed Leeson to make massive speculative trades and hide his losses. The most serious flaw was

The case was prepared by Mark S. Beasley, Ph.D. and Frank A. Buckless, Ph.D. of North Carolina State University and Steven M. Glover, Ph.D. and Douglas F. Prawitt, Ph.D. of Brigham Young University, as a basis for class discussion. It is not intended to illustrate either effective or ineffective handling of an administrative situation.

that Leeson was allowed to function both as Chief Trader and to settle his own trades; functions that are typically segregated. This weakness in the design of controls at Barings proved fatal to the storied bank. For his crimes, including taking unauthorized actions that he did not disclose to his employer, Leeson served nearly 5 years in prison.

Many believed Leeson's $1.3 billion debacle would be the last of its kind as banks learned through Barings' demise how important appropriate risk assessment and strong controls are to the health of a bank. However, Jérôme Kerviel's trading losses would dwarf Leeson's.

BACKGROUND ON THE TRADER

Jérôme Kerviel, a 31-year-old low-level trader in Société Générale's European equities arbitrage unit, covered up unauthorized speculative trades that led to $7.2 billion loss. Kerviel claimed he didn't want to hurt the bank or embezzle funds; he was just out to enhance his reputation as a trader and increase his bonuses.

Kerviel was assigned to the "Delta One" desk, comprised of traders who specialized in low-risk, low-return trades. Kerviel's job was to limit the bank's risk by placing trading positions on whether a stock market index would rise or fall. However, Kerviel was required to have offsetting positions to limit the bank's exposure. Such hedging requirements not only limit the potential loss but also the potential gain from any single transaction; profits are generated through large volumes of transactions. While Kerviel's hedged positions would not completely offset, he was required to keep his net exposure to under 500,000 Euros.

Kerviel earned $147,0000 a year, a far smaller amount than the millions earned by higher-flying traders. Ironically, Kerviel was so low on the bank's pecking order that many didn't consider him a trader at all. That perception motivated him, and in some ways may have allowed him, to pull off the large-scale fraud. Kerviel confessed to police that he gambled in the markets and hid his activities from superiors because he wanted to be a star trader.

Société Générale's traders held little regard for the Delta One desk. For Mr. Kerviel, just getting to Delta One had been an achievement. For his first five years at the bank he labored in the back office, a place other traders derisively referred to as "the mine." While toiling away in the back office, Kerviel became expertly familiar with the bank's trading operations as well as internal controls and monitoring activities associated with trades.

Had Kerviel been one of the A-league traders in Société Générale's most prestigious trading area - the desks that handle complex equity derivatives - his actions likely would have drawn more attention. But the Delta One desk on the seventh floor of the bank's headquarters in western Paris dealt with a "boring" corner of the equities market. "We all lived in fear that something within the exotic products would blow up in our face. It never came to our mind that we might have a problem with Delta One," said a top Société Générale official.[1]

HOW HE CONCEALED FAKE TRADES

Kerviel was confident that he could make his mark if he were allowed to place bets on market movements without being constrained by offsetting trading positions. However, Kerviel knew he had to show offsetting trades in his book of business in order to make it look like he was following his company's guidelines. Kerviel decided to use his knowledge of the trading system and related controls to enter fake trades into the system to offset his real trades. While the bank's risk management group did monitor the overall positions closely, it did not verify the data Kerviel entered into the bank's trading system, accepting his fake contracts at face value. Kerviel's superiors focused on his net trading positions to ensure he had appropriate offsetting trades, but they had no mechanism to detect fictitious entries. For over 2 years, Kerviel built up

---

1   David Gauthier-Villars and Carrick Mollenkamp, "How Kerviel turned fake trades into real losses," *Wall Street Journal*, January 28, 2008.

massive exposures by placing unhedged real trades on stock index futures as well as buying options and warrants on individual stocks. This went undiscovered because he was always able to balance his books for the Delta One desk and never report a net large profit or loss (when his fictitious trades were considered).

Kerviel knew that certain nightly system checks and reconciliations built into the trading controls would check for particular features of trades that would likely reveal his ficticious trades. Because of his back-office experience, he knew when these reconciliations and other systems checks took place. To elude the controls, he simply erased all of his fictitious trades just before the system checks took place and then he re-created the fictitious positions immediately after the checks to keep his trading positions in balance. Temporary imbalances did not trigger alerts within the system. According to an internal probe on Kerviel's fraud compiled by 40 bank employees with oversight by PricewaterhouseCoopers (who was not Société Générale's external auditor), he was able to hide his losses and gains by entering pairs of fictitious transactions, one a purchase and the other a sale, for equal amounts of equities but for different prices; thus creating a fictitious loss or gain to cover his real losses and gains.[2]

Kerviel's trading volume grew beyond what would normally be expected of a Delta One trader. He knew that back-office controllers were organized into teams monitoring specific types of financial instruments and that they would be sensitive to abnormally large volumes of trades running through their balance sheets. Kerviel was careful to spread his trades, both real and fictitious, across a range of different financial instruments. Thus, even when one of Kerviel's trades did raise an alert, it appeared as an isolated incident associated with only one type of financial instrument.

Kerviel also avoided detection by using forward instead of futures contracts. Futures contracts are agreements to pay a certain price for a given commodity in the future. For example, the trader could enter into a futures contract for oil at $130 a barrel in 3 months. If oil is trading for more than $130 in 3 months, the trader has a gain; if the price is lower than $130, the trader has a loss. Futures contracts are usually zeroed or balanced daily with cash flows to cover the difference in prices. In contrast, forward contracts are only settled on the final day of the contract. Thus, by using forward contracts, Kerviel ensured that no money exchanged hands until the settlement date. To avoid having his fictitious contracts sent to actual institutions for approval, Kerviel "cancelled fictitious trades before they gave rise to any confirmation, settlement or control. In order to do so, he used features that left him time to cancel these trades and to replace them with new false trades."[3]

When documentation was required to support a trade, Kerviel would fabricate support. For example, Kerviel confessed that "I fabricated fake mail using a feature in our in-house messaging system, a function which allows you to reuse the electronic letterhead I had received and change the body of the text," he said.[4] Kerviel also told investigators that he frequently used logins and passwords of colleagues.

Kerviel's tactics to enter into large speculative bets on market movements, without an offsetting position, initially paid off handsomely. Questions from securities regulators in late 2007 made him nervous and Kerviel closed all his positions and locked in an actual gain of 1.6 billion Euros ($2.35 billion U.S.). Quite an amazing feat for someone at the Delta One desk! However, he was frustrated because he was not able to report the full gain without revealing his unauthorized activities, and he felt his superiors did not recognize and appreciate his trading skill and success. Just a few short weeks later, Kerviel's strategy would lead to the largest trading loss in history.

---

2   Société Générale General Inspection Department, "Report Part 3," May 20, 2008.

3   Ibid.

4   David Gauthier-Villars and Stacy Meichtry, "Kerviel felt out of his league," *Wall Street Journal*, January 31, 2008.

CONTROLS AND ALERTS

Perhaps the first clear warning of Kerviel's activities came in late 2006 or early 2007, when Kerviel made a 500,000 Euro profit on a one-way bet. Kerviel's role on the Delta trading desk did not allow him to speculate with the bank's money, and he was reprimanded by his bosses, who said his profit would not be included in his year-end bonus calculation. This incident alone should have been sufficient grounds to fire Mr. Kerviel. However, French banking experts have indicated that this reaction to inappropriate behavior was consistent with a culture of risk taking at Société Générale. It wasn't uncommon for traders to be rewarded for making a profit on risky investments with the bank's money, even if they had exceeded their trading limits in doing so.

Another warning sign came in November 2007, when the surveillance office at Eurex, the derivatives exchange, sent two email messages to Société Générale's compliance department questioning large positions held by Kerviel that were entered into after regular trading hours. In the same correspondence, Eurex asked what Kerviel's trading strategy was. This inquiry led to questions directed to Kerviel and Delta One supervisors. Société Générale responded on November 20 indicating no irregularities and that volatility in the U.S. and European stock markets explained the need for afterhours trading. Eurex was not satisfied and requested more information. Société Générale responded on December 10, and Eurex considered the second response adequate.

Société Générale's system of controls was designed to alert compliance officers of unusual or unexpected trades and Kerviel's fictitious trades clearly should have triggered alarms. In fact, a subsequent internal probe indicated there were at least 75 alerts between June 2006 and the beginning of 2008 that should have led to the investigation of Kerviel's unauthorized trading activity. Some of the unusual or unexpected aspects of Kerviel's trades that triggered alerts included:

- A trade with a maturity date that fell on a Saturday
- Trades without identified counterparties
- Trades with counterparties within Société Générale itself
- Trades that exceeded the limits of counterparties
- Broker names missing or listed as "pending"
- Large increases in broker fees.

"Several times, Mr. Kerviel's supervisors spotted mistakes in the trader's books. But Mr. Kerviel would claim it was a mistake and fix it," said Jean-Pierre Mustier, head of Société Générale's investment banking arm. "Société Générale got caught just like someone who would have installed a highly sophisticated alarm… and gets robbed because he forgot to shut the window," said the Société Générale manager.[5]

The internal investigation found that Kerviel increased the size of his fraudulent positions in January 2007 after the resignation of his direct manager. The manager was not immediately replaced and for two-and-a-half months there was little effective control over the desk. When a replacement manager was hired, he did not carry out any detailed analyses of trader's earnings or positions thereby failing to fulfill one of the main tasks expected from a trading manager. Kerviel's exposure continued to grow.

According to the internal inspection report, throughout the period when Kerviel was concealing fake trades, there was an absence of certain controls that might have identified the fraud. However, even when the bank's controls did properly identify fraud-risk factors, compliance inspectors often conducted only routine reviews and "did not systematically carry out more detailed checks" to validate Kerviel's assertions, even when they lacked plausibility. In early 2008 when compliance inspectors did ask for additional information regarding a Kerviel trade, Kerviel's response was accepted and the inspector later apologized to Kerviel for his excessive zeal in investigating the trade. Insiders have described the relation between traders and back-office staff as difficult or even

---

5   David Gauthier-Villars and Carrick Mollenkamp, "The Loss Where No One Looked; How Low-Level Trader Cost Société Générale," *Wall Street Journal*, January 28, 2008.

antagonistic. The bank's inspectors only received vague answers from traders or their supervisors. As one bank employee explained, "the name of the game is to say as little as possible to the [internal] inspectors."[6]

The internal report indicated that back-office staff did not inform supervisors when they noticed irregularities in Kerviel's transactions, even when the trades involved abnormally high amounts, "because this was not specifically part of their job description."[7] When managers were alerted of seemingly suspicious behavior, the report indicated that, in some cases, they simply did not react.

One of the key failings was that bank controllers were instructed to monitor only the net, rather than the gross, risk exposures of the Delta One traders' activities. Furthermore, the controllers relied on the balances recorded in Kerviel's books.

For more than two years, Kerviel used his knowledge of the control procedures to hide his speculative bets with roughly equal fictitious trades supported by forged documents and e-mails.

Transcripts of email conversations between Kerviel and another trader, Moussa Bakir, reveal that Kerviel was well aware of the gravity of his actions. After being questioned by Société Générale compliance inspectors about Eurex's concerns, Kerviel indicated he was so nervous he had trouble sleeping and eating. Bakir wrote, "You absolutely must take a vacation."

"In jail," Kerviel replied.

Later, Kerviel bragged to Bakir about his trades. "This will show the power of Kerviel," he wrote.

Bakir relied, "Or his irresponsibility… a simple and discreet boy. Unassuming. Who makes a pile of dough. And not recognized for his true value."

On January 17, the day compliance officers began asking questions, Kerviel felt the noose tightening and he wrote to Bakir, "I'm dead in the water."

Later that same day, Bakir replied, "Good luck pal."

"This pal is dead," Kerviel wrote.[8]

DISCOVERY OF THE FRAUD

Mr. Citerne, Société Générale's co-chief executive described how Kerviel was caught: "He changed a tactic he had been using to conceal his trades and taking a position that prompted a possible margin call (or demand for funds). That triggered some alerts."[9] At about the same time the bank's controls flagged a trading partner whose account showed abnormally high levels. When asked about it, the partner denied knowing anything. Further investigation led to Kerviel.

The bank soon learned of the fictitious contracts and that Kerviel had secretly exposed the bank to $73.5 billion in speculative one-sided positions—more than the total market value of the bank. Over a three-day period, the bank closed these positions, resulting in a $7.2 billion loss.

Kerviel is accused of stealing computer passwords, sending fake e-mail messages, and illegally accessing the bank's computer system to exceed trading limits and cover up his actions. He bought futures contracts but ignored requirements to offset them with countervailing buys.

---

6   Nicola Clark, "More questions for bank chief; Société Générale leader to face lawmakers," *The International Herald Tribune*, April 9, 2008.

7   David Gauthier-Villars, "Société Générale Details Lapses; Probe Says Staff Entrusted to Verify Kerviel's Trades Failed to Dig Deep Enough," *Wall Street Journal*, February 21, 2008.

8   Katrin Bennhold, "Transcript Reveals Details of French Trader's Actions," *The New York Times*, February 10, 2008.

9   David Gauthier-Villars, "French Bank Rocked by Rogue Trader," *Wall Street Journal*, January 25, 2008.

AFTERMATH

Société Générale recognized the massive losses resulting from the fraud in fiscal year 2007. Chief executive officer Daniel Bouton resigned in the wake of the trading fraud. The governor of the Bank of France has said that central bank officials warned Société Générale before the trading scandal that its back offices were insufficiently staffed. Unlike peer banks, Société Générale was not shy about taking proprietary trading risks (i.e., trading with bank's money rather than just facilitating customer trades) and such trades represented a large percentage of the bank's revenue. Experts believe the business grew faster than risk management could cope.

Société Générale announced in April 2008 that it expected to spend as much as 100 million Euros in 2008 to improve the bank's risk-management systems. However, the bank cautioned that the additional investment could never fully guarantee against frauds. Société Générale said that risk-control employees represent 62 percent of its investment banking division; up from 55 percent in 2002 and that it is tightening controls after the trading scandal.[10] Société Générale has also set up a dedicated internal fraud investigation group of around 20 people that will be independent of the front- and back-office operations.

Kerviel told police that his supervisors in the Delta One office were aware that he had overreached his trading limits. He said he was told to "straighten it out."[11] Kerviel said he believes his supervisors knew about his fictitious trades, but as long as he was making money, they didn't care. He said, "I cannot believe that my superiors did not realize the amount I was risking. It is impossible to generate such profit with small positions. That's what leads me to say that while I was in the black, my supervisors closed their eyes on the methods I was using and the volumes I was trading."[12]

At a trading conference in London in April 2008, Nick Leeson said, "There's not enough investment that goes into control functions. A lot of money is still targeted at the front office where the actual money is made and that creates dangerous imbalances." Leeson, in comparing his trading activities to Kerviel's, indicated that much of the blame should go to poor systems and controls. He went on to say that, "There was also a lack of understanding in the organization of what I was doing so there was no one around to challenge me. That was similar to Jérôme Kerviel."[13]

While waiting trail, Kerviel took a job at a suburban computer company, and in a media campaign he depicted himself as a regular guy from a modest background. In 2010 a French judge found Kerviel guilty of breach of trust, forgery, and unauthorized computer use. He was sentenced to 3 years in prison and ordered to pay restitution of 4.9 billion euros to the Société Générale. A spokeswoman for the bank said the damage award was "symbolic" and the bank did not expect it would be collected.[14]

---

10 Nicola Clark, "Société Générale tightens controls after trading scandal," *International Herald Tribune*. Paris: April 10, 2008.

11 Nicola Clark, "French Trader's Bets Said to Have Set Off Alarms," *The New York Times*, February 15, 2008.

12 David Gauthier-Villars and Stacy Meichtry, "Kerviel felt out of his league," *Wall Street Journal*, January 31, 2008.

13 Nicola Clark, "More questions for bank chief; Société Générale leader to face lawmakers," *The International Herald Tribune*, April 9, 2008.

14 Nicola Clark, "Rogue Trader at Société Générale Gets 3 Years," *The New York Times*, October 5, 2010.

REQUIRED

[1] Using auditing standards or your textbook, define the following control-related terms:

    [a] Control environment

    [b] Segregation of duties

    [c] Restricted access

    [d] Preventative and detective controls

    [e] Design and operating effectiveness

[2] The term "tone at the top" is typically associated with a firm's control environment. How would you characterize Société Générale's tone at the top and what effect do you believe that had on oversight at the trading-desk level?

[3] Fraud research indicates three conditions must exist before a fraud occurs: (1) Pressure/Incentive, (2) Rationalization, and (3) Opportunity. What do you think were Jérôme Kerviel's incentives and rationalizations for committing fraud? What created the opportunity for fraud?

[4] In an independent audit of the financial statements of a large bank, why do auditors typically follow a controls reliance strategy (i.e., obtaining some audit assurance via controls testing)? In the case of Société Générale, do you believe the external auditors gathered much controls-related evidence regarding the Delta One trading desk? Why or why not?

[5] What do you believe were the three most serious control deficiencies at Société Générale? For each deficiency listed, indicate whether the deficiency related to poor design or poor operating effectiveness. Describe how you would remediate or fix each of the deficiencies listed.

[6] What are the advantages and disadvantages of promoting personnel across functional areas within a company (e.g., from risk and controls to operations)?

[7] The loss from Kerviel's rogue trading resulted in a loss many times greater than audit materiality. The external auditor did not discover the misstatement. Was this an audit failure? Conduct internet research to determine if the external auditors, Ernst & Young Audit and Deloitte & Associés, were named in law suits associated with the loss due to the trading fraud.

The Impact of Information Technology

CASES INCLUDED IN THIS SECTION

OTHER CASES THAT DISCUSS TOPICS RELATED TO THIS SECTION

Harley-Davidson, Inc.

Identifying eBusiness Risks and Related Assurance Services for the eBusiness Marketplace

MARK S. BEASLEY · FRANK A. BUCKLESS · STEVEN M. GLOVER · DOUGLAS F. PRAWITT

LEARNING OBJECTIVES

After completing and discussing this case you should be able to

[1] Identify business risks associated with eBusiness models used in today's supply-chain management systems

[2] Describe assurance services CPAs can provide to clients involved in eBusiness partnerships

[3] Recommend effective internal controls to address risks associated with eBusiness supply-chain systems

INTRODUCTION

The Harley-Davidson Motor Company (Harley-Davidson) began over 100 years ago, fulfilling a dream of 21-year-old William S. Harley and 20-year-old Arthur Davidson. In 1903, they made available to the public the first Harley-Davidson motorcycle, a bike built to be a racer. The factory in which they worked was a 10- by 15-feet wooden shed with the words "Harley-Davidson Motor Company" scrawled on the door. Arthur's brother Walter later joined their efforts.

Over one-hundred years later, Harley-Davidson's total assets and net sales have each grown to over $4 billion, with annual production of over 220,000 motorcycles and a 55% share of the U.S. heavyweight motorcycle market with 31 domestic models included in its 2010 model year.

The Milwaukee-based company has an avid following of motorcycle enthusiasts. The Harley-Davidson Owners Group, frequently referred to as "H.O.G.," is the largest factory-sponsored motorcycle club in the world, with over one million members worldwide. In 2002, *FORBES* summarized the tremendous success of Harley-Davidson to that point:

> *"In a disastrous year for hundreds of companies, Harley's estimated 2001 sales grew 15%, to $3.3 billion, and its earnings grew 26%, to $435 million. Its shares were up 40% in 2001, while the S&P dropped 15%. Recessions don't phase this profit machine. Harley grew right through the last one, too. In fact, since Harley's initial public offering in 1986, the company has put up 37% average annual earnings growth. Investors who went looking for tech sizzle and cover-boy chief executives would have done better with hogs. Since Harley went public, its shares have risen 15,000%. Intel? A mere 7,200% since 1986. GE? A paltry 1,056%."*[1]

---

1   Fahey, Jonathan. "Love Into Money." *FORBES*, January 7, 2002: 60-65.

The case was prepared by Mark S. Beasley, Ph.D. and Frank A. Buckless, Ph.D. of North Carolina State University and Steven M. Glover, Ph.D. and Douglas F. Prawitt, Ph.D. of Brigham Young University, as a basis for class discussion. It is not intended to illustrate either effective or ineffective handling of an administrative situation.

HARLEY-DAVIDSON'S eBUSINESS SUPPLY CHAIN

In the mid-1990s, Harley-Davidson faced the enormous challenge of meeting production demand for its motorcycles. Like many companies in today's global marketplace, Harley-Davidson struggled to manage all of its upstream suppliers (who provide parts and raw materials) to ensure the effective downstream manufacture and delivery of motorcycles to customers. Company leaders found that managing complex supply-chains, which involve material and information flows concerning new product development, systems management, operations and assembly, production scheduling, order processing, inventory management, transportation, warehousing and customer service, presents numerous challenges for large manufacturing organizations like Harley-Davidson.

Harley-Davidson attacked the supply-chain problem by streamlining its cumbersome and bureaucratic supply-chain into a vertically and technologically integrated system of suppliers directly interested in Harley-Davidson's success. To assist with the transformation, Harley-Davidson's Vice President of Materials Management, Garry Berryman, initiated a consolidation of Harley-Davidson's supply-chain to overhaul this vital aspect of company management. His plan involved a company-wide consolidation of its various purchasing departments, the formation of new business partnerships, and several technological innovations.

Consistent with other companies with complex supply-chain systems, Harley-Davidson faced huge hurdles associated with coordinating a large number of material requirements and suppliers. To effectively implement its internal supply chain makeover, Harley-Davidson had to radically alter its corporate purchasing philosophy and move to a more centralized purchasing process. Prior to initiating the overhaul, Harley-Davidson had nine separate purchasing systems, over 4,000 separate suppliers, and little or no central guidance for purchasing. The company consolidated its purchasing function by forming a select group of suppliers from its enormous supply chain and ultimately cut its supplier base by 80%, from 4,000 to 800 suppliers.

In addition to consolidating its purchasing function, Harley-Davidson also worked hard to foster new business partnerships with these key suppliers, but bringing the suppliers into strategic partnerships was difficult. Management had to show its business partners that being selected as a key supplier for a company like Harley-Davidson would have a tremendous positive impact. Then, the company had to convince suppliers to agree to certain conditions associated with its offer. For example, Georgia Pacific's Unisource division had to commit to double quality, cut product development time in half, and simultaneously lower the cost of goods in order to meet Harley-Davidson's requirements for inclusion in its supply chain. Fortunately, Unisource recognized the potential payoff. Unisource's revenues increased over ten times as a result of being selected as a key Harley-Davidson supplier.

Once suppliers were integrated into Harley-Davidson's supply chain, the company faced another problem: how to effectively and seamlessly share information with its new network of suppliers? Harley-Davidson turned to the Internet as the solution for integrating its supplier network. Use of the Internet enabled smaller suppliers, previously unable to connect to the company's legacy electronic data interface (EDI) systems, to participate in the supply-chain process. The versatility of the Internet provided an interface for transactions and interactions with the majority of its suppliers, removing costly hurdles imposed by the restrictive technology compatibility requirements of its old EDI systems.[2]

To provide the technological interface for communicating with its suppliers, Harley-Davidson selected Manugistics Group, Inc. to power the Harley-Davidson Supplier Network that provides real-time access to detailed order and inventory data. Manugistics is one of the leading suppliers of Enterprise Profit Optimization (EPO) services. These services use information technology (IT) innovations to allow companies and their suppliers to lower operating costs by simultaneously improving supply-chain management and supplier relationship management.[3]

---

2 Milligan, Bryan. "Harley-Davidson Wins by Getting Suppliers On Board." *Purchasing,* September 21, 2000: 52-65.

3 *PR Newswire,* September 27, 2001.

The Manugistics-designed private Internet trading network enables Harley-Davidson and its trading partners to communicate and collaborate around key aspects of the company's supply chain. The network provides transaction execution capability to the company's supply chain. Suppliers have the ability to initiate and monitor transactions related to the order lifecycle, from planning through order processing and invoicing. For example, the Harley-Davidson eBusiness supply-chain network enables suppliers to access information from Harley-Davidson about upcoming demand for parts and past order histories. The system includes supplier-reporting tools and even allows Harley and its suppliers to create collaborative forecasts for parts needs. This eBusiness site offers secure access to billing histories and a full year's forecast for total demand for various parts.

The company also encouraged cost reductions through innovation and efficiency. After whittling down the number of relationships to be managed, Berryman invited Harley-Davidson's key suppliers to place employees at Harley's facilities, thereby including key suppliers not only in purchasing decisions but also in product design and manufacturing discussions. These in-house suppliers were granted access to Harley's Intranet, which allows suppliers access to meeting minutes, schedules, plans, and other internal systems. With increased sharing of information between Harley-Davidson and its supply-chain through Harley-Davidson's Intranet, the company became a model for successfully using eBusiness and technologically-fueled partnerships to facilitate and enhance core business activities.

Dave Cotteleer, Harley-Davidson's Manager of Planning and Control explained some of the motives for the change:

> "We're using technology to cut back on communication times and administrative trivia, like invoice tracking, so we can focus the relationships on more strategic issues. We're not saying, "Here's a neat piece of technology. Let's jam it into our model...Our goal is to have the suppliers doing their own replenishing, using the site. They can see what our consumption rates are, rather than trying to project (them) based on historical information."[4]

Did these changes make a difference? By forming strategic alliances with all of its top suppliers, bringing them into the design and planning process, and integrating with them through the Internet, Harley-Davidson was able to dramatically reduce the cost of producing its famous "hogs." The company shaved $40 million off its materials costs over a five-year period. Product-development time fell by 30%. Defect levels on bike parts plummeted from an average of 10,000 defective parts per million to only 48 parts per million for over 75% of its suppliers.[5]

BENEFITS AND RISKS OF eBUSINESS MODELS[6]

eBusiness solutions, such as Harley-Davidson's supply-chain system, leverage the power of information technology (IT) and electronic communication networks, such as the Internet, to transform critical business strategies and processes. These eBusiness models remove traditional boundaries of time and geography and make possible the creation of new virtual communities of suppliers and customers.

Formally defined, eBusiness is the use of IT and electronic communication networks to exchange business information and conduct transactions in electronic, paperless form. As indicated in the definition, eBusiness includes the exchange of business information that may or may not directly relate to the purchase or sale of goods or services. For example, businesses are increasingly using electronic mechanisms to improve company performance by facilitating collaboration and data sharing among employees as well as to provide improved customer support. Participants in eBusiness transactions and information exchanges may be individuals (consumers and employees)

---

4   Sullivan, Missy, "High-Octane Hog." *FORBES,* September 10, 2001: 8-10.

5   Ibid.

6   See Glover, Liddle, Prawitt, *eBusiness: Principles & Strategies for Accountants,* Prentice Hall, 2001

or automated agents (information systems that are programmed to perform with little or no human intervention). Transactions and information exchanges can take place within a company, between companies, between companies and individuals, and between individuals.

As evidenced by Harley-Davidson's supply-chain network, the Internet is frequently one of the electronic mechanisms used by companies to support core business functions. Companies that recognize the ability of the Internet to assist in essential business operations often find synergies through the implementation of the technology. eBusiness is becoming an integral part of the way many companies conduct business.

The integration of technology at companies like Harley-Davidson, however, introduces new issues and risks that must be effectively managed. Companies must be sure they have the resources to integrate new technologies effectively and efficiently. This is often accomplished through strategic partnerships within the company's supply chain and by adding partners to obtain technical abilities not currently found within the organization.

eBusiness partnerships create interdependencies between business partners that can substantially increase the amount of business risk faced by each organization. The success of technology-linked partnerships is often determined by the ability of each partner to identify and mitigate risks to its business and IT systems. The integrity and quality of each partner's IT system and the communication system between partners are critical. Because of the amount of information access and sharing that takes place in eBusiness partnerships, participating companies must be concerned not only with the integrity of their own information systems, but also with the quality of the IT systems of their strategic business partners. An effectively integrated system involves not only an interdependent relationship between business partners, but also a complete system of hardware, software, people, procedures, and data that effectively isolates and manages the risks associated with eBusiness models. Because of the interdependencies often involved in an eBusiness environment, organizations must realize their responsibility to ensure that trading partners are using effective risk identification and management practices to protect the strength and the integrity of the entire network of interdependent enterprises.

Understanding the benefits and risks associated with eBusiness models is important to CPAs for several reasons. First, CPAs need a good understanding of the key technologies underlying eBusiness models to effectively identify, measure, and assess the related costs and benefits when potential eBusiness solutions are being evaluated. In addition, CPAs who are engaged as auditors to provide assurance about client financial statements need a good understanding of eBusiness systems to effectively evaluate business risks that may increase the likelihood of material misstatements in those financial statements. Such an understanding is particularly vital today given the new risk assessment standards. Further, auditors of public companies are required by the Sarbanes–Oxley Act of 2002 to provide an opinion on the operating effectiveness of internal control over financial reporting. To do so, they must understand the nature of eBusiness partnerships powered by the Internet and the risks and controls involved.

REQUIRED

[1] Identify the most significant new business risks facing Harley-Davidson as a result of integrating eBusiness into its supply-chain management system and by allowing suppliers to have access to the company's Intranet. If your instructor does not specify the number of risks for you to identify, list at least three.

[2] For each risk you identified in question number one above, identify a control Harley-Davidson might have implemented to mitigate that risk.

Note: Your instructor may request that you prepare your answers to questions 1 and 2 using the worksheet found on the website: www.pearsonhighered.com/beasley5e.

[3] Given the technology linkages between business partners in eBusiness systems, how might an eBusiness system like Harley-Davidson's increase business risks for its business partners?

[4] Research the *SysTrust* and *WebTrust* services from the information on the following website (or search the Internet or within the AICPA's Information Technology Center website for "Trust Services"): http://www.webtrust.org. Describe how *WebTrust* services differ from *SysTrust* services. Describe how they are related.

[5] What *Trust Services Principles* are examined in a *SysTrust* engagement? Describe the role of the criteria when evaluating these principles in a *SysTrust* engagement.

[6] According to the CICA website indicated in question number four, what professional standards must a CPA follow when providing assurance services that result in the expression of a *WebTrust* or *SysTrust* opinion?

[7] Assume Harley-Davidson asks your CPA firm about the *WebTrust* and *SysTrust* services that it provides. Write a brief memo to Gerry Berryman, Vice president of Materials Management, detailing the potential benefits of *WebTrust* and *SysTrust* for Harley-Davidson. Include in the memo a recommendation regarding which of these assurance services would be most appropriate for Harley-Davidson's supply chain management system. Be sure to explain to Mr. Berryman the nature of the two different services and why you are recommending the one you chose.

Jacksonville Jaguars
Evaluating IT Benefits and Risks and Identifying Trust Services Opportunities

MARK S. BEASLEY · FRANK A. BUCKLESS · STEVEN M. GLOVER · DOUGLAS F. PRAWITT

LEARNING OBJECTIVES

After completing and discussing this case you should be able to

[1] Identify benefits to businesses from implementing information technology

[2] Recognize risks that are associated with the use of information technology

[3] Understand the *Trust Services® Principles and Criteria* framework of assurance services

[4] Distinguish between *SysTrust®* and *WebTrust®* services

[5] Determine how CPAs can provide assurance about processes designed to reduce risks created when new information technology systems are introduced

INTRODUCTION

The Jacksonville Jaguars National Football League (NFL) team was one of the first major sporting organizations to take advantage of information technology (IT) tools in the sale of stadium snacks and souvenirs. Beginning in 1995, football fans at Alltel Stadium (which is now called the EverBank Field), where the Jaguars play their home games, began using Spot Cards to purchase soft drinks, beer, popcorn, and Jaguar souvenirs rather than fumble for cash and change when making their purchases.[1] These reloadable Spot Cards, which contain an embedded computer chip, operate in a manner similar to other smart cards such as Kinko's ExpressPay cards and many retail establishments including university student identification cards that are used for fee payment, meal and book purchases, and building access.

Not only does the Spot Card offer benefits to fans in the stadium, but the use of IT also offers advantages for snack and souvenir vendors by providing better information for monitoring their businesses. Although IT offers improvements for the fans and vendors, those who rely on the Spot Card to process sales need assurance that the technology and related information produced is accurate and reliable.

BACKGROUND

The implementation of the Spot Card at the stadium in Jacksonville in the fall of 1995 represents one the first uses of that type of IT in a major sports stadium. The stadium contracted with First Union Bank, (which was subsequently acquired by the Wachovia Corporation that is now part of Wells Fargo Bank, one of the country's largest financial institutions), to develop and implement the Spot Card system. First Union contracted with Diebold Incorporated of Canton, Ohio, a manufacturer of card-based transaction systems, to develop the Spot Card system.

---

1 Many of the facts about the Spot Card system are based on an article titled, "Jacksonville Jaguars Fans Score Big with Smart Cards," by Maura McEnaney which appeared in *EC World*, January 1998, pp. 24 –27.

The case was prepared by Mark S. Beasley, Ph.D. and Frank A. Buckless, Ph.D. of North Carolina State University and Steven M. Glover, Ph.D. and Douglas F. Prawitt, Ph.D. of Brigham Young University, as a basis for class discussion. It is not intended to illustrate either effective or ineffective handling of an administrative situation.

A description of how the system was originally designed to function follows. Customers purchased Spot Cards in various denominations such as $20, $50, and $100. ATM-like machines in the stadium allowed fans to transfer funds from their bank or credit card onto an electronic chip on the Spot Card. Fans could also buy cards with cash or with a debit card. Other terminals were located in various bank branches around Jacksonville. Card readers located throughout the stadium allowed fans to check card balances.

Fans purchasing snacks and souvenirs presented their Spot Card to vendors at concession and souvenir stands who calculated sales amounts and swiped the cards through point-of-sale (POS) machines. Software tracked each transaction for vendors. Before the transaction was complete, fans reviewed the amount to be deducted and punched the "Yes" key on the POS machine. At that point, the POS device deducted the purchase amount from the chip-embedded balance on the fan's Spot Card. These cards could also be used at battery-operated POS computers carried by vendors who roamed the stadium stands selling merchandise during the game.

The POS machines captured information about each transaction. The system recorded the card number, location code, and the date and time of the transaction as well as the items sold. That information was later summarized for vendors.

Once the game was over, vendors linked their POS machines to a network that allowed the transfer of data stored on each POS machine to a computer located in the stadium counting room. Once all the data were downloaded to that computer, the information was then transmitted to a host computer at the bank in Jacksonville. The host computer used the transmitted data to settle that day's sales with each vendor in the stadium. The host computer produced various reports, which provided vendors detailed information to track sales volume for specific products in specific sections of the stadium.

The bank received a fee from every Spot Card transaction, and the bank collected whatever remained on an unused Spot Card at the end of two years. Soon after implementation, the bank also began selling player-signature Spot Cards with pictures of selected Jaguar players on the front for an additional fee. Other stadiums around the country, such as the Carolina Panthers' stadium in North Carolina, have used similar technologies.

OPPORTUNITIES FOR CPAS TO PROVIDE ASSURANCE

In the mid-1990s, the American Institute of Certified Public Accountants (AICPA) began to develop CPA "assurance services" opportunities designed to allow CPAs to provide assurance about the reliability and relevance of information decision-makers use to run their businesses.

Certain forms of assurance services have always been performed by CPAs. For example, auditors of historical financial statements provide assurance about whether those financial statements are in conformity with generally accepted accounting principles. Continuous changes in IT provide new opportunities for CPAs to provide assurance regarding the accuracy, reliability and relevance of information produced by these technologies. As IT continues to play a larger role in business, some argue that the need for assurance on IT systems and controls will continue.

In response to this perceived need, the AICPA developed *Trust Services Principles and Criteria* that provide a framework for CPAs to assess and report on various aspects of information system reliability and accuracy. The *Trust Services Principles and Criteria* are developed within the framework of the Statement on Standards for Attestation Engagements (the "attestation standards"). Only CPAs may provide *Trust Services* that result in a *Trust Services* opinion.

Under the *Trust Services* framework, CPAs can be engaged to perform an AICPA *SysTrust* service to provide assurance regarding the reliability of IT systems. In these engagements, CPAs can provide users with assurance that an IT system has been properly designed and produces reliable data. In doing so, CPAs might test the integrity of an information system by analyzing sample IT output for accuracy. Assurance providers can also provide valuable services to help organizations determine whether systems are secure and whether adequate contingency plans are in place in the event of system failure or disaster.

REQUIRED – PART A

[1] To become more familiar with these assurance service opportunities, obtain a copy of the *Trust Services Principles and Criteria*, which can be located on the Internet. Use your internet browser to locate a copy of the framework by conducting a search for "Trust Services Principles and Criteria." Most likely you will find a link to the framework posted on the AICPA's website (http://www.aicpa.org) by entering "trust services principles" in the search box. Use the framework to complete the following exercises:

[a] Summarize in your own words the objective of a *Trust Services* engagement.

[b] What are the five *Trust Services Principles*? Provide a brief description of each Principle.

[c] For each of the five *Trust Services Principles*, describe why management at Alltel Stadium or fans in the stadium could have benefitted from assurance about how the Spot Card technology complies with each of the five *Trust Services Principles*. For example, why might management be interested in obtaining assurance about the Spot Card's system's compliance with the "Security" principle?

[d] What are the purposes of "Principles" and "Criteria?" How do they relate and how do they differ?

[e] What is the relationship between a *SysTrust* engagement and the *Trust Services Principles and Criteria*? You may need to conduct an Internet-based search to locate more information about *SystTrust* services.

[f] What is the difference between a *SysTrust* engagement and a *WebTrust* engagement? You may need to conduct an Internet-based search to locate more information about these services.

[2] The use of IT offers tremendous advantages. At the time of implementation, what benefits did the use of Spot Cards offer to the following groups:

- Jaguar stadium snack and souvenir vendors?
- Fans in the stadium?
- First Union Bank?

[3] While the Spot Card offered several benefits, the use of the related information technology to process snack and souvenir transactions did create new risks. Identify risks for the following groups:

- Snack and souvenir vendors
- Fans in the stadium
- First Union Bank

[4] What processes or controls might the stadium and First Union have implemented to help reduce these risks?

[5] What kind of information could the CPA examine and evaluate in order to assure stadium vendors that they could reasonably rely on the Spot Card system to conduct business?

[6] Using *Trust Services Principles and Criteria* for the "Online Privacy Principle," develop an online privacy policy for Alltel Stadium that could be posted on the stadium's website for customers to review before using the Spot Card technology.

Jacksonville Jaguars Part B
Do not proceed to this part of the case
unless requested to do so by your instructor.

BACKGROUND

Congratulations!!! You were recently promoted to manager within your firm. Your strong work ethic and, of course, your excellent college training have propelled your career to new heights.

One of the challenges of your new role is that you are now held accountable for finding new business opportunities for the firm. You have been regularly reading the financial business press (i.e., newspapers, business magazines) to see if you can identify new service opportunities.

The firm's managing partner came to you today and asked if you knew of any companies that recently introduced new IT that could lead to *Trust Services* engagement opportunities. After you indicated you are actually working on a couple of ideas, he was excited to hear more. He asked you to prepare a memorandum outlining your answers to address the following issues:

REQUIRED – PART B

[1] Please describe a situation where a company recently introduced a new information technology into its business operations. You should look for a real world example from the business press. Look for a business that recently increased its reliance on IT. The Spot Card technology used at the Jacksonville Jaguars stadium is a good example. Please attach a copy of the article you use to prepare your memorandum.

[2] Please describe the new technology and how it is used. Provide enough information for the partner to understand the technology without having to go back to the attached article.

[3] Explain why the company introduced the technology. Highlight the benefits to various constituents affected by the technology. The benefits related to the technology are probably easily identified and may even be discussed in the related article. However, the article does not likely address risks that are introduced. Please provide a thorough discussion of the risks to all parties affected by the new technology.

[4] Given the risks identified, describe whether there are any related *Trust Services* opportunities and discuss why you might be engaged to provide those services for the company situation you identified. Describe IT-related risks about which your firm could provide *Trust Services*. Your memo will serve as the basis for the formal business proposal that will be sent to the potential client. Please be sure to briefly outline in your memo what *Trust Services* are because the potential client may be unfamiliar with the term. Make sure you explain the term in your own words so that the potential client has a better idea of exactly what services you propose to provide.

[5] In describing the nature of the services that you plan to provide, please highlight the types of evidence you would want to gather as a basis for providing the assurance. For example, you might consider evaluating the contingency plan describing how the company would deal with breakdowns in technology hardware or software or in the communication infrastructure. In this example, you would want to specifically describe what types of information you would look for in that plan.

Your partner is very busy and doesn't want your memo to be too long. So, strive to be clear and concise and be sure to attach the related article(s) to your memo. Try to step out of the typical accountant's box and be creative!!! You'll be expected to do so in the real world.

Planning Materiality

CASES INCLUDED IN THIS SECTION

OTHER CASES THAT DISCUSS TOPICS RELATED TO THIS SECTION

Anne Aylor, Inc.
Determination of Planning Materiality and Tolerable Misstatement

Mark S. Beasley · Frank A. Buckless · Steven M. Glover · Douglas F. Prawitt

LEARNING OBJECTIVES

After completing and discussing this case you should be able to

[1] Determine planning materiality for an audit client

[2] Provide support for your materiality decisions

[3] Allocate planning materiality to financial statement elements

INTRODUCTION

Anne Aylor, Inc. (Anne Aylor) is a leading national specialty retailer of high-quality women's apparel, shoes, and accessories sold primarily under the "Anne Aylor" brand name. Anne Aylor is a highly recognized national brand that defines a distinct fashion point of view. Anne Aylor merchandise represents classic styles, updated to reflect current fashion trends. Company stores offer a full range of career and casual separates, dresses, tops, weekend wear, shoes and accessories coordinated as part of a total wardrobing strategy. The company places a significant emphasis on customer service. Company sales associates are trained to assist customers in merchandise selection and wardrobe coordination, helping them achieve the "Anne Aylor" look while maintaining the customers' personal styles.

The company follows the standard fiscal year of the retail industry, which is a 52-or 53-week period ending on the Saturday closest to January 31 of the following year. Net revenue for the year ended January 29, 2011 (referred to as fiscal 2011) was $1.4 billion and net income was $58 million.

At the end of fiscal 2011, the company operated approximately 584 retail stores located in 46 states under the name Anne Aylor. The company's core business focuses on relatively affluent, fashion-conscious professional women with limited shopping time. Substantially all of the company's merchandise is developed in-house by its product design and development teams. Production of merchandise is sourced to 131 independent manufacturers located in 19 countries. Approximately 45 percent, 16 percent, 13 percent, 12 percent, and 9 percent of the company's merchandise is manufactured in China, Philippines, Indonesia, India, and Vietnam, respectively. Merchandise is distributed to the company's retail stores through a single distribution center, located in Louisville, Kentucky.

Anne Aylor stock trades on The New York Stock Exchange and Anne Aylor is required to have an integrated audit of its consolidated financial statements and its internal control over financial reporting in accordance with the standards of the Public Company Accounting Oversight Board (United States). As of the close of business on March 11, 2011 Anne Aylor had 48,879,663 shares of common stock outstanding with a trading price of $22.57.

The case was prepared by Mark S. Beasley, Ph.D. and Frank A. Buckless, Ph.D. of North Carolina State University and Steven M. Glover, Ph.D. and Douglas F. Prawitt, Ph.D. of Brigham Young University, as a basis for class discussion. Anne Aylor, Inc. is a fictitious company. All characters and names represented are fictitious; any similarity to existing companies or persons is purely coincidental.

BACKGROUND

Your firm, Smith and Jones, P.A., is in the initial planning phase for the fiscal 2012 audit of Anne Aylor, Inc. (i.e., the audit for the year that will end on January 28, 2012). As the audit manager, you have been assigned responsibility for determining planning materiality and tolerable misstatement for key financial statement accounts. Your firm's materiality and tolerable misstatement guidelines have been provided to assist you with this assignment (see Exhibit 1).

Donna Fontain, the audit partner, has performed a preliminary analysis of the company and its performance and believes the likelihood of management fraud is low. Donna's initial analysis of the company's performance is documented in the memo referenced as G-3 (top right hand corner of the document). Additionally, Donna has documented current events/issues noted while performing the preliminary analysis in a separate memo, G-4. You have recorded the audited fiscal 2011 and projected fiscal 2012 financial statement numbers on audit schedule G-7. The company's accounting policies are provided in Exhibit 2. Assume no material misstatements were discovered during the fiscal 2011 audit.

REQUIRED

[1] Review Exhibits 1 and 2; audit memos G-3, and G-4; and audit schedules G-5, G-6 and G-7. Based on your review, answer each of the following questions:

[a] Why are different materiality bases considered when determining planning materiality?

[b] Why are different materiality thresholds relevant for different audit engagements?

[c] Why is the materiality base that results in the smallest threshold generally used for planning purposes?

[d] Why is the risk of management fraud considered when determining tolerable misstatement?

[e] Why might an auditor not use the same tolerable misstatement amount or percentage of account balance for all financial statement accounts?

[f] Why does the combined total of individual account tolerable misstatements commonly exceed the estimate of planning materiality?

[g] Why might certain trial balance amounts be projected when considering planning materiality?

[2] Based on your review of the Exhibits (1 and 2), audit memos (G-3, and G-4), and audit schedules (G-5, G 6-1, and G 6-2), complete audit schedules G-5, G-6 and G-7.

EXHIBIT 1

Smith and Jones, PA.
Policy Statement: Planning Materiality

This policy statement provides general guidelines for firm personnel when establishing planning materiality and tolerable misstatement for purposes of determining the nature, timing, and extent of audit procedures. The intent of this policy statement is not to suggest that these materiality guidelines must be followed on all audit engagements. The appropriateness of these materiality guidelines must be determined on an engagement by engagement basis, using professional judgment.

Planning Materiality Guidelines

Planning materiality represents the maximum, combined financial statement misstatement or omission that could occur before influencing the decisions of reasonable individuals relying on the financial statements. The magnitude and nature of financial statement misstatements or omissions will not have the same influence on all financial statement users. For example, a 5 percent misstatement with current assets may be more relevant for a creditor than a stockholder, while a 5 percent misstatement with net income before income taxes may be more relevant for a stockholder than a creditor. Therefore, the primary consideration when determining materiality is the expected users of the financial statements.

Relevant financial statement elements and presumptions on the effect of combined misstatements or omissions that would be considered immaterial and material are provided below:

- **Net Income Before Income Taxes** – combined misstatements or omissions less than 2 percent of Net Income Before Income Taxes are presumed to be immaterial and combined misstatements or omissions greater than 7 percent are presumed to be material. (Note: Net Income Before Income Taxes may not be an appropriate base if the client's Net Income Before Income Taxes is substantially below other companies of equal size or is highly variable.)
- **Net Revenue** – combined misstatements or omissions less than 0.5 percent of Net Revenue are presumed to be immaterial, and combined misstatements or omissions greater than 2 percent are presumed to be material.
- **Current Assets** – combined misstatements or omissions less than 2 percent of Current Assets are presumed to be immaterial, and combined misstatements or omissions greater than 7 percent are presumed to be material.
- **Current Liabilities** – combined misstatements or omissions less than 2 percent of Current Liabilities are presumed to be immaterial and combined misstatements or omissions greater than 7 percent are presumed to be material.
- **Total Assets** – combined misstatements or omissions less than 0.5 percent of Total Assets are presumed to be immaterial, and combined misstatements or omissions greater than 2 percent are presumed to be material. (Note: Total Assets may not be an appropriate base for service organizations or other organizations that have few operating assets.)

The specific amounts established for each financial statement element must be determined by considering the primary users as well as qualitative factors. For example, if the client is close to violating the minimum current ratio requirement for a loan agreement, a smaller planning materiality amount should be used for current assets and liabilities. Conversely, if the client is substantially above the minimum current ratio requirement for a loan agreement, it would be reasonable to use a higher planning materiality amount for current assets and current liabilities.

Planning materiality should be based on the smallest amount established from relevant materiality bases to provide reasonable assurance that the financial statements, taken as a whole, are not materially misstated for any user.

Tolerable Misstatement Guidelines

In addition to establishing materiality for the overall financial statements, materiality for individual financial statement accounts should be established. The amount established for individual accounts is referred to as "tolerable misstatement." Tolerable misstatement represents the amount individual financial statement accounts can differ from their true amount without affecting the fair presentation of the financial statements taken as a whole. Establishment of tolerable misstatement for individual accounts enables the auditor to design and execute an audit strategy for each audit cycle.

The objective in setting tolerable misstatement for individual financial statement accounts is to provide reasonable assurance that the financial statements taken as a whole are fairly presented in all material respects at the lowest cost.

To provide reasonable assurance that the financial statements taken as a whole do not contain material misstatements, the tolerable misstatement established for individual financial statement accounts should not exceed 75 percent of planning materiality. The percentage threshold should be lower as the expectation for management fraud increases. In many audits it is reasonable to expect that individual financial accounts misstatements identified will be less than tolerable misstatement and that misstatements across accounts will offset each other (some identified misstatements will overstate net income and some identified misstatements will understate net income). This expectation is not reasonable when the likelihood of management fraud is high. If management is intentionally trying to misstate the financial statements, it is likely that misstatements will be systematically biased in one direction across accounts.

The tolerable misstatement percentage threshold should not exceed:

- 75 percent of planning materiality if low likelihood of management fraud
- 50 percent of planning materiality if reasonably low likelihood of management fraud, and
- 25 percent of planning materiality if moderate likelihood of management fraud

Finally a lower tolerable misstatement may be required for specific accounts because of the relevance of the account to users. Tolerable misstatement for a specific account should not exceed that amount that would influence the decision of reasonable users.

Approved: April 24, 2009

EXHIBIT 2

Anne Aylor, Inc.
Accounting Policies

Revenue Recognition – The Company records revenue as merchandise is sold to clients. The Company's policy with respect to gift certificates and gift cards is to record revenue as they are redeemed for merchandise. Prior to their redemption, these gift certificates and gift cards are recorded as a liability. While the Company honors all gift certificates and gift cards presented for payment, management reviews unclaimed property laws to determine gift certificate and gift card balances required for escheatment to the appropriate government agency. Amounts related to shipping and handling billed to clients in a sales transaction are classified as revenue and the costs related to shipping product to clients are classified as cost of sales. A reserve for estimated returns is established when sales are recorded. The Company excludes sales taxes collected from customers from net sales in its Statement of Operations.

Cost of Sales and Selling, General and Administrative Expenses – The following table illustrates the primary costs classified in each major expense category:

Cost of Sales	Selling, General and Administrative Expenses
• Cost of merchandise sold;	• Payroll, bonus and benefit costs for retail and corporate associates;
• Freight costs associated with moving merchandise from our suppliers to our distribution center;	• Design and merchandising costs;
• Costs associated with the movement of merchandise through customs;	• Occupancy costs for retail and corporate facilities;
• Costs associated with the fulfillment of online customer orders;	• Depreciation related to retail and corporate assets;
• Depreciation related to merchandise management systems;	• Advertising and marketing costs;
• Sample development costs;	• Occupancy and other costs associated with operating our distribution center;
• Merchandise shortage; and	• Freight expenses associated with moving merchandise from our distribution center to our retail stores; and
• Client shipping costs.	• Legal, finance, information systems and other corporate overhead costs.

Advertising – Costs associated with the production of advertising, such as printing and other costs, as well as costs associated with communicating advertising that has been produced, such as magazine ads, are expensed when the advertising first appears in print. Costs of direct mail catalogs and postcards are fully expensed when the advertising is scheduled to first arrive in clients' homes.

Leases and Deferred Rent Obligations – Retail stores and administrative facilities are occupied under operating leases, most of which are non-cancelable. Some of the store leases grant the right to extend the term for one or two additional five-year periods under substantially the same terms and conditions as the original leases. Some store leases also contain early termination options, which can be exercised by the Company under specific conditions. Most of the store leases require payment of a specified minimum rent, plus a contingent rent based on a percentage of the store's net sales in excess of a specified threshold. In addition, most of the leases require payment of real estate taxes, insurance and certain common area and maintenance costs in addition to the future minimum lease payments. Rent expense under non-cancelable operating leases with scheduled rent increases or free rent periods is accounted for on a straight-line basis over the initial lease term beginning on the date of initial possession, which is generally when the Company enters the space and begins construction build-out. Any reasonably assured renewals are considered. The amount of the excess of straight-line rent expense over scheduled payments is recorded as a deferred liability.

Construction allowances and other such lease incentives are recorded as deferred credits, and are amortized on a straight-line basis as a reduction of rent expense beginning in the period they are deemed to be earned, which often is subsequent to the date of initial possession and generally coincides with the store opening date. The current portion of unamortized deferred lease costs and construction allowances is included in "Accrued tenancy", and the long-term portion is included in "Deferred lease costs" on the Company's Balance Sheets.

Restructuring Costs – On January 30, 2008, the Company initiated a multi-year restructuring program designed to enhance profitability and improve overall operating effectiveness. The restructuring program, includes closing underperforming stores over a three-year period, reducing the Company's corporate staff by approximately 10% and undertaking a broad-based productivity initiative that includes, among other things, the strategic procurement of non-merchandise goods and services. Restructuring costs include non-cash expenses, primarily associated with the write-down of assets related to store closures, cash charges related primarily to severance and various other costs to implement the restructuring program. Liabilities associated with restructuring charges are included in "Accrued salaties and bonus," Accrued tenancy," "Accrued expenses and other current liabilities," and "Other liabilities."

Cash and Cash Equivalents – Cash and short-term highly liquid investments with original maturity dates of 3 months or less are considered cash or cash equivalents. The Company invests excess cash primarily in money market accounts and short-term commercial paper.

Financial Instruments – The Company's auction rate securities are classified as available-for-sale and are carried at cost or par value, which approximates fair market value. These securities have stated maturities beyond three months but are priced and traded as short-term instruments due to the liquidity provided through the interest rate reset mechanism of 28 or 35 days.

Merchandise Inventories – Merchandise inventories are valued at the lower of average cost or market, at the individual item level. Market is determined based on the estimated net realizable value, which is generally the merchandise selling price. Merchandise inventory levels are monitored to identify slow-moving items and broken assortments (items no longer in stock in a sufficient range of sizes) and markdowns are used to clear such merchandise. Merchandise inventory value is reduced if the selling price is marked below cost. Physical inventory counts are performed annually in January, and estimates are made for any shortage between the date of the physical inventory count and the balance sheet date.

Store Pre-Opening Costs – Non-capital expenditures, such as rent, advertising and payroll costs incurred prior to the opening of a new store are charged to expense in the period they are incurred.

Property and Equipment – Property and equipment are recorded at cost. Depreciation and amortization are computed on a straight-line basis over the following estimated useful lives:

Building...40 years

Leasehold improvements ....10 years or term of lease, if shorter

Furniture, fixtures and equipment..................................2-10 years

Software ....5 years

Accounting for the Impairment or Disposal of Long-Lived Assets – The assessment of possible impairment is based on the Company's ability to recover the carrying value of the long-lived asset from the expected future pre-tax cash flows (undiscounted and without interest charges). If these cash flows are less than the carrying value of such assets, an impairment loss is recognized for the difference between estimated fair value and carrying value. The primary measure of fair value is based on discounted cash flows. The measurement of impairment requires management to make estimates of these cash flows related to long-lived assets, as well as other fair value determinations.

Goodwill and Indefinite-lived Intangible Assets – The Company performs annual impairment testing related to the carrying value of the Company's recorded goodwill and indefinite-lived intangible assets.

Deferred Financing Costs – Deferred financing costs are amortized using the effective interest method over the term of the related debt.

Self Insurance – The Company is self-insured for certain losses related to its employee point of service medical and dental plans, its workers' compensation plan and for short-term disability up to certain thresholds. Costs for self-insurance claims filed, as well as claims incurred but not reported, are accrued based on management's estimates, using information received from plan administrators, third party activities, historical analysis, and other relevant data. Costs for self-insurance claims filed and claims incurred but not reported are accrued based on known claims and historical experience.

Income Taxes – The Company accounts for income using the asset and liability method. Under the asset and liability method, deferred tax assets and liabilities are recognized, and income or expense is recorded, for the estimated future tax consequences attributable to differences between the financial statement carrying amounts of existing assets and liabilities and their respective tax bases.

Treasury Stock Repurchases – The Company repurchases common stock from time to time, subject to market conditions and at prevailing market prices, through open market purchases or in privately negotiated transactions. Repurchased shares of common stock are recorded using the cost method.

Stock-based Compensation – The Company uses the modified prospective method to record stock-based compensation. The calculation of stock-based compensation expense requires the input of highly subjective assumptions, including the expected term of the stock-based awards, stock price volatility, and pre-vesting forfeitures. The Company estimates the expected life of shares granted in connection with stock-based awards using historical exercise patterns, which is assumed to be representative of future behavior. The volatility of common stock at the date of grant is estimated based on an average of the historical volatility and the implied volatility of publicly traded options on the common stock. In addition, the expected forfeiture rate is estimated and expense is only recorded for those shares expected to vest. Forfeitures are estimated based on historical experience of stock-based awards granted, exercised and cancelled, as well as considering future expected behavior.

Savings Plan and Pension Plan – In June 2006, the Company's Board of Directors authorized management to freeze its non-contributory defined benefit pension plan (the "Pension Plan") and enhance its defined contribution 401(k) savings plan (the "401(k) Plan"). These plan changes became effective on October 1, 2006.

Savings Plan – Substantially all employees of the Company and its subsidiaries who work at least 30 hours per week or who work 1,000 hours during a consecutive 12 month period are eligible to participate in the Company's 401(k) Plan. Under the plan, participants can contribute an aggregate of up to 75% of their annual earnings in any combination of pre-tax and after-tax contributions, subject to certain limitations. The Company makes a matching contribution of 100% with respect to the first 3% of each participant's contributions to the 401(k) Plan and makes a matching contribution of 50% with respect to the second 3% of each participant's contributions to the 401(k) Plan.

Pension Plan – Substantially all employees of the Company who began employment prior to October 1, 2006, and completed 1,000 hours of service during a consecutive 12 month period prior to that date are eligible for benefits under the Company's Pension Plan. The Pension Plan calculates benefits based on a career average formula. Only those associates who were eligible under the Pension Plan on or before September 30, 2006 are eligible to receive benefits from the Pension Plan once they have completed the five years of service required to become fully vested. As a result of the Pension Plan freeze, no associate may become a participant in the Pension Plan on or after October 1, 2006, and no additional benefits will be earned under the Pension Plan on or after October 1, 2006.

The Company records the net over- or under-funded position of a defined benefit postretirement plan as an other asset or other liability, with any unrecognized prior service costs, transition obligations or actuarial gains/losses reported as a component of accumulated other comprehensive income in stockholders' equity.

Other Liabilities – Other liabilities includes liabilities associated with the Company's restructuring program, pension plan, borrowings for the purchase of fixed assets, and obligation for excess corporate office space.

Anne Aylor, Inc.
Memo: Analysis of Performance First Quarter
Year Ended: January 28, 2012

Reference:	G 3
Prepared by:	DF
Date:	6/15/11
Reviewed by:	

Net sales for the first quarter of fiscal 2012 increased 7.5 percent from the first quarter of fiscal 2011. Comparable store sales for the first quarter of fiscal 2012 increased 5.1 percent, compared to a comparable store sales increase of 2.5 percent in the first quarter of fiscal 2011. The Company saw improvement in same store sales as a result of a targeted promotional strategy that helped drive increased traffic to Company stores. The Company also continues to experience growth in e-commerce sales that are up by more than 20% over the previous comparable period.

Gross margin as a percentage of net sales increased to 54.5 percent in the first quarter of fiscal 2012, compared to 53.0 percent in the first quarter of fiscal 2011. The increase in gross margin as a percentage of net sales for the first quarter of fiscal 2012 as compared to the comparable fiscal 2011 period was due primarily to higher full price sales as a percentage of total sales coupled with higher margin rates achieved on both full price and non-full price sales at stores. This performance was the result of improved product offerings, effective marketing initiatives and the success of the Company's strategy to appropriately position inventory levels.

Selling, general and administrative expenses as a percentage of net sales decreased to 48.1 percent, in the first quarter of fiscal 2012, compared to 50.8 percent of net sales in the first quarter of fiscal 2011. The decrease in selling, general and administrative expenses as a percentage of net sales was primarily due to improved operating leverage as a result of higher net sales, payroll and tenancy related savings associated with the restructuring program, and continued focus on cost savings initiatives. The decrease in selling, general and administrative expenses was partially offset by higher marketing and performance-based compensation expenses.

Net income as a percentage of net sales increased to 3.8 percent in the first quarter of fiscal 2012, compared to 2.6 percent in the first quarter of fiscal 2011. The increase in net income as a percentage of net sales is due to strong full price selling at Company stores and improved operating efficiencies.

Anne Aylor, Inc.	Reference:	*G 4*
Memo: Current Events/Issues	Prepared by:	*DF*
Year Ended: January 28, 2012	Date:	*6/15/11*
	Reviewed by:	

The company plans to focus on optimizing store productivity and enhancing the in-store environment of existing stores. Last year the Company remodeled 4 stores with updated aesthetics and reducing the square footage 30-40%. The Company intends remodel an additional 20 stores during fiscal 2012 following the remodeled prototype developed last year. The remodeling will be funded with operating cash flows.

On March 18, 2011 the Company entered into the credit facility with First Bank and a syndicate of lenders, which amended its then existing $100 million senior secured revolving credit facility which was due to expire in October 2011. The credit facility provides the Company with an option to increase the total facility and the aggregate commitments thereunder up to $200 million, subject to the lenders' agreement to increase their commitment for the requested amount. The credit facility expires on September 30, 2016 and may be used for working capital, letters of credit and other general corporate purposes. Should certain liquidity and other requirements not be met, as defined in the credit facility, any outstanding borrowings may become immediately due and payable. The Company is required to maintain a quick ratio of 0.8 and current ratio of 2.0. Additionally, the Company is only allowed to repurchase common stock held by employees up to $100,000 in any fiscal year.

Anne Aylor, Inc.
Planning Materiality Assessment
Year Ended: January 28, 2012

Reference: _G 5_
Prepared by: _____
Date: _____
Reviewed by: _____

Primary Users of Financial Statements (list):

Materiality Bases (in thousands):

Base	Fiscal 2011 Actual Financial Statement Amounts	Fiscal 2012 Projected Financial Statement Amounts	Planning Materiality Levels			
			Lower Limit		Upper Limit	
			Percent	Dollar Amount	Percent	Dollar Amount
Income Before Taxes			2		7	
Net Revenues			0.5		2	
Current Liabilities			2		7	
Current Assets			2		7	
Total Assets			0.5		2	

Planning Materiality (in thousands): $ _____

Explanation:

Anne Aylor, Inc.
Tolerable Misstatement Assessment
Year Ended: January 28, 2012

Reference: _____ G 6 _____
Prepared by: _____
Date: _____
Reviewed by: _____

Likelihood of Management Fraud (check one):

_____ Low Likelihood of Management Fraud
_____ Reasonably Low Likelihood of Management Fraud
_____ Moderate Likelihood of Management Fraud

Tolerable Misstatement (in thousands):

Planning Materiality:	$
Multiplication Factor (0.75 if low likelihood of management fraud, 0.50 if reasonably low likelihood of management fraud, and 0.25 if moderate likelihood of management fraud).	X
Tolerable Misstatement (in thousands)	$

Specific Accounts Requiring Lower Tolerable Misstatement:

Account	Tolerable Misstatement
Explanation:	
Explanation:	
Explanation:	
Explanation:	
Explanation:	
Explanation:	

Anne Aylor, Inc.
Planning Materiality Financial Information
Year Ended: January 28, 2012

Reference:	G 7
Prepared by:	
Date:	
Reviewed by:	

All amounts are in thousands	1/28/2012 Projected	1/29/2011 Actual
Net sales	$ 1,355,400	$ 1,243,788
Cost of sales	599,700	562,427
Gross margin	755,700	681,361
Selling, general and administrative expenses	659,800	627,622
Restructuring charges	0	3,856
Operating income/(loss	95,900	49,883
Interest income	700	636
Interest expense	1,200	1,009
Income/(loss) before income taxes	95,400	49,510
Income tax provision/(benefit)	36,900	18,408
Net income/(loss)	$ 58,500	$ 31,102
Assets		
Current assets		
Cash and cash equivalents	$ 156,600	$ 138,194
Accounts receivable	12,100	12,670
Merchandise inventories	133,800	111,229
Refundable income taxes	18,400	16,394
Deferred income taxes	19,400	23,542
Prepaid expenses and other current assets	39,600	29,995
Total current assets	379,900	332,024
Property and equipment, net	229,700	240,641
Deferred financing costs, net	500	640
Deferred income taxes	21,600	15,574
Other assets	8,600	4,376
Total assets	$ 640,300	$ 593,255
Liabilities and Stockholders' Equity		
Current liabilities		
Accounts payable	$ 67,200	$ 50,615
Accrued salaries and bonus	20,300	21,154
Accrued tenancy	29,400	29,512
Gift certificates and merchandise credits redeemable	33,900	31,273
Accrued expenses and other current liabilities	43,900	48,534
Total current liabilities	194,700	181,088
Deferred lease costs	114,200	120,945
Deferred income taxes	600	1,042
Long-term performance compensation	22,300	6,200
Other liabilities	15,900	9,635
Total liabilities	347,700	318,910
Stockholders' equity		
Common stock and paid in capital	553,900	511,847
Retained earnings	291,243	232,443
Accumulated other comprehensive loss	(1,600)	(2,734)
Treasury stock	(550,943)	(467,211)
Total stockholders' equity	292,600	274,345
Total liabilities and stockholders' equity	$ 640,300	$ 593,255

Analytical Procedures

CASES INCLUDED IN THIS SECTION

OTHER CASES THAT DISCUSS TOPICS RELATED TO THIS SECTION

Laramie Wire Manufacturing
Using Analytical Procedures in Audit Planning

MARK S. BEASLEY · FRANK A. BUCKLESS · STEVEN M. GLOVER · DOUGLAS F. PRAWITT

LEARNING OBJECTIVES

After completing and discussing this case you should be able to

[1] Review and analyze information relating to a company's inventory and related accounts

[2] Identify potential risks and areas requiring a greater amount of substantive audit attention

[3] Understand how preliminary analytical procedures can help in planning the audit of inventory

INTRODUCTION

Analytical procedures can be powerful tools in conducting an audit. They help the auditor understand a client's business and are useful in identifying potential risks and problem areas requiring greater substantive audit attention. If formulated carefully, they allow the auditor to arrive at a precise expectation of what an account balance *ought* to be; the balance per the client's books is then compared against this expectation. Thus, "analytics" can sometimes provide a source of inexpensive and powerful substantive evidence that complements or even replaces time-consuming detailed testing. Finally, analytical procedures are useful in helping the auditor assess whether a client faces a going-concern issue and whether a client's financial statements "make sense" after required audit adjustments are made.

The three general uses of analytical procedures listed above correspond to the three stages of an audit in which they are typically used—planning, evidence gathering, and final review. Auditing standards provide guidance to auditors on how and when to use analytical procedures. The standards *require* auditors to use analytics in the planning and final review stages, and encourage—but do not require—the use of analytics in the substantive evidence-gathering stage of the audit.

This case addresses the use of analytical procedures in the planning stage of the audit. During planning, analytics help the auditor gain an overall understanding of the client and its business environment. They also help the auditor plan the evidence that will be gathered in various audit areas by helping the auditor identify potential risks and problem areas requiring more extensive substantive testing.

BACKGROUND

You are a senior auditor assigned to the Laramie Wire Manufacturing audit. This is the first year your firm has conducted the audit for this particular client. In fact, although Laramie has previously engaged accountants to perform limited review services for the purpose of obtaining bank loans, this is the first year Laramie has contracted for a full-scale audit of its financial statements. The company is planning an initial public offering (IPO) of its stock in the next two or three years and has hired your firm to conduct its first financial statement audit in preparation for the upcoming IPO.

The case was prepared by Mark S. Beasley, Ph.D. and Frank A. Buckless, Ph.D. of North Carolina State University and Steven M. Glover, Ph.D. and Douglas F. Prawitt, Ph.D. of Brigham Young University, as a basis for class discussion. It is not intended to illustrate either effective or ineffective handling of an administrative situation.

Laramie is a medium-sized company that buys copper rod and plastic materials used to make insulated copper wiring. Laramie operates out of a single building complex totaling 400,000 square feet, which includes office space (3%), production area (57%), shipping and receiving (15%), and finished goods and raw materials inventory warehousing (25%). Laramie supplies insulated copper wiring in the northeastern part of the United States. The company has a good reputation for quality products and has had a good working relationship with its outside accountants over the past 10 years. You have been assigned responsibility for auditing Laramie's inventories. You are in the planning stages of the audit, and you are preparing to conduct some analytical procedures to identify areas that may represent heightened risk and that thus may require further attention.

Your staff assistant assembled information relating to inventories and other items, including a brief description of Laramie's production and inventory areas. Because your assistant is new, he is not very good about weeding out irrelevant information, so you may not need to use every piece of information he has provided. The information is listed below.

	2011	2010
Sales	$ 8,350,000	$ 8,050,000
Cost of Sales	$ 6,142,500	$ 5,980,000
Finished Goods Inventory (Approx. 250 million ft.)	$ 1,554,500	$ 1,075,500
Copper Rod Inventory (Approx. 5.5 million lbs.)	$ 2,525,000	$ 1,550,000
Plastics Inventory (Approx. 1 million lbs.)	$ 214,500	$ 172,000
Accounts Payable (for Inv. purchases)	$ 440,000	$ 415,000
Days Purchases in A/P	25.4 days	27.1 days
Days Sales in Receivables	55.8 days	47.9 days
Market Price of Insulated Wire (per foot)	$ 0.007	$ 0.009
Market Price of Copper Rod (per lb.)	$ 0.470	$ 0.470
Market Price of Plastics (per lb.)	$ 0.130	$ 0.190

Laramie makes several different gauges and types of insulated copper wire for use in applications ranging from residential telephone and electrical wiring to industrial-grade, high-voltage power cables. The production area is divided into three areas, with each area specializing in a particular product group, including residential products, industrial products, and special-order products. Production is done in batches according to orders placed with the firm. For each batch, machinery is adjusted and calibrated according to the type and size of product to be manufactured, and the size of the batch depends on the amount of product needed. Average machine setup time from start to finish is approximately four hours, which is slightly better than the industry average.

The different types of products Laramie manufactures all use similar raw materials, so raw materials inventory is stored in a single location, divided into copper and plastics. Finished goods (i.e., insulated copper wire) are stored on large stackable spools of various sizes, with approximately 500,000 feet of wire per spool. Copper rod inventory is stored on pallets, which are not stackable. Each pallet measures 6 feet by 6 feet, stands 5 feet tall, and holds 1,500 pounds of copper rod. Plastics inventory is stored in 4-feet-tall stackable barrels, with approximately 350 lbs. of plastic per barrel. The raw materials inventory storage area is located near the shipping and receiving area for convenience. Inbound and outbound shipments of inventory are trucked to the nearest rail yard, from which they are distributed around the northeastern region of the U.S. A single 18-wheeler can carry up to 15 pallets of copper rod, 40 barrels of plastics, or 24 spools of finished insulated copper wire.

Laramie's production process includes some automation but still requires a relatively large amount of labor. Thus, Laramie's conversion costs are fairly evenly divided between direct labor and factory overhead. Overhead consists primarily of the costs of the production facilities and depreciation and maintenance on the machinery. Laramie uses a hybrid product costing system (i.e., a system that combines characteristics of both job-order and process costing systems) to accommodate both the continuous and homogeneous nature of the manufacturing process and the fact that production runs are performed in separately identifiable batches. In accordance with the relatively homogenous nature of Laramie's products, overhead is allocated from a single cost pool based on a combination of machine and direct labor hours.

As the insulated copper wire product is completed, it is rolled onto large spools of various sizes, usually in lengths of about 500,000 linear feet. These spools of finished goods inventory are stored next to the raw materials inventory near the facility's eight loading and unloading docks. In many cases, the inventory is produced in response to specific customer orders received. The spools are tagged for shipment to customers according to date requested. Inventory that has been produced to provide a "cushion" for rush orders is stored toward the far end of the finished goods storage area, away from the shipping area.

The inventory and production areas are well organized and seem to flow smoothly. Machines appear to be well maintained. A cursory visual examination of inventories reveals no problems. Two spools in the finished goods area were tagged as being of a type of residential wiring recently banned by federal safety guidelines. These spools are clearly marked, and the inventories supervisor indicated they are to be destroyed within the next week. Procedures and records for tracking materials upon arrival, through the production process, and into finished goods and shipping, appear to be well designed.

REQUIRED

[1] Perform analytical procedures to help you identify relatively risky areas that indicate the need for further attention during the audit, if any.

[2] Focus specifically on each of the following balance-related management assertions for the inventory account: existence, completeness, valuation, and rights and obligations. Link any risks you identified for this account in question 1 to the related management assertion. Briefly explain identified risks for the inventory account that require further attention, if any.

Northwest Bank
Developing Expectations for Analytical Procedures

Mark S. Beasley · Frank A. Buckless · Steven M. Glover · Douglas F. Prawitt

LEARNING OBJECTIVES

After completing and discussing this case you should be able to

[1] Use analytical procedures as a reasonableness test of interest income

[2] Recognize factors that lead to the development of more precise expectations

[3] Understand the relationship between the precision of an expectation and the level of assurance derived from an analytical procedure

[4] Understand the limitations of imprecise expectations

BACKGROUND

Northwest Bank (NWB) has banking operations in 35 communities in the states of Washington, Oregon, and Idaho. Headquarters for the bank are in Walla Walla, Washington. NWB's loan portfolio consists primarily of agricultural loans, commercial loans, real estate loans, and loans to individuals. Credit-granting authority is primarily centralized in Walla Walla; however, certain seasoned loan officers have decision authority for small loans in their local area. Loan portfolio performance, monitoring, and ongoing credit quality assessments are performed in Walla Walla for all loans.

NWB has been an audit client for three years. Because of NWB's strong controls over bank loans, the audit team places high reliance on controls (i.e., control risk is assessed as low). The audit approach calls for the audit team to gain assurance on the fairness of loan interest income primarily through the performance of analytical procedures. Additional detailed testing will only be performed if analytical procedures suggest interest income is materially misstated. Total reported interest income for 2011 is $35,337,204, and reported net income for the bank is $12,484,000. A misstatement of $525,000 is considered material.

In addition to comparing the 2010 interest income to 2009 interest income, last year's audit team also developed an expectation for loan interest income using the average loan volume multiplied by the weighted average interest rate. Last year's audit file indicates that the average loan volume agrees to numbers tested elsewhere in the audit file and that the interest rates used to compute the weighted average rate were comparable to rates published in a Washington State Banking Commission publication.

The case was prepared by Mark S. Beasley, Ph.D. and Frank A. Buckless, Ph.D. of North Carolina State University and Steven M. Glover, Ph.D. and Douglas F. Prawitt, Ph.D. of Brigham Young University, as a basis for class discussion. It was adapted from an article authored by S. Glover, D. Prawitt, and J. Wilks appearing in the 25th Anniversary edition of Auditing: A Journal of Practice and Theory (2005). Northwest Bank is a fictitious company. All characters and names represented are fictitious; any similarity to existing companies or persons is purely coincidental.

Section 8: Analytical Procedures

The following computation was performed last year.

NWB's Loan Interest Analytical Procedure 2010 (in thousands)

Average Loan Volume (or balance) 2010	$ 361,225
Multiplied by Weighted Average Annual Interest Rate (2010)	× 8.65%
Computed 2010 Loan Interest Income per Audit	$ 31,246
2010 Loan Interest Income per NWB	$ 31,435
Difference (in thousands)	**$ 189**

The following information was available for an analysis of the current audit year.

NWB's Loan Interest Analytical Procedure Updated for 2011 (in thousands)

Aggregate Loan Volume (or balance) as of Dec. 31, 2010	$ 388,110
Aggregate Loan Volume as of December 31, 2011	$ 383,860
Average Loan Volume (or balance) for 2011	$ 385,985
Multiplied by Weighted Average Annual Interest Rate (2011)	× 9.115%
Computed 2011 Loan Interest Income	$ 35,183
2011 Loan Interest Income per NWB	$ 35,337
Difference (in thousands)	**$ 154**

REQUIRED – PART A

[1] As part of the year-end audit and using the analytical-procedure approach similar to last year's audit (average loan volume multiplied by weighted-average interest rate), determine if Northwest Bank's interest income from loans reported at December 31, 2011 appears fairly stated. Do the results of the analytical procedure indicate that you accept 2011 interest income as reported?

Yes _____   No _____   Please briefly explain your answer.

[2] Based on the results of the analytical procedure, how likely is it that 2011 interest income is materially misstated?

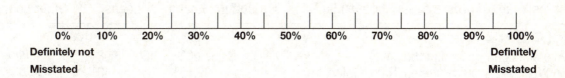

| 0% | 10% | 20% | 30% | 40% | 50% | 60% | 70% | 80% | 90% | 100% |

Definitely not Misstated   **Definitely Misstated**

[3] Please indicate on the scale below your assessment of the strength (quality and sufficiency) of evidence provided by the interest income analytical procedure:

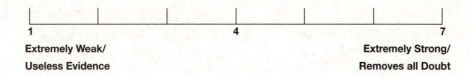

1   4   7

Extremely Weak/ Useless Evidence   **Extremely Strong/ Removes all Doubt**

DO NOT CONTINUE ON TO PART B UNTIL INSTRUCTED TO DO SO **STOP**

Northwest Bank Part B
Do <u>NOT</u> begin this part of the case until instructed to do so

In an effort to develop a more precise (i.e., higher quality) expectation, you asked an associate to collect more detailed information, which is provided below. The quarterly rates are comparable to those reported in a Washington State Bank Commission publication. The quarterly loan volumes have been tied to audit work in other areas of the audit file. You decided not to have the associate track down detailed information for the "Individual and Other Loans" category because it is relatively small and is made up of heterogeneous loans. However, for the loans in the Individual and Other Loans category you do have the loan volume and weighted average interest rate as of December 31, 2010 and December 31, 2011. Recall that materiality for this area is $525,000.

For the Year 2011 (balances in thousands)	Commercial and Agricultural Loans	Real Estate Loans	Individual and Other Loans
First Quarter			
Average Loan Volume (or Balance)	$ 267,003	$ 99,998	*See Info Below**
× Weighted Average Interest Rate (Qrtly)	2.15%	2.40%	
Expected Interest Income, First Quarter ❶	5,741	2,400	
Second Quarter			
Average Loan Volume	263,868	101,200	*See Info Below**
× Weighted Average Interest Rate (Qrtly)	2.08%	2.35%	
Expected Interest Income, Second Quarter ❷	5,488	2,378	
Third Quarter			
Average Loan Volume	264,400	95,608	*See Info Below**
× Weighted Average Interest Rate (Qrtly)	2.13%	2.35%	
Expected Interest Income, Third Quarter ❸	5,632	2,247	
Fourth Quarter			
Average Loan Volume	$ 266,510	$ 96,200	*See Info Below**
× Weighted Average Interest Rate (Qrtly)	2.17%	2.43%	
Expected Interest Income, Fourth Quarter ❹	5,783	2,338	

	Commercial and Agricultural Loans	Real Estate Loans	Individual and Other Loans
Annual Expected Interest Income by Loan Type based on Quarterly Data ❶ + ❷ + ❸ + ❹	$ 22,644	$ 9,363	$ 2,515*
Computed Total Interest Income per Audit ($22,644 + $9,363 + $2,515, in thousands)			$ 34,522
2011 Loan Interest Income per NWB			$ 35,337
Difference (in thousands)			$ 815

*Computation of Individual and Other Loans	12/31/2010	12/31/2011	Average
Average Annual Loan Volume	$ 21,109	$ 21,152	$ 21,131
× Weighted Average Interest Rate	11.7%	12.1%	11.9%
Annual Expected Interest, Individual and Other (in thousands)			$ 2,515

REQUIRED – PART B

[1] Given the additional information provided in Part B (i.e., quarterly information by loan type), please determine if Northwest Bank's interest income from loans reported at December 31, 2011 appears fairly stated. Can you accept 2011 interest income as reported?

Yes _____ No _____ Please briefly explain your answer.

[2] Based on the results of the analytical procedure preformed in Part B, how likely do you think it is that 2011 interest income is materially misstated?

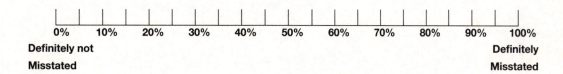

[3] Please indicate on the scale below your assessment of the strength (quality and sufficiency) of evidence provided by the interest income analytical procedure:

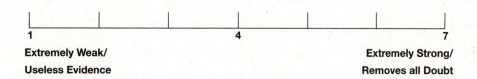

[4] Now reevaluate the first analytical procedure you performed (i.e., based only on average aggregate loan and interest averages). Using hindsight, please indicate on the scale below your assessment of the strength (quality and sufficiency) of evidence provided by that high-level interest income analytical procedure:

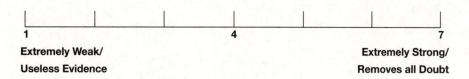

Burlingham Bees
Using Analytical Procedures as Substantive Tests

Mark S. Beasley · Frank A. Buckless · Steven M. Glover · Douglas F. Prawitt

LEARNING OBJECTIVES

After completing and discussing this case you should be able to

[1] Use analytical procedures to develop expectations for revenue accounts

[2] Appreciate the degree of professional judgment involved in evaluating differences between expected and reported account balances

[3] Recognize factors that lead to precise expectations of account balances

[4] Understand the audit planning implications of using analytical procedures as substantive tests of account balances

BACKGROUND

Burlingham Bees, an independent, minor league baseball team, competes in the Northwest Coast League. The team finished in second place in 2011 with an 92-52 record. The Bees' 2011 cumulative season attendance of 516,783 spectators set a new record high for the team, up more than 8% from the prior season's attendance.

Bank-loan covenants require the Bees to submit audited financial statements annually to the bank. The accounting firm of Hickman and Snowden, CPAs, has served as the Bees' auditor for the past five years.

One of the major audit areas involves testing ticket revenues. Ticket revenues reached nearly $3.95 million in 2010. In 2011 the unaudited ticket revenues are reported to be $4,292,970 with net income before tax of $731,845. In prior years, the audit plan called for extensive detail testing of revenue accounts to gain assurance that reported ticket revenues were fairly stated.

Michelle Andrews, a new audit manager, just received the assignment to be the manager on the 2011 audit. Michelle worked previously on the Bees' prior-year audits as a staff auditor. When she learned she would be managing the current-year engagement, she immediately thought back to all the hours of detailed testing of ticket sales she performed. On some of her other clients, Michelle has been successful at redesigning audit plans to make better use of analytical procedures as substantive tests. She is beginning to wonder if there is a more efficient way to gather effective substantive evidence related to ticket revenues on the Bees' engagement.

In her first meeting with Bees' management for the 2011 audit, Michelle learned that the Bees now use an outside company, Tickets R Us, to operate ticket gates for home games. The terms of the contract require Tickets R Us to collect ticket stubs so that it can later report total tickets collected per game. While Tickets R Us does not break down the total ticket sales into the various price categories, Michelle thinks there may be a way to develop an analytical procedure using the independently generated total ticket numbers and data from prior audits. To investigate this possibility, Michelle asked a staff person to gather some information related to reported sales.

The case was prepared by Mark S. Beasley, Ph.D. and Frank A. Buckless, Ph.D. of North Carolina State University and Steven M. Glover, Ph.D. and Douglas F. Prawitt, Ph.D. of Brigham Young University, as a basis for class discussion. Burlingham Bees is a fictitious team. All characters and names represented are fictitious; any similarity to existing teams, companies or persons is purely coincidental.

Section 8: Analytical Procedures

Here is the information the staff person gathered from the records of the client, Tickets R Us, and prior-year audit files:

2011 Park Attendance (all games)
Total park attendance   516,783

2011 Number of Games
Weekday games	44
Weekend games	28

Information from prior-year audit files indicates a similar number of home games in total, although in the prior year there were 26 weekend games. The audit file indicates that average per-game attendance for weekend games was 20% higher than average per-game attendance for weekday games.

2011 Per-Game Ticket Prices
Club seats		$ 12
Box seats		$ 10
General seats:	Adult	$ 6
	Child (Senior Citizens)	$ 4

Comparison of 2010 ticket prices to 2011 ticket prices reveals an average increase of 9% between the two years.

Sales Mix
	Weekday	Weekend
Club seats	25%	26%
Box seats	30%	29%
General seats:		
Adult	23%	24%
Child (Senior Citizens)	22%	21%

Information from prior-year audit files shows that sales mix has remained fairly constant over the last several years.

2011 Promotions: Number of Games
Weekday	8
Weekend	9

Information from prior-year audit files shows that attendance generally increases by 15% when there is a promotion (e.g., free baseball cap, poster, or special entertainment). In the prior year there were only 15 total promotional days.

REQUIRED

[1] Research auditing professional standards and list the requirements related to developing an expectation and conducting analytical procedures when those procedures are intended to provide substantive evidence. What are the advantages of developing an expectation at a detailed level (i.e., using disaggregated data) rather than at an overall or aggregated level?

[2] Using the information provided, please develop a precise expectation (i.e., using the detailed or disaggregated data provided) for ticket revenues for the 2011 fiscal year.

[3] (a) How close does the Bees' reported ticket revenue for 2011 have to be to your expectation for you to consider reported ticket revenue reasonable or fairly stated? (b) If reported ticket revenues were outside your "reasonableness range," what could explain the difference?

[4] (a) What are the advantages of using analytical procedures as substantive tests? (b) If the engagement team decides to use analytical procedures for the Bees' audit, how will the audit plan differ from prior years? (c) Discuss whether you believe analytical procedures should be used as substantive tests for the Bees 2011 audit?

Auditing Cash, Fair Value, and Revenues

Wally's Billboard & Sign Supply
The Audit of Cash

MARK S. BEASLEY · FRANK A. BUCKLESS · STEVEN M. GLOVER · DOUGLAS F. PRAWITT

LEARNING OBJECTIVES

After completing and discussing this case you should be able to

[1] Understand the objectives of substantive audit procedures relating to the audit of cash balances

[2] Consider the effectiveness and reliability of audit procedures

[3] Identify and assess factors important when evaluating the sufficiency and appropriateness of different types of audit evidence

[4] Understand the layout and content of the standardized bank confirmation form.

INTRODUCTION

Wally's Billboard & Sign Supply, Inc. was founded four years ago by Walter Johnson. The company specializes in providing locations for sign and billboard advertising and has recently begun to enter the sign design market. After working several years in the marketing department of a large corporation, Wally decided that there was a need in his area for a company specializing in signs and billboards. Drawing on his marketing experiences, he started his own company.

The company is now preparing to expand its business and has enlisted the help of your firm, Taylor & Jones, LLP. Over the past two years your firm has provided auditing and assurance services to prepare the company to seek badly needed outside funding. Along with Bill Thompson, a senior auditor, you have been assigned to help with the annual audit.

Your assignment is to conduct substantive testing of the company's cash balances. Bill has already conducted tests of controls for each of the company's transaction cycles and has assessed control risk as relatively low in those cycles. He has also inquired of management regarding any restrictions imposed by external parties on the use of cash. Management assured him there are no such restrictions, but you plan to corroborate this response using bank confirmations.

Wally's Billboard & Sign Supply currently has three separate bank accounts. The first is a general account used mostly for business expenses and receipts. When payments are collected they are deposited, along with any cash sale receipts, in the general account. The second account is a payroll account. Funds are transferred twice a month to this account from the general account to cover payroll. The third account is an interest bearing account that the company uses to maintain extra cash for future needs. For this assignment, you will not be required to test intrabank transfers.

The case was prepared by Mark S. Beasley, Ph.D. and Frank A. Buckless, Ph.D. of North Carolina State University and Steven M. Glover, Ph.D. and Douglas F. Prawitt, Ph.D. of Brigham Young University, as a basis for class discussion. Wally's is a fictitious company. All characters and names represented are fictitious; any similarity to existing companies or persons is purely coincidental.

REQUIRED

Complete the audit program found on working paper C 2, recording all your work on the audit program and marking the provided documents (using auditing tick marks such as the ones used on the cash lead sheet—working paper C 1) to serve as your working papers. Document the results of your work on the Audit Summary sheet (working paper C 3), noting any errors, concerns, adjustments, and/or recommendations. If you make adjustments to the ending account balances, enter the adjustments on the cash lead sheet. Note, you may also download electronic versions of the working papers from www.pearsonhighered.com/beasley5e.

After completing the audit program, answer the following questions:

[1] Why is the audit of cash an important part of the audit?

[2] Bill performed tests of controls for all transaction cycles with good results. Why is it important to also perform substantive audit procedures for the ending cash balance even when tests of controls over transactions that affect the cash account indicate that those controls are operating effectively?

[3] According to AICPA auditing standards, what are the necessary ingredients for audit evidence to be considered "appropriate"?

[4] For each procedure listed in the audit program (schedule C 2), indicate the primary assertion(s) targeted by the procedure.

[5] For each error, concern, or adjustment you listed on the Audit Summary (schedule C 3), briefly describe at least one additional test you could perform to gain evidence as to whether or not the cash account is materially misstated.

[6] The AICPA and the American Banker's Association developed a standardized bank confirmation form—see working paper C 6. What is the purpose for confirming information in item number two on the bank confirmation form? Identify the accounts and related audit assertion(s) to which the information in item number two is relevant.

[7] What audit procedures might you perform if you were to decide that the risk of fraud involving the cash account was relatively high for this client?

[8] Perform an online search for "electronic bank confirmations." Summarize in one page or less what you learn about recent developments in the use of web-based bank confirmations. Include a brief discussion of the advantages of electronic confirmations in your write-up.

Reference:	*C-1*
Prepared by:	
Date:	*1/16/12*
Reviewed by:	

Wally's Billboard & Sign Supply
Cash Lead Sheet
For the Year Ended December 31, 2011

Account Number and Name	2011 Ending Balance	Net Adjustments	2011 Adjusted Ending Balance	2010 Ending Balance	% Change (before adjustment)
10100 Petty Cash	$ 216 ‡ *G/L*	0	216	$ 200 *PY*	8.00%
10200 Bank, General	100,750 *G/L*			97,431 *PY*	3.41%
10225 Bank, Payroll	1,500 *G/L*			3,923 *PY*	-61.76%
10250 Bank, Savings	84,024 *G/L*			73,341 *PY*	14.57%
Total	$ 186,490 *F*			$ 174,895 *F*	

Tickmark Legend

G/L - Agreed to General Ledger

PY - Agreed to prior years' workpapers

F - Footed without Exception

‡ - Traced amount to physical count on working paper C-14

Reference:	*C-2*
Prepared by:	
Date:	*1/16/12*
Reviewed by:	

Wally's Billboard & Sign Supply
Audit Program for Cash
For the Year Ended December 31, 2011

Audit Procedures	Initial	Date	Ref.
1. Obtain Cutoff Bank Statements and Confirmations returned by the bank, scan and review.			
2. Obtain copies of client's bank reconciliations and perform the following for each account:			
A. Test the mathematical accuracy of each bank reconciliation.			
B. Trace the line item "*Balance Per Bank Statement*" on each bank reconciliation to the related Bank Confirmation and to the Cutoff Bank Statement.			
C. Trace the check number and amount of outstanding items on each bank reconciliation to the corresponding Cutoff Bank Statement.			
D. Trace the date, check number, and amount of outstanding items on each bank reconciliation to the corresponding entry in the Cash Disbursement Journal.			
E. Trace the amount of any deposits in transit on the bank reconciliation to the Cutoff Bank Statement and then to the Cash Receipts Journal. Investigate unexpected timing differences.			
F. Trace the line item "*Undeposited Cash Receipts*" from each bank reconciliation to the Undeposited Cash Receipts List.			
3. In the presence of client personnel, count cash on hand following proper procedure.	*BT*	*1/12/12*	*C-13*
4. Inquire with management about cash restrictions and review response for disclosure needs.	*BT*	*1/12/12*	

Reference:	C-3
Prepared by:	
Date:	1/16/12
Reviewed by:	

Wally's Billboard & Sign Supply
Audit Summary
For the Year Ended December 31, 2011

Working Paper Reference	Description of Error or Concern

Wally's Billboard & Sign Supply
Selected Portions of the Cash Receipts Journal

Wally's Billboard & Sign Supply					
Cash Receipts Journal					
		Bank Account Debit		Credit	
Date	Description	General	Payroll	A/R	Other
12/23	Brought Forward	$13,750	$0	$7,500	$6,250
12/24	Total Cash Sales	400			400
12/27	Daily A/R Collections	755		755	
12/27	Total Cash Sales	400			400
12/28	Daily A/R Collections	800		800	
12/28	Total Cash Sales	425			425
12/28	Payroll from General Account		5,725		5,725
12/29	Daily A/R Collections	725		725	
12/29	Total Cash Sales	390			390
12/30	Daily A/R Collections	740		740	
12/30	Total Cash Sales	315			315
12/31	Daily A/R Collections	730		730	
12/31	Total Cash Sales	300			300
	December Totals	**$19,730**	**$5,725**	**$11,250**	**$14,205**
1/1	Beginning Balance				
1/3	Daily A/R Collections	825		825	
1/3	Total Cash Sales	725			725
1/4	Total Cash Sales	400			400
1/4	Daily A/R Collections	725		725	
1/5	Total Cash Sales	425			425
1/5	Daily A/R Collections	800		800	
1/6	Total Cash Sales	400			400
1/7	Total Cash Sales	415			415
1/7	Daily A/R Collections	745		745	
	Totals	**$5,460**		**$3,095**	**$2,365**

Reference:	*C-5*
Prepared by:	
Date:	*1/16/12*
Reviewed by:	

Wally's Billboard & Sign Supply
Selected Portions of the Cash Disbursements Journal

			Wally's Billboard & Sign Supply Cash Disbursements Journal			Cash Credit	
Date	Check #	Description	Payee	G/L Account #		General	Payroll
12/23		Brought Forward				$3,250	$0
12/24	5721	Inventory	Greg's Signs	80100		700	
12/24	5722	Inventory	Jones Printing	80100		950	
12/26	5723	Inventory	Western Paper	80100		650	
12/27	5724	Inventory	Taylor Inc	80100		700	
12/27	5725	Utilities	Waszte Removal Inc.	82000		75	
12/28	5726	Inventory	Newport Promotions	80100		85	
12/28	5727	Inventory	Magneto Industrial	80100		225	
12/29	5728	Utilities	Aurora City Power	82000		210	
12/29	5729	Office Supply	Office City	67000		75	
12/29	5730	Advertising	Young Promotions	66000		150	
12/30	5731	Inventory	Sign Solutions	80100		675	
12/30		Payroll Bank Transfer	Sunnydale Bank	10000		5,725	
12/30	10123	Paycheck	Wally Johnson	69100			2,310
12/30	10124	Paycheck	Tricia Holmes	69100			1,200
12/30	10125	Paycheck	John Riley	69100			925
12/30	10126	Paycheck	Jane Harris	69100			665
12/30	10127	Paycheck	Steve Norton	69100			625
12/31	**December Totals**					**$13,470**	**$5,725**
1/3	5732	Rent Payment	LLD Property Inc.	69000		1,750	
1/3	5733	Inventory	Merida Manufacturing	80170		525	
1/3	5734	Inventory	Greg's Signs	80100		430	
1/3	5735	Inventory	Jones Printing	80100		350	
1/4	5736	Building Supply	Haroldson Hardware	68010		50	
1/4	5737	Board Dues	Colorado Board	69200		125	
1/4	5738	Janitorial	TTC Janitorial	68000		100	
1/6	5739	New Printer	Duff Computers	67000		225	
1/7.	5740	Janitorial	W Lawn Care	68000		50	
Carried Forward						**$3,605**	**$0**

Reference:	C-6
Prepared by:	
Date:	1/16/12
Reviewed by:	

STANDARD FORM TO CONFIRM ACCOUNT
BALANCE INFORMATION WITH FINANCIAL INSTITUTIONS

ORIGINAL
To be mailed to accountant

Wally's Billboard & Sign Supply
CUSTOMER NAME

We have provided to our accountants the following information as of the close of the business on _December 31_ , 20 _11_, regarding our deposit and loan balances. Please confirm the accuracy of the information, noting any exceptions to the information provided. If the balances have been left blank, please complete this form by furnishing the balance in the appropriate space below.* Although we do not request nor expect you to conduct a comprehensive, detailed search of your records, if during the process of completing this confirmation additional information about other deposit and loan accounts we may have with you comes to your attention, please include such information below. Please use the enclosed envelope to return the form directly to our accountants.

Financial Institution's Name and Address
[*Woodland National Bank*]
530 Stadium Ave
Provo, UT 84604
[ ]

1. At the close of business on the date listed above, our records indicated the following deposit balance(s):

ACCOUNT NAME	ACCOUNT NO.	INTEREST RATE	BALANCE*
Wally's Billboard & Sign Supply	*0504-02*	*N/A*	*$100,515*

2. We were directly liable to the financial institution for loans at the close of business on the date listed above as follows:

ACCOUNT NO./ DESCRIPTION	BALANCE*	DATE DUE	INTEREST RATE	DATE THROUGH WHICH INTEREST IS PAID	DESCRIPTION OF COLLATERAL

Wally Johnson
(Customer's Authorized Signature)

_1/2/2012_
(Date)

The information presented above by the customer is in agreement with our records. Although we have not conducted a comprehensive, detailed search of our records, no other deposit or loan accounts have come to our attention except as noted below.

Cindy Lunt
(Financial Institution Authorized Signature)

_01/10/2012_
(Date)

Clerk
(Title)

EXCEPTIONS AND OR COMMENTS

Please return this form directly to our accountants:
[*Taylor & Jones LLP*]
Certified Public Accountants
717 East Bay Drive
Aurora, CO 73442
[ ]

* Ordinarily, balances are intentionally left blank if they are not available at the time the form is prepared.

Approved 1990 by American Bankers Association, American Institute of Certified Public Accountants, Bank Administration Institute. Additional forms available from: AICPA – Order Department, P.O. Box 1003, NY, NY 10108-1003

D451 5951

Wally's Billboard & Sign Supply
Cutoff Bank Statement from Woodland National Bank

Woodland National Bank
530 Stadium Ave
Provo, UT 84604

Statement of account # 0504-02
Statement Date: 01/01/12-01/10/12   Cutoff Statement

Wally's Billboard & Sign Supply

Date	Transaction Description	Amount	New Balance
1/1	Previous Balance		$100,515
1/3	Check # 5723	-650	99,865
	Deposit	1,030	100,895
1/4	Check # 5725	-75	100,820
1/5	Check # 5729	-75	100,745
	Check # 5727	-225	100,520
	Deposit	825	101,345
1/6	Check # 5731	-675	100,670
	Deposit	725	101,395
1/9	Check # 5732	-1,750	99,645
	Check # 5734	-430	99,215
	Deposit	1,125	100,340
	Check # 5735	-350	99,990
	Check # 5736	-50	99,940
	Deposit	1,055	100,995
1/10	Deposit	1,225	102,220
1/11	Balance		$102,220

Reference:	C-8
Prepared by:	PBC
Date:	1/16/12
Reviewed by:	

Wally's Billboard & Sign Supply
Bank Reconciliation for Woodland National Bank (Prepared by Client)
For the Month Ended December 31, 2011

Wally's Billboard & Sign Supply
Bank Reconciliation for Woodland National Bank
For the Month Ended December 31, 2011

Balance Per Bank Statement: $100,515

Add:

	Date	Amount
Deposits in Transit:	12/30	1,055
Undeposited Cash Receipts:	12/31	1,030

2,085

Deduct:

Outstanding Checks

Date Issued	Number	Amount
12/26	5723	650
12/27	5725	75
12/28	5727	225
12/29	5729	75
12/29	5730	150
12/30	5731	675

(1,850)

Book Balance $100,750

Reference: _C-9_
Prepared by: _____
Date: _1/16/12_
Reviewed by: _____

STANDARD FORM TO CONFIRM ACCOUNT
BALANCE INFORMATION WITH FINANCIAL INSTITUTIONS

ORIGINAL
To be mailed to accountant

Wally's Billboard & Sign Supply
CUSTOMER NAME

We have provided to our accountants the following information as of the close of the business on *December 31*, 20 *11*, regarding our deposit and loan balances. Please confirm the accuracy of the information, noting any exceptions to the information provided. If the balances have been left blank, please complete this form by furnishing the balance in the appropriate space below.* Although we do not request nor expect you to conduct a comprehensive, detailed search of your records, if during the process of completing this confirmation additional information about other deposit and loan accounts we may have with you comes to your attention, please include such information below. Please use the enclosed envelope to return the form directly to our accountants.

Financial Institution's Name and Address
[*Sunnydale Banking Co.*
267 West Irvine St.
Aurora, CO 73454]

[ ]

1. At the close of business on the date listed above, our records indicated the following deposit balance(s):

ACCOUNT NAME	ACCOUNT NO.	INTEREST RATE	BALANCE*
Wally's Billboard & Sign Supply Payroll Account	6315-789	N/A	$3,625

2. We were directly liable to the financial institution for loans at the close of business on the date listed above as follows:

ACCOUNT NO./ DESCRIPTION	BALANCE*	DATE DUE	INTEREST RATE	DATE THROUGH WHICH INTEREST IS PAID	DESCRIPTION OF COLLATERAL

Wally Johnson
(Customer's Authorized Signature)

_1/2/2012_
(Date)

The information presented above by the customer is in agreement with our records. Although we have not conducted a comprehensive, detailed search of our records, no other deposit or loan accounts have come to our attention except as noted below.

Tim Merkley
(Financial Institution Authorized Signature)

_01/11/2012_
(Date)

Clerk
(Title)

EXCEPTIONS AND OR COMMENTS

Please return this form directly to our accountants: [ ]

Taylor & Jones LLP
Certified Public Accountants
717 East Bay Drive
Aurora, CO 73442

[ ]

* Ordinarily, balances are intentionally left blank if they are not available at the time the form is prepared.

Approved 1990 by American Bankers Association, American Institute of Certified Public Accountants, Bank Administration Institute. Additional forms available from: AICPA – Order Department, P.O. Box 1003, NY, NY 10108-1003

D451 5951

Reference:	*C-10*
Prepared by:	
Date:	*1/16/12*
Reviewed by:	

Wally's Billboard & Sign Supply
Cutoff Bank Statement from Sunnydale Banking Co.

Sunnydale Banking Co.
267 West Irvine St.
Aurora, CO 73454

Statement of account # 6315-789
Statement Date: 01/01/12-01/10/12 Cutoff Statement

Wally's Billboard & Sign Supply

Date	Transaction Description	Amount	New Balance
1/1	Previous Balance		$3,625
1/4	Check # 10124	-1,200	2,425
1/4	Check # 10125	-925	1,500
1/10	Balance		$1,500

Reference: _C-11_
Prepared by: _____
Date: _1/16/12_
Reviewed by: _____

Wally's Billboard & Sign Supply
Bank Reconciliation for Sunnydale Bank Co. (Prepared by Client)
For the Month Ended December 31, 2011

Wally's Billboard & Sign Supply
Bank Reconciliation for Sunnydale Bank Co.
For the Month Ended December 31, 2011

Balance Per Bank Statement: $ 3,652

Add:

	Date	Amount
Deposits in Transit:		0
Undeposited Cash Receipts:		0

0

Deduct:

Outstanding Checks

Date Issued	Number	Amount
12/30	10124	1,200
12/30	10125	925

(2,125)

Book Balance $ 1,500

FEB-26-2012 THR 01:15 PM Brigham Nat'Bank   FAX NO. 3037586842   P.01/01

BRIGHAM NATIONAL BANK
155 North State, Aurora, CO 73451

February 26, 2012

Taylor & Jones
Certified Public Accountants
717 East Bay Drive
Aurora, CO 73442

Dear Taylor and Jones,

In response to your request of confirmation for audit purposes of Wally's Billboard & Sign Supply, Inc., we have provided the following account balance information:

Account Name	Account Number	Interest Rate	Balance
Wally's Billboard & Sign Supply, Inc.	73647-1234	N/A	$ 84,024

This information is CONFIDENTIAL and is provided by the written permission of the party named herein. Any use of this information without consent of all parties is strictly prohibited.

Sincerely,

Gretchen Larson
Gretchen Larson

Reference: _C-13_

Prepared by:

Date: _1/16/12_

Reviewed by:

Wally's Billboard & Sign Supply
Bank Reconciliation for Brigham National Bank (Prepared by Client)
For the Month Ended December 31, 2011

Wally's Billboard & Sign Supply
Bank Reconciliation for Brigham National Bank
For the Month Ended December 31, 2011

Balance Per Bank Statement: $84,024

Add:

	Date	Amount
Deposits in Transit:		0
Undeposited Cash Receipts:		0

0

Deduct:

Outstanding Checks

Date Issued	Number	Amount

0

Book Balance $84,024

Reference:	C-14
Prepared by:	
Date:	1/16/12
Reviewed by:	

Wally's Billboard & Sign Supply
Undeposited Receipts and Cash on-hand
For the Month Ended December 31, 2011

Wally's Billboard & Sign Supply
Undeposited Cash Receipts
All for deposit in Woodland National Bank
For the month ended December 31, 2011

Date	Name	Amount
12/31	Hardy Real Estate	$200
12/31	Hamilton Homes	315
12/31	Washington Banker	215
12/31	Daily Cash Sales	300
	Total	$1,030

Cash on hand for general business purpose.

Denomination	# counted	Total
$20	7	$140
10	4	40
5	5	25
1	11	11
		$216 ‡

The above cash receipts for deposit and cash on hand have been examined and verified as of the close of business on 12/31/11.

Bill Thompson- Senior Auditor

Tickmark Legend
‡ - Traced amount to cash lead sheet on working paper C-1.

Henrico Retail, Inc.
Understanding the IT Accounting System and Identifying Audit Evidence for Retail Sales

MARK S. BEASLEY · FRANK A. BUCKLESS · STEVEN M. GLOVER · DOUGLAS F. PRAWITT

LEARNING OBJECTIVES

After completing and discussing this case you should be able to

[1] Outline the audit trail for processing retail sales transactions

[2] Recognize when audit evidence must be gathered electronically if a traditional paper trail is absent

[3] Develop audit plans for gathering evidence to test the occurrence and accuracy assertions for retail sales transactions

INTRODUCTION

Henrico Retail, Inc. is a first year audit client. The audit partner obtained the following description of the sales system after recently meeting with client personnel at the corporate office.

DESCRIPTION OF THE SALES SYSTEM

Henrico's sales system is IT-based with computerized cash registers on the floors of all of its stores. At the point of sale, Henrico's sales clerks scan the bar code on the price tag of the product being sold to read the product number. If the quantity of a product being sold exceeds one, sales clerks can either enter the quantity being sold for that particular product code or scan the bar code for each individual item being purchased. At that point, the computerized cash register performs the following:

- Identifies correct unit price for that product number from the online price master file stored on the store server
- Notifies the clerk if product number is invalid
- Calculates total price of purchase (price × quantity)
- Extends totals, calculates sales taxes, and determines final transaction amount.

Before the sale can be completed, sales clerks must indicate whether this is a cash, debit, or credit sale. For credit sales, Henrico only accepts VISA or MasterCard credit cards. Customers swipe their credit card through a card reader directly linked to VISA and MasterCard to initiate the online credit card approval process. When the credit card agency's electronic approval is transmitted back to the cash register system, the credit approval code is electronically recorded on the cash register hard drive before the charge slip is generated for customer signature. When credit is denied, customers must either pay by cash or the sales clerk voids the sale. The original signed copy of the credit charge slip is maintained in the cash drawer. Debit card transactions work virtually in the same manner as credit sales except that the online system seeks authorization from the customer's bank.

The case was prepared by Mark S. Beasley, Ph.D. and Frank A. Buckless, Ph.D. of North Carolina State University and Steven M. Glover, Ph.D. and Douglas F. Prawitt, Ph.D. of Brigham Young University, as a basis for class discussion. Henrico is a fictitious company. All characters and names represented are fictitious; any similarity to existing companies or persons is purely coincidental.

For all types of sales, the cash register generates a customer paper-based receipt while a duplicate record of the transaction is stored on the cash register's hard drive in an online file that is backed up hourly to the store's computer server. This electronic transaction information documents on the register's hard drive the product number, unit price, quantity sold, the extended transaction totals, and credit card agency or bank approval information.

Sales clerks have no access to the transaction electronic file. In addition, sales clerks can only read unit price information and have no access to change unit prices in the online price master file. Only the store manager's staff has access to the price master file. Each week, the store manager's staff approves price changes and new product listings to be added to the price list master files. And, only the store's human resources manager is authorized to input changes to the employee master file of valid employee identification numbers.

Store clerks are allowed to operate any machine on the floor as long as the clerk has a valid employee identification number. If a cash register is not currently being used, all the sales clerk has to do is enter his or her employee identification number before scanning any product being sold. The system will not proceed without a valid employee identification number. Generally, operation of the cash register is self-explanatory although some problems have occurred previously. New sales clerks receive two hours of training on the operation of the cash register before serving customers on the sales floor. Henrico management believes "on the job experience" is most effective.

At the end of each day, sales clerks select the "register closing" option on the cash register. That process automatically updates both the transaction online file stored on the cash register's hard drive and the backup file stored on the store's server. The closing process generates a receipt printout at the register that summarizes the total amount of cash sales, debit and credit sales, sales returns, and any other miscellaneous transactions for the day. The sales clerks count the cash in the drawer and list the total cash count on a Daily Deposit Sheet (a preprinted blank form). In addition, sales clerks summarize total debit and credit sales on the Daily Deposit Sheet by listing total amounts from the debit and credit sales slips in the register. The sales clerks also record on the Daily Deposit Sheet the cash, debit, credit, and other transaction totals indicated on the cash register receipt generated by the register closing process. The sales clerks reconcile their cash, debit, and credit slip counts to these transaction totals and indicate any differences in amount. At that point, the sales clerks take the cash drawer, which includes debit and credit slips, to the store cashier who is located in the store cashier's office. The store cashier verifies the Daily Deposit Sheet and initials the total cash and debit and credit sales columns listed on the Daily Deposit Sheet for each register closed indicating that the amounts in the drawer reconcile to the amounts on the Daily Deposit Sheet.

The cashier leaves $200 in each cash drawer to begin the following day. Cash drawers are stored overnight in the store's vault. Each night, a local Brinks security service picks up the cash, debit transaction receipts, and credit charge slips collected during the day for delivery to the overnight depository at the store's local bank. The next day, the bank immediately gives the store cash credits for all charge slips presented based on the bank's arrangement with VISA and MasterCard and funds from debit transactions are electronically transmitted to Henrico's bank account from the customers' banks. And, the bank automatically credits the store's bank account for all cash received. The bank emails the store accountant and the store cashier a confirmation of the deposit processed each day.

An independent person in accounting for each store verifies that the sum of the cash, debit transactions, and credit card slip totals on all Daily Deposit Sheets for the prior day reconcile to the confirmation received from the bank of the deposit processed. After the reconciliation is performed, the bank's email confirmation is printed and attached to the Daily Deposit Sheets, which are filed together by date.

Overnight, the store computer server processes all transactions downloaded from each cash register through the register closing process and summarizes that information in a Daily Sales Report, which is an electronic file stored on the store's server. Each night, an electronic copy of the Daily Sales Report file from each store is transmitted automatically at midnight to the corporate office main server. The store server also automatically generates a paper copy of the Daily Sales Report for each store nightly. It summarizes total store sales, as well as subtotals of cash transactions, debit transactions, and credit sales, by store cash register. These reports are filed by date at each store.

Each night, the store computer server automatically updates perpetual inventory records, which are stored on the store's computer server. Once the perpetual inventory records are updated, an electronic copy of the perpetual inventory record is transmitted to the corporate office main server. No paper reports of daily updates to the perpetual inventory record are generated by the computer.

At month end, the store computer server generates an Inventory Report from the perpetual inventory file. The Inventory Report provides inventory quantity information by product number. Also, the store computer server uses each day's Daily Sales Report file to generate a Monthly Sales Report file for each store. This file contains daily sales totals for the store for each day of the month. This Monthly Sales Report information is electronically transmitted to the corporate office. Each store's server generates a printout of the Monthly Sales Report at month end. The corporate office computer server uses this information to prepare and print a consolidated General Ledger, which summarizes the postings of monthly sales totals from each store to the consolidated sales account.

REQUIRED

You are the audit senior assigned to the audit of Henrico Retail Inc. The audit partner recently asked you to assist in planning the audit of the sales system based on your review of the client-prepared sales system narrative. The partner has asked you to address the following issues:

[1] Describe the sales transaction audit trail from the point of sale to the general ledger posting to the consolidated sales accounts at the corporate office. Be sure to emphasize which aspects of the audit trail are in paper or electronic form.

[2] Develop a proposed strategy for auditing the *occurrence* assertion for sales transactions. Describe whether there is a sufficient paper-based audit trail to audit that assertion without relying on IT audit specialists to test electronic only processes.

[3] What evidence source would you use to select a sample of sales transactions to test the *occurrence* of sales transactions at one store? Why would you use this source? What evidence would you examine for each transaction selected?

[4] Develop a proposed strategy for auditing the *accuracy* assertion for sales transactions. Describe whether there is a sufficient paper-based audit trail to audit that assertion without relying on IT audit specialists to test electronic only processes.

[5] What portion, if any, of the accounting system will likely require the assistance of an IT systems auditor, who evaluates evidence existing only in electronic form?

[6] What control deficiencies can you identify in the existing sales system?

Longeta Corporation
Auditing Revenue Contracts

MARK S. BEASLEY · FRANK A. BUCKLESS · STEVEN M. GLOVER · DOUGLAS F. PRAWITT

LEARNING OBJECTIVES

After completing and discussing this case you should be able to

[1] Analyze complex revenue transactions for fair GAAP presentation

[2] Document final conclusions about the fair presentation of accounts

[3] Understand criteria for recording revenue

[4] Assess client accounting treatment when oral or written arrangements are made outside normal contract arrangements

BACKGROUND

You couldn't be more excited about being on your first financial statement audit as you launch into your new professional accounting career. Having recently graduated with a Master of Accountancy degree, you are thrilled to be employing all the skills acquired in your rigorous accounting program.

The client engagement you're now working on is Longeta Corporation, which is a California-based developer and marketer of software used to manage data storage functions for complex computer networks. Longeta particularly markets its products to other companies who serve as intermediaries for government purchasers. These intermediaries purchase Longeta's products and then "resell" them to government purchasers and other organizations. The company's stock is quoted on the NASDAQ National Market System.

The audit manager in charge of the engagement assigned you responsibility for auditing revenues for Longeta. You are excited to be in charge of this highly significant account and are enjoying the work you've done so far in the audit of some of the significant revenue transactions recorded during the year. The financial statements under audit are for the fiscal period ended September 30, 2012.

ASSESSING EVIDENCE OBTAINED

You have gathered quite a bit of information about several of the revenue transactions for the year. One of the transactions particularly caught your attention given its size. So, you're in the process of assessing the evidence obtained to determine if the revenues from this transaction are fairly stated. You obtained this information from reviewing documentation related to the transaction and from inquiries you made of the vice president of sales and the controller. You made the following notes about what you've learned and are now preparing for a meeting with the audit manager to discuss issues related to the transaction. Here's what you've noted so far:

- During July 2012, Longeta's vice president of sales sent a proposal to Magicon Inc, to sell $7 million worth of Longeta software and services to the U.S. Air Force. Longeta approached Magicon because Magicon has a relationship with the U.S. Air Force while Longeta does not. Magicon is a necessary intermediary under the government's procurement regulations.

The case was prepared by Mark S. Beasley, Ph.D. and Frank A. Buckless, Ph.D. of North Carolina State University and Steven M. Glover, Ph.D. and Douglas F. Prawitt, Ph.D. of Brigham Young University, as a basis for class discussion. It is not intended to illustrate either effective or ineffective handling of an administrative situation.

- Under terms of the proposal, Magicon would place a $7 million order for Longeta software and services by September 30, 2012, which is the last day of Longeta's fiscal year. In exchange, Magicon would receive a sizeable commission and become an exclusive reseller of Longeta products for the Air Force.

- Longeta normally must enter into "reseller agreements" with intermediaries such as Magicon in order to complete transactions. However, given the short timetable, Magicon was unable to obtain necessary corporate approvals from its legal department to sign a reseller agreement with Longeta before year end on September 30.

- As a substitute for the reseller agreement, Magicon's buyers agreed to place its order through an "order letter" that would later be followed by a purchase order and the reseller agreement.

- Before the order letter was submitted, Magicon's legal department requested that Longeta grant Magicon the right to cancel its obligation to pay Longeta the $7 million if Longeta and Magicon were unable to negotiate a mutually acceptable reseller agreement within 30 days.

- In late September, Longeta's vice president of sales emailed and faxed a letter on Longeta letterhead to Magicon legal specialists. Here is an excerpt from the letter:

  > "Per our discussion, the following is a clarification of the intent of the order letter dated September 30, 2012 between Longeta Corporation and Magicon Inc. The order letter meets GAAP requirement 97-4 for revenue recognition. The order letter allows Longeta to recognize revenue for our year ended September 30, 2012… The order letter gives us 30 days to reach mutually agreeable terms and conditions. In the unlikely event that we do not reach "mutually agreeable terms and conditions," Magicon will have the right to terminate the order letter and all obligations. This contingency may not be expressly stated in the order letter. However, you have my assurance that in the event that we cannot reach terms we will not hold you to the commitment to pay referenced in the order letter."

- On September 30, 2012, the Magicon legal department approved the deal and Magicon's purchasers signed and transmitted an order letter from Magicon to Longeta to buy $7 million worth of software and support services. The separate letter from the vice president of sales to Magicon, however, was not attached to the order letter and it was not referenced in the order letter.

- The order letter was submitted to Longeta's finance department. At that point, Longeta's made an accounting entry to record $5.8 million as current revenue for the product Longeta had shipped. The remaining $1.2 million was to be separately invoiced for updates and technical support services and was therefore recorded as deferred revenue.

REQUIRED

You want to be thoroughly prepared for the meeting with the audit manager. Perform the following procedures to be certain you have all necessary information about the transaction's treatment.

[1] Research required accounting treatment criteria related to revenue recognition to make sure you have a clear understanding of the explicit criteria that must be satisfied before revenue can be recognized. The Securities and Exchange Commission's (SEC) Staff Accounting Bulletin No. 101, *Revenue Recognition in Financial Statements*, provides a good summary of the key required elements. Read the SEC's guidance and document the four criteria the SEC believes must be satisfied for revenue recognition.

[2] In your own words, explain the company's reasoning for recording $5.8 million as current revenue while recording the remaining $1.2 million as deferred revenue. Also, document where on the financial statements the deferred revenue account would be presented.

[3] Assess the content of the separate letter issued by Longeta's vice president of sales to Magicon. Document your conclusion about how the content of the letter affects or does not affect revenue recognition for Longeta for the year ended September 30, 2012.

[4] Given that the letter from the vice president of sales was not attached to or documented in the order letter submitted by Magicon to Longeta, document your conclusion as to the impact, if any, the vice president's letter has on the accounting treatment for the transaction since it was not part of the order letter.

[5] The separate letter from the vice president of sales was emailed and faxed to Magicon representatives. What would be the impact if Longeta's vice president had only provided that information orally to Magicon representatives and not forwarded the information in written form?

[6] As of September 30, 2012, Magicon had only submitted the order letter. Document your conclusion about the impact on the accounting for the transaction if Longeta and Magicon (a) sign the reseller agreement within 30 days or (b) do not sign the reseller agreement within 30 days.

[7] Document your final conclusion about the accounting treatment of this transaction between Longeta and Magicon. Be sure to provide a basis for your conclusion.

Bud's Big Blue Manufacturing
Accounts Receivable Confirmations

MARK S. BEASLEY · FRANK A. BUCKLESS · STEVEN M. GLOVER · DOUGLAS F. PRAWITT

LEARNING OBJECTIVES

After completing and discussing this case you should be able to

[1] Understand requirements in the auditing standards relating to confirmations of receivables

[2] Understand the factors influencing the reliability of confirmations

[3] Describe how the receivables confirmation process should be handled in order to provide reliable audit evidence

INTRODUCTION

Confirmations of accounts receivable play an important role in the accumulation of sufficient, appropriate audit evidence. One of the principal strengths of confirmations is that they provide evidence obtained directly from third-parties. Auditing Standards provide guidance to auditors on how and when to use confirmations.

Generally Accepted Auditing Standards require accounts receivable (A/R) to be confirmed unless the gross amount of receivables is immaterial or confirmations are deemed to be ineffective given the audit client's circumstances. While they take various forms, A/R confirmations are typically prepared in the form of a letter from the audit client to its customers. The letter requests a response as to whether or not the customer agrees with the balance on the audit client's books, as indicated in the letter.[1]

Although a typical A/R confirmation letter is signed by the audit client, the auditor controls the process by mailing the confirmations to the client's customers and requesting that the confirmation responses be returned directly to the auditor. It is important that the auditor mail and receive the confirmations to minimize the potential that the client can manipulate the results. If proper control is not maintained throughout the process, bias could be introduced through the interception and alteration of the confirmation requests or responses.

When the recipient of a confirmation request fails to respond, the auditor generally follows-up with a second or even a third request. In the event the auditor does not receive a response to repeated requests, alternative procedures such as examining subsequent cash receipts are usually performed to gain evidence about the balance for the non-responding customer.

BACKGROUND

Bud's Big Blue Manufacturing (BBB), based in Kansas City, manufactures standard flight instruments for small aircraft. BBB's primary market consists of small aircraft manufacturers and repair shops.

You are a staff auditor in your second year with a public accounting firm. This week you have been assigned to work on the BBB audit, which is already nearing completion. The staff auditor who

---

1   This type of confirmation is known as a non-blank, positive confirmation.

This case was prepared by Mark S. Beasley, Ph.D. and Frank A. Buckless, Ph.D. of North Carolina State University and Steven M. Glover, Ph.D. and Douglas F. Prawitt, Ph.D. of Brigham Young University, as a basis for class discussion. Bud's Big Blue is a fictitious company. All characters and names represented are fictitious; any similarity to existing companies or persons is purely coincidental.

was working on the BBB audit was just reassigned to a new out-of-town client and was not able to complete her work on BBB. As you arrive at the client's headquarters, you are met by the audit senior assigned to BBB, Jenna Checketts. Jenna asks you to start by finishing the evaluation of accounts receivable balances. Confirmations were mailed to selected customers a few weeks ago. The former staff auditor completed an evaluation of all but seven of the receivables confirmations before being reassigned. The seven remaining confirmations either indicated a potential misstatement or were not received before the staff member left. Jenna also said some of the returned confirmations may require additional follow-up to determine if differences highlighted by customers represent actual misstatements or can be explained (e.g., timing differences).

It's been a while since you have evaluated confirmations, so you decide to review the relevant requirements in the auditing standards. After refreshing your memory, you begin your evaluation of the last seven confirmations for BBB's accounts receivable.

REQUIRED

[1] List the four factors auditors should consider when evaluating the results of confirmation procedures. Also, what are three of the characteristics of a reliable confirmation? (For this and other questions, you may wish to refer relevant auditing standards).

[2] What does it mean to "maintain control" over the confirmation requests and responses? What could go wrong if the auditor doesn't maintain control over the confirmation process?

[3] Complete the audit log provided on the next page for each of the seven remaining confirmations. Consider whether each confirmation provides sufficient, appropriate audit evidence, whether sufficient alternative procedures have been performed for non-responses, and whether additional procedures should be performed before concluding that the confirmation provides evidence supporting the client's account balance. Be as precise and concise as possible.

[4] What is the difference between a positive and a negative confirmation? What are the advantages and disadvantages of each type?

[5] Search the internet to identify a real-life situation where an auditor apparently did not maintain sufficient control over the confirmation process. Briefly describe the situation you found.

Bud's Big Blue, Mfg.
Accounts Receivable Confirmation Log
For the Year Ended December 31, 2011

Confirmation Tracking Number	Date Sent	Date Received	Difference Noted By Customer? (Y/N)	Is the noted difference an audit difference (i.e., not a timing difference)?	Has sufficient appropriate evidence been obtained? If no, describe additional procedures you believe should be performed.
71	1/12	1/22			
72	1/12	2/5			
73	1/12	1/26			
74	1/12	2/9			
75	1/12	2/6			
76	1/12	1/30			
77	1/12	1/19			

BUD'S BIG BLUE, MFG.

1599 West Ranch Road
Kansas City, Kansas 66131

January 12, 2012

Private Planes Plus, Mfg.
122 Courier Blvd.
Indianapolis, IN 46987
Attn: Sandy Donner

With regard to our annual audit, please complete the bottom portion of this letter and return the entire letter to our auditors, S&T LLP, PO Box 3221, Kansas City, 66122. Our records indicate your balance with our company as of December 31, 2011 amounted to $257,449.

If the amount listed above is in agreement with your records, please mark "A" below.

If the amount listed above is not in agreement with your records, please mark "B" below.

After marking the appropriate response, please sign and date this confirmation letter and return it directly to our auditors in the enclosed envelope. This is not a request for payment; please DO NOT SEND PAYMENT to our auditors.

Sincerely,

Patty Rice

Patty Rice
Controller

A. ☐   The above balance agrees with my record.

B. ☒   My records show a balance of $ _207,449_.

The difference may be attributable to the following:

Our records show that we made a payment in the

the amount of $50,000 on December 29, 2011.

_____

Sandy Donner
(Signed by)

_01/19/2012_
(Date)

DATE: FEB-05-2012 3:20 PM   NewHeights, LLC   302-223-9271 P.01/01

BUD'S BIG BLUE, MFG.

Received by fax: 2/5/12

1599 West Ranch Road
Kansas City, Kansas 66131

January 12, 2012

NewHeights, LLC
9750 Kingly St.
Omaha, NE 69375
Attn: James Kindel

With regard to our annual audit, please complete the bottom portion of this letter and return the entire letter to our auditors, S&T LLP, PO Box 3221, Kansas City, 66122. Our records indicate your balance with our company as of December 31, 2011 amounted to $177,821.

If the amount listed above is in agreement with your records, please mark "A" below.

If the amount listed above is not in agreement with your records, please mark "B" below.

After marking the appropriate response, please sign and date this confirmation letter and return it directly to our auditors in the enclosed envelope. This is not a request for payment; please DO NOT SEND PAYMENT to our auditors.

Sincerely,

Patty Rice

Patty Rice
Controller

A. ☒   The above balance agrees with my record.

B. ☐   My records show a balance of $_____.

The difference may be attributable to the following:

_____

_____

_____

James Kindel
(Signed by)

February 05, 2012
(Date)

268

Confirmation Tracking No.   73

Received: 1/26/12

BUD'S BIG BLUE, MFG.

1599 West Ranch Road
Kansas City, Kansas 66131

January 12, 2012

Pilot's Passion, Mfg.
4544 West Carter Cir.
Lavina, MT 59599
Attn: Paula Sutton

With regard to our annual audit, please complete the bottom portion of this letter and return the entire letter to our auditors, S&T LLP, PO Box 3221, Kansas City, 66122. Our records indicate your balance with our company as of December 31, 2011 amounted to $257,449.

If the amount listed above is in agreement with your records, please mark "A" below.

If the amount listed above is not in agreement with your records, please mark "B" below.

After marking the appropriate response, please sign and date this confirmation letter and return it directly to our auditors in the enclosed envelope. This is not a request for payment; please DO NOT SEND PAYMENT to our auditors.

Sincerely,

Patty Rice

Patty Rice
Controller

A. ☒   The above balance agrees with my record.

B. ☐   My records show a balance of $_____.

The difference may be attributable to the following:

_____

_____

_____

_____
Paula Sutton
(Signed by)

_____
1/21/2012
(Date)

Confirmation Tracking No. _____74_____

Received: 2/9/12

Via E-MAIL

Jenna Checketts
_____

From: Carl Metser [cmets@highflyer.com]
Sent: Monday, February 9, 2012 11:46 AM
To: jenna.checketts@stllp.com
Subject: A/R Confirmation

Jenna:

I received your email address from Patty. This is to confirm that our outstanding balance with Bud's per our books matches the balance noted in your letter.

Best Regards,

Carl Metser
High Flyer, Corp.
Controller
cmets@highflyer.com

Confirmation Tracking No. _____75_____
Received by auditor: 2/6/12

BUD'S BIG BLUE, MFG.

1599 West Ranch Road
Kansas City, Kansas 66131

January 12, 2012

Bird Buddies, LLP.
7220 Industrial Loop.
Rapid City, SD 57400
Attn: Victoria Holman

With regard to our annual audit, please complete the bottom portion of this letter and return the entire letter to our auditors, S&T LLP, PO Box 3221, Kansas City, 66122. Our records indicate your balance with our company as of December 31, 2011 amounted to $343,810.

If the amount listed above is in agreement with your records, please mark "A" below.

If the amount listed above is not in agreement with your records, please mark "B" below.

After marking the appropriate response, please sign and date this confirmation letter and return it directly to our auditors in the enclosed envelope. This is not a request for payment; please DO NOT SEND PAYMENT to our auditors.

Sincerely,

Patty Rice

Patty Rice
Controller

A. ☒   The above balance agrees with my record.

B. ☐   My records show a balance of $_____.

The difference may be attributable to the following:

_____

_____

_____

_____Vicki Holman_____
(Signed by)

_____01/30/2012_____
(Date)

Confirmation Tracking No. ____76____

Received: ___1/30/12___

BUD'S BIG BLUE, MFG.

1599 West Ranch Road
Kansas City, Kansas 66131

January 12, 2012

Higher Flyers, Mfg.
410 Mountain Pass Road
Boise, ID 83680
Attn: Phillip Bramwell

With regard to our annual audit, please complete the bottom portion of this letter and return the entire letter to our auditors, S&T LLP, PO Box 3221, Kansas City, 66122. Our records indicate your balance with our company as of December 31, 2011 amounted to $98,033.

If the amount listed above is in agreement with your records, please mark "A" below.

If the amount listed above is not in agreement with your records, please mark "B" below.

After marking the appropriate response, please sign and date this confirmation letter and return it directly to our auditors in the enclosed envelope. This is not a request for payment; please DO NOT SEND PAYMENT to our auditors.

Sincerely,

Patty Rice

Patty Rice
Controller

A. ☐ The above balance agrees with my record.

B. ☐ My records show a balance of $_____.

The difference may be attributable to the following:

Seems Reasonable.

_____

_____

Phillip Bramwell
(Signed by)

01/26/2012
(Date)

Confirmation Tracking No. _____77_____

Received: 1/19/12

BUD'S BIG BLUE, MFG.

1599 West Ranch Road
Kansas City, Kansas 66131

January 12, 2012

Aviator's Assembly, Corp.
3100 Steer Dr. Suite 207
Choctaw, OK 73099
Attn: Jason DeVue

With regard to our annual audit, please complete the bottom portion of this letter and return the entire letter to our auditors, S&T LLP, PO Box 3221, Kansas City, 66122. Our records indicate your balance with our company as of December 31, 2011 amounted to $302,717.

If the amount listed above is in agreement with your records, please mark "A" below.

If the amount listed above is not in agreement with your records, please mark "B" below.

After marking the appropriate response, please sign and date this confirmation letter and return it directly to our auditors in the enclosed envelope. This is not a request for payment; please DO NOT SEND PAYMENT to our auditors.

Sincerely,

Patty Rice

Patty Rice
Controller

    A. ☐   The above balance agrees with my record.

    B. ☒   My records show a balance of $ _302,177_ .

        The difference may be attributable to the following:

        _____

        _____

        _____

_____*Jason DeVue*_____
(Signed by)

_____*Jan. 14, 2012*_____
(Date)

Morris Mining Corporation
Auditing Fair Value

MARK S. BEASLEY · FRANK A. BUCKLESS · STEVEN M. GLOVER · DOUGLAS F. PRAWITT

LEARNING OBJECTIVES

After completing and discussing this case you should be able to

[1] Understand common audit procedures used to audit fair value estimates

[2] Comprehend the challenges inherent in auditing fair value estimates

[3] Appreciate how estimation uncertainty and sensitivity to small changes in fair value inputs can affect reported values

[4] Understand and appreciate the degree of judgment required to formulate and audit Level 3 fair value estimates

INTRODUCTION

The Financial Accounting Standard Board's Accounting Standards Codification Topic 820, "Fair Value Measurement," (ASC 820) provides a framework for measuring or estimating the fair value of certain assets and liabilities. It provides a hierarchy with three levels that are differentiated by the inputs used to derive estimates. Level 1 valuations are based on quoted prices in active markets for identical assets or liabilities. Level 2 valuations are based on directly or indirectly observable market data for similar or comparable assets or liabilities. Orderly transactions between market participants may not be observable at the valuation date; therefore, Level 3 valuations are based on management's judgments and assumptions about unobservable inputs. While standard setters and most users believe an appropriately developed Level 3 valuation provides valuable information and is better than the alternative (e.g., possibly irrelevant historical), some critics of Level 3 valuations refer to such valuations as being marked to "make believe."[1] There are a number of valuation models that are commonly used for Level 3 measurement: stock option pricing models (e.g., the Black Scholes model), discounted cash flows method, discounted dividend method, and others. Even though some inputs into these models could qualify for Level 1 or Level 2 treatment, the overall model and the related asset or liability being estimated would be considered a Level 3 model/valuation if any of the significant inputs are unobservable because the level of the asset or liability is determined based on the lowest level input.

In the next section you will find a dialogue between an audit manager and an audit senior discussing the fair value method and assumptions used by audit client Morris Mining Corporation to form a fair value estimate. Morris Mining, Corp., with a fiscal year-end of December 31, owns and operates mining facilities in the U.S. and Canada and distributes various extracted ores and minerals to customers throughout the world.

In January 2012, Morris Mining acquired another mining company called King Co. The acquisition is expected to be synergistic, as the location and nature of King's operations fit well with

---

1 Weil, J. "Mark-to-make-believe perfumes rotten bank loans," Bloomberg Opinion available at http://www.bloomberg.com/news/2010-11-18/mark-to-make-believe-perfumes-rotten-loans-commentary-by-jonathan-weil.html.

Morris Mining's long-term strategy. The combined firm controls greater market share in key ores and minerals and some redundant overhead costs can be streamlined to improve overall profitability. According to valuation analyses conducted by Morris Mining and its advisors in preparation of the acquisition, the purchase price will exceed the value of identifiable net assets. As a result Morris Mining will record goodwill and the identifiable assets and liabilities of King Co. will be recorded on the books of Morris Mining at fair value.

One of the assets that will require fair value measurement is a patent that King Co. was granted two years ago. King Co. engineers developed and patented the design for a new mining machine that significantly improves mining efficiency. The patent obtained by King Co. gives the company the right to exclude others from commercial exploitation of the invention for a period of 20 years. King Co. developed some prototypes of the new mining machine, the "Extract-o-Matic 1000," and then entered into an agreement with a manufacturing firm called Build-IT, Inc. The agreement gives Build-IT the exclusive rights to manufacture and sell the Extract-o-Matic 1000 machines for a period of 12 years. In exchange, King Co. receives a yearly royalty payment in the amount of 10 percent of the revenue from sales of the Extract-o-Matic 1000. After acquiring King Co., Morris Mining is now the legal patent holder and as such is entitled to receive the royalty payments.

Sales of the Extract-o-Matic have gone well as the machines allow mines to significantly reduce the amount of waste during the mineral extraction process. In fact, Morris Mining purchased one of the machines before the acquisition, and it is performing as promised.

PHONE CONVERSATION ABOUT FAIR VALUE ESTIMATE

The following is a phone conversation between Rob, a new audit manager on the Morris Mining engagement, and Gabriela, the audit senior, regarding Morris Mining's accounting for the Extract-o-Matic patent.

[ROB]   Gabriela, I understand you have tracked down more information on the valuation of the patent Morris obtained in the acquisition of King Co.

[GABRIELA]   Yes, I did. I met with Morris Mining's CFO, Chris Carter, this morning, and he walked me through their thinking on developing a fair value estimate for the patent on the Extract-o-Matic 1000.

[ROB]   Well, if the machine is as impressive as its name, it must really be something. I understand the equipment reduces waste and that the company is using the equipment in its operations. I also understand that the company has an agreement to receive yearly patent royalties from sales. Is that correct?

[GABRIELA]   Right. The company is currently using the equipment and has 10 years left on a royalty agreement with Build-IT, Inc. Under the agreement, Build-IT has the exclusive right to manufacture and sell the Extract-o-Matic and Morris Mining receives a 10 percent royalty payment on the revenue from sales of Extract-o-Matics each year, paid annually at the end of each year. Sales growth in the first couple of years was significant and is expected to continue for at least another few years before leveling out and then declining for the remaining useful life of the patent. Reports back from customers are extremely positive—the Extract-o-Matics are reported to really reduce waste and improve overall yield. The fact that the equipment is performing well, on top of the granting of the patent and the agreement with Build-IT, really has the company excited about the potential royalty cash flows that Extract-o-Matic sales will generate over the next 10 years.

[ROB]   Okay, the equipment is in production, there is already a track record on sales, and there is positive buzz in the marketplace—that is all good news and suggests the patent is a valuable asset. How is the company proposing to value the patent? I'm guessing no one else has a directly comparable product or patent.

[GABRIELA] Correct. Certainly, there are other patents in the industry that we will want to consider in our evaluation of the company's estimate, but the Extract-o-Matic is definitely unique in the market. The company is using a discounted cash flow approach to estimate the fair value of the patent. Key inputs include: expected life of the asset, discount rate, royalties on sales, and expected sales growth. The machines are not cheap; they sell for about $2 million each.

[ROB] Ok, a discounted cash flow approach sounds reasonable. What other approaches did they consider? Did they compute the value using more than one approach?

[GABRIELA] The CFO did mention they considered other models before concluding that the discounted cash flow method is the most appropriate approach. As you know, for valuing assets, three common approaches are the market approach, cost approach, and income approach. The market approach would value the patent based on sales of similar assets or patents in the market. The problem with this approach is that patents are so unique that it becomes very difficult to find a comparable sale to base a value on. That's definitely the case with the Extract-o-Matic. There just doesn't appear to be a good comparison in the marketplace.

[ROB] Okay, makes sense. How about the cost approach?

[GABRIELA] The cost approach would measure the fair value of the patent based on the costs that would be necessary to replace it. But this method is generally not used because patents can't really be replaced like many other assets. Plus, capturing specific development costs is non-trivial, especially because King Co. did not track separately the development costs that led to the patent design. So it doesn't seem that a replacement cost approach is sensible. After discussing with the CFO, I agree with the use of the income or discounted cash flows approach.

[ROB] Yeah, that makes sense. The fair value of the patent is computed by estimating the present value of the estimated cash flows that will be earned in royalty payments. Based on past experience, applying the discounted cash flow approach requires a great deal of effort to ensure that inputs used in the model are reasonable and supportable. Fortunately, it sounds like the company has focused a lot of time and attention on formulating the estimate and providing support for its inputs. I appreciate you walking me through all this. So what amount have they computed for the fair value under the discounted cash flow method?

[GABRIELA] Well, it is a pretty big number; the present value of the projected discounted cash flows is just over $25.7 million. Morris Mining obtained estimates from Build-IT regarding the expected future cash flows to be generated from sales of the Extract-o-Matic 1000. These cash flow estimates were then used to value the patent. Build-IT had $30 million in Extract-o-Matic sales last year and expects sales to increase 15 percent per year for the next four years, and then decline at 5 percent per year for three years, and finally decline 15 percent per year for the last three years of the agreement. Morris Mining obtained a 10-year discounted cash flow projection from Build-IT, and based on that they were able to compute the present value of the royalties that will be received each year for the life of the licensing agreement (see Appendix A). While the actual patent grants exclusive rights for up to 20 years, experience in the industry is that the patent will likely produce a competitive advantage for 12 years, as other competing technology will eventually come online. In this situation, the remaining useful life matches up with the 10-year remaining life of the agreement with Build-IT. I've looked at the model. They're using a discount rate of 10 percent and the expected sales trend provided by Build-IT.

[ROB]   Well, all of those numbers are estimates and they all will impact the fair value estimate and of course the future amortization. What do you think about the inputs, do they seem reasonable to you?

[GABRIELA]   Well, I did some research, and based on relevant rate indices and industry norms, the discount rate seems to be reasonable, but you know how much rates have fluctuated in the past few years. Given a 10-year remaining useful life, I'm not sure 10 percent is the best rate to use in the valuation model. A reasonable range for the interest rate appears to be 8 to 11 percent, but it seems the lower end of the range is more likely and probably more supportable. They are at the higher end of that range, which decreases the net present value of the asset and thus the future amortization they will be recognizing. It also increases the amount recorded as goodwill, as compared to what it would be if they used a lower discount rate. As for the growth rate in the first four years, Chris tells me that the President of Build-IT doesn't believe the growth rate of 25 percent in the first couple of years is sustainable, but based on his experience with sales of equipment like this he is confident that they can achieve a 15 percent growth rate over the first four years. He also believes that sales will then start to decline because technological improvements in mining have limited useful lives.

[ROB]   Well, I'm glad Chris and the President of Built-IT feel comfortable with the forecasts, but unfortunately it doesn't seem like there's enough support for us to buy-off on the estimated growth and subsequent decline projections. Do you or the company have any benchmark data for similar mining machinery that's been patented and sold in recent years?

[GABRIELA]   I've done some research on that as well, and given my preliminary findings, I think the 15 percent growth rate that's been suggested for the first four years may actually be too conservative given the rapid growth in the first two years and the other information I found. Several years ago, another mining company in the western U.S. manufactured and sold newly patented equipment that represented a pretty big step over existing technology at the time. The company was quite successful in marketing and selling the equipment, and in the first few years averaged just over 22 percent growth, with the highest years at about 25 percent, which is about what Build-IT experienced in the first two years of sales. The decline in the middle and later years of the useful life seem reasonable, although in the last year or two I think it could drop more than 15 percent.

[ROB]   We'll need to do some more research on this and we'll have to challenge the client to provide additional support for the expected pattern of cash flows in terms of initial growth and subsequent decline. The chosen discount rate and sales growth in the early years relative to what you have determined so far as reasonable ranges will tend to reduce the net present value of the cash flows. What do you think about the estimated length of the asset's useful life?

[GABRIELA]   Their numbers seem reasonable in that regard. In researching footnotes of other mining companies' financials, it seems pretty common for patent assets to have a useful life of 10 to 12 years. In this case, it seems reasonable to estimate the remaining useful life at 10 years, which as I mentioned is the same as the term remaining in the royalty agreement with Build-IT. I also gathered more evidence from Chris on how they are supporting the estimated life.

[ROB]   Gabriela, you've done a great job on the patent valuation so far. Thanks for your good work. Now we need to make sure we can get comfortable with the model and the inputs. To the extent we disagree with Morris on any of the inputs, we will want to compute our own estimated value and then look at the sensitivity of the estimated value to changes in inputs. We'll want to see how big the ranges are relative to materiality.

[GABRIELA] Right. Even slight changes in the input estimates the Company is using could have a significant impact on the financial statements. I'll continue researching the projected growth rate and discount rate and I'll run some sensitivity analyses and keep you posted.

REQUIRED

[1] What is the definition of fair value according to ASC 820? Do you believe the discounted cash flow method is capable of computing an estimate that would be considered a reasonably reliable fair value for the patent held by Morris Mining? Why or why not?

[2] Should Gabriela and Rob be concerned about the fair value estimate Morris Mining has computed? Why? What incentive does the company likely have in terms of valuing the patent (over or understatement)? Explain your answer.

[3] Research auditing standards and describe the typical procedures that an auditor would perform in auditing a fair value estimate such as the value of Morris Mining's patent. Is the patent a Level 1, Level 2, or Level 3 fair value asset? Why?

[4] Examine the 10-year discounted cash flow analysis provided by the client in Appendix A and also available electronically at www.pearsonhighered.com/beasley5e and verify that the model is producing a mathematically sound fair value estimate based on the inputs used by Morris Mining. Assuming planning or performance materiality for Morris Mining is $10 million, answer the following questions:

[a] How sensitive is the fair value estimate to changes in the discount rate? How much would the discount rate estimate have to change for it to have a material impact on the financial statements?

[b] How sensitive is the fair value estimate to changes in the estimated growth rates? How much would the estimated growth percentages have to change to have a material impact on the fair value estimate? Do rate changes in early years or later years have a larger impact? Why?

[5] Now, assuming planning or performance materiality at Morris Mining is $600,000, answer the following questions. (Note: as indicated earlier, you can obtain an electronic copy of the 10-year discounted cash flow analysis at www.pearsonhighered.com/beasley5e)

[a] How sensitive is the fair value estimate to changes in the discount rate? How much would the discount rate estimate have to change for it to have a material impact on the financial statements?

[b] How sensitive is the fair value estimate to changes in the estimated growth rates? How much would the estimated growth percentages have to change to have a material impact on the fair value estimate? Do rate changes in early years or later years have a larger impact? Why?

[c] A great deal of judgment is required when estimating some fair values and sometimes a "reasonable range" for the possible estimate value is very large relative to materiality. What implications do the judgment involved and the estimate's sensitivity to small changes to inputs have when it comes to auditing fair value estimates?

[6] What are the most significant audit risks associated with the fair value estimate of the patent? Assuming performance materiality of $600,000, what additional steps can the auditor take to improve the sufficiency and appropriateness of the evidence gathered to support the fair value estimate for the patent?

APPENDIX A

Royalty Discounted Cash Flow Analysis
Prepared by Chris Carter, Morris Mining CFO

2011 Revenue	$30,000,000									
Discount rate:	10%									
Royalty rate:	10%									

Growth Rates:		
Years 1 - 4	15%	
Years 5 - 7	-5%	
Years 8 - 10	-15%	

Morris Mining, Corp.										
Year	1	2	3	4	5	6	7	8	9	10
	2012	2013	2014	2015	2016	2017	2018	2019	2020	2021
Extract-o-Matic Revenues	$34,500,000	$39,675,000	$45,626,250	$52,470,188	$49,846,678	$47,354,344	$44,996,627	$38,238,633	$32,502,838	$27,627,412
Patent Royalty (10%)	3,450,000	3,967,500	4,562,625	5,247,019	4,984,668	4,735,434	4,498,663	3,823,863	3,250,284	2,762,741
Present Value of Cash Flow from Royalty	3,136,364	3,278,926	3,427,968	3,583,784	3,095,087	2,673,029	2,308,525	1,783,860	1,378,438	1,065,156
Total Present Value of Cash Flow from Royalty	**$ 25,731,137**									
Patent Royalty (10%)	3,450,000	3,967,500	4,562,625	5,247,019	4,984,668	4,735,434	4,498,663	3,823,863	3,250,284	2,762,741
Amortization per year	2,573,114	2,573,114	2,573,114	2,573,114	2,573,114	2,573,114	2,573,114	2,573,114	2,573,114	2,573,114
Annual Net Royalty Income	$ 876,886	$ 1,394,386	$ 1,989,511	$ 2,673,905	$ 2,411,554	$ 2,162,321	$ 1,925,549	$ 1,250,750	$ 677,170	$ 189,628

Hooplah, Inc.

Applying Audit Sampling Concepts to Tests of Controls and Substantive Testing in the Revenue Cycle

MARK S. BEASLEY · FRANK A. BUCKLESS · STEVEN M. GLOVER · DOUGLAS F. PRAWITT

LEARNING OBJECTIVES

After completing and discussing this case you should be able to

[1] Understand the differences between statistical and non-statistical sampling

[2] Appreciate the professional judgment involved in determining the extent of sampling to be performed

[3] Appreciate the role of sampling risk in determining sample size and in evaluating results

[4] Understand how to perform attribute sampling for tests of controls

[5] Know how and why it is important to consider size- and risk-based substantive testing prior to obtaining evidence using audit sampling

[6] Understand the implications of the results of tests of controls on substantive testing

INTRODUCTION

Your audit firm, Garrett and Schulzke LLP, is engaged to perform the annual audit of Hooplah, Inc., for the year ending December 31, 2011. Hooplah is a privately-held company that sells electronics components to companies that manufacture various appliances. The company hires a public accounting firm to provide an audit of its financial statements in order to get favorable terms on its bank loans. Your firm has audited Hooplah for the past three years. For the current audit engagement, your team has already performed most of the audit work; however, there are a few loose ends for you to tie up. Portions of Garrett and Schulzke's audit policy relating to audit sampling are provided to assist you in completing the procedures.

AUDIT SAMPLING

Audit sampling is commonly applied in performing tests of controls and tests of details. Audit sampling involves the application of audit procedures to less than 100 percent of the items in a population of audit relevance, selected in such a way that the auditor expects the sample to be representative of the population and thus likely to provide a reasonable basis for conclusions about the population. A sample is usually selected either randomly (using some form of random-number generator) or haphazardly (where the auditor attempts to select items randomly but without using a formal random-number generator).

Auditors often use sampling approaches that involve formal statistical theories and principles, similar to those you may have learned in an introductory statistics class. Statistical sampling applications require the use of random selection, based on a formal random-number generator (such as the one built in to Microsoft Excel or audit software such as ACL). Auditing standards also allow auditors to use "non-statistical" sampling approaches. Non-statistical audit sampling approaches are based on a foundation of statistical principles, but allow certain departures from formal statistics in order to simplify the auditor's task. One such simplification is that non-statistical sampling allows the use of haphazard selection of the items to be examined.

When an auditor examines only a sample instead of all of the items in the population, an element of uncertainty enters into the auditor's conclusions. This uncertainty, referred to as sampling risk, is due to the possibility that the sample selected is not representative of the population and that as a result the auditor will reach an incorrect conclusion about the population. It is crucial that sampling risk be taken into account when evaluating the results of any audit procedures that involve sampling.

Sampling approaches also differ depending on the nature of the items the auditor is examining and the objectives of the auditor. Depending on the method of sampling used, different formulas and tables are available to help you determine the number of items to include in the sample. This case has two parts. In Part A you will be asked to use statistical attribute sampling for testing controls. In Part B you will use non-statistical substantive sampling for testing accounts receivable.

PART A: TESTS OF CONTROLS

Before beginning substantive tests for accounts receivable, you and Darrell need to perform tests of important controls over the revenue process to justify the preliminary control risk assessment of low control risk and to determine whether a reliance approach is appropriate for substantive testing. You have decided to test three controls in Hooplah's revenue process:

1. Sales are properly authorized for credit approval.

2. Sales are reviewed by the sales manager to ensure that they are properly priced.

3. Credit memos for sales returns are properly authorized once all goods have been returned.

Garrett and Schulzke's sampling guidance for testing controls is based on attribute sampling. In testing the operating effectiveness of controls you are interested in determining the likely "deviation rate," or the rate at which a control is not properly operating. Testing controls to measure the deviation rate provides evidence about whether the control is operating effectively an acceptably high percentage of the time and helps the auditor determine whether or not the control can be relied upon. Garrett and Schulzke's sample size table for attribute sampling can be found in Appendix A. Use the table to determine the appropriate sample size for tests of controls given a specified tolerable deviation rate and estimated deviation rate. Garrett and Schulzke's controls testing sampling policy indicates that to place high reliance on controls (i.e., to support a low level of remaining control risk) the test must be performed at a high level of assurance, which they define as 95 percent confidence. Thus, only the sample size table associated with 95 percent confidence is provided. In addition to the sample size table, an evaluation table is provided in Appendix A that will help you determine the computed upper deviation rate for the control given the number of detected deviations and the sample size used. The computed upper deviation rate is the sum of the sample deviation rate and an appropriate allowance for sampling risk. In other words, it represents the upper end of the 95 percent confidence interval for the deviation rate in the population. If the computed upper deviation rate indicated is greater than the tolerable deviation rate for the control, the auditor should not rely on the control.

In order to determine the appropriate sample size for your tests, the importance of the control to be tested needs to be assessed. Garrett and Schulzke's policy indicates that any controls the auditor might consider relying on are either "highly important" or "moderately important." According to the firm's policies, a deviation rate of only four percent can be tolerated for controls deemed "highly important," while a tolerable deviation rate of eight percent can be tolerated for controls deemed "moderately important." Some "tolerance" for error must always exist when using audit sampling because sampling involves sampling risk. The higher the tolerable deviation rate, the lower the sample size.

Based on your knowledge of Hoopla's systems, you decide that the first two controls are moderately important, and that the third control is highly important. The other input needed to determine sample size is the estimated population deviation rate. Based on past experience with the client and considering historical rates, you determine that the estimated population deviation rates for the three controls are one percent, two percent, and zero percent, respectively.[1]

Darrell decided that since all sales pass through the first two controls and since the tolerable deviation rate for those controls is the same, he could be more efficient by using the same sample of transactions to test both controls. He randomly chose 58 sales transactions and tested the documentation for evidence of proper credit approval and review of pricing by the sales manager. After finding only one exception for the first control and two exceptions for the second control, Darrell determined that both controls are operating effectively.

Now that Darrell has tested the first two controls, you need to test the third one before moving on to substantive testing.

REQUIRED (CONTINUED ON NEXT PAGE)

[1] Evaluate the appropriateness of Darrell's conclusions relating to the first two controls:

[a] Is it acceptable to use the same set of transactions and the same sample size to test two different controls?

[b] Do you agree with Darrell's conclusions with respect to these first two controls? If not, why not? In evaluating Darrell's conclusions, you may wish to refer to the attribute sampling evaluation table available in Appendix A.

[c] What additional work, if any, is necessary to support his assessment that both controls are operating effectively?

[2] Evaluate each of the following questions independently:

[a] Referring to Garrett and Schulzke's sample size table (Appendix A), determine an appropriate sample size for the test of the control relating to authorization of credit memos.

[b] Regardless of your answer to question [a], assume that Darrell randomly selected a sample of 75 credit memo packages, each of which contains a credit memo with a matching receiving report and inventory warehouse receipt, and has reviewed all but the last five credit memo packages and found no exceptions. Each credit memo authorizing a customer refund or reduction in the amount owed due to the return of goods should be authorized by Brian Thompson, the accounting supervisor over accounts receivable. When a customer wants to return unwanted or defective product, they go to Hooplah's website and download a "Customer Return Report" and fill in their information as well as a description and quantity of goods being returned. Chris Jacobs in the receiving department at Hooplah uses the Customer Return Report as the receiving report when the shipment comes in, and Felix Katt counts and inspects the goods to make sure they're all in good condition. The goods are then transferred back to Jed Baxter in the warehouse, who issues an "Inventory Receipt." Once the Inventory Receipt is attached to the Customer Return Report, the documents are forwarded to Brian so that he can approve a credit memo. Brian examines the Customer

---

1   To be effective, most controls do not need to operate 100 percent of the time so long as the times the control fails to operate are not predictable and the person(s) performing the control investigates processing exceptions observed during the proper application of the control. To be effective, however, a control does need to operate effectively a reasonably high percentage of the time.

Return Report and the Inventory Receipt to ensure that credit is only authorized when goods have been received and for the quantity actually received. He then documents his authorization by marking his initials on the credit memo. You have agreed to help Darrell by examining the remaining five credit memo packages. You will find the last five credit memo packages at www.pearsonhighered.com/beasley5e. Examine these documents for Brian Thompson's initials indicating the memos were approved (for this question, just focus on his initials for audit evidence that the control is operating effectively) and then evaluate the test results for the full sample. Provide support for your assessment on the effectiveness of the control based on testing performed.

[3] In question 2[b] you gathered evidence on the operation of the control by examining the five credit memos for Brian's initials. While this provides some evidence of control, higher quality evidence that the control is actually operating effectively can be obtained by reperforming Brian's control procedure. This would be done by verifying that each credit memo is supported by a Customer Return Report and Inventory Receipt and that the quantity and description of goods on the credit memo is supported by the quantity and description on the supporting documents. If Brian's initials are on the credit memo, but the quantity or description of goods on the memo is not consistent with the quantity and description on the supporting documents, this would be considered a control deviation. Assume Darrell reperformed the control for the first 70 credit memo packages and found no exceptions.

[a] Reperform the control for the remaining five credit memo packages and evaluate the test results for the full sample. Provide support for your assessment on the effectiveness of the control based on testing performed.

[b] If you came to a different conclusion in 2[b] and 3[a], which conclusion is more supportable and why?

[4] Assuming the controls testing is not expanded to provide additional support regarding the effectiveness of the controls tested, what are the implications of the controls testing in question 3[a] with respect to the nature, timing, and extent of substantive evidence that must be gathered to support the fairness of the accounts receivable balance?

PART B: TESTS OF DETAILS

Regardless of what you found in Part A, for Part B assume that you are able to place moderate reliance on the controls tested and that you have already obtained some substantive evidence supporting the fairness of accounts receivable from substantive analytical procedures. While you have already obtained some assurance regarding the fairness of the ending accounts receivable balance, you do not yet have sufficient evidence given the size of accounts receivable and the remaining risk of misstatement. You plan to request that some of Hooplah's customers confirm their accounts receivable balance directly to you. In the prior year's audit, aggregate misstatements of less than 0.5% of the accounts receivable balance were discovered via customer confirmation testing. The few misstatements that were found were promptly corrected by Hooplah.

The current-year information that follows will help you in determining the nature and extent of detail testing in order to have sufficient appropriate evidence to conclude on the fairness of the accounts receivable balance.

Current Year Information:
Net income = $9 million
Total assets = $85 million
Total accounts receivable = $12,881,551
Accounts receivable greater than 90 days past due = $2 million
Tolerable misstatement for accounts receivable = $400,000

In most cases, the selection of items to be detail tested is based on two approaches, which can be used singly or in combination to achieve the desired level of assurance with respect to the population being tested:

1 - Directed Testing
2 - Audit sampling

Directed testing, also known as "targeted testing" or "key item testing," is a technique that involves selecting items to examine based on a particular characteristic of interest such as size or risk. Unlike audit sampling, the items are not randomly (or haphazardly) selected. Instead, selection is "directed" or "targeted" based on a particular characteristic. Thus, directed testing is not considered "sampling" per se, because the subset of selected items is not expected to be representative of the population. Garrett and Schulzke's audit policy requires that teams direct test all individual items in the account that are greater than tolerable misstatement. Thus, even if the auditor intends to perform audit sampling to test an account (e.g., accounts receivable), the auditor must first examine all items (e.g., individual customer accounts) that are individually greater than tolerable misstatement.

After testing all such items, it is often appropriate to expand the directed testing to specifically select relatively high risk items, if such items can be identified. The auditor may also expand directed testing to select relatively large items other than those that are larger than tolerable misstatement in order to achieve "coverage" of a higher dollar percentage of the total account. Selection criteria for directed testing can include a combination of risk and size components. Expanding the number of items examined in directed testing can often provide sufficient assurance in combination with the assurance already obtained from other audit procedures (e.g., risk assessment, controls testing, substantive analytical procedures, testing in related accounts, etc.). In such cases, the use of an audit sampling approach is unnecessary.

Garrett and Schulzke's substantive audit sampling policy uses a nonstatistical sampling approach. Items are selected from the population either randomly or haphazardly, at the auditor's discretion. To determine the appropriate sample size, the firm provides the following formula:

$$Sample\ size = \left(\frac{Sampling\ population\ book\ value}{Tolerable - Expected\ misstatement}\right) \times Confidence\ factor$$

The sampling population book value is the total book value of all the items available to be selected in the sample. This total does not include items already removed for direct testing (i.e., all items greater than tolerable misstatement and other items selected based on size and/or risk characteristics). Tolerable misstatement is the greatest amount of misstatement that can be tolerated for the account being tested without concluding that the account is materially misstated. Expected misstatement is the amount of misstatement that the auditor expects to find in the account being tested. The "confidence factor" included in the above equation is determined based on the assessed risk of material misstatement for the account and the desired level of confidence from the sample. The confidence factor table below is from Garrett and Schulzke's sampling policy.

Confidence Factors for Nonstatistical Sampling

Assessment of Risk of Material Misstatement	Desired Level of Confidence		
	High	Moderate	Low
High	3.0	2.3	2.0
Moderate	2.3	1.6	1.2
Low	2.0	1.2	1.0

The purpose of audit sampling is to draw conclusions about the entire population through testing a subset of the population. To draw inferences about the entire population, sample results must be projected to the population. Garrett and Schulzke's sampling policy provides two projection methods: ratio projection and difference projection. Ratio projection is performed by calculating the ratio of the misstatement to the sample book value and projecting it to the sampling population book value according to the following formula:

$$Projected\ misstatement = \frac{Sample\ misstatement}{Sample\ book\ value} \times Sampling\ population\ book\ value$$

Difference projection is performed by calculating the average misstatement per sample item (e.g. individual customer account) and projecting it to the number of items in the sampling population according to the following formula:

$$Projected\ misstatement = \frac{Sample\ misstatement}{Sample\ size} \times \#\ Items\ in\ sampling\ population$$

REQUIRED (CONTINUED ON NEXT PAGE)

[1] In selecting which customer balances to detail test via accounts receivable confirmations, assume that you have decided to direct test only the minimum number of customer accounts required; that is, you will direct test only customer accounts that are greater than tolerable misstatement, and you will use audit sampling to test the remainder of the population. You can find the accounts receivable detail listing at www.pearsonhighered.com/beasley5e. As noted there, Hooplah has a total of 357 customers, with an accounts receivable balance totaling $12,881,551. Based on the engagement team's knowledge of Hooplah's accounts receivable processes and policies, experience in prior year's audits, and the results of tests of controls and substantive analytical procedures, the assessment of risk of material misstatement for accounts receivable has been set at "moderate." Prepare a schedule that includes the following

[a] List the customer number and related balance for all customers you plan to direct test.

[b] Indicate your computed sample size (using the sample size formula provided on prior page). Provide supporting calculations and justification for your sample size, including justification for the confidence factor and the level of expected misstatement you used to compute your sample size.

[2] Based on the same background information as was used for question 1, but assuming that in selecting which customer balances to detail test you want to expand directed testing by selecting additional items based on risk and size, reevaluate the mix of directed testing and audit sampling. If you believe it would be efficient and effective to increase your directed testing, prepare a schedule that includes the following:

[a] Identify what characteristic can be used to select riskier items.

[b] List the customer numbers and related balances you would select for directed testing based on risk and provide the characteristics you used.

[c] List the additional customer accounts you would select for directed testing based on size and "coverage."

[d] Determine whether it would be necessary to test the remaining population using audit sampling; if so, compute your sample size for testing the remaining population through audit sampling and justify the inputs you used in the sample size formula.

[3] Which detail testing approach seems most appropriate in this situation: the minimum level of directed testing together with a larger audit sample, expanded directed testing with no audit sampling, or both expanded directed testing and audit sampling? Be sure to consider the effectiveness and efficiency of the approach, as well as the level of assurance needed in view of the evidence already obtained from controls testing, substantive analytical procedures, etc.

[4] Independent of your responses to prior questions, assume that you direct tested customer balances greater than tolerable misstatement and randomly selected a sample of 40 additional customer balances for confirmation. The total book value of the 40 items sampled is $761,030. No differences were noted in the directed testing, and the sample yielded a combined overstatement in Hooplah's records of $4,215. Brian Thompson, the accounts receivable supervisor agrees that the differences noted are misstatements due to pricing errors. Please answer the following questions:

[a] How much is the known misstatement in the accounts receivable balance?

[b] How much is the projected misstatement in the population (i.e., the total accounts receivable account) using ratio projection?

[c] How much is the projected misstatement in the population using difference projection?

[d] Explain why the two projections produce different results and describe the circumstances under which one projection approach might be more appropriate than the other.

[e] Based on the results of the detail testing outlined in this requirement, as well as the assurance obtained from controls testing and substantive analytical procedures, do the audit procedures support the assertion that the accounts receivable account is fairly stated? Why or why not?

APPENDIX A

Statistical Sample Sizes for Attribute Sampling—95-Percent Desired Confidence Level

Expected Population Deviation Rate	Tolerable Deviation Rate						
	2%	3%	4%	5%	6%	7%	8%
0%	149(0)	99(0)	74(0)	59(0)	49(0)	42(0)	36(0)
0.25%	236(1)	157(1)	117(1)	93(1)	78(1)	66(1)	58(1)
0.50%	*	157(1)	117(1)	93(1)	78(1)	66(1)	58(1)
0.75%	*	208(2)	117(1)	93(1)	78(1)	66(1)	58(1)
1.00%	*	*	156(2)	93(1)	78(1)	66(1)	58(1)
1.25%	*	*	156(2)	124(2)	78(1)	66(1)	58(1)
1.50%	*	*	192(3)	124(2)	103(2)	66(1)	58(1)
1.75%	*	*	227(4)	153(3)	103(2)	88(2)	77(2)
2.00%	*	*	*	181(4)	127(3)	88(2)	77(2)

*Sample size is too large to be cost-effective for most audit applications. The number in parentheses represents the maximum number of deviations in a sample of that size that allows the auditor to conclude that the tolerable deviation rate is not exceeded.

Statistical Sample Results Evaluation Table (Computed Upper Deviation Rates) for Attribute Sampling—95-Percent Desired Confidence Level

Sample Size	Actual Number of Deviations Found			
	0	1	2	3
25	11.3	17.6	*	*
30	9.5	14.9	19.6	*
35	8.3	12.9	17	*
40	7.3	11.4	15	18.3
45	6.5	10.2	13.4	16.4
50	5.9	9.2	12.1	14.8
55	5.4	8.4	11.1	13.5
60	4.9	7.7	10.2	12.5
65	4.6	7.1	9.4	11.5
70	4.2	6.6	8.8	10.8
75	4	6.2	8.2	10.1
80	3.7	5.8	7.7	9.5

*Over 20 percent.

Planning and Performing Audit Procedures in the Revenue and Expenditure Cycles

An Audit Simulation

CASES INCLUDED IN THIS SECTION

Southeast Shoe Distributor, Inc.
Identification of Tests of Controls for the Revenue Cycle (Sales and Cash Receipts)

MARK S. BEASLEY · FRANK A. BUCKLESS · STEVEN M. GLOVER · DOUGLAS F. PRAWITT

LEARNING OBJECTIVES

After completing and discussing this case you should be able to

[1] Recognize common documents and records used to record transactions in the revenue cycle

[2] Recognize common control activities used to process transactions in the revenue cycle

[3] Identify client control activities that reduce the likelihood of material misstatements

[4] Link client control activities to management assertions

[5] Identify tests of controls for each control activity identified

INTRODUCTION

Southeast Shoe Distributor (SSD) is a closely owned business that was founded ten years ago by Stewart Green and Paul Williams. SSD is a distributor that purchases and sells men's, women's, and children's shoes to retail shoe stores located in small to midsize communities. The company's basic strategy is to obtain a broad selection of designer label and name brand merchandise at low prices and resell the merchandise to small one-location retail stores that have difficulty obtaining reasonable quantities of designer and name brand merchandise. The company is able to keep the cost of merchandise low by (1) selectively purchasing large blocks of production over-runs, over-orders, mid- and late-season deliveries and last season's stock from manufacturers and other retailers at significant discounts, (2) sourcing in-season name brand and branded designer merchandise directly from factories in Brazil, Italy, and Spain, and (3) negotiating favorable prices with manufacturers by ordering merchandise during off-peak production periods and taking delivery at one central warehouse.

During the year the company purchased merchandise from over 50 domestic and international vendors, independent resellers, manufacturers and other retailers that frequently had excess inventory. Designer and name brand footwear sold by the company during the year include the following: Amalfi, Clarks, Dexter, Fila, Florsheim, Naturalizer, and Rockport. At the present time, SSD has one warehouse located in Atlanta, Georgia. Last year SSD had 123 retail shoe store customers and had net sales of $7,311,214. Sales are strongest in the second and fourth calendar year quarters with the first calendar year quarter substantially weaker than the rest.

.

The case was prepared by Mark S. Beasley, Ph.D. and Frank A. Buckless, Ph.D. of North Carolina State University and Steven M. Glover, Ph.D. and Douglas F. Prawitt, Ph.D. of Brigham Young University, as a basis for class discussion. SSD is a fictitious company. All characters and names represented are fictitious; any similarity to existing companies or persons is purely coincidental.

BACKGROUND

SSD is required to have an audit of its annual financial statements to fulfill requirements of loan agreements with financial institutions. This audit is to be completed in accordance with the AICPA professional standards for the audit of nonpublic companies. Your audit firm is currently planning for the Fiscal 2011 audit in accordance with these professional standards. SSD has the following general ledger accounts related to sales and cash collection activities:

- Sales
- Sales Discounts
- Sales Returns and Allowances

- Uncollectible Accounts Expense
- Accounts Receivable
- Allowance for Uncollectible Accounts

In accordance with the professional standards, Susan Mansfield, audit manager, reviewed SSD's control environment, risk assessment process, and monitoring system and has assessed them as strong. Bill Zander, staff auditor, reviewed SSD's information system and control activities related to sales and cash receipts and prepared the enclosed flowcharts (referenced in the top right hand corner as *R 30-1, R 30-2, R 30-3*, and *R 30-4*). The number and size of sales returns and allowances and write-offs of specific customer accounts is relatively small. Thus Susan has decided there is no need to document SSD's policies nor perform tests of controls for these two business activities. As the audit senior, you have been assigned responsibility for (1) identifying internal control activities that assure that transactions, accounts and disclosures related to sales and cash collection activities are not materially misstated and (2) identifying tests of controls that would test the design and operating effectiveness of internal control activities identified for sales and cash collection activities.

REQUIRED

[1] Identify SSD's control activities by completing step 5 of the audit program *R 1-1*.
Document your work in audit schedules *R 1-1, R 31-1, R 31-2*, and *R 31-3* (Note: you should assume that only the control activities identified in the flowcharts exist).

[2] Identify potential tests of controls by completing step 6 of the audit program *R 1-1*. Document your work in audit schedules *R 1-1, R 40-1, R 40-2*, and *R 40-3* (Note: number your tests similar to the example provided).

[3] Complete step 7 of the audit program *R 1-1* by identifying any internal control deficiencies SSD may have and document your work in audit schedule *R 1-1* and *R 32*.

[4] How would your work differ if SSD was a public company? What other factors would you need to consider?

[5] For each internal control deficiency you listed in audit schedule *R 32* (requirement 3), identify at least one control activity that would remediate the deficiency.

[6] Describe the importance of SSD's control activities given its large number of customers and vendors.

Reference:	R 1-1
Prepared by:	BZ
Date:	6/10/11
Reviewed by:	

Southeast Shoe Distributor, Inc.
Revenue Cycle Planning Audit Program - Identification of Tests of Controls
For the Year Ended December 31, 2011

Audit Procedures	Initial	Date	Ref.
1. Obtain and study a copy of the client's policies and procedures manuals related to sales and cash receipts.	BZ	6/10/11	N/A
2. Discuss with and observe client personnel performing control activities related to sales and cash receipts.	BZ	6/10/11	N/A
3. Perform a document walk-through of the client's polices and procedures related to sales and cash receipts.	BZ	6/10/11	N/A
4. Obtain or prepare a flowchart for sales and cash receipts showing control activities, document flows, and records.	BZ	6/10/11	R30-1 R30-2 R30-3 R30-4
5. Use the control activities matrix to identify client control activities that reduce the likelihood of material misstatements for management assertions related to sales and cash receipts.			R31-1 R31-2 R31-3
6. Use the planning audit test matrices to identify potential tests of controls.			R40-1 R40-2 R40-3
7. Based on the previous procedures, identify internal control deficiencies that may need to be reported to the client on the internal control deficiencies schedule.			R32

Reference:	R 30-1
Prepared by:	BZ
Date:	6/10/11
Reviewed by:	

Southeast Shoe Distributor, Inc.
Revenue Cycle - Sales Flowchart
For the Year Ended December 31, 2011

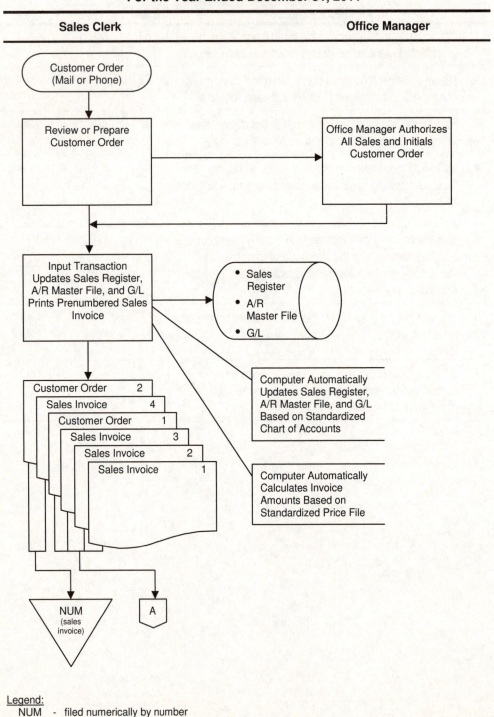

Legend:
NUM — filed numerically by number
A — off-page connector

Reference:	R 30-2
Prepared by:	BZ
Date:	6/10/11
Reviewed by:	

Southeast Shoe Distributor, Inc.
Revenue Cycle - Sales Flowchart
For the Year Ended December 31, 2011

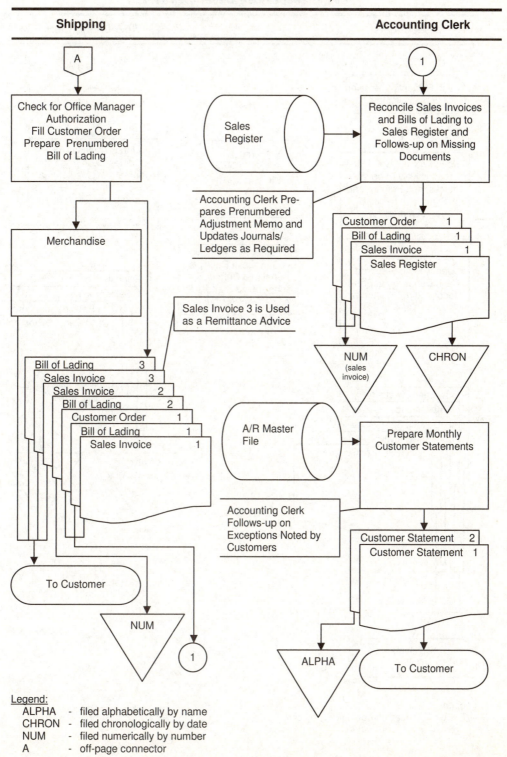

Legend:
ALPHA - filed alphabetically by name
CHRON - filed chronologically by date
NUM - filed numerically by number
A - off-page connector

Reference:	R 30-3
Prepared by:	BZ
Date:	6/10/11
Reviewed by:	

Southeast Shoe Distributor, Inc.
Revenue Cycle - Cash Receipts Flowchart
For the Year Ended December 31, 2011

Receptionist	Accounting Clerk

Cash Receipts (Received from Customers)

Two Individuals Open Mail, Restrictively Endorse Checks, and Prepare and Sign Cash Receipt Summary

Deposit Slip Prepared
Cash Deposited at Bank
Deposit Slip Validated by Bank

- C/R Journal
- A/R Master File
- G/L

Computer Automatically Updates Cash Receipts Journal and General Ledger Using Standardized Chart of Accounts

Customer Checks
Deposit Slip   1
Deposit Slip   2
Sales Invoice   3
Cash Receipt Summary

To Bank (Daily)

1

1

Input Transactions Updates Cash Receipts Journal, A/R Master File, and G/L for Cash Receipts and Sales Discounts

Deposit Slip   2
Sales Invoice   3
Cash Receipt Summary
Cash Receipts Journal

CHRON (summary)

CHRON

Legend:
CHRON - filed chronologically by date.

296

Reference:	R 30-4
Prepared by:	BZ
Date:	6/10/11
Reviewed by:	

Southeast Shoe Distributor, Inc.
Revenue Cycle - Cash Receipts Flowchart
For the Year Ended December 31, 2011

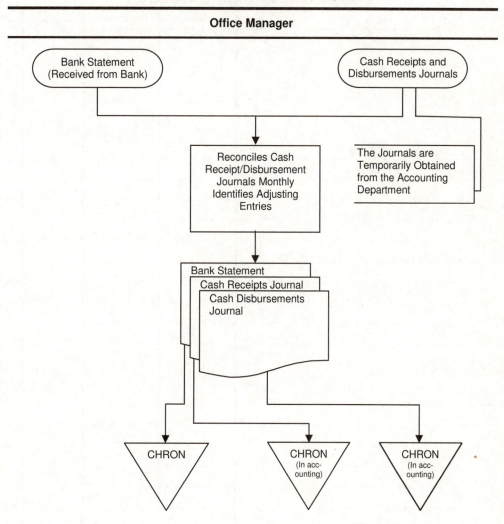

Office Manager

Bank Statement (Received from Bank)

Cash Receipts and Disbursements Journals

Reconciles Cash Receipt/Disbursement Journals Monthly Identifies Adjusting Entries

The Journals are Temporarily Obtained from the Accounting Department

Bank Statement
Cash Receipts Journal
Cash Disbursements Journal

CHRON

CHRON (In accounting)

CHRON (In accounting)

Legend:
CHRON   -   filed chronologically by date.

Reference: _R 31-1_
Prepared by: _____
Date: _____
Reviewed by: _____

Southeast Shoe Distributor, Inc.
Revenue Cycle - Control Activities Matrix
For the Year Ended December 31, 2011

Control Activities	Sales					Cash Receipts					Accounts Receivable				Disclosure			
	Occurrence	Completeness	Accuracy	Cutoff	Classification	Occurrence	Completeness	Accuracy	Cutoff	Classification	Existence	Rights/Obligations	Completeness	Valuation	Occurrence/Rights/Obligations	Completeness	Classification/Understandability	Accuracy/Valuation
CA1) All sales are approved by the office manager.	X													X				

Identify the management assertion(s) each control activity affects with an "X."

Reference: *R 31-2*
Prepared by: _____
Date: _____
Reviewed by: _____

Southeast Shoe Distributor, Inc.
Revenue Cycle - Control Activities Matrix
For the Year Ended December 31, 2011

Control Activities	Sales					Cash Receipts					Accounts Receivable				Disclosure			
	Occurrence	Completeness	Accuracy	Cutoff	Classification	Occurrence	Completeness	Accuracy	Cutoff	Classification	Existence	Rights/Obligations	Completeness	Valuation	Occurrence/Rights/Obligations	Completeness	Classification/Understandability	Accuracy/Valuation

Identify the management assertion(s) each control activity affects with an "X."

Reference: *R 31-3*

Prepared by: _____

Date: _____

Reviewed by: _____

Southeast Shoe Distributor, Inc.
Revenue Cycle - Control Activities Matrix
For the Year Ended December 31, 2011

Control Activities	Sales					Cash Receipts					Accounts Receivable				Disclosure			
	Occurrence	Completeness	Accuracy	Cutoff	Classification	Occurrence	Completeness	Accuracy	Cutoff	Classification	Existence	Rights/Obligations	Completeness	Valuation	Occurrence/Rights/Obligations	Completeness	Classification/Understandability	Accuracy/Valuation

Identify the management assertion(s) each control activity affects with an "X."

Reference: _R 32_
Prepared by: _____
Date: _____
Reviewed by: _____

Southeast Shoe Distributor, Inc.
Revenue Cycle – Internal Control Deficiencies
For the Year Ended December 31, 2011

Internal Control Deficiencies	Client Personnel Discussed With
1) The client does not internally verify the proper general ledger account classification for sales and cash receipt transactions.	

Reference: _R 40-1_
Prepared by: _____
Date: _____
Reviewed by: _____

Southeast Shoe Distributor, Inc.
Revenue Cycle – Audit Tests Planning Matrix
For the Year Ended December 31, 2011

Tests of Controls	Sales					Cash Receipts					Accounts Receivable				Disclosure			
	Occurrence	Completeness	Accuracy	Cutoff	Classification	Occurrence	Completeness	Accuracy	Cutoff	Classification	Existence	Rights/Obligations	Completeness	Valuation	Occurrence/Rights/Obligations	Completeness	Classification/Understandability	Accuracy/Valuation
TC1) Inquire and observe the office manager authorizing sales.	W													W				

Indicate whether the test provides Strong (S), Moderate (M), or Weak (W) evidence for the specific management assertion.

Reference: _R 40-2_
Prepared by: _____
Date: _____
Reviewed by: _____

Southeast Shoe Distributor, Inc.
Revenue Cycle - Audit Tests Planning Matrix
For the Year Ended December 31, 2011

Tests of Controls	Sales					Cash Receipts					Accounts Receivable				Disclosure			
	Occurrence	Completeness	Accuracy	Cutoff	Classification	Occurrence	Completeness	Accuracy	Cutoff	Classification	Existence	Rights/Obligations	Completeness	Valuation	Occurrence/Rights/Obligations	Completeness	Classification/Understandability	Accuracy/Valuation

Indicate whether the test provides Strong (S), Moderate (M), or Weak (W) evidence for the specific management assertion.

Reference: _R 40-3_
Prepared by: _____
Date: _____
Reviewed by: _____

Southeast Shoe Distributor, Inc.
Revenue Cycle - Audit Tests Planning Matrix
For the Year Ended December 31, 2011

Tests of Controls	Sales					Cash Receipts					Accounts Receivable				Disclosure			
	Occurrence	Completeness	Accuracy	Cutoff	Classification	Occurrence	Completeness	Accuracy	Cutoff	Classification	Existence	Rights/Obligations	Completeness	Valuation	Occurrence/Rights/Obligations	Completeness	Classification/Understandability	Accuracy/Valuation

Indicate whether the test provides Strong (S), Moderate (M), or Weak (W) evidence for the specific management assertion.

Southeast Shoe Distributor, Inc.
Identification of Substantive Tests for the Revenue Cycle (Sales and Cash Receipts)

MARK S. BEASLEY · FRANK A. BUCKLESS · STEVEN M. GLOVER · DOUGLAS F. PRAWITT

LEARNING OBJECTIVES

After completing and discussing this case you should be able to

[1] Recognize common documents and records used in the revenue cycle

[2] Link audit tests to management assertions

[3] Identify analytical tests to detect material misstatements

[4] Identify substantive tests of transactions to detect material misstatements

[5] Identify substantive tests of balances to detect material misstatements

INTRODUCTION

Southeast Shoe Distributor (SSD) is a closely owned business that was founded 10 years ago by Stewart Green and Paul Williams. SSD is a distributor that purchases and sells men's, women's, and children's shoes to retail shoe stores located in small- to mid-size communities. The company's basic strategy is to obtain a broad selection of designer-label and name brand merchandise at low prices and resell the merchandise to small, one-location, retail stores that have difficulty obtaining reasonable quantities of designer and name brand merchandise. The company is able to keep the cost of merchandise low by (1) selectively purchasing large blocks of production overruns, overorders, mid- and late- season deliveries and last season's stock from manufacturers and other retailers at significant discounts, (2) sourcing in-season name-brand and branded designer merchandise directly from factories in Brazil, Italy, and Spain, and (3) negotiating favorable prices with manufacturers by ordering merchandise during off-peak production periods and taking delivery at one central warehouse.

During the year the company purchased merchandise from over 50 domestic and international vendors, independent resellers, manufacturers and other retailers that frequently had excess inventory. Designer and name brand footwear sold by the company during the year include the following: Amalfi, Clarks, Dexter, Fila, Florsheim, Naturalizer, and Rockport. At the current time, SSD has one warehouse located in Atlanta, Georgia. Last year, SSD had 123 retail shoe store customers and had net sales of $7,311,214. Sales are strongest in the second and fourth calendar-year quarters, with the first calendar-year quarter substantially weaker than the rest.

The case was prepared by Mark S. Beasley, Ph.D. and Frank A. Buckless, Ph.D. of North Carolina State University and Steven M. Glover, Ph.D. and Douglas F. Prawitt, Ph.D. of Brigham Young University, as a basis for class discussion. SSD is a fictitious company. All characters and names represented are fictitious; any similarity to existing companies or persons is purely coincidental.

BACKGROUND

SSD is required to have an audit of its annual financial statements to fulfill requirements of loan agreements with financial institutions. This audit is to be completed in accordance with the AICPA professional standards for the audit of nonpublic companies. Your audit firm is currently planning for the Fiscal 2011 audit in accordance with these professional standards. SSD has the following general ledger accounts related to sales and cash collection activities:

- Sales
- Sales Discounts
- Sales Returns and Allowances
- Uncollectible Accounts Expense
- Accounts Receivable
- Allowance for Uncollectible Accounts

Bill Zander, staff auditor, reviewed SSD's information system and control activities related to sales and cash receipts and prepared the enclosed flowcharts (referenced in the top right hand corner as *R 30-1, R 30-2, R 30-3,* and *R 30-4*). The number and size of sales returns and uncollectible accounts is relatively small. Thus Susan Mansfield, audit manager, decided not to have Bill document the company's policies and procedures related to sales returns and allowances and uncollectible accounts.

As the audit senior, you have been assigned responsibility for identifying substantive tests to detect material misstatements related to revenue cycle accounts. You have conducted some preliminary discussions with client personnel and noted the following:

- Sales returns and allowances transactions are recorded in the sales register.
- Sales discounts are recorded in the cash receipts journal.
- The estimation and write-off of uncollectible accounts are recorded in the general journal and require preparation of a prenumbered adjustment memo.
- Misstatements to sales, cash receipts, and accounts receivable are recorded in the general journal and require preparation of a prenumbered adjustment memo.

REQUIRED

[1] Complete audit steps 1 and 2 from the audit program *R 1-2* to obtain an understanding of the documents and records used by SSD for sales and cash transactions. Document completion of your work in audit schedule *R 1-2*.

[2] Identify potential substantive tests by completing steps 3a, 3b, and 3c from the audit program *R 1-2.* Document your work in audit schedules *R 1-2, R 41-1, R 41-2,* and *R 41-3* and number your tests by following the examples provided. Each of these steps can be completely separately at the discretion of your instructor (Note: number your tests similar to the example provided).

[3] What are some of the factors that influence the level of assurance obtained through substantive audit tests?

[4] For a given account, why might an auditor choose to:

[a] not conduct substantive tests?

[b] conduct only substantive tests?

Reference:	R 1-2
Prepared by:	
Date:	
Reviewed by:	

Southeast Shoe Distributor, Inc.
Revenue Cycle Planning Audit Program – Identification of Substantive Tests
For the Year Ended December 31, 2011

Audit Procedures	Initial	Date	Ref.
1. Obtain an understanding of the documents and records used for sales and cash receipts transactions by reviewing the flowcharts documenting our understanding.			R 30-1 R 30-2 R 30-3 R 30-4
2. Obtain an understanding of the documents and records used for recording adjustments to sales, cash receipts, and accounts receivable by discussing with client personnel.			N/A
3. Use the planning audit test matrices to identify potential a. substantive tests of transactions, b. tests of balances, c. and analytical tests related to sales and cash collections accounts.			R 41-1 R 41-2 R 41-3

Reference:	R 30-1
Prepared by:	BZ
Date:	6/10/11
Reviewed by:	

Southeast Shoe Distributor, Inc.
Revenue Cycle - Sales Flowchart
For the Year Ended December 31, 2011

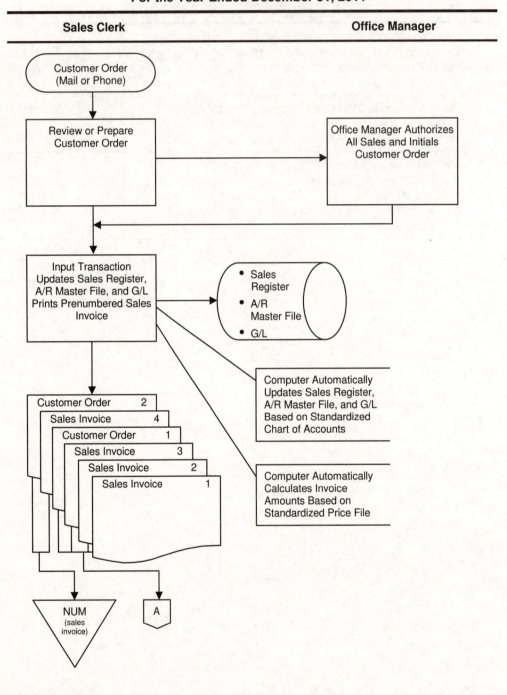

Legend:
NUM - filed numerically by number
A - off-page connector

Reference:	R 30-2
Prepared by:	BZ
Date:	6/10/11
Reviewed by:	

Southeast Shoe Distributor, Inc.
Revenue Cycle - Sales Flowchart
For the Year Ended December 31, 2011

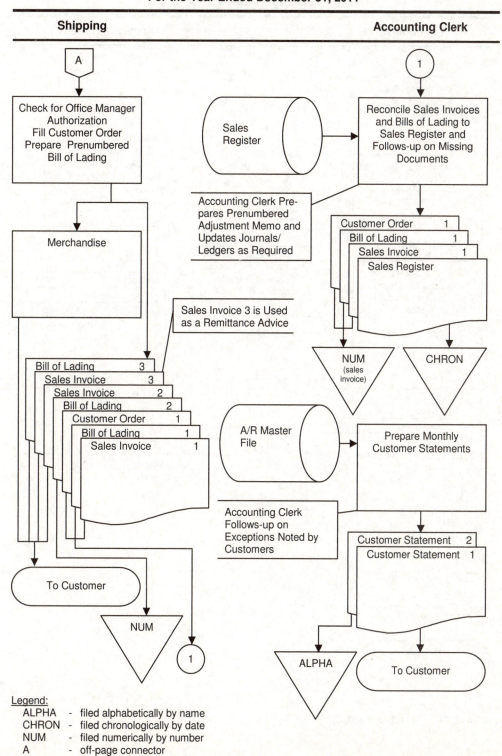

Shipping   **Accounting Clerk**

A

Check for Office Manager
Authorization
Fill Customer Order
Prepare Prenumbered
Bill of Lading

Merchandise

Sales
Register

1

Reconcile Sales Invoices
and Bills of Lading to
Sales Register and
Follows-up on Missing
Documents

Accounting Clerk Pre-
pares Prenumbered
Adjustment Memo and
Updates Journals/
Ledgers as Required

Customer Order   1
Bill of Lading   1
Sales Invoice   1
Sales Register

Sales Invoice 3 is Used
as a Remittance Advice

Bill of Lading   3
Sales Invoice   3
Sales Invoice   2
Bill of Lading   2
Customer Order   1
Bill of Lading   1
Sales Invoice   1

NUM
(sales
invoice)

CHRON

A/R Master
File

Prepare Monthly
Customer Statements

Accounting Clerk
Follows-up on
Exceptions Noted by
Customers

Customer Statement   2
Customer Statement   1

To Customer

NUM

1

ALPHA

To Customer

Legend:
    ALPHA   -   filed alphabetically by name
    CHRON   -   filed chronologically by date
    NUM   -   filed numerically by number
    A   -   off-page connector

Reference:	_R 30-3_
Prepared by:	_BZ_
Date:	_6/10/11_
Reviewed by:	

Southeast Shoe Distributor, Inc.
Revenue Cycle - Cash Receipts Flowchart
For the Year Ended December 31, 2011

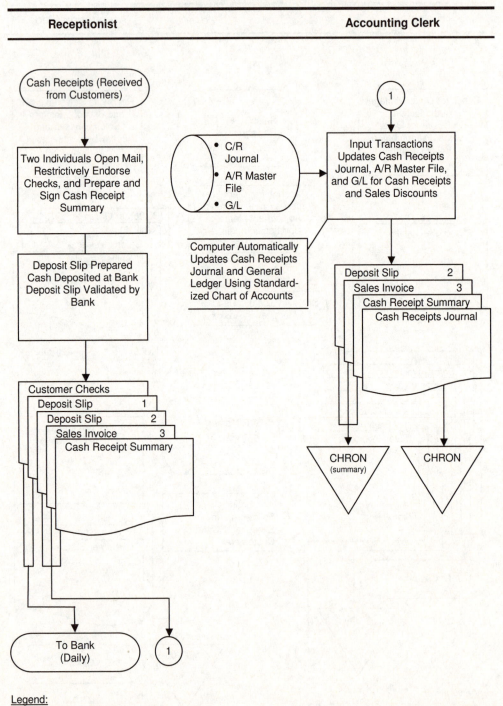

Legend:
CHRON - filed chronologically by date.

Reference:	*R 30-4*
Prepared by:	*BZ*
Date:	*6/10/11*
Reviewed by:	

Southeast Shoe Distributor, Inc.
Revenue Cycle - Cash Receipts Flowchart
For the Year Ended December 31, 2011

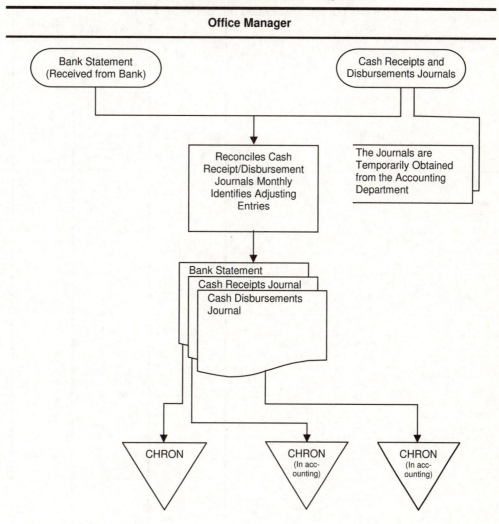

Office Manager

Bank Statement (Received from Bank)

Cash Receipts and Disbursements Journals

Reconciles Cash Receipt/Disbursement Journals Monthly Identifies Adjusting Entries

The Journals are Temporarily Obtained from the Accounting Department

Bank Statement
Cash Receipts Journal
Cash Disbursements Journal

CHRON

CHRON (In accounting)

CHRON (In accounting)

Legend:
CHRON - filed chronologically by date.

Reference: _R 41-1_
Prepared by: _____
Date: _____
Reviewed by: _____

Southeast Shoe Distributor, Inc.
Revenue Cycle – Audit Tests Planning Matrix
For the Year Ended December 31, 2011

Substantive Audit Tests	Sales					Cash Receipts					Accounts Receivable				Disclosure			
	Occurrence	Completeness	Accuracy	Cutoff	Classification	Occurrence	Completeness	Accuracy	Cutoff	Classification	Existence	Rights/Obligations	Completeness	Valuation	Occurrence/Rights/Obligations	Completeness	Classification/Understandability	Accuracy/Valuation
TTS1) Vouch sales transactions recorded in the sales register to supporting documents.	M		M		M						M			M				

Indicate whether the test provides Strong (S), Moderate (M), or Weak (W) evidence for the specific management assertion.

Reference: _____R 41-2_____
Prepared by: _____
Date: _____
Reviewed by: _____

Southeast Shoe Distributor, Inc.
Revenue Cycle - Audit Tests Planning Matrix
For the Year Ended December 31, 2011

Substantive Audit Tests	Sales					Cash Receipts					Accounts Receivable				Disclosure			
	Occurrence	Completeness	Accuracy	Cutoff	Classification	Occurrence	Completeness	Accuracy	Cutoff	Classification	Existence	Rights/Obligations	Completeness	Valuation	Occurrence/Rights/Obligations	Completeness	Classification/Understandability	Accuracy/Valuation
STB1) Confirm accounts receivable using positive confirmations.	S		M	M			S	M	M		S	W		M				

Indicate whether the test provides Strong (S), Moderate (M), or Weak (W) evidence for the specific management assertion.

Reference: _R 41-3_
Prepared by: _____
Date: _____
Reviewed by: _____

Southeast Shoe Distributor, Inc.
Revenue Cycle - Audit Tests Planning Matrix
For the Year Ended December 31, 2011

Substantive Audit Tests	Sales					Cash Receipts					Accounts Receivable				Disclosure			
	Occurrence	Completeness	Accuracy	Cutoff	Classification	Occurrence	Completeness	Accuracy	Cutoff	Classification	Existence	Rights/Obligations	Completeness	Valuation	Occurrence/Rights/Obligations	Completeness	Classification/Understandability	Accuracy/Valuation
SAT1) Scan the sales register for related party, large, or unusual transactions.	M		M		M						M			M	M			

Indicate whether the test provides Strong (S), Moderate (M), or Weak (W) evidence for the specific management assertion.

Southeast Shoe Distributor, Inc.
Selection of Audit Tests and Risk Assessment for the Revenue Cycle (Sales and Cash Receipts)

MARK S. BEASLEY · FRANK A. BUCKLESS · STEVEN M. GLOVER · DOUGLAS F. PRAWITT

LEARNING OBJECTIVES

After completing and discussing this case you should be able to

[1] Design an overall audit strategy for the revenue cycle (i.e., select tests of controls, substantive tests of transactions, analytical tests, and tests of balances to be performed)

[2] Assess planned control risk for the revenue cycle based on the tests of controls selected

[3] Assess planned detection risk for the revenue cycle based on the substantive tests selected

INTRODUCTION

Southeast Shoe Distributor (SSD) is a closely owned business that was founded 10 years ago by Stewart Green and Paul Williams. SSD is a distributor that purchases and sells men's, women's, and children's shoes to retail shoe stores located in small- to mid-size communities. The company's basic strategy is to obtain a broad selection of designer-label and name brand merchandise at low prices and resell the merchandise to small one-location retail stores that have difficulty obtaining reasonable quantities of designer and name brand merchandise. The company is able to keep the cost of merchandise low by (1) selectively purchasing large blocks of production overruns, overorders, mid- and late-season deliveries and last season's stock from manufacturers and other retailers at significant discounts, (2) sourcing in-season name-brand and branded designer merchandise directly from factories in Brazil, Italy, and Spain, and (3) negotiating favorable prices with manufacturers by ordering merchandise during off-peak production periods and taking delivery at one central warehouse.

During the year, the company purchased merchandise from over 50 domestic and international vendors, independent resellers, manufacturers and other retailers that frequently had excess inventory. Designer and name brand footwear sold by the company during the year include the following: Amalfi, Clarks, Dexter, Fila, Florsheim, Naturalizer, and Rockport. At the current time, SSD has one warehouse located in Atlanta, Georgia. Last year, SSD had 123 retail shoe store customers and had net sales of $7,311,214. Sales are strongest in the second and fourth calendar-year quarters with the first calendar-year quarter substantially weaker than the rest.

The case was prepared by Mark S. Beasley, Ph.D. and Frank A. Buckless, Ph.D. of North Carolina State University and Steven M. Glover, Ph.D. and Douglas F. Prawitt, Ph.D. of Brigham Young University, as a basis for class discussion. SSD is a fictitious company. All characters and names represented are fictitious; any similarity to existing companies or persons is purely coincidental.

BACKGROUND

SSD is required to have an audit of its annual financial statements to fulfill requirements of loan agreements with financial institutions. This audit is to be completed in accordance with the AICPA professional standards for the audit of nonpublic companies. Your audit firm is currently planning for the Fiscal 2011 audit in accordance with these professional standards. SSD has the following general ledger accounts related to sales and cash collection activities:

- Sales
- Sales Discounts
- Sales Returns and Allowances

- Uncollectible Accounts Expense
- Accounts Receivable
- Allowance for Uncollectible Accounts

In accordance with the professional standards, Susan Mansfield, audit manager, reviewed SSD's control environment, risk assessment process, and monitoring system and has assessed them as strong. Additionally, Susan determined that tolerable misstatement should be $40,000 for the revenue cycle and that acceptable audit risk should be low. Bill Zander, staff auditor, assessed inherent risk related to sales, cash receipts, and accounts receivable and prepared the enclosed audit risk matrix (referenced in the top right hand corner as R 50 and R 50-1). As the audit senior, you have been assigned responsibility for selecting audit procedures to perform for the revenue cycle that will achieve the desired acceptable audit risk at the lowest possible cost.

REQUIRED

[1] Complete step 3 of the audit program R 1-3 by selecting specific audit tests from your work in the previous two SSD audit case assignments (see R 40-1, R 40-2, R 40-3, R 41-1, R 41-2, and R 41-3). Document your work in audit schedules R 1-3, R 40-1, R 40-2, R 40-3, R 41-1, R 41-2, and R 41-3.

[2] Assess planned control and detection risk by completing step 4 of the audit program R 1-3. Document completion of your work in audit program R 1-3. Record your assessment in audit schedule R-50. Document in audit schedules R 50-2 and R 50-3 the specific tests by number that you have chosen, the assertion(s) covered by each test, and the level of assurance (high, medium, or low risk) provided.

Reference:	R 1-3
Prepared by:	BZ
Date:	6/10/11
Reviewed by:	

Southeast Shoe Distributor, Inc.
Revenue Cycle Planning Audit Program –
Risk Assessment and Selection of Audit Tests
For the Year Ended December 31, 2011

Audit Procedures	Initial	Date	Ref.
1. Complete the acceptable audit risk section of the revenue cycle "planning audit risk" matrix by obtaining the acceptable audit risk from the general planning audit schedules.	BZ	6/10/11	R 50
2. Form an initial assessment of inherent risk related to revenue cycle accounts and complete the initial inherent risk assessment section of the "planning audit risk" matrix.	BZ	6/10/11	R 50 R 50-1
3. Select audit tests to perform by circling the procedure number on the audit tests planning matrices.			R 40-1 R 40-2 R 40-3 R 41-1 R 41-2 R 41-3
4. Based on the procedures selected in audit step 3, complete the planned control risk and detection risk sections of the revenue cycle "planning audit risk" matrix.			R 50 R 50-2 R 50-3

Reference:	R 50
Prepared by:	BZ
Date:	6/10/11
Reviewed by:	

Southeast Shoe Distributor, Inc.
Revenue Cycle - Planning Audit Risk Matrix
For the Year Ended December 31, 2011

	Reference	Transactions					Balances				Disclosure			
		Occurrence	Completeness	Accuracy	Cutoff	Classification	Existence	Rights/Obligations	Completeness	Valuation	Occurrence/Rights/Obligations	Completeness	Classification/Understandability	Accuracy/Valuation
Tolerable Misstatement: $40,000, G6														
Acceptable Audit Risk	G5	L	L	L	L	L	L	L	L	L	L	L	L	L
Initial Inherent Risk – Sales	R50-1	H	H	H	H	L					L	L	L	L
Initial Inherent Risk – Cash Receipts		H	H	H	H	L					L	L	L	L
Initial Inherent Risk – Accounts Receivable							H	L	L	H	L	L	L	L
Planned Control Risk – Sales														
Planned Control Risk – Cash Receipts														
Planned Control Risk – Accounts Receivable														
Planned Detection Risk – Sales														
Planned Detection Risk – Cash Receipts														
Planned Detection Risk – Accounts Receivable														

Initial Inherent Risk should be assessed as:

High (H) unless the combination of inherent risk factors present justify a lower assessment.

Low (L) if the combination of inherent risk factors present justify this assessment.

Factors justifying a lower inherent risk assessment are:
High management integrity, Low motivation to materially misstate for external parties, Repeat engagement, No material prior year misstatements, No related party transactions, Routine transactions, Limited judgment required to correctly record transactions, Low susceptibility to defalcation, Stable business environment.

Planned Control Risk should be assessed as:

Low (L) if control activity(ies) reduces the likelihood of a material misstatement to a negligible level and tests of controls are planned to be performed.

High (H) if control activity(ies) does not reduce the likelihood of a material misstatement to a reasonable level or no tests of controls are planned.

Planned Detection Risk should be assessed at:

Low (L) if persuasive substantive tests are planned to be performed.

Medium (M) if moderately persuasive substantive tests are planned to be performed.

High (H) if minimal substantive tests are planned to be performed.

Reference:	*R 50-1*
Prepared by:	*BZ*
Date:	*6/10/11*
Reviewed by:	

Southeast Shoe Distributor
Revenue Cycle - Comments Initial Inherent Risk Assessment
For the Year Ended December 31, 2011

Comments:

The inherent risk assessment for the occurrence of sales transactions is set at a high level even though no misstatements were discovered in previous years because of the external incentives for management and employees to inflate sales.

The inherent risk assessment for the completeness of sales transactions is set at a high level even though no misstatements were discovered in previous years because of the susceptibility of cash to theft.

The inherent risk assessment for the accuracy of sales transactions is set at a high level even though no misstatements were discovered in previous years because of the large number of products and price points offered.

The inherent risk assessment for the cutoff of sales transactions and cash receipt transactions is set at a high level even though no misstatements were discovered in previous years because of the higher volume in the last quarter of the year.

The inherent risk assessment for the classification of sales transactions is set at a low level because no misstatements were discovered in prior years and few non-trade sales occur during any year.

The inherent risk assessment for the occurrence, completeness, accuracy, and cutoff of cash receipt transactions is set at a high level even though no misstatements were discovered in previous years because of the susceptibility of cash to theft.

The inherent risk assessment for the classification of cash receipt transactions is set at a low level because of the lack of external incentives and discovered misstatements in previous years.

The inherent risk assessment for the completeness and rights and obligations of accounts receivable is set at a low level because of the lack of external incentives and absence of any discovered misstatements in previous years.

The inherent risk assessment for the existence of accounts receivable is set at a high level even though no misstatements were discovered in prior years because of the management and employee external incentives to inflate accounts receivable.

The inherent risk assessment for the valuation assertion for accounts receivable is set at a high level even though no misstatements were observed in prior years because of the subjectivity of estimating uncollectible accounts and the large number of products and price points offered.

The inherent risk assessment for the occurrence, completeness, classification, and accuracy of disclosures related cash receipt transactions, sales transactions and accounts receivable is set at a low level because of the lack of external incentives and discovered misstatements in previous years.

Reference: _R 50-2_
Prepared by: _____
Date: _____
Reviewed by: _____

Southeast Shoe Distributor
Revenue Cycle - Comments Planned Control Risk Assessment
For the Year Ended December 31, 2011

Comments:

Reference: _R 50-3_
Prepared by: _____
Date: _____
Reviewed by: _____

Southeast Shoe Distributor
Revenue Cycle - Comments Planned Detection Risk Assessment
For the Year Ended December 31, 2011

Comments:

Southeast Shoe Distributor, Inc.
Performance of Tests of Transactions for the Expenditure Cycle (Acquisitions and Cash Disbursements)

Mark S. Beasley · Frank A. Buckless · Steven M. Glover · Douglas F. Prawitt

LEARNING OBJECTIVES

After completing and discussing this case you should be able to

[1] Recognize common documents and records used to record purchase and cash disbursement transactions

[2] Recognize common control activities used to process purchase and cash disbursement transactions

[3] Recognize potential tests of controls and substantive tests of transactions for auditing purchase and cash disbursement transactions

[4] Perform tests of controls and substantive tests of transactions for purchase and cash disbursement transactions

[5] Evaluate the results of tests of controls and substantive tests of transactions for purchase and cash disbursement transactions using a non-statistical approach

[6] Recognize the linkage between control activities, tests of controls and management assertions

[7] Recognize the linkage between substantive tests of transactions and management assertions

INTRODUCTION

Southeast Shoe Distributor (SSD) is a closely owned business founded 10 years ago by Stewart Green and Paul Williams. SSD is a distributor that purchases and resells men's, women's, and children's shoes to retail shoe stores located in small to midsize communities. The company's basic strategy is to obtain a broad selection of designer-label and name-brand footwear at low prices to resell to small one-location retail stores. SSD targets stores that have a difficult time obtaining reasonable quantities of designer and name-brand footwear. The company is able to keep the cost of footwear low by (1) selectively purchasing large blocks of production overruns, overorders, mid- and late-season deliveries, and last season's stock from manufacturers and other retailers at significant discounts, (2) sourcing in-season name-brand and branded designer footwear directly from factories in Brazil, Italy, and Spain, and (3) negotiating favorable prices with manufacturers by ordering footwear during off-peak production periods and taking delivery at one central warehouse.

During the year, the company purchased merchandise from over 50 domestic and international vendors, independent resellers, manufacturers, and other retailers that have frequent excess inventory. Designer and name-brand footwear sold by the company include the following: Amalfi, Clarks, Dexter, Fila, Florsheim, Naturalizer, and Rockport. At the present time, SSD has one warehouse located in Atlanta, Georgia. Last year, SSD had net sales of $7,311,214. Sales are strongest in the second and fourth calendar-year quarters, with the first calendar-year quarter substantially weaker than the rest.

The case was prepared by Mark S. Beasley, Ph.D. and Frank A. Buckless, Ph.D. of North Carolina State University and Steven M. Glover, Ph.D. and Douglas F. Prawitt, Ph.D. of Brigham Young University, as a basis for class discussion. SSD is a fictitious company. All characters and names represented are fictitious; any similarity to existing companies or persons is purely coincidental.

BACKGROUND

SSD is required to have an audit of its annual financial statements to fulfill requirements of loan agreements with financial institutions. This audit is to be completed in accordance with the AICPA professional standards for the audit of nonpublic companies. Your audit firm is in the process of completing the audit for the Fiscal 2011 financial statements in accordance with these professional standards. Jorge Hernandez, audit senior, reviewed SSD policies and procedures related to acquisitions and cash disbursements and prepared the enclosed flowcharts (referenced in the top right hand corner as *E 20-1, E 20-2,* and *E 21*) and planned control risk matrix (audit schedule *E 22*). As a result of this process, Jorge developed the enclosed audit program (audit schedules *E 1-1* and *E 1-2*). The audit program was approved by Susan Mansfield, audit manager, and Katherine Smith, audit partner. The two staff auditors assigned to this engagement are Joy Avery and you. Together, you and Joy are responsible for performing the tests of transactions outlined in the expenditure cycle audit program (audit schedules *E 1-1* and *E 1-2*). The general ledger accounts related to purchasing and cash disbursement activities at SSD include the following:

- Inventory Purchases
- Purchase Discounts
- Purchase Returns and Allowances
- Freight In
- Administrative Expenses

- Warehousing Expenses
- Selling Expenses
- Prepaid Assets
- Accounts Payable

Joy Avery has already selected the audit samples for purchases and cash disbursements and completed audit procedures 2, 3, 5, 6, and 7. Joy's work is documented on audit schedules *E 1-1, E 1-2, E 30, E 32, E 33, E 34, E 40, E 41, E 42, E 43,* and *E 44.*

REQUIRED

[1] Review the flowcharts on audit schedules *E 20-1* and *E 20-2* and become familiar with the accounting documents and records used with purchases. Also review Joy Avery's work documented on audit schedules *E 1-1, E 1-2, E 30, E 32, E 33, E 34, E 40, E 41, E 42, E 43,* and *E 44* in order to understand the work you will perform and how to document your work in the audit schedules. Note that purchase orders are not required to be generated for recurring services such as utilities and cleaning.

[2] Complete steps 1a-h from the audit program *E 1-1*. Assume you have already completed step 1g and h and no deviations were found. Also assume that you have already tested 35 of the selected sample items, observing no misstatements. The documents and records for the remaining five sample items are provided at the following website www.pearsonhighered.com/beasley5e. Additionally, note that the audit firm has a policy of using the same audit sample for planned tests of controls and substantive tests of transactions (dual-purpose tests) whenever possible to maximize audit efficiency. Thus, the results of the test-of-controls aspect of audit steps 1a-h should be documented in audit schedules *E 1-1* and *E 31*, whereas the substantive test aspect should be documented in audit schedules *E 1-1* and *E 35*.

[3] Complete step 4a from the audit program *E 1-1*. Assume you have already completed this step for 55 of the 60 sample items and no deviations or misstatements were found. The documents and records for the remaining five sample items are provided at the following website www.pearsonhighered.com/beasley5e. Document the results of your work in audit schedules *E 1-1* and *E35*.

[4] Document any adjusting entries you propose on audit schedule *E 11* for any observed misstatements. You should assume that there was no systematic pattern or intent to commit a fraud based on a review and discussion with client personnel concerning observed deviations and misstatements.

Reference:	E 1-1
Prepared by:	JA
Date:	2/17/12
Reviewed by:	

Southeast Shoe Distributor
Expenditure Cycle Audit Program for
Analytical Procedures and Tests of Transactions
For the Year Ended December 31, 2011

Audit Procedures	Initial	Date	Ref.
1. Select a sample of 40 transactions recorded in the purchase journal throughout the year and perform the following:	JA	2/14/12	E 30
a. Determine if vendor invoices, purchase orders, and receiving reports were properly included in the voucher packages or the invoices were properly initialed by the executive secretary (Karen Tucci as "KT").			E 31
b. Examine vendor invoices, purchase orders, and receiving reports for authenticity and reasonableness.			E 31 E 35
c. Determine if the purchase orders were signed by the supervisor (Bruce Penny).			E 31
d. Determine if the voucher cover was initialed by the supervisor (Janet Sotiriadis as "JS").			E 31
e. Determine if the purchase journal amounts were correct based on the voucher package documents.			E 31 E 35
f. Determine if the vouchers had correct general ledger account code.			E 31 E 35
g. Determine if the vouchers were posted to the correct general ledger accounts.			E 31 E 35
h. Determine if the vouchers were posted to the correct vendor's accounts payable subsidiary file.			E 31 E 35
2. Scan the purchase journal for related party, large, or unusual transactions and perform follow-up procedures for each one identified.	JA	2/15/12	E 32
3. Examine the weekly exception reports for receiving reports and determine if proper follow-up procedures were performed.	JA	2/15/12	E 33
60, JA			
4. Select a sample of 40 receiving reports issued during the current year and perform the following:	JA	2/14/12	E 34
a. Obtain the related purchase order and vendor invoice and determine if receiving report was properly accounted for in the purchase journal.			E 35

Reference:	E 1-2
Prepared by:	JA
Date:	2/17/12
Reviewed by:	

Southeast Shoe Distributor
Expenditure Cycle Audit Program
For the Year Ended December 31, 2011

Audit Procedures	Initial	Date	Ref.
5. Scan the cash disbursement journal for related party, large, or unusual transactions and perform follow-up procedures for each one identified.	JA	2/15/12	E 42
6. Select a sample of 40 transactions recorded in the cash disbursement journal throughout the year and perform the following:	JA	2/14/12	E 40
a. Determine if the voucher packages were properly stamped "paid."	JA	2/17/12	E 41
b. Examine cancelled checks for proper endorsement and reasonableness.	JA	2/17/12	E 41 E 44
c. Determine if cash disbursement journal amounts agree with the cancelled checks.	JA	2/17/12	E 41 E 44
d. Determine if disbursements were posted to the correct general ledger accounts.	JA	2/17/12	E 41 E 44
e. Determine if disbursements were posted to the correct vendor accounts payable subsidiary file.	JA	2/17/12	E 41 E 44
7. Obtain the bank reconciliations completed during the year and perform the following:	JA	2/16/12	E 43
a. Determine who prepared the bank reconciliations.	JA	2/16/12	E 43
b. Review the bank reconciliations for reasonableness.	JA	2/16/12	E 43
c. Reperform the bank reconciliation for one month.	JA	2/16/12	E 43

Reference: _E 11_
Prepared by: _____
Date: _____
Reviewed by: _____

Southeast Shoe Distributor
Expenditure Cycle - Proposed Adjusting Entry Schedule
For the Year Ended December 31, 2011

Account	Debit	Credit
Explanation:		
Explanation:		
Explanation:		
Explanation:		

Reference:	*E 20-1*
Prepared by:	*JH*
Date:	*9/16/11*
Reviewed by:	

Southeast Shoe Distributor
Expenditure Cycle - Purchases Flowchart
For the Year Ended December 31, 2011

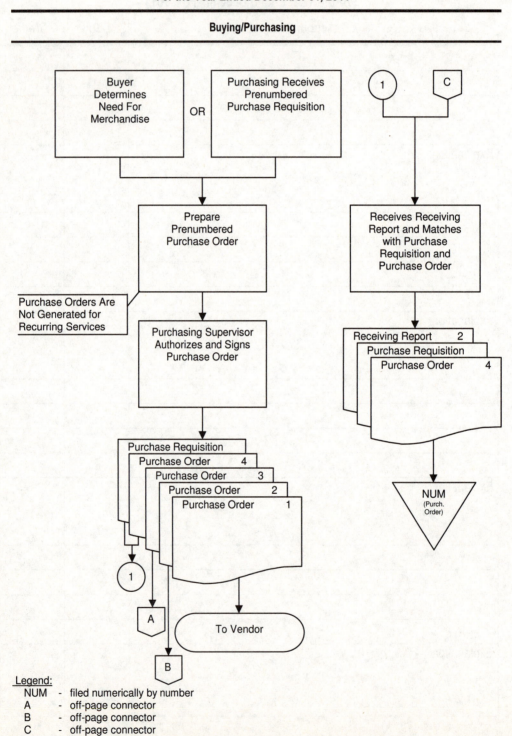

Buying/Purchasing

Legend:
NUM - filed numerically by number
A   - off-page connector
B   - off-page connector
C   - off-page connector

Reference:	E 20-2
Prepared by:	JH
Date:	9/16/11
Reviewed by:	

Southeast Shoe Distributor
Expenditure Cycle - Purchases Flowchart
For the Year Ended December 31, 2011

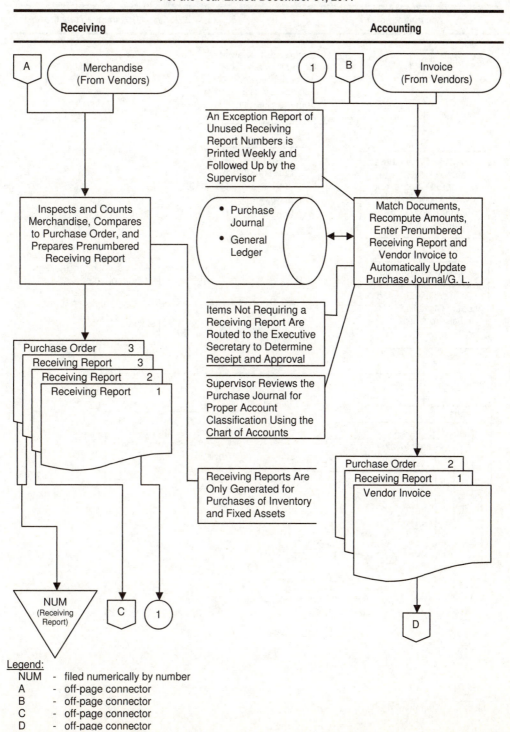

Legend:
NUM - filed numerically by number
A   - off-page connector
B   - off-page connector
C   - off-page connector
D   - off-page connector

Reference:	*E 21*
Prepared by:	*JH*
Date:	*9/16/11*
Reviewed by:	

Southeast Shoe Distributor
Expenditure Cycle - Cash Disbursement Flowchart
For the Year Ended December 31, 2011

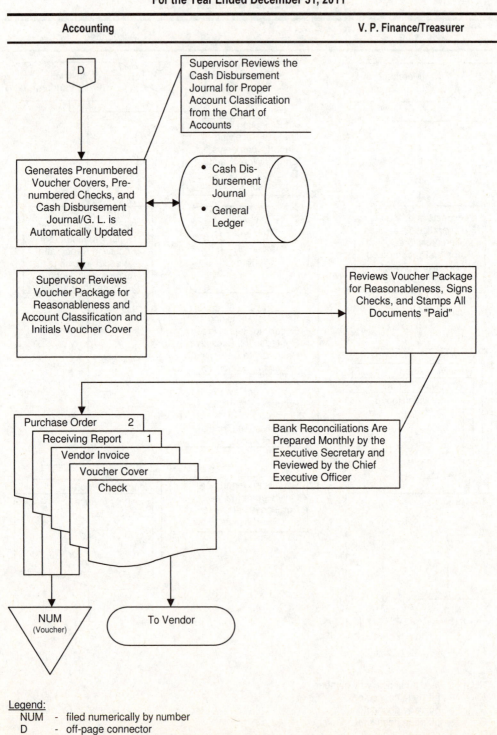

Reference:	*E 22*
Prepared by:	*JH*
Date:	*9/16/11*
Reviewed by:	

Southeast Shoe Distributor
Expenditure Cycle - Planned Audit Risk Matrix
For the Year Ended December 31, 2011

	Reference	Transactions					Balances				Disclosure			
		Occurrence	Completeness	Accuracy	Cutoff	Classification	Existence	Rights/Obligations	Completeness	Valuation	Occurrence/Rights/Obligations	Completeness	Classification/Understandability	Accuracy/Valuation
Tolerable Misstatement: *$40,000, G6*														
Acceptable Audit Risk	G5	L	L	L	L	L	L	L	L	L	L	L	L	L
Initial Inherent Risk – Purchases		H	H	L	H	L					L	L	L	L
Initial Inherent Risk – Cash Disbursements		H	H	L	H	L					L	L	L	L
Initial Inherent Risk – Accounts Payable							L	L	H	H	L	L	L	L
Planned Control Risk – Purchases		L	L	L	H	L					H	H	H	H
Planned Control Risk – Cash Disbursements		L	L	L	L	L					H	H	H	H
Planned Control Risk – Accounts Payable							L	L	L	L	H	H	H	H
Planned Detection Risk – Purchases		M	M	H	L	H					M	M	M	M
Planned Detection Risk – Cash Disbursements		M	M	H	M	H					M	M	M	M
Planned Detection Risk – Accounts Payable							L	L	M	M	M	M	M	M

Initial Inherent Risk should be assessed as:
High (H) unless the combination of inherent risk factors present justify a lower assessment.

Low (L) if the combination of inherent risk factors present justify this assessment.

Factors justifying a lower inherent risk assessment are:
High management integrity, Low motivation to materially misstate for external parties, Repeat engagement, No material prior year misstatements, No related party transactions, Routine transactions, Limited judgment required to correctly record transactions, Low susceptibility to defalcation, Stable business environment.

Planned Control Risk should be assessed as:
Low (L) if control activity(ies) reduces the likelihood of a material misstatement to a negligible level and tests of controls are planned to be performed.

High (H) if control activity(ies) does not reduce the likelihood of a material misstatement to a reasonable level or no tests of controls are planned.

Planned Detection Risk should be assessed at:
Low (L) if persuasive substantive tests are planned to be performed.

Medium (M) if moderately persuasive substantive tests are planned to be performed.

High (H) if minimal substantive tests are planned to be performed.

Reference:	E 30
Prepared by:	JA
Date:	2/14/12
Reviewed by:	

Southeast Shoe Distributor
Nonstatistical Tests of Transactions Sample Plan - Expenditure Cycle Purchases
For the Year Ended December 31, 2011

Sampling Frame	Beg. Doc. # or Page #	End. Doc. # or Page #	Sample Size
Lines recorded in the purchase journal during the year	*Page 1 (Line 1)*	*Page 100 (Line 1,293)*	*40*

Sample Selection Method:

The sample was selected by using the "=randbetween(1,1293)" Microsoft Excel spreadsheet function. Line numbers drawn twice were discarded and a new line number was selected using the Excel "randbetween" function.

Sample: *Line number starting with line 1 on page 1 to line 1,293 on page 100*

Sample Item	Sample Ref.	Sample Item	Sample Ref.	Sample Item	Sample Ref.	Sample Item	Sample Ref.
1	39	16	363	31	953		
2	43	17	368	32	969		
3	68	18	484	33	1,025		
4	79	19	514	34	1,054		
5	87	20	582	35	1,070		
6	91	21	586	36	1,159		
7	99	22	604	37	1,161		
8	219	23	606	38	1,254		
9	235	24	652	39	1,272		
10	237	25	682	40	1,281		
11	238	26	811				
12	301	27	903				
13	326	28	907				
14	341	29	918				
15	356	30	942				

Reference: _____E 31_____
Prepared by: _____
Date: _____
Reviewed by: _____

Southeast Shoe Distributor
Nonstatistical Tests of Controls Evaluation - Expenditure Cycle Purchases
For the Year Ended December 31, 2011

Sampling Frame: *Lines recorded in the purchase journal during the year*

Attribute	RCL	Sample Size	SDR	TDR	ASR
Voucher contains Vendor Invoice, Purchase Order, and Receiving Report (if necessary).	M	40		5%	
Vendor Invoice, Purchase Order, and Receiving Report look authentic and reasonable.	M	40		5%	
Purchase Order is signed by Bruce Penny or Vendor Invoice is initialed by Karen Tucci.	M	40		5%	
Voucher Cover is initialed by Janet Sotiriadis.	M	40		5%	
Purchase journal amount is correct based on voucher package documents.	M	40		5%	
Voucher Cover has correct general ledger account code.	M	40		5%	
Voucher is posted to the correct general ledger account.	M	40	0	5%	5%
Voucher is posted to correct vendor accounts payable subsidiary file.	M	40	0	5%	5%

Conclusions:

Legend:
ASR - Allowance for Sampling Risk (TDR-SDR)
RCL - Risk of Assessing Control Risk Too Low (L – Low or M – Moderate)
SDR - Sample Deviation Rate
TDR - Tolerable Deviation Rate

Reference: E 32

Prepared by: JA

Date: 2/15/12

Reviewed by: _____

Southeast Shoe Distributor
Unusual Transactions – Expenditure Cycle Purchases
For the Year Ended December 31, 2011

Date	Account Description or Payee	Check or Voucher #	Account IDs	Amount
	No large, unusual, or related-party			
	transactions noted. See conclusion below.			

Follow-up procedures performed:
No large, unusual, or related-party purchase transactions were identified from scanning the purchase journal (audit step 2). Thus, no follow-up procedures are needed.

Reference:	E 33
Prepared by:	JA
Date:	2/15/12
Reviewed by:	

Southeast Shoe Distributor
Nonsampling Tests of Transactions – Expenditure Cycle Purchases
For the Year Ended December 31, 2011

Procedure:

The weekly exception reports of unused vouchers and receiving reports were scanned and the follow-up procedures were discussed with Janet Sotiriadis, Accounting Manager (audit step 3).

Exceptions/Misstatements:

Janet indicated she did not resolve all unmatched receiving reports because she did not have enough time to follow-up on them. Janet indicated that unmatched receiving reports always resulted from vendors not invoicing SSD on a timely basis and that these unmatched receiving reports were eventually captured in the system when the invoice was received from the vendor. No specific misstatements were noted as a result of this audit procedure.

Conclusion:

The results of this procedure do not support a lower control risk assessment related to the completeness of purchases (i.e., there may be unrecorded purchases) and completeness and valuation of accounts payable. Control risk for the completeness of purchases and the completeness and valuation of accounts payable will be increased to the maximum level and additional substantive audit procedures will be performed. The sample size for audit step 4 will be increased from its planned size of 40 to 60 receiving reports. Additionally, more emphasis will be placed on purchase transactions occurring in the last calendar year quarter to ensure that there are no material unrecorded purchases and payables at year-end.

Reference:	E 34
Prepared by:	JA
Date:	2/14/12
Reviewed by:	

Southeast Shoe Distributor
Nonstatistical Tests of Transactions Sample Plan - Expenditure Cycle Purchases
For the Year Ended December 31, 2011

Sampling Frame	Beg. Doc. # or Page #	End. Doc. # or Page #	Sample Size
Receiving reports issued during the year	2,387	2,810	60

Sample Selection Method:

The first 40 sample items were selected from the first three calendar-year quarters by using the "=randbetween(2387,2673)" Microsoft Excel spreadsheet function. The last 20 sample items were selected from the last calendar year quarter by using the "=randbetween(2674,2810)" Microsoft Excel spreadsheet function. Receiving report numbers drawn twice were discarded and a new random number was selected using the Excel "randbetween" function.

Sample: *Receiving Report Number*

Sample Item	Sample Ref.	Sample Item	Sample Ref.	Sample Item	Sample Ref.	Sample Item	Sample Ref.
1	2,389	16	2,529	31	2,598	46	2,695
2	2,394	17	2,533	32	2,599	47	2,696
3	2,395	18	2,539	33	2,610	48	2,702
4	2,409	19	2,540	34	2,624	49	2,703
5	2,412	20	2,548	35	2,633	50	2,706
6	2,415	21	2,549	36	2,635	51	2,709
7	2,419	22	2,563	37	2,636	52	2,723
8	2,421	23	2,568	38	2,647	53	2,726
9	2,424	24	2,570	39	2,666	54	2,741
10	2,450	25	2,579	40	2,668	55	2,759
11	2,463	26	2,584	41	2,674	56	2,764
12	2,490	27	2,587	42	2,677	57	2,778
13	2,494	28	2,588	43	2,679	58	2,784
14	2,522	29	2,593	44	2,685	59	2,787
15	2,523	30	2,597	45	2,694	60	2,801

Reference: _____E 35_____
Prepared by: _____
Date: _____
Reviewed by: _____

Southeast Shoe Distributor
Nonstatistical Substantive Tests Evaluation - Expenditure Cycle Purchases
For the Year Ended December 31, 2011

Misstatements:	Recorded Amount	Audited Amount	Misstatement Amount
Total Sample Misstatement			
Projected Misstatement:			
Total Sample Misstatement			
Dollar Value of Sample		÷	$1,061,410.43
Percentage Sample Dollar Misstatement		=	
Dollar Value of Population per Journal		×	$6,206,243.81
Projected Population Dollar Misstatement		=	
Allowance for Sampling Risk			
Tolerable Misstatement			$40,000.00
Projected Population Dollar Misstatement		−	
Recorded Adjustments		+	
Allowance for Sampling Risk		=	
Conclusions:			

Reference:	E 40
Prepared by:	JA
Date:	2/14/12
Reviewed by:	

Southeast Shoe Distributor
Nonstatistical Tests of Transactions Sample Plan –
Expenditure Cycle Cash Disbursements
For the Year Ended December 31, 2011

Sampling Frame	Beg. Doc. # or Page #	End. Doc. # or Page #	Sample Size
Lines recorded in the cash disbursement journal during the year	Page 1 (Line 1)	Page 47 (Line 1,032)	40

Sample Selection Method:

The sample was selected by using the "=randbetween(1,1032)" Microsoft Excel spreadsheet function. Line numbers drawn twice were discarded and a new line number was selected using the Excel "randbetween" function.

Sample: *Cash disbursement journal line number*

Sample Item	Sample Ref.	Sample Item	Sample Ref.	Sample Item	Sample Ref.	Sample Item	Sample Ref.
1	37	16	446	31	819		
2	117	17	449	32	845		
3	139	18	499	33	867		
4	159	19	516	34	884		
5	168	20	536	35	902		
6	197	21	539	36	914		
7	232	22	579	37	987		
8	271	23	612	38	992		
9	273	24	636	39	997		
10	285	25	648	40	1,000		
11	321	26	670				
12	345	27	694				
13	374	28	720				
14	396	29	736				
15	403	30	739				

Reference:	E 41
Prepared by:	JA
Date:	2/17/12
Reviewed by:	

Southeast Shoe Distributor
Nonstatistical Tests of Controls Evaluation –
Expenditure Cycle Cash Disbursements
For the Year Ended December 31, 2011

Sampling Frame: *Lines recorded in the cash disbursement journal during the year*

Attribute	RCL	Sample Size	SDR	TDR	ASR
Voucher package documents stamped "paid."	M	40	0%	5%	5%
Canceled check and endorsement look authentic and reasonable.	M	40	0%	5%	5%
Cash disbursement journal amount agrees with cancelled check.	M	40	0%	5%	5%
Disbursement posted to correct general ledger accounts.	M	40	0%	5%	5%
Disbursement posted to correct vendor accounts payable subsidiary file.	M	40	0%	5%	5%

Conclusions:
No deviations were noted as a result of performing test of controls 6a-e for cash disbursements. The magnitude of the allowance for sampling risk is sufficient to support a reduced control risk assessment for the occurrence of purchases; the occurrence, accuracy, and classification of cash disbursements; and the occurrence and valuation of accounts payable.

Legend:
ASR - Allowance for Sampling Risk (TDR-SDR)
RCL - Risk of Assessing Control Risk Too Low (L – Low or M – Moderate)
SDR - Sample Deviation Rate
TDR - Tolerable Deviation Rate

			Reference:	E 42
			Prepared by:	JA
			Date:	2/15/12
			Reviewed by:	

Southeast Shoe Distributor
Unusual Transactions – Expenditure Cycle Cash Disbursements
For the Year Ended December 31, 2011

Date	Account Description or Payee	Check or Voucher #	Account IDs	Amount
	No large, unusual, or related-party transactions			
	were noted. See conclusion below.			

Follow-up procedures performed:
  No large, unusual, or related-party cash disbursement transactions were identified from scanning the cash disbursement journal (audit step 5). Thus, no follow-up procedures are needed.

Reference:	E 43
Prepared by:	JA
Date:	2/16/12
Reviewed by:	

Southeast Shoe Distributor
Nonsampling Tests of Transactions – Expenditure Cycle Cash Disbursements
For the Year Ended December 31, 2011

Procedure:

The monthly bank reconciliations were scanned and the bank reconciliation process was discussed with Karen Tucci, Executive Secretary (audit steps 7a and b). Additionally, the April 2011 bank reconciliation was reperformed (audit step 7c).

Exceptions/Misstatements:

Review of the monthly bank reconciliations and reperformance of the April 2011 bank reconciliation revealed that the bank reconciliation process is consistent with stated company policy, no exceptions or misstatements were identified.

Conclusion:

The results of these tests support a reduced control risk assessment for the occurrence, completeness, and accuracy of cash disbursements and the existence and valuation of accounts payable.

Reference:	E 44
Prepared by:	JA
Date:	2/17/12
Reviewed by:	

Southeast Shoe Distributor
Non-Statistical Substantive Tests Evaluation - Expenditure Cycle Cash Disbursements
For the Year Ended December 31, 2011

Misstatements:	Recorded Amount	Audited Amount	Misstatement Amount
No misstatements were identified as a			
result of performing audit steps 6b-e	—	—	—
Total Sample Misstatement			*$0.00*
Projected Misstatement:			
Total Sample Misstatement			*$0.00*
Dollar Value of Sample		÷	*$316,319.78*
Percentage Sample Dollar Misstatement		=	*0.00%*
Dollar Value of Population per Journal		×	*$8,151,977.17*
Projected Population Dollar Misstatement		=	*$0.00*
Allowance for Sampling Risk			
Tolerable Misstatement			*$40,000.00*
Projected Population Dollar Misstatement		—	*$0.00*
Recorded Adjustments		+	*$0.00*
Allowance for Sampling Risk		=	*$40,000.00*

Conclusions:

No misstatements were noted as a result of performing substantive tests 6b-e for cash disbursements. The magnitude of the allowance for sampling risk is sufficient to support performing a reduced level of substantive tests of balances for the valuation, existence, and completeness of accounts payable.

Southeast Shoe Distributor, Inc.
Performance of Tests of Balances for the Expenditure Cycle (Acquisitions and Cash Disbursements)

Mark S. Beasley · Frank A. Buckless · Steven M. Glover · Douglas F. Prawitt

LEARNING OBJECTIVES

After completing and discussing this case you should be able to

[1] Recognize common documents and records used in the expenditure cycle

[2] Recognize common tests of balances for accounts payable

[3] Perform tests of balances for accounts payable

[4] Evaluate the results of tests of balances for accounts payable using a nonstatistical approach

[5] Recognize the linkage of substantive tests of balances to management assertions

INTRODUCTION

Southeast Shoe Distributor (SSD) is a closely-owned business that was founded 10 years ago by Stewart Green and Paul Williams. SSD is a distributor that purchases and resells men's, women's, and children's shoes to retail shoe stores located in small to midsize communities. The company's basic strategy is to obtain a broad selection of designer-label and name-brand footwear at low prices for resell to small one-location retail stores. SSD targets stores that have a difficult time obtaining reasonable quantities of designer and name-brand footwear. The company is able to keep the cost of footwear low by (1) selectively purchasing large blocks of production overruns, overorders, mid- and late- season deliveries and last season's stock from manufacturers and other retailers at significant discounts, (2) sourcing in-season name-brand and branded designer footwear directly from factories in Brazil, Italy, and Spain, and (3) negotiating favorable prices with manufacturers by ordering footwear during off-peak production periods and taking delivery at one central warehouse.

During the year, the company purchased merchandise from over 50 domestic and international vendors, independent resellers, manufacturers and other retailers that have frequent excess inventory. Designer and name-brand footwear sold by the company include the following: Amalfi, Clarks, Dexter, Fila, Florsheim, Naturalizer, and Rockport. At the present time, SSD has one warehouse located in Atlanta, Georgia. Last year SSD had net sales of $7,311,214. Sales are strongest in the second and fourth calendar-year quarters, with the first calendar-year quarter substantially weaker than the rest.

The case was prepared by Mark S. Beasley, Ph.D. and Frank A. Buckless, Ph.D. of North Carolina State University and Steven M. Glover, Ph.D. and Douglas F. Prawitt, Ph.D. of Brigham Young University, as a basis for class discussion. SSD is a fictitious company. All characters and names represented are fictitious; any similarity to existing companies or persons is purely coincidental.

BACKGROUND

SSD is required to have an audit of its annual financial statements to fulfill requirements of loan agreements with financial institutions. This audit is to be completed in accordance with the AICPA professional standards for the audit of nonpublic companies. Your audit firm is in the process of completing the audit for the fiscal 2011 financial statements in accordance with these professional standards. The audit senior for this engagement is Jorge Hernandez. The two audit staff assigned to this engagement are Joy Avery and you. The two of you are responsible for performing the tests of balances and analytical tests outlined in the expenditure cycle audit program (referenced in the top right-hand corner as *E 2*).

The general ledger accounts related to purchasing and cash disbursement activities at SSD include the following:

- Inventory Purchases
- Purchase Discounts
- Purchase Returns and Allowances
- Freight In
- Administrative Expenses

- Warehousing Expenses
- Selling Expenses
- Prepaid Assets
- Accounts Payable

Joy Avery has already performed audit procedures 1 and 2 listed on audit schedule *E 2*. Her work is documented on audit schedules *E 2, E 10, E 50,* and *E 51*. Additionally, Joy has selected the audit sample for audit procedure 3 as noted on audit schedule *E 52*.

REQUIRED

[1] Complete audit procedure 3a listed on audit program *E 2*. The supporting documents to be examined for this audit procedure are vouchers, vendor invoices, receiving reports, and purchase orders. Assume you have already tested 35 of the selected sample items, observing no misstatements. The documents and records for the remaining five sample items are provided at the following website www.pearsonhighered.com/beasley5e. SSD's polices only require the generation of receiving reports for purchases of inventory and fixed assets. Additionally, purchase orders are not required to be generated for recurring services such as utilities and cleaning. The results from performing audit procedure 3a should be documented in audit schedule *E 53*. Document completion of audit procedure 3a in the audit program *E 2*.

[2] Document your adjusting entries for any observed misstatements that you propose on schedule *E 11*. Then update the accounts payable lead schedule on audit schedule *E 10*. Assume that there was no systematic pattern or intent to commit a fraud based on a review and discussion with client personnel concerning observed misstatements, if any.

Reference:	E 2
Prepared by:	JA
Date:	2/28/12
Reviewed by:	

Southeast Shoe Distributor
Expenditure Cycle Audit Program for
Year End Analytical Procedures and Tests of Balances
For the Year Ended December 31, 2011

Audit Procedures	Initial	Date	Ref.
1. Obtain a lead schedule for Accounts Payable and perform the following:	JA	2/14/12	E 10
a. Agree prior year balance to prior year audit schedule.	JA	2/14/12	E 10
b. Agree current year balance to the general ledger.	JA	2/14/12	E 10
2. Obtain a printout of the accounts payable vendor ledgers as of the end of the year and perform the following:	JA	2/17/12	N/A
a. Foot the year-end vendor ledgers and agree it to the lead schedule.	JA	2/17/12	E 10
b. Scan the year-end vendor ledgers for large, unusual, related-party or debit balances and perform follow-up procedures for each one identified.	JA	2/17/12	E 50
c. Obtain the last five receiving reports issued before year-end and determine if they were properly included in the year-end vendor ledgers.	JA	2/20/12	E 51
d. Obtain the first five receiving reports issued after year-end and determine if they were properly excluded from the year-end vendor ledgers.	JA	2/20/12	E 51
3. Select a sample of checks issued after year-end and perform the following:	JA	2/28/12	E 52
a. Examine the voucher package and determine if the related payable was properly included or excluded from the year-end vendor ledgers.			E 53

Reference:	*E 10*	
Prepared by:	*JA*	
Date:	2/17/12	
Reviewed by:		

Southeast Shoe Distributor
Accounts Payable - Lead Schedule
For the Year Ended December 31, 2011

Account	Audited Balance 12/31/10	Unaudited Balance 12/31/11	Adjustments		Adjusted Balance 12/31/11
			Debit	Credit	
Accounts Payable	$453,370 √	$742,704 *f, GL*			

<u>*Tickmark Legend*</u>
√   - *Agreed to prior year audit schedule without exception (audit step 1a).*
GL - *Agreed to 12/31/2011 general ledger without exception (audit step 1b).*
f   - *Agreed to the footed balance of the 12/31/2011 accounts payable vendor ledgers without exception (audit step 2a).*

Reference: _E 11_
Prepared by: _____
Date: _____
Reviewed by: _____

Southeast Shoe Distributor
Expenditure Cycle - Proposed Adjusting Entries Schedule
For the Year Ended December 31, 2011

Account	Debit	Credit
Explanation:		
Explanation:		
Explanation:		
Explanation:		

347

Reference:	_E 50_
Prepared by:	_JA_
Date:	_2/17/12_
Reviewed by:	

Southeast Shoe Distributor
Unusual Balances – Expenditure Cycle Accounts Payable
For the Year Ended December 31, 2011

Vendor	Balance
No large, unusual, related-party or debit balances were noted. See conclusion below.	

Follow-up procedures performed:
  No large, unusual, related-party or debit accounts payable balances were identified as a result of scanning the year-end vendor ledgers (audit step 2b). Thus, no follow-up procedures are needed.

Reference:	*E 51*
Prepared by:	*JA*
Date:	*2/20/12*
Reviewed by:	

Southeast Shoe Distributor
Nonsampling Tests of Balances – Expenditure Cycle Accounts Payable
For the Year Ended December 31, 2011

Procedure:

The last receiving report issued before December 31, 2011 was 2810. The vouchers, vendor invoices, and purchase orders supporting the last five receiving reports issued before year-end and first five receiving reports issued after year-end were examined and traced to proper inclusion/exclusion in/from the December 31, 2011 vendor ledgers (audit steps 2c and d).

Exceptions/Misstatements:

No misstatements were noted.

Conclusion:

The results of audit steps 2c and d support that there were no material cutoff misstatements for purchase transactions occurring just before and after year-end.

Reference:	E 52
Prepared by:	JA
Date:	2/28/12
Reviewed by:	

Southeast Shoe Distributor
Nonstatistical Tests of Balances Sampling Plan - Expenditure Cycle
For the Year Ended December 31, 2011

Sampling Frame	Beg. Doc. # or Page #	End. Doc. # or Page #	Sample Size
Checks issued subsequent to year-end	7,431	7,584	40

Sample Selection Method:
   The sample of checks issued subsequent to year-end were selected using the haphazard selection method.

Sample: *Check Number*

Sample Item	Sample Ref.	Sample Item	Sample Ref.	Sample Item	Sample Ref.	Sample Item	Sample Ref.
1	7,434	16	7,488	31	7,531		
2	7,441	17	7,496	32	7,536		
3	7,442	18	7,498	33	7,541		
4	7,444	19	7,501	34	7,546		
5	7,452	20	7,502	35	7,552		
6	7,453	21	7,503	36	7,553		
7	7,456	22	7,505	37	7,560		
8	7,459	23	7,506	38	7,573		
9	7,466	24	7,514	39	7,579		
10	7,467	25	7,515	40	7,581		
11	7,468	26	7,518				
12	7,473	27	7,520				
13	7,476	28	7,521				
14	7,479	29	7,523				
15	7,486	30	7,527				

Reference: *E 53*
Prepared by:
Date:
Reviewed by:

**Southeast Shoe Distributor
Nonstatistical Tests of Balance Evaluation –
Expenditure Cycle Accounts Payable
For the Year Ended December 31, 2011**

Misstatements:	Recorded Amount	Audited Amount	Misstatement Amount
Total Sample Misstatement			

Projected Misstatement:

Total Sample Misstatement		
Dollar Value of Sample	÷	$184,583.10
Percentage Sample Dollar Misstatement	=	
Dollar Value of Population per Journal	×	$742,704.11
Projected Population Dollar Misstatement	=	

Allowance for Sampling Risk

Tolerable Misstatement		$40,000.00
Projected Population Dollar Misstatement	−	
Recorded Adjustments	+	
Allowance for Sampling Risk	=	

Conclusions:

Developing and Evaluating Audit Documentation

The Runners Shop
Litigation Support Review of Audit
Documentation for Notes Payable

MARK S. BEASLEY · FRANK A. BUCKLESS · STEVEN M. GLOVER · DOUGLAS F. PRAWITT

LEARNING OBJECTIVES

After completing and discussing this case you should be able to

[1] Read audit documentation prepared by audit staff to support management assertions related to Notes Payable

[2] Identify deficiencies with the preparation of the Notes Payable audit documentation

[3] Highlight implications of auditors' failure to properly document work performed

INTRODUCTION

The Runners Shop (TRS) was a family-owned business founded 17 years ago by Robert and Andrea Johnson. In July of 2011, TRS found itself experiencing a severe cash shortage that forced it to file for bankruptcy protection. Prior to shutting down its operations, TRS was engaged in the retail sale of athletic footwear and related products for runners. TRS's 2010 audited financial statements reported net sales of $2,217,292 and a net loss of $50,980. Consistent with prior years, sales were strongest in the second and fourth calendar-year quarters, with the first calendar-year quarter substantially weaker than the rest.

The company's basic strategy was to provide superior customer service compared to competing sporting goods and mass merchandiser retail stores. The company attempted to provide superior service by hiring college-age runners as sales staff and then training them on shoes and strategies that would correct common running ailments. This approach helped TRS develop a very loyal customer base for its first store located in Charlottesville, Virginia. Sales at the Charlottesville store were so strong that Robert and Andrea decided to expand into three other markets: Richmond, Virginia; College Park, Maryland; and Raleigh, North Carolina.

Unfortunately, the expansion effort did not go as well as Robert and Andrea had anticipated. They expected that the first three years of operations at the new locations would be difficult, but after that point they had hoped to experience significant improvement. However, the expected performance improvement did not materialize and after four years of operations the expansion stores were still running at a loss. In July 2011, Robert and Andrea, with almost all of their personal assets exhausted, realized they could no longer hang on and filed for bankruptcy protection.

BANKCRUPTCY PROMPTS CREDITORS TO SUE TRS

First Commercial Bank provided a short-term line of credit that allowed TRS to borrow up to $100,000 to cover cash disbursements for merchandise purchases prior to peak sales periods. This loan agreement required TRS to pay off its outstanding balance before the last business day in July.

National Bank and Trust provided an installment loan to TRS when it expanded from one to four locations. This loan agreement required TRS to remit monthly interest and principal payments. Both lenders required TRS to have its annual financial statements audited as a condition of the loan agreements.

Unfortunately, as a result of the bankruptcy both lending institutions lost the outstanding principal balances owed them by TRS. The two lending institutions jointly filed a lawsuit against the firm that audited TRS's financial statements, Green and Brown, LLP. The lawsuit alleges that the audit firm did not perform the audit in accordance with generally accepted auditing standards and as a result the two banks were misled and were unable to recover their outstanding loan balances.

The law firms representing the defendant (Green and Brown, LLP) and the plaintiffs (First Commercial Bank and National Bank and Trust) are now conducting discovery procedures. The objectives of the discovery process are to ensure that all evidence is equally available to all parties and to facilitate settlement of the case.

INFORMATION ABOUT THE AUDIT

Green and Brown, LLP audited the financial statements of TRS for the previous 10 years. Because TRS is not publicly traded, Green and Brown performed their audits under professional standards for audits of nonpublic companies. The audit report issued for the 2010 and 2009 financial statements is shown in Exhibit 1.

The audit staff for the 2010 audit of TRS's financial statements consisted of four individuals: Pete Letterman, audit partner; Carol Maddox, audit manager; Mary Lewis, audit senior, and Joe Manaker, staff auditor. All of these individuals also worked on the previous year's audit of TRS. The audit program and audit documentation related to TRS's Notes Payable are enclosed. Joe performed the audit work in this area and Mary reviewed his work. Green and Brown, LLP's guidelines for the preparation of audit documentation have also been provided for your information.

INFORMATION ABOUT THE ENGAGEMENT

You are working for the litigation support firm hired to identify deficiencies in the audit work performed by Green and Brown, LLP. You have been asked to review the audit documentation prepared by the audit firm related to TRS's Notes Payable. The purpose of reviewing this section of the audit documentation is to demonstrate a pattern of careless behavior on the part of the auditors and thereby build a case in support of an allegation of auditor negligence.

REQUIRED

[1] Describe the purposes of audit documentation and explain why each purpose is important.

[2] Review Green and Brown, LLP's audit documentation guidelines and explain why an audit firm would want to include each of the listed items in its audit documentation.

[3] Review the audit documentation prepared by Green and Brown, LLP, related to TRS's Notes Payable and list deficiencies on the enclosed schedules.

[4] Green and Brown, LLP would not be required to comply with the auditing standards of the Public Company Accounting Oversight Board (PCAOB) for the TRS audit because TRS is a private company. Setting this fact aside for the moment, go to the PCAOB Website and review Standard No. 3, "Audit Documentation" (see www.pcaob.org). This standard requires that documentation of audit work contain sufficient information to enable an experienced auditor not involved with the engagement to achieve two objectives. What are those two objectives? Explain whether you believe the audit documentation in this case achieves these objectives.

EXHIBIT 1

Independent Auditor's Report

To Robert and Andrea Johnson, President and Treasurer of The Runners Shop

We have audited the accompanying balance sheets of The Runners Shop as of December 31, 2010 and 2009, and the related statements of income, retained earnings, and cash flows for the years then ended. These financial statements are the responsibility of the company's management. Our responsibility is to express an opinion on these statements based on our audits.

We conducted our audits in accordance with auditing standards generally accepted in the United States of America. Those standards require that we plan and perform the audit to obtain reasonable assurance about whether the financial statements are free of material misstatement. An audit includes examining, on a test basis, evidence supporting the amounts and disclosures in the financial statements. An audit also includes assessing the accounting principles used and significant estimates made by management, as well as evaluating the overall financial statement presentation. We believe that our audits provide a reasonable basis for our opinion.

In our opinion, the financial statements referred to above present fairly, in all material respects, the financial position of The Runners Shop as of December 31, 2010 and 2009, and the results of its operations and its cash flows for the years then ended in conformity with accounting principles generally accepted in the United States of America.

Green and Brown, LLP

Charlottesville, VA
March 4, 2011

GREEN AND BROWN, LLP
FIRM GUIDELINES – AUDIT DOCUMENTATION

Provided below are firm guidelines related to the preparation of audit documentation:

- *Title* – each schedule/document included in the audit documentation should indicate the client name, description of content, and year-end financial statement date.
- *Source of schedule/document* – schedules/documents prepared by the client should be clearly indicated.
- *Work performed* – each schedule/document should include the initials of the audit staff who performed work related to the schedule/document, as well as the date the work was completed.
- *Indexing* – each schedule/document should be indexed to facilitate filing and referencing between documents.
- *Cross-referencing* – information on a schedule/document shared or used on another schedule/document should be cross-referenced by indicating on both schedules/documents the index (as close to the information as possible) of the other schedule/document.
- *Tickmark (footnote) explanations* – should be included on each schedule/document to indicate the work performed.

Approved December 7, 2009

Reference:	FI 4
Prepared by:	JM
Date:	1/14/11
Reviewed by:	ML

The Runners Shop
Financing and Investing Cycle—Short- and
Long-term Debt Audit Program
Year Ended: December 31, 2010

Audit Procedures	Initial	Date	A/D Ref.
1. Confirm terms and balances of Notes Payable with lenders.	JM	12/31/10	FI 114-1 FI 114-2
2. Obtain the client-prepared lead schedule for short- and long-term debt.	JM	1/14/11	FI 110
A. Crossfoot the lead schedule.	JM	1/14/11	FI 110
B. Agree the prior-year balances to prior-year audit documentation.	JM	1/14/11	FI 110
C. Agree the current-year balances to the general ledger and trial balance.	JM	1/14/11	FI 110
3. Obtain the client-prepared supporting schedule(s) for Notes Payable.	JM	1/14/11	FI 111
A. Foot and crossfoot the schedule(s).	JM	1/14/11	FI 111
B. Agree the prior-year balances to prior-year audit documentation.	JM	1/14/11	FI 111
C. Agree the current-year balances to the general ledger and trial balance.	JM	1/14/11	FI 111
D. Agree the reported balances to the lead schedule.	JM	1/14/11	FI 111
E. Agree terms and year-end balances with the confirmations.	JM	1/14/11	FI 111 FI 114
F. Recompute the current and long-term portion of notes using the loan agreement.	JM	1/14/11	FI 111
G. Review the cash receipts journal and schedule of fixed-asset additions to determine that all debt is properly included on the schedule.	JM	1/14/11	N/A
H. Review bank cash confirmations to determine that all debt is properly included on the schedule.	JM	1/14/11	FI 111
4. Recompute year-end accrued interest for each outstanding loan based on the last date interest was paid.	JM	1/14/11	FI 112
5. Test the reasonableness of interest expense by multiplying the average outstanding balance by the appropriate interest rate.	JM	1/14/11	FI 113
6. Review the provisions of the loan agreements to determine if there are any violations.	JM	1/14/11	FI 111
7. Conclude to the fair presentation of Notes Payable.	JM	1/14/11	FI 110

PBC

Reference:	FI 110
Prepared by:	JM
Date:	1/14/11
Reviewed by:	ML

The Runners Shop
Financing and Investing Cycle—Short- and Long-Term Debt Lead Schedule
For the Year Ended December 31, 2010

Account Name And Description	12/31/09 Balance	12/31/10 Balance	Adjustments	12/31/10 Adjusted Balance	
Accrued Interest	$747.67	$1,344.71	—	$1,344.71	cf
	FI 112, PY	FI 112, GL			
Notes Payable—Short-term	$51,803.40	$65,676.52	—	$65,676.52	cf
	PY	FI 111, GL			
Notes Payable—Long-term	$66,053.47	$48,836.95	—	$48,836.95	cf
	PY	FI 111, GL			
Interest Expense	$14,669.79	$14,199.73	—	$14,199.73	cf
	FI 113, PY	FI 113, GL			

$117,856.87
FI 111, Σ

Tickmark Legend

PY - *Agreed to prior-year audit documentation without exception.*

GL - *Agreed to 12/31/2010 general ledger and trial balance without exception.*

cf - *Crossfooted amount without exception.*

PBC

Reference:	FI 111
Prepared by:	JM
Date:	1/14/11
Reviewed by:	ML

The Runners Shop
Financing and Investing Cycle—Notes Payable Schedule
For the Year Ended December 31, 2010

Lender	Loan Terms	12/31/09 Balance	Additions	Reductions	12/31/10 Balance	Current Portion	Non-Current Portion	
First Commercial Bank√	10%√ $100,000 short-term line of credit,√ interest due on last day of each month, out-standing balance due on last day of July, no collateral.√	$43,090.00 PY	$149,360.00 cj	$143,990.00 cj	$48,460.00 √	$48,460.00 rc	$0	Σ
National Bank and Trust√	12%√ installment note,√ principal and interest due on first day of each month, no collateral.√	$74,766.87 PY	$0	$8,713.40	$66,053.47 √	$17,216.52 rc	$48,836.95	Σ
Total		$117,856.87	$149,360.00	$152,703.40	$114,513.47	$65,676.52	$48,836.95	Σ
		FI 110 PY f	f	f	f	FI 110 GL f	FI 110 GL f	

Tickmark Legend

PY - Agreed to prior-year audit documentation without exception.

GL - Agreed to 12/31/2010 general ledger and trial balance without exception.

f - Footed amount without exception.

√ - Agreed to confirmation without exception.

cj - Agreed to amounts recorded in the 2010 cash receipt/ disbursement journals without exception.

rc - Recomputed based on the terms of the note without exception.

Σ - The current and non-current balances were summed and agreed to the total balance without exception.

Notes

A) Per review of the bank confirmations, no debt is excluded from this schedule.

C) The cash receipts journal was reviewed to determine if any large cash receipts related to new loan amounts. The only receipts identified were included in the additions column for First Commercial Bank above.

B) Per review of the two loan agreements, TRS is in violation of the covenant with National Bank and Trust that prohibits loans to officers. Robert Johnson has had a small $5,000 loan from TRS for the last two years. Per Robert Johnson National Bank and Trust is okay with the loan.

Reference:	*FI 112*
Prepared by:	*JM*
Date:	*1/14/11*
Reviewed by:	*ML*

PBC

The Runners Shop
Financing and Investing Cycle—Accrued Interest Schedule
For the Year Ended December 31, 2010

Lender	12/31/09 Balance	12/31/10 Balance	Last Interest Payment
First Commercial Bank	$0 *PY*	$0 *rc*	12/31/10
National Bank and Trust	$747.67 *PY*	$1,344.71 *rc*	12/01/10
Total Accrued Interest	$747.67 *PY, FI 110, ƒ*	$1,344.71 *GL, FI 110, ƒ*	

Tickmark Legend

PY - *Agreed to prior-year audit documentation without exception.*

GL - *Agreed to 12/31/2010 general ledger and trial balance without exception.*

rc - *Recomputed based on the terms of the note and last interest payment date without exception.*

ƒ - *Footed by auditor.*

Reference:	FI 113
Prepared by:	JM
Date:	1/14/11
Reviewed by:	ML

The Runners Shop
Financing and Investing Cycle—Interest Expense Schedule
For the Year Ended December 31, 2010

Lender	12/31/09 Interest Expense	12/31/10 Interest Expense
First Commercial Bank	$5,185.97 PY	$5,696.61
National Bank and Trust	$9,483.82 PY	$8,503.12
Total Interest Expense	$14,669.79	$14,199.73
	PY, FI 110, f	GL, FI 110, f

<u>Interest Expense Analytical Procedure</u>

$(43,090 + 48,460)/2 \times 10\%$ = 4,577.50 c
   FI 111   FI111   FI 111

$(74,766.87 + 66,053.47)/2 \times 12\%$ = 8,629.22 c
   FI 111   FI111   FI 111

Estimated Interest Expense = 13,206.72

f

<u>Tickmark Legend</u>

PY - *Agreed to prior-year audit documentation without exception.*

GL - *Agreed to 12/31/2010 general ledger and trial balance without exception.*

f - *Footed by auditor.*

c - *Computed by auditor.*

<u>Notes:</u>

The difference between the actual and estimated interest expense of $993.01 ($14,199.73 - $13,206.72) results from the fact that the outstanding balance for the short-term line of credit varies substantially from month to month consistent with the company's sales activity. The estimated amount is not materially different from the actual amount; therefore, no further work is needed.

The Runners Shop
1000 Barracks Road
Charlottesville, VA 22908

Reference:	FI 114-1
Prepared by:	JM
Date:	1/14/11
Reviewed by:	ML

December 31, 2010

Mr. Charles M. Banker
First Commercial Bank
Washington, DC 20001

Dear Mr. Banker:

In connection with an audit of the financial statements of The Runners Shop as of December 31, 2010, and for the year then ended, we have advised our independent auditors of the information listed below, which we believe is a complete and accurate description of our line of credit from your institution as of the close of business on December 31, 2010. Although we do not request nor expect you to conduct a comprehensive, detailed search of your records, if during the process of completing this confirmation additional information about other lines of credit from your financial institution comes to your attention, please include such information below.

- The company has available at the financial institution a line of credit totaling $100,000. The current terms of the line of credit are contained in the agreement letter dated November 15, 2001. The related debt outstanding at the close of business on December 31, 2010, was $48,460.
- The amount of the unused line of credit, subject to the terms of the related agreement letter, at December 31, 2010, was $51,540.
- The interest rate at the close of business on December 31, 2010, was 10%.
- There are no requirements for compensating balances in connection with this line of credit.
- The line of credit does not support commercial paper or any other borrowing arrangement.

Please confirm whether the information about lines of credit presented above is correct by signing below and returning this letter directly to our independent auditors, Green and Brown, LLP, 1 Hill Street, Charlottesville, VA, 22905.

Sincerely,

Robert Johnson

Robert Johnson
President, The Runners Shop

Dear Green and Brown, LLP:

The above information regarding the line-of-credit arrangement agrees with the records of this financial institution. Although we have not conducted a comprehensive, detailed search of our records, no information about other lines of credit came to our attention. [Note exceptions below or in attached letter.]

No exceptions.

First Commercial Bank

By: *Charles M. Banker, Vice President, Loans*   *January 10, 2011*
    (Officer and Title)   (Date)

Reference:	FI 114-2
Prepared by:	JM
Date:	1/14/11
Reviewed by:	ML

STANDARD FORM TO CONFIRM ACCOUNT
BALANCE INFORMATION WITH FINANCIAL INSTITUTIONS

ORIGINAL
To be mailed to accountant

The Runners Shop
CUSTOMER NAME

We have provided to our accountants the following information as of the close of the business on <u>December 31</u>, 20 <u>10</u>, regarding our deposit and loan balances. Please confirm the accuracy of the information, noting any exceptions to the information provided. If the balances have been left blank, please complete this form by furnishing the balance in the appropriate space below.* Although we do not request nor expect you to conduct a comprehensive, detailed search of your records, if during the process of completing this confirmation additional information about other deposit and loan accounts we may have with you comes to your attention, please include such information below. Please use the enclosed envelope to return the form directly to our accountants.

Financial Institution's Name and Address
[*National Bank and Trust*
100 Main Street
Roanoke, VA 24014]

[ ]

1. At the close of business on the date listed above, our records indicated the following deposit balance(s):

ACCOUNT NAME	ACCOUNT NO.	INTEREST RATE	BALANCE*
None			

2. We were directly liable to the financial institution for loans at the close of business on the date listed above as follows:

ACCOUNT NO./ DESCRIPTION	BALANCE*	DATE DUE	INTEREST RATE	DATE THROUGH WHICH INTEREST IS PAID	DESCRIPTION OF COLLATERAL
086-738950/ Installment Note	$66,053.47	Monthly Installments Matures 02/01/09	12%	12/01/10	None

_____
Robert Johnson
(Customer's Authorized Signature)

_____
12 / 31 / 10
(Date)

The information presented above by the customer is in agreement with our records. Although we have not conducted a comprehensive, detailed search of our records, no other deposit or loan accounts have come to our attention except as noted below.

_____
Brian G. Lender
(Financial Institution Authorized Signature)

_____
01 / 11 / 11
(Date)

Vice President of Loans
(Title)

EXCEPTIONS AND OR COMMENTS

No exceptions.

Please return this form directly to our accountants: [*Brown and Green, LLP*
1 Hill Street
Charlottesville, VA 22905]

[ ]

* Ordinarily, balances are intentionally left blank if they are not available at the time the form is prepared.

Approved 1990 by American Bankers Association, American Institute of Certified Public Accountants, Bank Administration Institute. Additional forms available from: AICPA – Order Department, P.O. Box 1003, NY, NY 10108-1003

D451 5951

Index: _____
Prepared by: _____
Date: _____

The Runners Shop
Audit Review Schedule
For 12/31/2010 Audit

#	Description of Deficiency
1)	*The tickmark legend on schedule FI 110 does not define PBC.*
2)	*No conclusion was noted on schedule FI 110 regarding the fair presentation of*
	Notes Payable (audit step 7).

Index: _____
Prepared by: _____
Date: _____

The Runners Shop
Audit Review Schedule
For 12/31/2010 Audit

#	Description of Deficiency

SECTION 12

Completing the Audit, Reporting to Management, and External Reporting

CASES INCLUDED IN THIS SECTION

EyeMax Corporation
Evaluation of Audit Differences

MARK S. BEASLEY · FRANK A. BUCKLESS · STEVEN M. GLOVER · DOUGLAS F. PRAWITT

LEARNING OBJECTIVES

After completing and discussing this case you should be able to

[1] Evaluate proposed adjustments to client financial statements

[2] Know how to support your decision to either record or exclude adjustments

[3] Appreciate the degree of judgment involved in determining a minimum adjustment, particularly when the client's preference is to not adjust

INTRODUCTION

The information below relates to the audit of EyeMax Corporation, a client with a calendar year-end. EyeMax has debt agreements associated with publicly traded bonds that require audited financial statements. The company is currently, and historically has been, in compliance with the covenants in the debt agreements. Further, management believes that having audited financial statements prepared in accordance with GAAP is important to shareholders and is "simply a good business practice."

Assume that audit fieldwork has been completed. At this point you are considering several items that have been posted to a "Summary of Unadjusted Misstatements." The Summary of Unadjusted Misstatements is a listing auditors compile during an audit as they uncover potential or proposed corrections to the client's financial statements. Additional detailed information about the items posted to the Summary of Unadjusted Misstatements is provided on the following pages. Based on the information provided, you will be asked to decide the minimum adjustment (if any) to the financial statements that would be necessary before issuing a "clean opinion."

Make sure you carefully consider materiality as you evaluate the misstatements because auditors do not require their clients to book immaterial adjustments. While it is considered best practice to correct errors discovered during the audit, there are situations where it is justifiable to make the corrections in the following period. Therefore, even if, for example, a client has followed a non-GAAP procedure, no adjustment would necessarily be required unless the impact is material (i.e., an individual adjustment(s) is greater than individual account tolerable misstatement or the aggregated sum of all misstatements is greater than overall materiality after considering relevant qualitative factors). At the end of this case you will also be asked several questions related to your decisions. Please carefully consider the following information before you answer the questions.

The case was prepared by Mark S. Beasley, Ph.D. and Frank A. Buckless, Ph.D. of North Carolina State University and Steven M. Glover, Ph.D. and Douglas F. Prawitt, Ph.D. of Brigham Young University, as a basis for class discussion. It was adapted from an article authored by D. Burgstahler, S. Glover, and J. Jiambalvo, *Auditing: A Journal of Practice and Theory*, (2000, Vol. 1, page 79). EyeMax is a fictitious company. All characters and names represented are fictitious; any similarity to existing companies or persons is purely coincidental.

BACKGROUND

Nature of client's business.

EyeMax is engaged in research and development, manufacture, and sale of medical devices used by ophthalmologists during eye surgeries. Customers of the product lines are primarily doctors of ophthalmology and laser-eye clinics. Wayne Carruth, MD, founded the company in 1986 to produce and market a line of devices he designed for use in optic surgery. Several years ago, EyeMax began to exploit the future prospects of laser technology in optic surgery. EyeMax has grown rapidly, especially in recent years, and has made significant strides in market share. EyeMax is currently the third largest supplier of optical equipment, with a 25 percent market share, and employs 425 people, up from only 285 employees just two years ago. Thirty percent of the stock in EyeMax is owned by Wayne Carruth and his immediate family. An additional 40 percent of the stock is owned by company employees, with the largest individual holding equal to about ten percent of the company's shares. Venture capitalists and a few outside investors hold the remaining shares. The company's shares currently trade on the over-the-counter bulletin-board market.[1]

Accounting environment, risk assessments, and audit approach.

The accounting department employs eight people with various backgrounds: the controller is a CPA, the accounting supervisor and payroll supervisor each have college degrees in business, and the remaining five clerks have limited training and experience. Although the company has no material weaknesses in internal controls, the accounting department has not kept pace with the demands created by growth in production and sales. The department is overworked. Key controls appear to be functioning but are not always performed on a timely basis. In the planning phase of the audit, both inherent risk and control risk were assessed at less than the maximum, but the audit plan specifies an audit approach that relies primarily on substantive testing.

Management's position regarding audit adjustments.

EyeMax has been an audit client for five years. Prior audits have generally detected accounting misstatements, and EyeMax's management has readily made the recommended adjustments. As the client has booked all identified prior-year differences, there are no "turn-around" effects to be considered from the prior year. However, in the past, audit reports have been dated before the end of February. This year, because of deadlines imposed by other clients and staffing problems at your audit firm, fieldwork at EyeMax was not completed by the end of February. Nonetheless, the president of EyeMax, without prior consultation with your firm, provided shareholders and creditors with preliminary earnings information in the last week of February. It is now the middle of March, and the president strongly prefers to minimize adjustments to the financial statements because he believes that such adjustments will unduly reduce shareholder and creditor confidence. In his opinion, no adjustment should be made unless it is absolutely essential for fair presentation. The managing partner of your office has been notified of the situation and the client's request. She has not yet reviewed the supporting detail presented below, but at this point she agrees that the audit team should not require adjustments be made unless the firm has no choice based on firm audit-practice standards.

Materiality.

For purposes of planning and conducting the audit, total financial statement materiality was set at $625,000. This amount is equal to approximately 5% of earnings before taxes. (Note that because materiality is stated on a before-tax basis, all of the information below is also presented on a before-tax basis.) According to firm policy, tolerable misstatement for any one financial statement account cannot exceed 75% of overall materiality.

---

1 The OTC Bulletin Board® (OTCBB) is a regulated quotation service that displays real-time quotes, last-sale prices, and volume information in over-the-counter (OTC) equity securities. An OTC equity security generally is any equity that is not listed or traded on NASDAQ or a national securities exchange. OTCBB securities include national, regional, and foreign equity issues, warrants, units, American Depositary Receipts, and Direct Participation Programs. For more information see www.otcbb.com.

MISSTATEMENTS POSTED TO THE SUMMARY OF UNADJUSTED MISSTATEMENTS

Four proposed adjustments are posted to the Summary of Unadjusted Misstatements. These differences are related to warranty expense, repair and maintenance expense, litigation expense, and accounts receivable. All items posted to the Summary of Unadjusted Misstatements have been discussed with the client and the client agrees with our (the auditors') position on each item. However, for the reasons discussed above, the client would prefer not to book any of the items in the fiscal year under audit. The first three adjustments have been calculated/estimated based on nonsampling procedures. Information about the last difference is based on audit sampling. A sample was selected from accounts receivables. The sample size was determined based on the tolerable misstatement for the account, the expected misstatement in the population tested, and the acceptable level of risk.

Warranty expense.

Warranty expense in the current year is estimated to be understated by $130,000 based on the following information: EyeMax grants a written one-year warranty for all products and estimates warranty expense based on current-year sales. However, during the last two years, the company has been making verbal commitments to repair or replace all products for a two-year period. The company has been complying with its verbal commitments and intends to continue the practice to improve customer relations. Because of this change in warranty policy, analysis of warranty repair and replacement data supports a $130,000 addition to the warranty expense estimate for the current year.

Repair and maintenance expense.

Repair expense in the current year is understated by $200,000. The client inappropriately capitalized $240,000 of cost related to modifications to its production process. Because the modifications were unsuccessful, the full amount should be written off in the current year. The client has included one-sixth of the capitalized amount in depreciation expense for the year; therefore, net of the amount included in depreciation expense for the current year, overall expense in the current year is understated by $200,000.

Litigation expense.

Product liability expense is overstated by $50,000. The client maintains product liability insurance with a $50,000 per occurrence deductible. The client has an excellent record relating to product liability. One liability case was pending at year-end and the client had conservatively accrued $50,000 at year-end to provide for the potential loss even though the likelihood of loss was remote. A judge ruled the case was without merit shortly after year-end.

Accounts Receivable.

The major audit work in the accounts receivable area was confirmation of customer balances. At year-end, EyeMax had receivables from 1,545 customers with a book value of approximately $12,600,000. Based on preliminary estimates, a random sample of 40 accounts was selected for positive confirmation. Customer-reported differences and alternative audit procedures applied to nonreplies revealed misstatements in four accounts that are detailed in Exhibit 1. The misstatements all appeared to be unintentional (e.g., using an incorrect price in billing). The net effect of the misstatements is an overstatement of Accounts Receivable (and Sales) at year-end.

EXHIBIT 1

Item Number	Customer Number	Customer Name	Balance Per Client	Balance Per Audit	Difference
1	998	Clear Vision Clinic	14,226	10,562	3,664
2	1963	South Cleveland Ophthalmologists	6,871	4,332	2,539
3	1133	Saint Luke's Medical Center	1,955	1,551	404
4	2479	Speedy Eye Center	25,587	23,532	2,055
5 to 40		All other receivables in sample	277,457	277,457	0
		Totals	**326,096**	**317,434**	**8,662**

SUMMARY OF UNADJUSTED MISSTATEMENTS

The following items have been recorded on the Summary of Unadjusted Misstatements:

	Known Misstatement
Warranty expense	130,000
Repair and maintenance expense	200,000
Litigation expense	(50,000)
Accounts Receivables (Sales)	8,662
Net overstatement of earnings	**$288,662**

REQUIRED (CONTINUED ON NEXT PAGE)

Assume that you are the auditor responsible for the EyeMax audit. It is now March 30, and all planned fieldwork has been completed. Recall that total financial statement materiality has been set at $625,000. Taking into account the information provided, please answer the following question.

[1] Which of the following three alternatives best describes the conditions under which you would issue a clean opinion for EyeMax? (select one)

_____ a. I would not be willing to issue a clean opinion even if EyeMax is willing to make adjustments for items on the Summary of Unadjusted Misstatements.

_____ b. I would be willing to issue a clean opinion without any adjustments.

_____ c. I would be willing to issue a clean opinion only if EyeMax is willing to make some adjustments to their financial statements for items on the Summary of Unadjusted Misstatements.

Briefly explain your choice:

CONTINUED ON NEXT PAGE

[2] If you selected options "a" or "b" in question 1, assume now that the client has decided that they will make an adjustment of up to $250,000 to their financial statements. Please decompose the total adjustment you would recommend into the individual account classifications included on the Summary of Unadjusted Misstatements in the space provided below (e.g., what adjustment would you require for warranty expense, repair and maintenance expense, etc? The dollar values of your individual account adjustments should sum to no more than $250,000).

If you selected item "c" in question 1, what is the minimum total adjustment that you would require before issuing a clean opinion? $ _____. Please decompose this total adjustment into the individual account classifications included on the Summary of Unadjusted Misstatements in the space provided below (e.g., what adjustment, if any, would you require for warranty expense, repair and maintenance expense, etc? The dollar values of your individual account adjustments should sum to your required minimum adjustment).

Warranty expense	_____
Repair and maintenance expense	_____
Litigation expense	_____
Accounts Receivables/Sales	_____
Total	_____

Please briefly explain your decisions:

Auto Parts, Inc.
Considering Materiality When Evaluating Accounting Policies and Footnote Disclosures

MARK S. BEASLEY · FRANK A. BUCKLESS · STEVEN M. GLOVER · DOUGLAS F. PRAWITT

LEARNING OBJECTIVES

After completing and discussing this case you should be able to

[1] Develop a reasonable estimate for financial statement materiality and identify qualitative issues that may affect materiality estimates

[2] Understand audit and footnote-disclosure issues associated with changes in accounting policies

[3] Evaluate the reasonableness of a client's proposed accounting and disclosure preference

BACKGROUND

Auto Parts, Inc. ("the Company") manufactures automobile subassemblies marketed primarily to the "big three" U.S. automakers. The publicly held Company's unaudited financial statements for the year ended December 31, 2011, reflect total assets of $56 million, total revenues of approximately $73 million, and pre-tax income of $6 million. The Company's audited financial statements for the year ended December 31, 2010, reflected total assets of $47 million, total revenues of approximately $60 million, and pre-tax income of $5 million. Earnings per share have increased steadily over the past five years, with a cumulative return of 140% over that period.

During 2011, the Company significantly expanded its plant and fixed asset spending to accommodate increased orders received by its brake valve division. The company also accumulated significant levels of tooling supplies, which primarily consist of drill bits and machine parts utilized in the manufacturing process. The nature of the tooling supplies is such that the parts wear out relatively quickly and require continual replacement.

In prior years, the Company expensed tooling supplies as they were purchased. However, at the beginning of 2011 the controller and chief financial officer (CFO) determined that capitalization of the tooling supplies would be the preferable method of accounting. The Company changed its accounting policy accordingly and began to include the tooling supplies in "other current assets" until the supplies are placed into service, at which time the Company enters a journal entry to remove the assets and record the costs of the used supplies as an expense.

During the prior year, 2010, the Company incurred roughly $650,000 of tooling expense and held approximately $35,000 of the tooling supplies on hand at year-end. The on-hand supplies were not included in assets on Auto Parts' balance sheet at December 31, 2010. The amount of supplies on hand at December 31, 2009 was trivial. In 2011 the Company purchased $1,330,000 of tooling supplies, of which the company used $1,000,000 during the year (in addition to the approximately $35,000 on hand at the beginning of the year). The increase of tooling supplies at year-end reflects the company's belief that prices would rise on the supplies in the first or second quarter of 2012.

The case was prepared by Mark S. Beasley, Ph.D. and Frank A. Buckless, Ph.D. of North Carolina State University and Steven M. Glover, Ph.D. and Douglas F. Prawitt, Ph.D. of Brigham Young University, as a basis for class discussion. Auto Parts, Inc. is a fictitious company. All characters and names represented are fictitious; any similarity to existing companies or persons is purely coincidental.

As such, the unaudited financial statements for the year ended December 31, 2011 reflect $1,000,000 of tooling expense on the income statement and $330,000 of tooling supplies as current assets on the balance sheet. The approximately $35,000 of tooling supplies on-hand at the end of last year were not included in the $1,000,000 tooling expense recorded in 2011 because those costs were expensed in 2010 under the old accounting policy.

Because your accounting firm serves as external auditor for Auto Parts, the CFO and the controller asked your firm for advice on whether the Company would be required to account for and disclose the accounting policy change as a change in accounting principle, a change in estimate, or an error correction. In the client's opinion, the change is not material to the financial statements and, therefore, would not require disclosure in the 2011 financial statements. The client strongly prefers to not make any disclosure related to the policy change, as such the 2010 comparative statements would not be adjusted and the 2011 statements would simply reflect the new policy (i.e., in 2011 there would be a decrease in expense and increase in other current assets relative to the prior accounting policy) without the added attention of a disclosure.

REQUIRED

[1] Describe whether you agree that capitalization of the tooling supplies is the preferable method of accounting for Auto Parts, Inc.

[2] Assuming the policy change is considered material, how should it be reported and disclosed in the 2011 financial statements and what would be the effect, if any, of the accounting change on the auditor's report?

[3] In general, how do auditors develop an estimate of financial statement materiality? For Auto Parts, Inc., what is your estimate of financial statement materiality? Are there qualitative factors that might impact your decision about the materiality of the accounting treatment and the related disclosure?

[4] Do you concur with management's assessment that the accounting change is immaterial and, therefore, requires no disclosure? Why or why not?

K&K, Inc.
Leveraging Audit Findings to Provide Value-Added Insights in a Manufacturing Environment

Mark S. Beasley · Frank A. Buckless · Steven M. Glover · Douglas F. Prawitt

LEARNING OBJECTIVES

After completing and discussing this case you should be able to

[1] List key issues to consider when auditing the production process and inventory balances for a manufacturing firm

[2] Understand the role of a manufacturing client's costing system in the context of a financial statement audit

[3] Understand how insights gained through the conduct of a financial statement audit can be used as a foundation to add additional value to auditing services provided for a client

[4] Leverage knowledge of concepts from many different disciplines to generate useful business insights for audit clients

INTRODUCTION

Spencer and Loveland, LLP is a medium-sized, regional accounting firm based in the western part of the United States. A new client of the firm, K&K, Inc., which manufactures a variety of picture frames, recently contracted with Spencer and Loveland to perform an audit of the company's financial statements for the year ended December 31, 2011. K&K, which is privately owned, expects to use the audited financial statements to obtain a more favorable line of credit with its bank.

Spencer and Loveland has a reputation for providing value to its clients above and beyond the high-quality auditing services the firm provides. The firm successfully looks for opportunities to leverage insights obtained during the audit as a basis for offering advice to its clients as a business advisor. K&K management is eager to receive Spencer and Loveland's financial advice, which is especially needed because the company's current accounting personnel primarily have clerical backgrounds. Thus, the audit engagement team has been instructed to generate suggestions that might help improve the growth and profitability of K&K, which have taken a turn for the worse during the past year.

K&K's original, labor-intensive custom-frame line appears to be struggling. Given rising costs for skilled labor over the past several years, K&K's production manager has long believed that it was only a matter of time before the company's older custom-frame line would begin to lose the long-term profitability it had enjoyed. He believes the custom line's declining profitability over the past year confirms the decision to expand the company's product line into new areas. At the beginning of last year, K&K invested in the RX-1000 system to mass-produce plastic frames. Internal cost accounting reports indicate that the new plastic-frame line has been quite profitable,

The case was prepared by Mark S. Beasley, Ph.D. and Frank A. Buckless, Ph.D. of North Carolina State University and Steven M. Glover, Ph.D. and Douglas F. Prawitt, Ph.D. of Brigham Young University, as a basis for class discussion. K&K is a fictitious company. All characters and names represented are fictitious; any similarity to existing companies or persons is purely coincidental.

despite operating at low volume levels relative to its capacity. The production manager recently recommended to K&K's president that the company consider discontinuing the labor-intensive custom-frame line to focus on expanding the less labor-intensive, higher-volume, higher-margin line of plastic frames.

You are a second-year audit senior at Spencer and Loveland. You and your audit staff are currently auditing the inventory and production costing systems at K&K. You and the junior staff auditor on the team have performed most of the audit procedures outlined on the audit program and have documented your findings in the audit papers.

As audit senior, you are responsible for reviewing the audit schedules and reporting to the audit engagement manager any areas of concern with respect to the audit. In addition, the manager asked you to analyze the client's inventory and production situation to indicate any areas where you believe the firm can provide value-added constructive suggestions to the client.

BACKGROUND

K&K, Inc. was founded 25 years ago when brothers Kent and Kevin Shaw started manufacturing custom-made picture frames for local artists using their father's workshop. They soon realized there was profit to be made in building large frames for use by painting and portrait studios. Over the years, K&K has become a well-known picture frame manufacturer in the western part of the United States, and has distinguished itself as a company that produces and sells high-quality picture frames. K&K manufactures and sells three basic sizes of frames, which are relatively large and ornate. K&K sells wholesale to portrait studios, retailers, and other users of large hardwood picture frames.

Due to the nature of the frames produced, the production process for custom frames at K&K is labor intensive. Most of the work is done essentially by hand, with the aid of specialized carving and shaping tools. Skilled workers use these tools to craft the wood pieces used in making the picture frames. K&K uses a traditional job-order costing system and allocates overhead costs to the frames on the basis of direct labor hours. While the company makes all sizes of frames, K&K's custom frames generally can be categorized into three basic sizes (small, medium, and large) that use a variety of designs and materials.

K&K has grown slowly over the past 25 years, generating reasonable profits along the way. Early last year, management decided to accelerate its growth by entering the market for smaller, mass-produced picture frames of the type sold in most craft and discount retail stores. The company first experimented with inexpensive metal frames. They purchased two used machines to produce these frames, which manufactured a large quantity of metal frames in a relatively short time. However, the frames produced were of varying quality and did not sell well. Thus, the machines remained idle through the second half of last year, and the company does not plan to produce any more of this type of frame.

K&K currently produces around 4,000 custom hardwood frames a month, or 48,000 a year. After the failed experiment with mass-produced metal frames, K&K invested in new machinery called the RX-1000 system. This new system is capable of producing standard-sized (5x7, 8x10, and 11x14 inch) plastic picture frames at a rate of up to 60,000 frames a month, with little variation in quality. The new machinery fit easily into K&K's existing plant facilities.

Even though the machinery was quite expensive, the plastic frame line is much less labor-intensive than the custom hardwood frame line. Based on the past year's cost data, the production manager is convinced that the new machinery will pay for itself in a matter of two or three years as production and sales volumes for the new frame line increase. Production volumes for the new frames averaged around 24,000 frames a month over the past year, which is close to the production level of 288,000 K&K had budgeted, but well below the RX-1000's capacity.

Sales prices on these mass-produced plastic frames are obviously much lower than those for the custom frames, but management expects to generate a reasonable profit through high-volume production and higher percentage profit margins. So far, K&K's internal data indicates that the new line is far more profitable than had been hoped even at current production volumes, with gross margins just under 50%. By contrast, the gross margin percentage for the custom frame line dropped from its usual average between 9% and 10% to an even more anemic 4.9% over the past year. The production foreman prepared a cost summary for the company's two product lines, which is provided on the pages that follow (see Exhibits 1 and 2).

The RX-1000 system consists of three machines integrated into a single system. The first machine mixes appropriate quantities of the resins and other liquid and powder materials needed to produce a molded plastic frame. The second machine injects the mixed raw materials into a large sheet of molds of a particular size, depending on the production run. When the material is cool, the machine breaks the hardened frames free of the molds, and the frames are then manually fed into the third stage. Here, the third machine polishes the frames to remove any burrs or tabs and inserts a clear, hard plastic sheet, which serves as a picture protector. Workers manually place a glossy paper picture of an attractive young couple behind the clear plastic in each frame (for marketing purposes), and the frames are then packaged for sale and shipment.

The RX-1000 system initially cost $400,000. Management estimates each of the three machines will have a useful life of six years. K&K depreciates the machinery using the straight-line method. These new machines do not require nearly as much direct labor as the custom frame line. Other than a specially trained employee to operate and monitor the system, the only manual labor required is to place the promotional photo and package the frames.

The system is costly to maintain, requiring regular maintenance every two weeks to keep it running effectively. Each regular maintenance cycle requires replacement of parts and lubricants, costing approximately $2,300 a month for labor and parts that must be replaced regularly. A breakdown of expected maintenance and other costs is found in the production foreman's analysis of production costs in the following pages.

Early on, the RX-1000 was so effective at mass-producing defect-free frames that management rented out an additional storage facility to hold the finished inventory produced by the new machinery. Later in the year, production rates had to be scaled back, and the system periodically sat idle until plastic frame inventories shrank to more reasonable levels. Management wants to be in a position to fill orders on a timely basis and avoid stock-outs, and thus is content to have a considerable amount of both finished goods and raw materials inventories on hand.

Inventory costs consist of direct materials, direct labor, and overhead. Overhead continues to be allocated to both product lines (i.e., the custom frames and the plastic frames) from a common, company-wide cost pool using direct labor hours as the activity base. Further detail on K&K's production costs are found in the following exhibits.

REQUIRED

[1] Briefly list and explain the primary audit risks in the production and inventory area of the K&K audit.

[2] Identify any accounting or auditing issues in the way K&K handles its product costs, including overhead allocation, that need to be addressed in the current audit.

[3] Review the analysis performed by K&K on the two product lines. K&K's management is debating the elimination of the manual line given that it is no longer profitable. Should K&K discontinue the labor-intensive custom frame product line? Why or why not?

[4] Based on your analysis, prepare a memo to the audit manager suggesting areas in K&K's inventory and production-costing systems where your firm could provide advice and value-added services to the client. In addition, given K&K is a non-public company, suggest any areas in which your firm might be able to provide consulting services that would be of value to the client.

EXHIBIT 1—COST BREAKDOWN

Direct Materials

Custom (cost per foot)[1]		Plastic (cost per oz.)[2]	
Maple	$ 1.90	Tan	$ 0.07
Oak	$ 2.60	Brown	$ 0.07
Cherry	$ 3.35	Black	$ 0.07

Glass or Plastic Sheeting (per unit)—Regular

Custom		Plastic	
Size Small	$ 4.75	Size 5x7	$ 0.08
Size Medium	$ 5.25	Size 8x10	$ 0.11
Size Large	$ 6.25	Size 11x14	$ 0.13

Glass or Plastic Sheeting (per unit)—Non-Glare

Custom		Plastic	
Size Small	$ 5.25	Size 5x7	$ 0.10
Size Medium	$ 6.00	Size 8x10	$ 0.13
Size Large	$ 7.35	Size 11x14	$ 0.16

Direct Labor

Custom				Plastic			
DL Rate / hour:	$ 16.00	Hrs./unit	Unit Labor Cost	DL Rate / hour:	$ 14.00	Hrs./unit	Unit Labor Cost
Size Small		1.0	$ 16.00	Size 5x7		0.015	$ 0.21
Size Medium		1.5	$ 24.00	Size 8x10		0.015	$ 0.21
Size Large		2.0	$ 32.00	Size 11x14		0.015	$ 0.21

Overhead per Direct Labor Hour

Budgeted Direct Labor Hours:[3]	76,320
Overhead Rate per Direct Labor Hour:[4]	$ 2.30 ($175,872 ÷ 76,320)

Breakdown of Overhead Costs

Production Facility Rent	$ 5,000 /month
Production Facility Utilities	$ 650 /month
Misc. Indirect Materials	$ 300 /month[5]
Sales Bonuses	$ 225 /month
Maintenance on RX-1000 system	$ 1,600 /month
Replacement Parts for RX-1000 system	$ 700 /month
Depreciation for RX-1000 system	$ 5,556 /month[6]
Depreciation for Custom Frame Machinery	$ 625 /month
Total **Annual** Overhead Costs	$ 175,872 /year

[1] Size Small requires 5 feet, Size Medium requires 8 feet, and Size Large requires 10 feet.

[2] Size 5x7 requires 2 oz., Size 8x10 requires 3 oz., and Size 11x14 requires 5 oz.

[3] Based on a production level of 48,000 custom frames and 288,000 plastic frames. K&K produces approximately equal proportions of the three frame sizes in both product lines.

[4] Overhead rate per DLH equals total annual overhead costs divided by budgeted total direct labor hours. Assume for simplicity that budgeted direct labor hours equal actual direct labor hours, and that budgeted costs equal actual costs. Thus, there is no over/under applied overhead for the year.

[5] Assume approximately 1/2 of indirect materials costs are attributable to each product line.

[6] $5,556=$400,000 ÷ 72 mos.

EXHIBIT 2—COMPARISON COST BREAKDOWN

CUSTOM

Total Costs	Size Small	Size Medium	Size Large
Maple w/ regular	$ 32.55	$ 47.91	$ 60.71
Maple w/ nonglare	$ 33.05	$ 48.66	$ 61.81
Oak w/ regular	$ 36.05	$ 53.51	$ 67.71
Oak w/ nonglare	$ 36.55	$ 54.26	$ 68.81
Cherry w/ regular	$ 39.80	$ 59.51	$ 75.21
Cherry w/ nonglare	$ 40.30	$ 60.26	$ 76.31

Sales Price (Wholesale)	Size Small	Size Medium	Size Large
Maple w/ regular	$ 32.50	$ 49.50	$ 66.00
Maple w/ nonglare	$ 33.50	$ 50.75	$ 68.00
Oak w/ regular	$ 35.00	$ 55.50	$ 73.00
Oak w/ nonglare	$ 36.00	$ 56.50	$ 75.00
Cherry w/ regular	$ 42.75	$ 62.00	$ 81.00
Cherry w/ nonglare	$ 43.75	$ 63.00	$ 83.00

Margin	Size Small	Size Medium	Size Large
Maple w/ regular	$ (0.05)	$ 1.59	$ 5.29
Maple w/ nonglare	$ 0.45	$ 2.09	$ 6.19
Oak w/ regular	$ (1.05)	$ 1.99	$ 5.29
Oak w/ nonglare	$ (0.55)	$ 2.24	$ 6.19
Cherry w/ regular	$ 2.95	$ 2.49	$ 5.79
Cherry w/ nonglare	$ 3.45	$ 2.74	$ 6.69

PLASTIC

Total Costs	Size 5x7	Size 8x10	Size 11x14
Tan w/ regular	$ 0.46	$ 0.56	$ 0.72
Tan w/ nonglare	$ 0.48	$ 0.58	$ 0.75
Brown w/ regular	$ 0.46	$ 0.56	$ 0.72
Brown w/ nonglare	$ 0.48	$ 0.58	$ 0.75
Black w/ regular	$ 0.46	$ 0.56	$ 0.72
Black w/ nonglare	$ 0.48	$ 0.58	$ 0.75

Sales Price (Wholesale)	Size 5x7	Size 8x10	Size 11x14
Tan w/ regular	$ 0.70	$ 0.85	$ 1.00
Tan w/ nonglare	$ 0.75	$ 0.90	$ 1.07
Brown w/ regular	$ 0.70	$ 0.85	$ 1.00
Brown w/ nonglare	$ 0.75	$ 0.90	$ 1.07
Black w/ regular	$ 0.70	$ 0.85	$ 1.00
Black w/ nonglare	$ 0.75	$ 0.90	$ 1.07

Margin	Size 5x7	Size 8x10	Size 11x14
Tan w/ regular	$ 0.24	$ 0.29	$ 0.28
Tan w/ nonglare	$ 0.27	$ 0.32	$ 0.32
Brown w/ regular	$ 0.24	$ 0.29	$ 0.28
Brown w/ nonglare	$ 0.27	$ 0.32	$ 0.32
Black w/ regular	$ 0.24	$ 0.29	$ 0.28
Black w/ nonglare	$ 0.27	$ 0.32	$ 0.32

K&K arrived at the per unit margin numbers by using the following summarized unit cost data :

CUSTOM

Wood	Size Small	Size Medium	Size Large
Maple	$ 9.50	$ 15.20	$ 19.00
Oak	$ 13.00	$ 20.80	$ 26.00
Cherry	$ 16.75	$ 26.80	$ 33.50

Glass			
Regular	$ 4.75	$ 5.25	$ 6.25
Nonglare	$ 5.25	$ 6.00	$ 7.35

Labor	$ 16.00	$ 24.00	$ 31.00

Overhead[1]	$ 2.30	$ 3.46	$ 4.46

PLASTIC

Plastic	Size 5x7	Size 8x10	Size 11x14
Tan	$ 0.14	$ 0.21	$ 0.35
Brown	$ 0.14	$ 0.21	$ 0.35
Black	$ 0.14	$ 0.21	$ 0.35

Glass			
Regular	$ 0.08	$ 0.11	$ 0.13
Nonglare	$ 0.10	$ 0.13	$ 0.16

Labor	$ 0.21	$ 0.21	$ 0.21

Overhead[1]	$ 0.03	$ 0.03	$ 0.03

[1] Overhead is allocated based on Direct Labor Hours from a common cost pool.

Surfer Dude Duds, Inc.
Considering the Going-Concern Assumption

MARK S. BEASLEY · FRANK A. BUCKLESS · STEVEN M. GLOVER · DOUGLAS F. PRAWITT

LEARNING OBJECTIVES

After completing and discussing this case you should be able to

[1] Appreciate and articulate the complexities involved in assessing the going-concern assumption for a client

[2] Describe the "self-fulfilling prophecy" aspect of an auditor's report that includes a going-concern paragraph

[3] Identify factors that encourage objective auditor judgments despite the presence of friendly client-auditor relationships

BACKGROUND

Mark glanced up at the clock on his office wall. It read 2:30 P.M. He had scheduled a 3:00 P.M. meeting with George "Hang-ten" Baldwin, chief executive officer of Surfer Dude Duds, Inc. Surfer Dude specialized in selling clothing and accessories popularized by the California "surfer" culture. Mark had served as audit partner on the Surfer Dude Duds audit for the past six years and was about ready to wrap up this year's engagement.

He enjoyed a strong client relationship with George Baldwin, who was ordinarily a relaxed and easygoing man, now going on 50 years of age. For several years running, Mark had received a personal invitation from George to attend a special Christmas party held only for George's employees and close associates. Mark considered George a good friend.

In his six years on the audit, Mark had never had any reason to give anything but a clean audit opinion for Surfer Dude Duds, Inc. But this year was different. The economy was in a mild recession, and given the faddishness of clothing trends, Surfer Dude's retail chain was hurting. As sales decreased, Surfer Dude was struggling to meet all its financial obligations. Retail analysts foresaw continuing hard times for clothing retailers in general, and current fashion trends did not seem to be moving in Surfer Dude's direction. As a result, Mark was beginning to doubt Surfer Dude's ability to stay in business through the next year. In fact, after conferring with the concurring partner on the audit, Mark was reluctantly considering the addition of a going-concern explanatory paragraph to the audit report. When Mark broached this possibility with George several weeks ago, George brushed him off.

The purpose of the scheduled 3:00 P.M. meeting was to inform George of the decision to issue a going-concern report and to discuss the footnote disclosure of the issue. Mark went over in his mind several times what he was going to say, but remained uneasy about the task before him.

When Mark arrived at George Baldwin's office, a secretary greeted him and told Mr. Baldwin of Mark's arrival. When Mark heard George say, "Send him in," he took a deep breath and headed into George's office with a smile on his face. George was sprawled out in a large executive chair,

This case was prepared by Mark S. Beasley, Ph.D. and Frank A. Buckless, Ph.D. of North Carolina State University and Steven M. Glover, Ph.D. and Douglas F. Prawitt, Ph.D. of Brigham Young University, as a basis for class discussion. The case was inspired by discussions with Craig Isom, a former audit partner, and we gratefully acknowledge his contribution to its development. Surfer Dude Duds is a fictitious company. All characters and names represented are fictitious; any similarity to existing companies or persons is purely coincidental.

with his ever-present smile. Mark always marveled at how a person could invariably seem so relaxed and happy. "Hey Mark, what's up? You know I don't like meetings on Friday afternoons," George yawned.

"Well George, I'll get right to the point. As you well know, the retail clothing market has really gone south the past few months. I know I don't need to tell you that Surfer Dude is struggling right now."

"I know, but we'll pull out of it," George said. "When you wipe out, you've got to climb right back on to ride the next bomb, right? We always manage to come out on top. We just need to ride this one out, just like the other tough times we've been through."

"George, I know you're optimistic that things will get better soon, but this time things are a little different," Mark sighed. "I know you well enough to know that you might just be able to pull the company out of this. But given the circumstances, I think we're going to have to look at including a going-concern explanatory paragraph in the audit report. There is a non-trivial possibility that Surfer Dude will not be able to continue as a going concern for the next year. I also recommend that you include a footnote in your financial statements to the same effect."

"What? Mark, you can't go slapping a going-concern report on me! Surfer Dude will go belly-up for sure. No one will be willing to loan us any money. Shoot, nobody will even be willing to sell us anything on account—all our inventory purchases and everything else will be C.O.D. It'll be cash-and-carry only. And what about our customers? Will they buy if they're not sure we'll be there to stand behind our return policy? It'll be your report that puts us under, not the ripples we're hitting now. I've got a feeling things are going to get better soon. We just need a little more time."

"George, you've got to consider the consequences if...."

"Mark, if you slap me with a going-concern report, there is no way we'll be able to pull out of this. Think of all the people who will lose their jobs if Surfer Dude shuts down. Please, I'm asking you to think hard about this." George's ever-present smile was gone.

Mark was silent for what seemed even to him like an eternity. "Okay George, let's both think about it over the weekend. I'll drop by on Monday morning so we can figure out where to go from here. Thanks for your time."

Mark walked slowly out of the building and to his car. This was not going to be a relaxing weekend.

REQUIRED

[1] What are Mark's options?

[2] How might a going-concern explanatory paragraph become a "self-fulfilling prophecy" for Surfer Dude?

[3] What potential implications arise for the accounting firm if they issue an unqualified report without the going-concern explanatory paragraph?

[4] Discuss the importance of full and accurate auditor reporting to the public, and describe possible consequences for *both* parties if the going-concern explanatory paragraph and footnote are excluded. How might Mark convince George that a going-concern report is in the best interests of all parties involved?

[5] Is it appropriate for an audit partner to have a friendly personal relationship with a client? At what point could a personal relationship become an independence issue?

[6] What factors might motivate Mark to be objective in his decision, despite his personal concern for his friend?

[7] In your opinion, what should Mark do? Briefly justify your position and explain how you would approach George on Monday.

Murchison Technologies, Inc.
Evaluating an Attorney's Response
and Identifying the Proper Audit Report

MARK S. BEASLEY · FRANK A. BUCKLESS · STEVEN M. GLOVER · DOUGLAS F. PRAWITT

LEARNING OBJECTIVES

After completing and discussing this case you should be able to

[1] Understand the role and timing of client attorney responses to the auditor

[2] Interpret information contained in an attorney's response letter

[3] Evaluate proper accounting treatment for material uncertainties

[4] Identify the correct audit report in light of varying circumstances

INTRODUCTION

Murchison Technologies, Inc. recently developed a patient-billing software system that it markets to physicians and dentists. Jim Archer and Janice Johnson founded the company in Austin, Texas five years ago after working at IBM for more than 15 years. Jim worked as a software programmer and Janice worked as a sales representative, frequently calling on stand-alone medical practices. Together, they identified a need for software to help physician and dental offices track charges for patient services provided by doctors and their staff. With the initial backing of three local venture capitalists, they left IBM, created Murchison Technologies, and devoted their full-time efforts to the development of the billing system software.

For more than three years, they worked on developing the software. After extensive pilot testing, the company shipped its first product to customers in early 2009. Sales have been surprisingly strong for the product, which is marketed as MEDTECH Software. Feedback from physicians and dentists has been extremely positive. Most note that billing clerks and office staff find the system quite flexible in tracking numerous types of services for large numbers of patients. Most are pleased with the ability to customize system features for their unique practice needs. Another key to the product's success is the relative cost of the software and the minimal upgrades required of the office microcomputers and networks to operate the software.

The company has gradually added employees to its staff. Currently, Murchison employs about 60 people, including software programmers who continually update the software for emerging technological developments. Janice serves as chief executive officer (CEO), and Jim serves as president. While both serve on the board of directors, they ultimately are accountable to the board, which also includes representatives from the three venture capitalists and two local bankers who financed company expansions through commercial loans issued three years ago. Murchison continues to be privately held.

The case was prepared by Mark S. Beasley, Ph.D. and Frank A. Buckless, Ph.D. of North Carolina State University and Steven M. Glover, Ph.D. and Douglas F. Prawitt, Ph.D. of Brigham Young University, as a basis for class discussion. Murchison is a fictitious company. All characters and names represented are fictitious; any similarity to existing companies or persons is purely coincidental.

Your firm, Custer & Custer, LLP, was first engaged by Murchison to perform a review of its December 31, 2008 financial statements. In the subsequent year, the company engaged your firm to conduct the audit of its December 31, 2009 financial statements to fulfill requirements of the loan agreements. Custer & Custer issued standard, unqualified reports on both the 2009 and 2010 annual financial statements.

BACKGROUND

Your firm is in the process of completing the audit of the December 31, 2011 financial statements. Currently it is February 17, 2012 and most of the detailed audit testing is complete. As audit senior, you are wrapping up the review of staff audit files. The partner anticipates performing the review and signing off on audit files tomorrow. This should provide plenty of time for the audit team to complete the gathering and evaluation of audit evidence in the next day or two.

In preparation for completion of the audit, you recently worked with the client to send requests to outside legal counsel asking them to provide the standard attorney letter response regarding material outstanding claims against the company. You sent requests for attorney confirmations to three law firms providing legal representation for the company.

Based on all the audit work performed, you do not expect any substantive issues related to outstanding litigation claims against Murchison. Your only concern relates to an alleged copyright infringement claim against Murchison that apparently was filed in October 2011. You learned about this case during your review of the November 2011 minutes of the board of directors' meeting. The minutes made reference to the case being filed; however, based on notations about the board's discussion it appeared to you that the probability of an unsuccessful outcome related to this case is extremely low. Apparently, another software development company, Physicians Software, Inc., claims that Murchison's MEDTECH software violates a copyright held by Physicians Software. They are suing Murchison for $260,000.

Your subsequent inquiries of management about the case confirmed your expectation of a very low likelihood of unfavorable outcome. In addition, management believes the claim is immaterial relative to the December 31, 2011 financial statements. Those financial statements indicate that Murchison's total assets as of December 31, 2011 were $8.3 million, with revenues of $26 million and pretax income of $2.1 million for the year then ended.

You received two of the attorney confirmation letters in the mail yesterday. Your review of the attorney responses produced no surprises. Most of the issues being handled by those attorneys relate to collection efforts on delinquent receivables. Those same firms also helped management develop contracts for special sales agreements with two new customers.

One of your audit staff members just delivered mail from the office after running by the office during lunch to pick up a few supplies. You are pleased to see that today's mail includes the attorney confirmation from the third law firm. You quickly open the envelope to make sure everything is okay. You begin reading the letter, which is presented in the pages that follow.

You are a little surprised to read the attorney's assessment of the case, and some of the language referencing American Bar Association (ABA) policies puzzles you. You quickly link to professional standards stored on your laptop to review the relevant ABA policy statements. An excerpt of those statements, which are presented as an appendix to the auditing standard that addresses inquiries of the client's lawyer, is presented in Exhibit 1 on the pages that follow.

You want to closely evaluate the information contained in the letter to prepare for a meeting with the partner regarding possible accounting treatments and audit reporting issues. It is also likely that the partner will want to discuss those issues with Murchison's management. In order to properly prepare, please complete the items noted on the next page.

REQUIRED

[1] Review the requirements of Statement of Financial Accounting Standards (SFAS) that address the accounting for contingencies. Describe the three ranges of loss contingencies outlined in the accounting standards and summarize briefly the accounting and disclosure requirements for each of the three ranges.

[2] Based on your review of the attorney's confirmation, which of the three ranges of probability of loss do you think the Physicians Software Inc., claim falls? How does that assessment differ from management's assessment of the loss probability?

[3] Assuming that management and the attorney's assessments differ, how would you resolve such differences when assessing the potential for an unfavorable outcome associated with the claim? What are the pros and cons of relying on the attorney's assessment versus management's assessment?

[4] In preparation for tomorrow's meeting with the partner and likely subsequent meeting with Murchison management, develop recommended responses to the following possible scenarios. In developing your responses, assume that each scenario is independent of the others:

[a] If generally accepted accounting principles require disclosure of this contingency, how would you respond to management's decision against disclosure because they view the claim as immaterial to the December 31, 2011 financial statements? Do you believe the potential loss is material? Why or why not?

[b] Assume that even though you convince management that the claim is material, they refuse to provide any disclosure that might be required. Prepare a draft of the auditor's report that would be issued in that scenario.

[c] Assume that you determine, through subsequent discussions with the attorney, that a more likely estimate of the range of loss falls between $35,000 and $55,000. What type of financial statement disclosure do you believe is required in that case? Prepare a draft of the auditor's report that you would issue in that scenario.

[d] What if you learn that management has pertinent information available about the case (and the case is deemed material) but refuses to share that information with you? Prepare a draft of the auditor's report that you would issue in that scenario.

[e] Assume that you convinced management to disclose the contingency in the footnotes to the December 31, 2011 financial statements and that your audit report on those financial statements was a standard, unqualified audit report. What would your responsibilities be if you learned two months after the issuance of the report that Murchison settled the case for $225,000?

[f] Assume that the settlement of the litigation prohibits future sales of MEDTECH software. What implication would that have on the auditor's report on the December 31, 2011 financial statements?

[5] Discuss why the attorney's letter is being received so close to the completion of the audit. Was the request for the attorney's response an oversight that should have been taken care of closer to December 31, 2011, or was Custer & Custer appropriate in not requesting the response until close to the end of the audit?

[6] Assume that Custer & Custer was delayed a month in completing the collection of audit evidence. What actions would be appropriate relating to gathering evidence about potential contingencies?

[7] Review the ABA policy statement excerpts in Exhibit 1. What limitations exist as it relates to the attorney's response? To what extent should auditors rely solely on attorney responses to identify outstanding claims against audit clients?

Dunn & King, PLLC
First National Tower, Suite 2300
200 Church Street
Austin, Texas 78701

February 16, 2012

Custer & Custer, LLP
City National Plaza
16th Floor
435 Seventh Avenue, South
Austin, Texas 78702

Dear Sirs:

By letter dated, February 4, 2012, Mr. James Archer, President of Murchison Technologies, Inc., (the "Company") has requested us to furnish you with certain information in connection with your examination of the accounts of the Company as of December 31, 2011.

Subject to the foregoing and to the last paragraph of this letter, we advise you that since January 1, 2011 we have not been engaged to give substantive attention to, or represent the Company in connection with material loss contingencies coming within the scope of clause (a) of Paragraph 5 of the ABA Statement of Policy referred to in the last paragraph of this letter, except as follows:

On October 16, 2011, a suit was filed naming Murchison Technologies, Inc. as defendant in an alleged copyright infringement claim. The plaintiff, Physicians Software, Inc., ("Physicians") alleges that Murchison's MEDTECH software violates Physicians' copyright registered for Physicians' PHYSITRACK software. The PHYSITRACK software also is marketed as a medical-practice billing system software and is a direct competitor of Murchison. The pending litigation claim alleges that Murchison violated Physicians' copyright protection in the development of the MEDTECH software. Allegedly, a former software development programmer of Physicians was hired away by Murchison four years ago when Murchison was in the development phase of the MEDTECH software. Physicians claims that trade secrets on its PHYSITRACK software were pirated from Physicians and incorporated into the design of the MEDTECH software. The plaintiff is seeking damages of $260,000.

In preparation of providing this letter to you, we have reviewed the merits of the claim against Murchison, which is currently in the deposition phase. At this time, our assessment of the likelihood of a negative future outcome occurring against Murchison in this case, is more than remote but less than likely. The possible ranges of costs and damages are estimated to extend from $190,000 to $240,000.

The information set forth herein is as of February 16, 2012, the date on which we commenced our internal review procedures for purposes of preparing this letter, and we disclaim any undertaking to advise you of changes which thereafter may be brought to your attention.

This response is limited by, and in accordance with, the ABA Statement of Policy Regarding Lawyer's Responses to Auditor's Requests for Information (December 1975); without limiting the generality of the foregoing, the limitations set forth in such Statement on the scope and use of this response (Paragraphs 2 and 7) are specifically incorporated herein by reference, and any description herein of any "loss contingencies" is qualified in its entirety by Paragraph 5 of the Statement and the accompanying Commentary (which is an integral part of the Statement).

Consistent with the sentence of Paragraph 6 of the ABA Statement of Policy and pursuant to the Company's request, this will confirm as correct the Company's understanding as set forth in its audit inquiry letter to us that whenever, in the course of performing legal services for the Company with respect to a matter recognized to involve an unasserted possible claim or assessment that may call for financial statement disclosure, we have formed a professional conclusion that the Company must disclose or consider disclosure concerning such possible claim or assessment, we, as a matter of professional responsibility to the Company, will so advise the Company and will consult with the Company concerning the question of such disclosure and the applicable requirements of Statement of Financial Accounting Standards.

Very truly yours,

Dunn & King, PLLC

Austin, Texas

EXHIBIT 1

American Bar Association Statement on Policy Regarding Lawyers' Responses
to Auditor's Requests for Information[1]

Paragraph 2 – Limitations of Scope of Response

It is appropriate for the lawyer to set forth in his response, by way of limitation, the scope of his engagement by the client. It is also appropriate for the lawyer to indicate the date as of which information is furnished and to disclaim any undertaking to advise the auditor of changes which may thereafter be brought to the lawyer's attention. Unless the lawyer's response indicates otherwise, (a) it is properly limited to matters which have been given substantive attention by the lawyer in the form of legal consultation and, where appropriate, legal representation since the beginning of the period or periods being reported upon, and (b) if a law firm or a law department, the auditor may assume that the firm or department has endeavored, to the extent believed necessary by the firm or department, to determine from lawyers currently in the firm or department who have performed services for the client since the beginning of the fiscal period under audit whether such services involved substantive attention in the form of legal consultation concerning those contingencies referred to in Paragraph 5(a) below, but beyond that, no review has been made of any of the client's transactions or other matters for the purpose of identifying loss contingencies to be described in the response.

Paragraph 5 – Loss Contingencies

When properly requested by the client, it is appropriate for the lawyer to furnish to the auditor information concerning the following matters if the lawyer has been engaged by the client to represent or advise the client professionally with respect thereto and he has devoted substantive attention to them in the form of legal representation or consultation:

a. overtly threatened or pending litigation, whether or not specified by the client;
b. a contractually assumed obligation which the client has specifically identified and upon which the client has specifically requested, in the inquiry letter or a supplement thereto, comment to the auditor;
c. an unasserted possible claim or assessment which the client has specifically identified and upon which the client has specifically requested, in the inquiry letter or a supplement thereto, comment to the auditor....

Paragraph 6 – Lawyer's Professional Responsibility

Independent of the scope of his response to the auditor's request for information, the lawyer, depending upon the nature of the matters as to which he is engaged, may have as part of his professional responsibility to his client an obligation to advise the client concerning the need for or advisability of public disclosure of a wide range of events and circumstances. The lawyer has an obligation not knowingly to participate in any violation by the client of the disclosure requirements of the securities laws. In appropriate circumstances, the lawyer also may be required under the Code of Professional Responsibility to resign his engagement if his advice concerning disclosures is disregarded by the client. The auditor may properly assume that whenever, in the course of performing legal services for the client with respect to a matter recognized to involve an unasserted possible claim or assessment which may call for financial statement disclosure, the lawyer has formed a professional conclusion that the client must disclose or consider disclosure concerning such possible claim or assessment, the lawyer, as a matter of professional responsibility to the client, will so advise the client and will consult with the client concerning the question of such disclosure and the applicable requirements of FAS 5.

---

1   Source: Clarified Auditing Standards (AU) Section 501, Audit Evidence - Special Considerations for Selected Items.

Paragraph 7 – Limitation on Use of Response

Unless otherwise stated in the lawyer's response, it shall be solely for the auditor's information in connection with his audit of the financial condition of the client and is not to be quoted in whole or in part or otherwise referred to in any financial statements of the client or related documents, nor is it to be filed with any governmental agency or other person, without the lawyer's prior written consent. Notwithstanding such limitation, the response can be furnished to others in compliance with court process or when necessary to defend the auditor against a challenge of the audit by the client or a regulatory agency, provided that the lawyer is given written notice of the circumstances at least twenty days before the response is so to be furnished to others, or as long in advance as possible if the situation does not permit such period of notice.

Going Green
Sustainability and External Reporting

Mark S. Beasley · Frank A. Buckless · Steven M. Glover · Douglas F. Prawitt

LEARNING OBJECTIVES

After completing and discussing this case you should be able to

[1] Describe the major elements that should be included in a sustainability report following the Global Reporting Initiative (GRI) framework

[2] Describe the potential advantages and disadvantages associated with sustainability reporting

[3] Describe the types of assurance services accountants can provide to clients issuing sustainability reports to external parties

[4] Describe potential advantages and disadvantages of obtaining third party assurances about corporate sustainability reports

[5] Describe major challenges for accountants who may be asked to issue an assurance report on corporate sustainability reporting

[6] Evaluate a corporate sustainability report using the GRI framework

INTRODUCTION

A 2011 Gallup Poll[1] survey regarding Americans' concerns about environmental issues revealed the following:

Tell me if you personally worry about this problem a great deal, fair amount, only a little or not at all?	Worry Great Deal/ Fair Amount	Worry Little/ Not At All
Contamination of soil and water by toxic waste	79%	20%
Pollution of rivers, lake and reservoirs	79%	22%
Pollution of drinking water	77%	23%
Maintenance of nation's supply of fresh water for household needs	75%	24%
Air pollution	72%	28%
Extinction of plant and animal species	64%	36%
The loss of tropical rain forests	63%	35%
Urban sprawl and loss of open spaces	57%	42%
Global warming	51%	48%

Given results of surveys like the one above, it shouldn't be surprising that more and more business leaders are concerned with how their business is impacting the environment and increasingly want to demonstrate that they are being good stewards of the environment.

---

1 Saad, Lydia. "Water Issues Worry Americans Most, Global Warming Least" *Gallup.* March 28, 2011. See the following website: http://www.gallup.com/poll/146810/Water-Issues-Worry-Americans-Global-Warming-Least.aspx

The case was prepared by Mark S. Beasley, Ph.D. and Frank A. Buckless, Ph.D. of North Carolina State University and Steven M. Glover, Ph.D. and Douglas F. Prawitt, Ph.D. of Brigham Young University, as a basis for class discussion. It is not intended to illustrate either effective or ineffective handling of an administrative situation.

BACKGROUND

The term "sustainability" means different things to different people. A traditional view of sustainability is to "... meet society's present needs without compromising the ability of future generations to meet their own needs."[2] In this context, sustainability is concerned with meeting economic and social needs of society while minimizing negative environmental impacts. From a business perspective, sustainability is often viewed differently as the ability of a business organization to sustain its operations over the long term. From this perspective, the goal of sustainability is to create long term shareholder and social value while reducing the usage of nonrenewable resources and minimizing the negative environmental impacts. To achieve this goal, business organizations must employ practices that integrate economic, social and environmental considerations into their decision processes.

Paying attention to sustainability issues is not just a moral issue. Why else are business organizations showing growing interest in sustainability issues? Many are realizing that creating shareholder value doesn't have to be a trade-off between economic, social, and environmental factors. Instead, shareholder value can be enhanced by capturing the synergy between economic, social, and environmental factors. Business leaders are recognizing that a focus on sustainability can create competitive advantage.

What is the business case for implementing sustainability practices? Esty and Simmons identify four potential benefits of incorporating sustainability into a business organization's strategy. Those benefits are:[3]

- Operating cost reductions and efficiency gains.
- Environmental risk reductions.
- Revenue growth.
- Intangible value growth.

Operating cost reductions and efficiency gains can be achieved by elimination or reduction of scrap, waste, energy usage, and other reduced costs through regulatory compliance (e.g., avoidance of penalties and fines). Reductions of waste and pollution emissions help mitigate environmental risks thus minimizing government fines, product recalls and diminished brand/customer loyalty. Development of products that are viewed positively from an environmental perspective can provide a business organization competitive advantage with customers who are especially focused on the impact of the business on the environment. Other intangible benefits achieved by having a strategic focus on sustainability include improved brand/customer loyalty and improved attraction, retention and productivity of employees.

A recent survey of United Kingdom and North American business organizations conducted by the Chartered Institute of Management Accountants (CIMA), American Institute of Certified Public Accountants (AICPA) and Canadian Institute of Chartered Accountants (CICA) indicates that over two-thirds of the responding organizations measure some aspect of their sustainability efforts.[4] While most of the business organizations measure some aspect of their sustainability efforts, less than one-third of the respondents externally report sustainability information and only a third of those have a third party provide assurance on that sustainability information.

The 2010 GRI Sustainability Reporting Statistics publication[5] reveals that the number of business organizations issuing external sustainability reports has increased every year since 1999. In

---

2   U.S. Environmental Protection Agency. "Sustainability: Basic Information" See the following website: http://www.epa.gov/sustainability/basicinfo.htm#sustainability

3   Esty, Daniel C. and P. J. Simmons. "The Green to Gold Business Playbook." *John Wiley and Sons, Inc.* 2011.

4   AICPA, CICA and CIMA. "Evolution of corporate sustainability practices." December 2010. See the following website: http://www.aicpa.org/InterestAreas/BusinessIndustryAndGovernment/Resources/Sustainability/DownloadableDocuments/EvolutionofCorporateSustainabilityPractices.pdf

5   Global Reporting Initiative. "GRI Sustainability Reporting Statistics." 2010. See the following website: http://www.globalreporting.org/NR/rdonlyres/23A1D934-64BF-4934-ACB5-43CD4A41E48A/0/GRIReportingStats.pdf

1999, less than 200 organizations issued external sustainability reports while over 1,800 organizations issued external sustainability reports in 2010. This publication also reveals that the number of organizations obtaining third-party assurance on their sustainability information is growing. Finally, this publication highlights that organizations with a more comprehensive sustainability report are much more likely to obtain third party assurance on their sustainability information. As business organizations become more comfortable with measuring and reporting sustainability information, requests for assurance services on sustainability information will likely grow.

SUSTAINABILITY REPORTING GUIDELINES

Currently there is no generally accepted reporting standard for corporate sustainability reporting. The most widely used reporting guidelines for corporate sustainability reporting is the framework issued by the Global Reporting Initiative (GRI).[6] The GRI was started in 1997 by the non-profit organization "Coalition for Environmentally Responsible Economies" (CERES) based out of Boston, Massachusetts. Today the GRI is an independent organization, based out of Amsterdam, Netherlands, with the mission to "... make sustainability reporting standard practice by providing guidance and support to organizations."[7]

POTENTIAL ASSURANCE ENGAGEMENT

Several clients have approached your accounting firm, Green and Brown, LLP, about the possibility of engaging your firm to provide assurance on their sustainability report. One of the audit partners, Annette Crossland, asked you to conduct some background research on the feasibility of Green and Brown expanding its service lines to include assurances on corporate environmental and social performance reports.

REQUIRED (CONTINUED ON NEXT PAGE)

[1] Go to the Global Reporting Initiative's website (try http://www.globalreporting.org) and read the G3.1 Reporting Guidelines. What are the three types of standard disclosures and what type of information is included under each type of standard disclosure?

[2] Go to the Global Reporting Initiative's website (try http://www.globalreporting.org) and read the G3.1 Application Levels. What are the major differences between the three application levels? The G3.1 Application Levels identifies six key qualities for having external assurance provided on the sustainability report. What are the six key qualities and how do they compare to the ten generally accepted auditing standards for audits of financial statements?

[3] Read AICPA Attestation Standard Sections 50 and 101. What types of engagements do the attestation standards cover? Would the attestation standards allow accountants to provide assurance on an organization's sustainability report? Explain your answer. What level of assurance is allowed with the attestation standards? How do the eleven generally accepted attestation standards compare to the G3.1 Application Level six key qualities in terms of having external assurance provided on the sustainability report?

[4] Read International Standard on Assurance Engagements (ISAE) 3000. What types of engagements does ISAE 3000 cover? Would ISAE 3000 allow accountants to provide assurance on an organization's sustainability report? Explain your answer. What level of assurance is allowed with ISAE 3000? How do requirements for performing an assurance engagement using ISAE 3000 compare to the requirements for performing an assurance engagement using the

---

6   See the following website: http://www.globalreporting.org/Home
7   Global Reporting Initiative. "Mission." See the following website:
   http://www.globalreporting.org/AboutGRI/WhatIsGRI/VisionAndMission.htm

AICPA Attestation Standards? How do requirements for performing an assurance engagement using ISAE 3000 compare to the requirements for performing an audit of financial statements? How do the requirements for performing an assurance engagement using ISAE 3000 compare to the G3.1 Application Level six key qualities in terms of having external assurance provided on the sustainability report?

[5] Based on what you have read related to sustainability reporting, what do you believe are the possible advantages and disadvantages associated with issuing a sustainability report to external stakeholders? What do you believe are the major reasons why some business organizations are reluctant to issue sustainability reports to external stakeholders?

[6] Based on what you have read related to sustainability reporting, what do you believe are the possible advantages and disadvantages associated with having a third party provide assurance on a business organization's sustainability report? What do you believe are the major reasons why some business organizations are reluctant to have third party assurance provided on their sustainability report? What are the key challenges for accountants who might be asked to issue an attestation report on a business organization's sustainability report?

[7] The 2010 GRI Sustainability Reporting Statistics publication[8] indicates that 47 percent of the GRI sustainability reports obtained external assurance and that the majority of the external assurance was provided by the GRI. What are the advantages of having accountants as compared to other third party groups like the GRI provide assurance services on corporate sustainability reports? What are the advantages of having non-accountant third party groups, like the GRI, as compared to accountants provide assurance services on corporate sustainability reports?

[8] Go to Caterpillar Inc.'s website (try http://www.caterpillar.com) to locate Caterpillars' latest sustainability report. What aspect of sustainability reporting seems to be a priority for Caterpillar? Explain your answer. Based on your reading of the G3.1 Reporting Guidelines and G3.1 Application Levels, what application level would you assign to Caterpillar's sustainability report?

[9] Go to Caterpillar Inc.'s website (try http://www.caterpillar.com) to locate Caterpillar's latest sustainability report. Go to Caterpillar Inc.'s website (try http://www.caterpillar.com) to locate Caterpillar's latest 10-K report. How consistent is the business strategy discussed in the 10-K to the sustainability strategy discussed in the sustainability report? How well does the sustainability report connect to financial information reported in the 10-K report? Do these two reports provide information on how sustainability is embedded into management processes such as human resources, purchasing, finance, etc.? Explain your answers.

[10] The 2010 GRI Sustainability Reporting Statistics publication[9] reveals that 12 percent of the business organizations issuing GRI sustainability reports issued integrated reports. An integrated report combines in one report information on economic, social, and environmental performance. Go to Southwest Airlines' website (try http://www.southwest.com) to locate the "Southwest Airlines One Report." Based on your reading of the integrated report for Southwest Airlines, what are the advantages and disadvantages of a business organization issuing an integrated report instead of issuing a separate report for financial performance and sustainability performance?

---

8   Global Reporting Initiative. "GRI Sustainability Reporting Statistics." 2010. See the following website: http://www.globalreporting.org/NR/rdonlyres/23A1D934-64BF-4934-ACB5-43CD4A41E48A/0/GRIReportingStats.pdf

9   Ibid.